BRITISH BATTLES OF THE CRIMEAN WARS 1854-1856

DESPATCHES FROM THE FRONT

The Commanding Officers' Reports From the Field and At Sea.

BRITISH BATTLES OF THE CRIMEAN WARS 1854-1856

Alma, Inkerman, Sevastopol, Battle of
The Balaclava - the Charge of the Light Brigade

Compiled by John Grehan and Martin Mace

Pen & Sword
MILITARY

First published in Great Britain in 2014 by
Pen & Sword Military
an imprint of
Pen & Sword Books Ltd
47 Church Street
Barnsley
South Yorkshire
S70 2AS

ISBN 978 1 78159 330 1

Printed and bound in England by CPI Group (UK) Ltd, Croydon, CR0 4YY

Pen & Sword Books Ltd incorporates the Imprints of Pen & Sword
Aviation, Pen & Sword Maritime, Pen & Sword Military, Wharncliffe Local
History, Pen and Sword Select, Pen and Sword Military Classics and Leo
Cooper.

For a complete list of Pen & Sword titles please contact:
PEN & SWORD BOOKS LIMITED
47 Church Street, Barnsley, South Yorkshire, S70 2AS, England
E-mail: enquiries@pen-and-sword.co.uk

Website: www.pen-and-sword.co.uk

CONTENTS

INTRODUCTION

The Crimean War, the most destructive of the Victorian era, was notable for the appalling suffering of the troops, the outmoded and inefficient military organisation and the recognition at last of the courage of all ranks of soldiers and sailors with the instigation of the Victoria Cross. It was also notable for being the first conflict to be extensively photographed and the first to be reported in detail by a war correspondent, William Russell of *The Times*.

With the new steam-powered, propeller-driven ships now able to cross the Mediterranean in a matter of days and the recently-established telegraph system able to transmit a message from the front line to London in twenty-four hours, Russell's reports could be received in London shortly after the events he described had occurred. In past conflicts the commanding officer's despatches were usually the method by which both the Government and the British public were informed of the progress of the war, and this could be a matter of weeks after the event, depending on the weather and the state of the roads in the theatre of operations.

All that changed with the Crimean War. Before the British Commander-in-Chief, Lord Raglan and his successors, could compile a full-length report on a battle, it might already be front page news. No longer could detailed, considered despatches be sent at the end of an operation or engagement, as for example Wellington had from Spain and Portugal in the Peninsular War, instead reports had to be submitted to Horse Guards every few days in order to keep ahead, or at least abreast, of the newspaper reporting.

As a consequence there were a vast number of despatches sent from the Crimea during the two years of war. Many of these are necessarily brief and many contain little valuable information. Large numbers of despatches were also dedicated in part or in whole, to the casualty returns and the hospital reports on the sick and wounded, as well as to the general health of the troops. Though these were important considerations affecting the fighting ability and the morale of the Expeditionary Force, space has not permitted their inclusion in this compilation.

The speed of telegraphic communications also had its effect on military operations, as it meant that government leaders were able to relay their policies to the commanders in the field in a way that had never been possible before. This particularly annoyed the French General Pélissier after he had taken over command of the French army in the Crimea. The Emperor Napoleon persistently urged him to mount field operations against the Russian forces rather than persist with the siege of Sevastopol, which the general refused to do. Eventually he was forced to write: "Your Majesty must free me from the narrow limits to which you have assigned me or else allow me to resign a command impossible to exercise in co-operation with our loyal allies at the somewhat paralysing end of an electric wire."

**

The war of 1854-6 with Russia was fought on many fronts and when Britain joined France in declaring war on Russia in support of Turkey in March 1854, it was expected that her most significant contribution to the allied case would be naval rather than military. Since the days of Nelson, Britain had commanded the seas and it was the threat to her naval dominance which prompted the despatch of a large force to the Balkans.

Even before the official opening of hostilities a combined Anglo-French fleet sailed into the Bosporus and entered the Black Sea to assist Turkey which was already at war with Russia. Tsar Nicholas I sought full access to the Mediterranean for his warships and Turkey stood in her way. A Russian naval force in the eastern Mediterranean would seriously disrupt the balance of power in the region and would have the potential to disrupt to Britain's trade routes to India and the Far East, so Turkey had to be supported at all costs.

The aim of the allied force, therefore, was to defend Constantinople and confine the Russian Black Sea Fleet to its own waters. The justification for this move was the destruction of a Turkish squadron by a patrol from the Russian fleet's home port of Sebastopol at the end of November 1853. It was the capture of Sebastopol which would become the focus of the operations in the Crimea. At the same time that the allied fleet was establishing its presence in the Black Sea, another Anglo-French force opened a second front in the Baltic. Under the command of Vice Admiral Sir Charles John Napier, the Baltic fleet was the largest that had assembled since the Napoleonic Wars and in terms of armament was the most powerful naval force that had put to sea. It is unsurprising, consequently, that a considerable proportion of the despatches sent back to Britain from these two war fronts are those from the admirals and officers of the Royal Navy. Other naval operations, in the White Sea and the Pacific, were of a minor nature and have not been reproduced here.

The naval operations in the Mediterranean and the Black Sea were led by Vice Admiral James Dundas, those of the Army by Lord Raglan. The latter commanded 18,000 British soldiers, his French counterpart, Marshal St Arnaud, could count 32,000. The main allied base on the Black Sea was Varna, 180 miles north of Constantinople. From there the allies launched their attack upon Sevastopol, landing at Kalimita Bay in the Crimea on 14 September 1854.

Both the allied commanders were to die in the Crimea, with Lord Raglan being replaced by General Sir James Simpson in June 1855. After being repeatedly criticised in the Press, Simpson stood down, with command of the British forces being taken up by General Sir William Codrington.

Admiral Dundas was also replaced during the course of the war. In January 1855, having completed the usual term of command, he was succeeded by Sir Edmund

Lyons, and returned to England. Admiral Napier also returned to the UK, but under entirely different circumstances. Napier, like Simpson, had suffered at the hands of the British newspapers and had consequently come under pressure from the Admiralty to be more positive in his operations against the enemy. Napier's replies were not well received as the Secretary of the Admiralty explained in a letter sent to Napier on 13 January 1855, "... you have repeatedly thought fit to adopt a tone in your correspondence with their Lordships which is not respectful of their authority." As a result he was relieved of his command, which was handed to another Dundas, Admiral the Honourable Richard Saunders Dundas.

In support of the British Army's efforts to capture Sevastopol, the Royal Navy landed a contingent of sailors and marines. Formed into a Naval Brigade, these men formed part of the defence of the British base at Balaklava as well as manning guns taken from the Navy's warships in the bombardment of Sevastopol. The Naval Brigade operated under its own officers and reported independently back to the Admiralty.

The despatches were not always received in England in their strict chronological sequence and often despatches included enclosures from subordinate officers which related to incidents that occurred some days or even weeks earlier. This at times produces a somewhat confusing and disjointed narrative. In just a few instances the despatches have been moved so that they contiguous with the events to which they refer. This is only for complete despatches and no despatches or enclosures have been separated or divided in any respect.

With the exception of the casualty returns, those despatches, from both the naval and military commanders, on land and at sea, are reproduced here in the same form as when they were originally published They have not been modified or interpreted in any way and are therefore the unedited and unique words of the commanding officers as they saw things at the time. For instance Sevastopol was sometimes spelt Sebastopol, Balaklava was Bala Clava, Omar Pasha was Omar Pacha, Tchernaya was Techernaia, just to name a few. Any grammatical or spelling errors have also been left uncorrected to retain the authenticity of the documents. These include misspellings of 'a sistance', 'bivouack', 'shrapnell' 'istant' 'Cosaques' and many others. The despatches are presented just as they were when first revealed to the general public more than 150 years ago.

IMAGES

MAPS

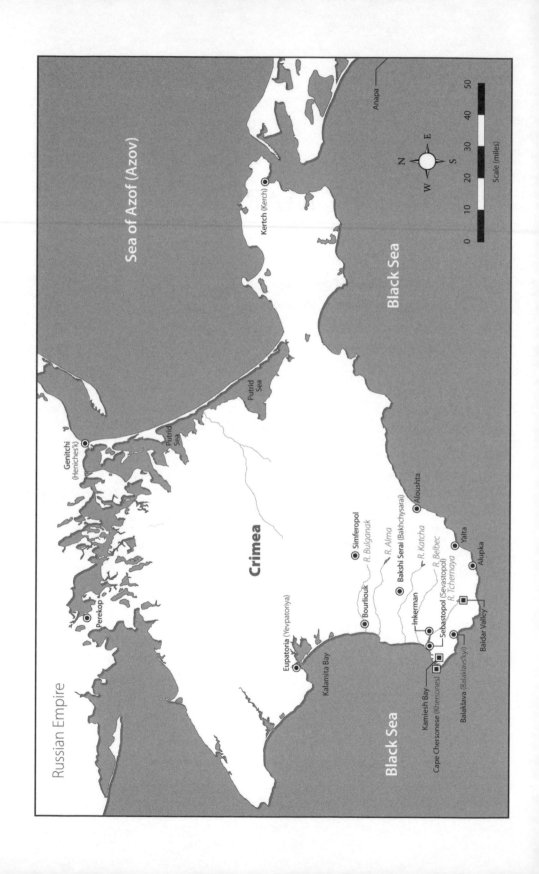

CHAPTER 1

THE BALTIC CAMPAIGN 1854

Admiralty, June 2, 1854.

DESPATCHES have been received at this Office from Vice-Admiral Sir Charles Napier, K.C.B, Commander-in-Chief of Her Majesty's ships and vessels in the Baltic, of which the following are copies:

No 96.
Her Majesty's Ship Duke of Wellington,
off Hango Head, May 20, 1854.

SIR,

I BEG to enclose a letter from Captain Yelverton, of the Arrogant, giving an account of a smart operation he performed at Ekness, 12 miles in the interior of the country. Great credit is due to him for his perseverance in threading up so narrow and intricate a navigation; and it will show the enemy they are not safe even in their country towns.

Captain Yelverton very properly abstained from damaging the town.

He speaks very highly of the gallantry of Captain Hall, of the Hecla (who I am sorry to say is slightly wounded), as also of Lieutenant Haggard, first of the Arrogant, and Lieutenant Crew Read, the senior lieutenant of the Hecla, which gallant officer has received a severe wound, which I fear has endangered the sight of his eye. All the officers and men behaved as British seamen and marines were wont to.

I have, &c.
(Signed) CHAS. NAPIER,
Vice-Admiral and Commander-in-Chief.

The Secretary of the Admiralty.
Her Majesty's Ship Arrogant,
SIR, Skagaedslenden, May 20, 1854.

I HAVE the honour to inform you that I came into the inner passage yesterday, in company with the Hecla, for the purpose of examining the channel.

At three in the afternoon, just as I was about to anchor a little beyond Teverminne, a strong force of the enemy's troops opened their fire upon both ships from behind an extensive sand-bank; the effect, however, of a few broadsides from Hecla and this ship soon dispersed them.

No one, I am glad to be able to say, was hurt in either vessel.

I did nothing to provoke this attack on the part of the enemy.

I ascertained from a pilot who lives here that three large Russian loaded merchant ships were at Ekness, eight miles to the northward. I lost no time in proceeding there early this morning; but did not expect to find the enemy so well prepared to receive me. Owing to the Hecla's light draught of water she led the way; a task not easy to perform in a narrow and intricate passage, exposed as she was to the first of the enemy's fire.

In addition to a field battery of five guns (two of which I dismounted) and one mortar, they had erected a strong battery which they supplied very efficiently; Captain Hall succeeded in dismounting and bringing off three of the guns. The engagement lasted longer than I expected, as they returned to their guns twice in the midst of our fire, and were only compelled to leave them when their guns were destroyed by our shot.

On reaching the anchorage of Ekness, I found that two of the merchantmen were aground, but Captain Hall brought out one under the fire of a battery, which my draught of water would not allow me to near sufficiently to completely destroy. I most carefully avoided firing one shot in or near the town of Ekness, directing the whole of the fire of the guns exclusively to the batteries and troops attacking us, which consisted, in addition to the brigade of Horse Artillery, of a considerable body of cavalry and infantry, moving abreast of the ship as she advanced.

I cannot give sufficient credit to Captain Hall for the assistance he rendered me on this, as on all occasions, since he has been under my orders; the admirable way in which he went in and brought out his prize, under a galling fire from the enemy, deserves the greatest praise.

I beg also to call to your favourable notice Lieut. H.V. Haggard, senior lieutenant of this ship, whose most zealous services at all times were particularly displayed on this occasion, and also that of the whole of the officers, seamen, and marines of Her Majesty's ship under my command.

I regret to say that I had one man killed, and five wounded. I must not omit to mention how very highly Captain Hall speaks of Lieutenant Crew Read, First Lieutenant of the Hecla, for the support he had from him, throughout the engagement) until he was unfortunately wounded and carried below), as also from the officers, seamen, and marines, of Her Majesty's ship under his command.

I beg leave to enclose herewith a list of casualties on board the Hecla and Arrogant, in the engagement.

I have, &c.
(Signed) H.R. YELVERTON,
Captain.

Admiralty, June 29, 1854.

DESPATCHES, of which the following are copies or extracts, have been received from Vice-Admiral Sir Charles Napier, K.C.B., Commander-in-Chief of Her Majesty's Ships and Vessels in the Baltic:-

ENCLOSING Admiral Plumridge's Report of his proceedings in the Gulf of Bothnia.

No. 151.
Duke of Wellington, Baro Sound,
June 18, 1854.

SIR,

I BEG leave to enclose Admiral Plumridge's Report of his proceedings in the Gulf of Bothnia, from the 5th May to the 10th June, by which their Lordships will observe that he has destroyed forty-six vessels, afloat and on the stocks, amounting to 11,000 tons; from 40,000 to 50,000 barrels of pitch and tar; 60,000 square yards of rough pitch; a great number of stacks of timber, spars, plank, and deals, sails, rope, and various kinds of naval Stores, to the amount of from 3 to £400,000, without the loss of a man. Admiral Plumridge has had to contend with innumerable rocks and shoals, incorrectly laid down in the charts, and met the ice up to the 30th May; nevertheless, though several of his squadron have touched the ground, I am happy to say they have received no damage that he is not able to repair with his own means.

2. The Rear-Admiral, their Lordships will observe, speaks in the highest terms of the captains, officers, seamen, and marines, and particularly of Lieutenant B.P. Priest, the first lieutenant of the Leopard, an old and deserving officer, and of Lieutenant Hammet, his flag lieutenant.

I have, &c.
CHAS. NAPIER, Vice-Admiral and
Commander-in-Chief.

The Secretary of the Admiralty.
Enclosure No. 1, in Sir Charles Napier's Letter,

No. 151.
Her Majesty's ship Leopard, at Sea,
10th June, 1854 – lat. 64° 1' N;
long. 22° 41' E At noon.

SIR,

IN obedience to your orders of 5th May, 1854, I proceeded with the squadron under my command to examine, as far as practicable, the Island of Aland, but not being able to procure a pilot, I found the hazard too great to proceed further in the execution of that duty; the reports of Captains Buckle and Giffard, numbered 1 and 2, will more fully inform you of the result and termination, for the present, of that service.

From thence I proceeded up the Gulf of Bothnia, and I have now the honour herewith to transmit letters and papers, numbered from 3 to 6, giving a detailed account of the squadron's proceedings up to the date hereof.

The summary of the large amount of mischief done to the enemy by the boats, as per margin, and the paper lettered A.

Boats of Leopard employed at Brahestad, Uleaborg, and Tornea.

1st Gig-
Lieutenant B.P. Priest.
Mr. Terence H. Wall, assistant-surgeon.
Mr. James Ray, passed clerk.

1st Cutter-
Lieutenant L.U. Hammet.
Mr. Richard Harington, midshipman.

Galley-
Lieutenant William Graham.
Mr. H. St. L. Palliser, naval cadet.

Barge-
Lieutenant G.W.E. Lloyd.
Mr. Arthur Salwey, mate.

1st Launch-
Mr. Henry G. Payne, mate.
Lieutenant E.D. Thelwall, R.M.A.
Pinnace-
Mr. James Laurence, second master.
Mr. W.D.M. Dalbin, naval cadet.

2nd Gig-
  Mr. J.G. O'Connell, master's assistant.

2nd Cutter-
  Mr. Augustus Jacob, naval cadet.

Valorous' Boats at Uleaborg and Tornea.

1st Launch-
  Lieutenant C.B.C. Dent.
  Lieutenant W.S. Davis, R.M.A.

Pinnace-
  Mr. R.F. Broadrick, mate.

1st Cutter-
  Mr. M.A.S. Hare, midshipman.

1st Gig-
  Mr. J.R. Trefusis, naval cadet.
  Mr. W. Ray (M.D.) assistant-surgeon.

2nd Gig-
  Mr. J. Bailey, cadet.
  Vulture's Boats, at Brahestad and Uleaborg.

1st Launch-
  Lieutenant C. Wise.
  Mr. N.J. Morphy, mate.
Barge-
  Mr. C.F. Hill, mate.
  Mr. Chapman, master's-assistant.
  Cutter-Mr. C.P. Fortescue, midshipman.

Gig-
  Mr. J.V.D. Butler, naval cadet.
  Mr. George Duncan, assistant-surgeon.

Odin's Boats at Brahestad and Uleaborg.

1st Launch-
  Lieutenant W. Mould.
  Mr. C.F. Montague, mate.
  Lieut. A.O. Lewis, R.M.A.

Pinnace-
> Lieutenant Carrington.
> Mr. Long, acting second master.

Barge-
> Lieutenant J.H.B. Fellowes.

Cutter-
> Mr. Henry Athorpe, midshipman.

1st Gig-
> Mr. C. Rice, naval cadet.

2nd Gig-
> Mr. H. Salmond, naval cadet.
> Mr. J.C. Hamilton, assistant-surgeon.

From the hindrances the squadron have encountered in this service, it has spread over a greater space of time than I at first contemplated; the intricacies of the ice, navigation, innumerable rocks, shoals, and the imperfect state of the charts as to soundings on the Russian side of the Gulf, together with the difficulties we experienced in disentangling the squadron, up to the 30th May, from the floes and fields of ice (of which we saw the last this morning), could not be surmounted in less time, or with less vigilance, by the officers in command, and that of the captain of my flag-ship, together with the constant perseverance and zeal evinced by Mr. George B.F. Swain, the master of the Leopard; which ship I may here observe, to the credit of these two officers, has led the squadron from leaving the Aland Islands.

I feel it incumbent on me to notice how sensibly I feel the zealous co-operation of Captains Buckle, Giffard, Glasse, and Scott, as well as the good arrangements of their ships' boats for service.

The letters from No. 3 to 6, show the names of the several lieutenants and boats commanded by Lieutenant B.P. Priest, of this ship, and seconded by my flag-lieutenant, L.U. Hammet. To them and the other, officers, those subordinate, the seamen, marines, and their lieutenants (Davis, Lewis, and Thelwall), my thanks are fully due.

Any credit that may arise from such extensive damage having been executed, will, I trust, pardon me for thus bringing to your special notice the name of that steady, old, and deserving officer, Lieutenant B. Priest, who held the boat command from Brahestad to Uleaborg and Tornea.

I cannot refrain from again reverting to the ability and exertions of Captain George Giffard, feeling as I do that it is my duty to take this opportunity of bringing some of his merits before you.

I have, &c.
(Signed) HANWAY PLUMRIDGE,
Rear-Admiral.

Return of Enemy's Property destroyed at Brahestad, Uleaborg, and on the Kemi River, near Tornea, between the 30th May and 8th June, 1854.

Her Majesty's ship Leopard,
June 9, 1854.

Burnt afloat and on shore, and totally destroyed:
Brahestad, May 30, 1854.

1 brig, 250 tons, under repair and empty.
1 barque, 450 tons, just launched and empty.
1 topsail schooner, 140 tons, }
2 F. and A. schooners, 60 to 80 tons, } in ballast.
5 sloops, 60 to 80 tons, }
4 large vessels, building, 300 to 500 tons.
Naval Stores destroyed:
About 25,000 barrels of pitch, tar, and oil.
A large quantity of timber, spars, plank and materials for ship building.
Three building yards, with workshops and storehouses.

Off Uleaborg, June 1, 1854.

3 schooners, 60 to 170 tons, 1 empty and 2 laden with tar, but burnt; they sank in the gale of 2nd June.
5 barques, 300 to 400 tons, building and nearly complete.

June 1 *and* 2, 1854.
8 schooners, 50 to 150 tons, hauled up on shore and purposely damaged.
Scuttled and purposely sunk:-
2 brigs, 600 tons, partially laden with tar.
1 brig, 400 tons, partially laden with tar.
1 brig, 350 tons, partially laden with tar.
1 cutter, 100 tons, contents not ascertained.
1 schooner, 150 tons, contents not ascertained.
1 brig, 300 tons, just launched and empty.

Ukovaryakka, June 1 *and* 2, 1854.

1 vessel, ready for launching, 204 feet long, about 1200 tons.
1 vessel, in frame, not measured.
1 barque, 600 tons, empty, but scuttled.

Killoncrusit, June 1 *and* 2, 1854.

1 schooner, 100 tons, laden with tar, purposely scuttled.
1 schooner, 70 tons, hauled up and fresh caulked.
3 schooners, 80 to 100 tons, empty.

Naval Stores destroyed:
Uleaborg, June 1 *and* 2, 1854.

From 40 to 50,000 barrels of tar and pitch.
6000 square yards of rough pitch.
A vast number of stacks of timber, spars, plank, deals, &c.
A large number of storehouses, containing sails, rope, and all kinds of stores.
Numerous workshops, with forges.
Several building yards, and a great extent of wharfage.

Kemi River, near Tornea, June 8, 1854.

1 schooner, of about 80 tons, empty.
80 stacks of timber.
Being a total of 46 vessels destroyed; and, at the lowest estimate, the enemy has suffered

damage to the extent of-

At Brahestad	£65,000
Uleaborg	£300,000
Kemi River	£15,000
	£380,000

(Signed) GEO. GIFFARD,
Captain.

Sub-Enclosure No. 1, in Enclosure No. 1, in Sir Charles Napier's Letter No. 151.

Her Majesty's ship Valorous at sea,
May 15, 1854.

SIR,

I HAVE the honour to report to you that in consequence of thick foggy weather, I did not reach Grisselhamn until noon of the 6th instant.

On landing to communicate, I found that the commandant was absent at Stockholm, but the officer in command, Captain Billbery, very obligingly afforded me all the information in his power, through the interpretation of Captain Fahnelyelm, the Director of the Electric Telegraph, which was to be in operation in about a week. No pilots for the Aland Islands could be obtained, and I believe they are not permitted to serve in our ships of war. The commandant observed that he believed there were not more than 1000 troops at Bomarsund, and that 300 of them had lately been relieved by 500 from Russia; he did not appear to know anything about the gun-boats.

The only information I could obtain relative to the Aland Islands was, that the inhabitants appeared to be well disposed towards the English, and that they had declined taking up arms to oppose us. He was anxious to know whether their Post-boat, Eckero, would be intercepted by us. I replied it would not, unless it contained military despatches to or from the Russian Government, but that I considered it advisable that a passport should be obtained from the Commander-in-Chief, to be produced when boarded by our cruizers.

2. I proceeded next morning in the direction of Wardo Island and Bomarsund, but in the afternoon found myself near some shoals, with ice on some of the patches; I therefore anchored to sound, and a fog soon came on which prevented my moving until noon on the following day. On standing to the southward, on the 8th instant; towards Wardo Island, I observed a barque running to the southward among the islands, and on my steering to cut her off, she bore up. I therefore stood in cautiously, and finding a good channel close to some rocks and small islands, I proceeded in, anchoring in 15 fathoms, with Vulture in company, within a mile of the barque, in a good harbour formed by the Island of Saggo and numerous others. On sending the boats, the barque was found to be aground and deserted, in a small cove. Russian colours. and a paper found on board proved her to be the Princess of Uleaborg, of 346 tons, with a cargo of salt (part having been landed), from St. Ubes, bound to Abo. Observing a boat pulling away from her, I sent a gig which brought her back, with the master, mate, and three men, the ship's papers and their private effects. I have sent her to Faro, with a prize crew of eleven men from the Valorous and Vulture, in charge of the second master of this ship. The village, consisting of half a dozen cottages, was deserted, with the exception of an old woman. I left a paper in the largest house, on which I caused the master of the captured vessel to state that the English would not molest them, or touch their property, but would pay for anything they had to dispose of, and this was likewise explained to the woman. We also found a cutter, of about 35 tons, deserted and empty, called the Alfred, which the master of the Princess said was a revenue vessel. The barque having been got afloat and brought out during the night, I started the following afternoon with the Vulture, towing the barque, and the cutter not being worth removing I directed her to be burnt.

3. While cutting the anchor, three or four cables' length from where we had been lying, the ship touched on a sunken rock.

4. The prize parted company in the evening, and I proceeded with the Vulture in the direction of Bomarsund. The master of the Princess stated that he had been three weeks at Marsund, and that the Russians had 500 troops there and 1500 at different parts among the islands, but principally at Bomarsund. Some, he said, were in the vicinity of the spot at which we had captured his vessel, and several watch-fires which were kept up during the night on the adjoining hills, which are rocky and covered with pine-trees, supported the assertion, though we saw none.

Next morning, the Vulture in company, I proceeded in the direction of Bomarsund, but found the channels very intricate between the innumerable small islands and rocks, which did not correspond with any of the charts, and which appear to be far from correct. Having no pilot, I proceeded cautiously by the eye and lead, the water being perfectly smooth. About two P.M. I observed a part of the works of Bomarsund, which proved to be two casemated batteries, one of which appeared to have double loop holes below, and both with embrasures on the summit, with chimneys appearing between them, a sketch of which, as I observed it to be from our mastheads, was taken by Mr. Broadrick, mate, is inclosed herewith, the distance was about five miles from Bomarsund. I was led there by observing the mastheads of several vessels over the land. In standing cautiously towards them the ship touched the ground once, but I succeeded in anchoring, in company with the Vulture, about a mile from the vessels. We made out six or seven, and I sent in seven boats from the two ships; they found them deserted, six being small schooners, and the other was a brigantine, – all empty and scarcely of any value. The boats brought out the brigantine and two schooners, the latter had the appearance of being fitted for gun-boats; I therefore burnt them. The others were apparently unseaworthy, except the brigantine; but as she was very badly found, and not fit for a voyage to England, and belonging apparently to the poorer people of the place, whose good-will I consider it advisable to gain, I left her untouched. The lights of Bomarsund were visible above the trees of the adjoining island from the masthead, and with the assistance of a glass the sketch was accurately made.

We started next morning without meeting with any opposition, only a few of the people of the village being seen at a distance. The channels between the innumerable rocks and islands are so intricate, and so different from the positions on the charts, that I considered it unsafe to proceed further south than Wardo without a pilot, nor could I find the channel track by which I entered; fortunately, the water was very smooth and clear, and the rocks bold, so that I could steer through them by the eye and lead, which generally indicated the approach to shoal water.

5. On the 12th instant I met the Odin, and received the rendezvous from her, since which I have been drawn away to the N.W. by chasing several vessels which proved to be Swedes and Norwegians.

I have, &c.
(Signed) C.H. BUCKLE,
Captain.
Rear-Admiral J.H. Plumridge.

Sub-Inclosure No. 2, in Enclosure No. 1, in Sir Charles Napier's Letter No. 151.

*Her Majesty's skip Leopard,
off Uleaborg, June 1, 1854.*

SIR,

I HAVE the honour to forward the enclosed report, from Lieutenant Benjamin P. Priest (senior lieutenant of this ship), of the operations of the boats of the squadron under his command, sent into Brahestad harbour on the 30th ultimo; and have great pleasure in reporting the very good conduct of every officer and man employed; the boats having been away upwards of seven hours, immediately after clearing the ice in which the squadron had been blocked up for the previous twenty-four hours.

Lieutenant Priest deserves credit for the able manner he conducted the operations, and I beg leave to bring his services under your notice.

I have, &c.
GEORGE GIFFARD,
Captain.

Rear-Admiral J. Hanway Plumridge.
Her Majesty's ship Leopard, off Brahestad,
May 30, 1854.

SIR,

IN obedience to your orders, I this afternoon proceeded with detachments of boats from Her Majesty's steam frigates Leopard, Vulture, and Odin, into the harbour of Brahestad, where I damaged enemy's property as follows:

Burnt on shore and totally destroyed, viz:

Four large vessels, building and nearly complete on the stocks, the largest being about 500 tons burden, and pierced for six guns.

Three detached stores of timber, fit for building ships of large scantling.

Two detached storehouses, containing some thousand barrels of pitch, tar, and oil, a large number of them marked with the imperial crown.

Burnt afloat and totally destroyed:

1 barque just launched, not masted, about 450 tons burden.
1 brig under repair.
1 topsail schooner.
2 fore and aft schooners.
5 sloops.
All in ballast.

As the inhabitants yielded immediately to our force, I was very careful not to damage the private houses; at the same time I satisfied myself by personal inspection, that there was no contraband of war within those storehouses, which were situated in the immediate vicinity of and inside the town, which I did not destroy.

Two large stores, on the outskirts of the town, were found to contain flour; these were not destroyed, as I had reason for supposing it to be private property.

All the officers placed under my orders, vied with me in preventing unnecessary alarm to the inhabitants; and I feel it to be my duty to report the alacrity, great steadiness, and good conduct shown by all the officers and seamen employed on this service.

It is almost superfluous to add that the royal marines under Lieutenants Thelwall, R.M.A., showed their admirable discipline.

I have, &c.
(Signed) BENJ. P. PRIEST,
Senior and Gunnery Lieut.
Captain Giffard, H.M.S. Leopard.

Destruction of enemy's property.

P.S. Being in all 14 vessels destroyed.
About 25,000 barrels of pitch, tar, and oil.
A large quantity of timber, spars, plank, and materials for ship-building.
3 building yards, with workshops and storehouses.

Boats employed on the 30th May, 1854.

Her Majesty's ship Leopard.

2nd Cutter-
   Lieutenant B.P. Priest.

1st Cutter-
   Lieutenant Hammet (next in command)
   Mr. Harrington, midshipman.

1st Launch-
   Mr. Payne, mate.
   Lieutenant Thelwall, R.M.A.

Pinnace-
   Mr. Lawrence, second master.

1st Gig-
   Mr. Wall, assistant-surgeon.
   Mr. Palliser, naval cadet.

Her Majesty's ship Vulture.

1st Launch-
   Lieutenant Wise.
   Mr. Hill, mate.

Barge-
   Mr. Morphy, mate.
   Mr. Chapman, master's assistant.

Gig-
   Mr. Duncan, assistant-surgeon.
   Mr. Butler, naval cadet.

Cutter-
   Mr. Fortescue, midshipman.

Her Majesty's ship Odin.

1st Launch-
   Lieutenant Mould.
   Lieutenant Lewis, R.M.A.
   Mr. Montagu, mate.

Pinnace-
   Lieutenant Carrington.
   Mr. Long, acting quartermaster.

Cutter-
   Mr. Athorpe, midshipman.

1st Gig-
   Mr. Hamilton, assistant-surgeon.
   Mr. Rice, naval cadet.

2nd Gig—
   Mr. Salmond, naval cadet

Total.

   3 gun-boats, each with 24-pounder howitzer.
   3 gun-boats, each with 12-pounder howitzer.
   25 officers.
   201 seamen.
   78 marines.

Grand Total.

   6 gun-boats.
   8 smaller boats.
   25 officers, and
   279 men.

Sub-Enclosure No. 3, in Enclosure No. 1, in Sir Charles Napier's Letter No. 151.

His Majesty's ship Leopard, off Uleaborg,
June 4, 1854.

SIR,

I HAVE the honour to enclose the reports of the officers commanding the several detachments of boats of the squadron sent from this ship on the 1st and 2nd instant, after the ships had anchored within range of the town of Uleaborg; and I have much pleasure in again bringing the zeal and ability of Lieutenant Benjamin P. Priest, who commanded the principal force, to your notice.

All the officers and men engaged in this trying duty for nearly 12 hours (and during a snow storm of six hours' duration) conducted themselves entirely to my satisfaction, and the destruction of enemy's shipping and property has been very great.

From the enemy having sunk all their shipping, it was found that no vessels could be rendered serviceable to embark any of the valuable property without great loss of time, and it was burnt without a murmur or thought of prize money.

I take this opportunity to report to you the unwearied zeal and ability of Mr. George B. Swain, master of this ship, assisted by Mr. D.M. Jago, the master of Her Majesty's ship Odin, and their assistants, in sounding and buoying the intricate and shallow channels for upwards of 30 miles leading to this port, they being employed day and night for 48 hours, and having no plan of the place.

I have, &c.
(Signed) GEORGE GIFFARD.
Captain.

Rear-Admiral J.H. Plumridge,
H.M.S. Leopard.

Total number of Vessels destroyed.

Lieutenant Priest's division	13 building, and on shore.
Lieutenant Priest's division	7 afloat, but scuttled.
Lieutenant Graham's division	2 building.
Lieutenant Graham's division	1 afloat, unseaworthy.
Lieutenant Lloyd's division	5 small vessels.
Captured by Lieutenant Young on the 31st May, and burnt	13 schooners.
	31

Naval Stores burnt.

From 40 to 50,000 barrels of tar and pitch.
6,000 square yards of rough pitch.
A vast number of stacks of timber, spars, planks, deals, &c.
A large number of storehouses, containing sails, rope, and all kinds of
stores, workshops, forges, &c.
Several building yards, and a great extent of wharfage.
Estimated damage to the enemy above £300,000.

Her Majesty's ship Leopard, off Uleaborg,
June 2,1854.

SIR,

IN compliance with your orders, I yesterday evening took under my command, the boats of Rear-Admiral Plumridge's squadron, as per margin,* and proceeded up the river to Uleaborg. Taking possession of the town of Uleaborg, I spent two hours in examining the buildings, of which none appeared to belong to the Russian Government, except the Cossacks' Barracks, situated in the very heart of the town; and as its destruction by fire would have involved the burning of a large number of private houses, if not of the whole town (containing several thousand inhabitants), I judged it better to spare it.

In thus acting I had the less reason to expect your disapprobation, as it was little better than a collection of hovels.

The storehouses within the town were for the most part cleared out; no naval stores were found in any of them, and as their burning would also have endangered the town, they were spared.

I next detached Lieutenant L.U. Hammet, (flag lieutenant) in command of a division to examine both the sides of a river, below the narrows, to recover any of the sunken vessels, if practicable in a short time; otherwise to destroy all the enemy's shipping and naval stores; impressing upon him your orders to be careful not to damage any private dwelling, a service which he performed with discretion and ability.

Proceeding myself with the other division to the island opposite to the town, I fired and destroyed all the ships building, together with the storehouses containing ship-building materials, and workshops, and continuing destroying as I passed down on both sides of the river, I rejoined Lieutenant Hammet and returned on board.

During the performance of this service, the men were exposed to great trials and temptations, both from the almost uninterrupted sleet, with very cold weather, and the large number of spirit stores open; yet, notwithstanding this their general behaviour gave me the greatest confidence in their devotion and daring, had the enemy shown opposition.

*

LEOPARD'S

1st Gig	Lieutenant B.P. Priest.
	W.J. Kay, passed clerk.
	W.T.C. Wall, acting-assistant-surgeon.
1st Cutter	Lieutenant Hammet (next in command).
	Mr. R. Harrington, midshipman.
1st Launch	Mr. Payne, mate.
	Lieutenant E.D. Thelwall, R.M.A.
Pinnace	W.J. Lawrence, second master.

VALOROUS'

1st Launch	Lieutenant C.C. Dent.
	Lieutenant W.S. Davies, R.M.A.
Pinnace	Mr. R.F. Broadrick, mate.
1st Cutler	Mr. Hare, midshipman.
2nd Gig	Mr. G. Trefusis, naval cadet.
	Mr. W. Ray, M.D., assistant-surgeon.

VULTURE'S

1st Launch	Lieutenant Wise.
Barge	Mr. C.F. Hill, mate.
Cutter	Mr. Fortescue, midshipman.
Gig	Mr. Butler, naval cadet.
	W.G. Duncan, assistant-surgeon.

ODIN'S

1st Launch	Lieutenant W. Mould.
	Mr. Montague, mate.
	Lieutenant A.O. Lewis, R.M.A.
Pinnace	Lieutenant Fellowes.
	Mr. R. Athorpe, midshipman.
Gig	Mr. C. Rice, naval cadet.
	Mr. J.E. Hamilton, assistant-surgeon.
Gig	Mr. Salmond, naval cadet.

TOTAL
4 gun-boats, each with 24-pounder howitzer.
4 gun-boats, each with 12-pounder howitzer.
27 officers.
203 seamen.
98 marines.

GRAND TOTAL.
8 gun-boats
8 smaller boats.
27 officers.
301 men.

Of the conduct and discipline of the marines under Lieutenant W.S. Davis, (R.M.A.) I cannot say too much in praise, exposed so much to temptation when sentries in the town.

All the shipping, boats, &c., were found scuttled and sunk; and as considerable time would have been required to weigh and load them, all were burnt and destroyed.

The whole service lasted nearly twelve hours, and the following list shows the loss which has been inflicted on the enemy, which, at a low estimate, cannot be valued under £200,000:

Burnt ashore and totally destroyed.

5 barques or ships, of from 300 to 400 tons, all nearly complete on the stocks.

8 schooners, sloops, and small vessels, hauled up on shore, and all damaged purposely, so as to render them unseaworthy unless extensively re-repaired.

A very large number of storehouses, containing sails, rope, shipwrights' gear, and other materials for fitting and building ships.

A vast number of stacks of timber, some of very large scantling.

Many stacks of deck planks.

Several heaps of spars.

A stack of crooked oak timber, apparently for stern and stem pieces of ships.

An enormous heap of unmanufactured pitch, extending over about 6000 square yards of surface, having an average height of about three feet.

8 stores facing the river, containing tar and pitch.

A large store at the back of this, containing tar, &c.

A large open space both before and behind those storehouses, containing barrels of pitch and tar. Calculating the contents, and taking the very lowest possible estimate, there must have been at least 30,000 barrels of pitch and tar on this portion of the banks of the river, as the conflagration was on each side of the river, and extended over a great length. Several storehouses containing salt were involved in their destruction. Eight storehouses on the right bank of the river were spared because their burning would have destroyed a private house. The contents, as far as regarded a small quantity of naval stores were taken possession of. There were many launches (most of them purposely scuttled and sunk) which were spared because they were reported to be the property of poor men.

Burnt afloat and partially destroyed.

2 vessels of about 300 tons, partially laden with tar.
1 vessel of 400 tons,   }
1 vessel of 350 tons,   } both laden with pitch, tar, &c.
1 cutter of 100 tons,
1 schooner of 150 tons,
1 brig of 300 tons, just launched and empty.

All the vessels had been scuttled and sunk purposely. They were burnt by us to the water's edge, and rendered quite unfit for their purpose without being almost rebuilt.

About 500 casks of tar were found in the river secured by spars. They were cut adrift after finding their burning impracticable.

I have, &c.,
(Signed) B.P. PRIEST,
Senior and Gunnery Lieutenant.

Captain George Giffard,
H.M.'s ship Leopard.
Her Majesty's ship Leopard, off Uleaborg,
June 2, 1854.

SIR,

I HAVE the honour to report to you, that in obedience to your orders, I proceeded in the boats of this ship, named in the margin,* to the Island of Ulkonargaick, and on arriving off the north-east point, I boarded a large barque, which on examination proved to be scuttled, and rendered otherwise unseaworthy. I then proceeded on shore, and searched several storehouses and work-shops, containing pitch, forges, and other materials requisite for ship-building, together, with two vessels on the stocks, one nearly ready for launching, and a second in a less advanced state; also a wharf, built at some distance from the shore, on which were sheers, capstans, &c., for masting ships, the whole of which were disposed of in the following manner, viz.:-

Large Storehouses, containing pitch – burnt.

2 blacksmiths' workshops, having two forges each – burnt.

1 large one-storied building, containing one launch, and apparently used for boat-building – burnt.

1 vessel ready for launching, extreme length 204 feet, breadth 36 feet – burnt.

1 vessel in frame, not measured – burnt.

1 barque lying at anchor, estimated size 600 tons – burnt.

I then searched the village on the adjacent island, but finding no stores contraband of war, I re-embarked and proceeded in search of three schooners, of which information was obtained from the pilot; and after pulling some distance through a creek to the south of the town, I met a division of boats under Lieutenant Hammet, by whom I found the vessel I was in search of had been destroyed.

I have, &c.
(Signed) W. GRAHAM,
Lieutenant.

Captain Giffard, H.M.S. Leopard.
* *Galley, Lieutenant Graham. 2. Cutter, Mr. Dolben, Naval Cadet*
Her Majesty's ship, Leopard, off
Uleaborg, June 3, 1854.

SIR,

I HAVE the honour to report that in obedience to your orders, I proceeded yesterday with the boats under my charge to take or destroy the vessels at Killoon Kraseli, that I found there five schooners, which were disposed of as follows.

Scuttled and aground, one laden with tar – burnt.

Empty, three – one burnt, two destroyed.

One hauled up and fresh caulked, burnt.

I have, &c.,
(Signed) G. LLOYD,
Lieutenant.

Captain Giffard, H.M.S. Leopard.

Boats employed.
1 cutter of Leopard, Lieutenant Lloyd.
1 cutter of Valorous.
1 cutter of Vulture.
1 cutter of Odin.

Sub-Enclosure No. 4, in Enclosure No. 1, to Sir Charles Napier's Letter No. 151.

Her Majesty's ship Leopard,
off Kemi, 9th June, 1854.

SIR,

I HAVE the honour to enclose Lieutenant B.P. Priest's report of his proceedings with a division of boats in the Tornea river and town, which, from the rapid current in the stream, he had great difficulty in reaching.

Also a letter from Lieutenant G.W.E. Lloyd, reporting the destruction of enemy's property in the Kemi River, with a division of boats under his command.

I have, &c.
(Signed) GEO. GIFFARD,
Captain.

Rear-Admiral J.H. Plumridge,
H.M.S. Leopard.
Her Majesty's ship Leopard, off
Kemi, June 9, 1854.

SIR,

I PROCEEDED yesterday morning with the boats, as per margin* to Tornea, in execution of your orders.

A strong wind, with extraordinary rapids in the river, delayed us, and it was 7 30

P.M. before the boats arrived off the town of Tornea, 13 hours after leaving the ship; the garrison left on our approach.

Having taken possession of the town I found the storehouses had been cleared out, and their contents conveyed across the barrier to the Swedish territory, and that the inhabitants had destroyed the barracks and public buildings; the purpose for which I was despatched having been thus completed, I therefore returned on board, after being 20 hours in the boats, and have great pleasure in stating every officer and man behaved to my satisfaction.

I have, &c.,
(Signed) B.P. PRIEST,
Senior and Gunnery Lieutenant.

Captain George Giffard,
H.M.S. Leopard.

	LEOPARD'S
*	
2nd Cutter	Lieutenant B.P. Priest.
	Mr. T. Wall, assistant-surgeon.
	Mr. Dolben, naval cadet.
1st Cutter	Lieutenant Hammet.
	Mr. Jacob, naval cadet.
1st Launch	Mr. H.C. Payne, mate.
	Lieutenant Thelwall, R.M.A.
Pinnace	Mr. Lawrence, second master.
	VALOROUS'
1st Launch	Lieutenant C.B.C. Dent.
	Lieutenant W.S. Davies, R.M.A.
Pinnace	Mr. Broadrick, mate.
1st Cutter	Mr. Hare, midshipman.
2nd Cutter	Mr. Trefusis, naval cadet.
Gig	Mr. Bailey, naval cadet.
	Mr. Ray, assistant-surgeon.

TOTAL.
4 gun-boats,
5 other boats,
15 officers, and
166 men.

off Kemi, June 9th, 1854.

SIR,

I HAVE the honour to report that in obedience to your orders I proceeded yesterday with the boats under my charge,* up the Kemi River, on the banks of which, and on the adjacent islands, I burnt eighty stacks of timber (covering about two miles of ground), and the hull of a vessel of about eighty tons burthen. A quantity of timber not fit for ship-building was spared at the request of the inhabitants.

I have, &c.,
GEO. LLOYD,
Lieutenant.

Captain George Giffard,

H.M.S. Leopard.

* *Boats employed, barge of Leopard, Mr. Salwey, mate; 2nd gig of Leopard, Mr. O'Connell, master's assistant.*

No. 152.
Duke of Wellington, Baro Sound,
June 10th, 1854.

SIR,

I BEG leave to transmit to their Lordships the accompanying letter from Rear-Admiral Plumridge, enclosing one from Captain Glasse, of the Vulture (which ship arrived here yesterday), giving an account of an unfortunate failure in an attack on Gamla Carleby, in the Gulf of Bothnia, by the boats of the Vulture and Odin.

2. I have expressed to Captain Glasse my disapproval of sending boats to attack a place so far distant from his ship, without any apparent object, which has led to the melancholy catastrophe on this occasion.

I have, &c.
(Signed) CHARLES NAPIER,
Vice-Admiral and Commander in Chief.

The Secretary of the Admiralty.
Enclosure No. 1, in Sir Charles Napier's Letter No. 152.
Her Majesty's ship Leopard,
Oreground, June 14, 1854.

SIR,

PREVIOUS to leaving the neighbourhood of Uleaborg, on the 4th instant, I gave Captain Glasse, of the Vulture, the accompanying order, and parted company from that ship and the Odin.

After having finished the service I went to perform at and near Tornea, with this ship and the Valorous, we rejoined the Vulture, and Odin, on the night of the 10th instant, at the previous appointed rendezvous (No. 6).

The accompanying letters, returns, and papers, I have received from Captain Glasse, detailing a failure in the service he intended to execute; the perusal of these letters and returns, has caused me considerable concern from the severe, and I am sorry to add very extensive, loss, sustained in officers and men killed and others wounded.

From what I am able to discern, it would appear to me that this serious catastrophe has resulted from surprise, and a subsequent want of suitable management.

I am, &c.
(Signed) HANWAY PLUMRIDGE,
Rear-Admiral.

Vice-Admiral Sir Charles Napier, K.C.B.
Sub-Enclosure No. 1, in Sir Charles Napier's Letter, No. 152.
Her Majesty's ship Leopard.
Memorandum. Uleaborg, June 3, 1854.

YOU will proceed off Old Carleby, taking with you the Odin.

After examining and operating, if practicable, on that place and its vicinity (where it is said they have a small screw steamer, which it is an object to obtain for the use of the squadron), you are then to rendezvous at Hallgrund Beacon, off Jacobstad; and as before directed, employ your force to the best advantage in its immediate neighbourhood, until rejoined by the Leopard, at Hallgrund Beacon (No. 1).

(Signed) HANWAY PLUMRIDGE,
Rear-Admiral.

Captain Glasse, H.M.S. Vulture.
Sub-Enclosure No. 2, in Rear-Admiral Sir Charles Napier's Letter No. 152.
Her Majesty's ship Vulture, at sea,
June 10, 1854.

SIR,

HAVING in obedience to your orders proceeded off Old Carleby, on the morning of the 6th instant, the state of the weather obliged me to put to sea again; but, on the following day, the 7th, the wind moderating, we were able to return, and anchored abreast of Trullön Island, as near as we prudently could to the bar, in four fathoms water, the Odin in Company.

The boats, as per enclosed list (1), were dispatched under charge of the senior lieutenant of the Vulture, Mr. Charles A. Wise, with signals and directions for his guidance, as per enclosures (Nos. 2 and 3).

It is my painful duty to report that they were met in force by the enemy, and beaten off, with the loss of the Vulture's paddle-box boat.

Immediately on perceiving the attack, the reserve was ordered away, consisting of one paddle-box boat from each ship, accompanied by Captain Francis Scott, in his gig, who having gallantly volunteered his services, I readily entrusted with the charge of bringing the boats out of action, as I observed the fire of the enemy evidently proceeded from an overwhelming force.

The following day under a flag of truce, Lieutenant Wise proceeded with a letter to the Governor of Gamla Carleby; he returned without communicating, the flag not being acknowledged, and reported that a regiment of regular troops were drawn up during the time the boat remained off the beach, and apparently a second regiment, from the difference of their uniforms, employed throwing up breastworks, with embrasures.

From there being only thirteen feet water on the deepest part of the bar, and the impossibility of getting ships of the draft of water of the Vulture and Odin over, I considered our further operations there impracticable, and sailed at six P.M., for the rendezvous at Hallgrund Beacon, off Jacobstad, but the unfavourable state of the weather has prevented our employing our force in its immediate neighbourhood.

Enclosed is Lieutenant Wise's report (No. 4), as also the returns of killed, wounded, and missing from the two ships (5 and 6), and a copy of my letter to the Governor of Carleby Gamla (7), and of my sailing orders (No. 8).

I have, &c.
(Signed) FREDERICK H.H. GLASSE,
Captain.

Rear-Admiral J. Hanway Plumridge.
Her Majesty's ship Vulture, off Gamla
Carleby, June 8, 1854.

SIR,

I HAVE the honour to report to you, that in obedience to your orders, I proceeded with the boats of Her Majesty's ships Vulture and Odin, named in the margin,* towards Gamla Carleby.

Having anchored the boats in line abreast, their guns pointed towards the beach, I landed in the gig with a flag of truce, for the purpose of communicating with some persons whom I observed on the adjacent shore. The flag was duly received, and I addressed one who styled himself the Burgomaster, demanding that all the property of the Emperor of Russia should be given up to me, and that on this condition, in compliance with Admiral Plumridge's notice, the town and private property would be respected. Not being able to obtain a satisfactory answer, and assistance in communicating with the Governor being denied me, re-embarked and directing Lieutenant Carrington to proceed ahead in a boat of light draught to sound, ordered the boats to weigh and form in two lines abreast, but before this was executed the enemy's fire from storehouses on our right, opened with field pieces and musketry, which was promptly returned by our guns and small arms.

The enemy being in great force and rapidly increasing – their position well chosen, and protected among wood and houses, behind which they were completely concealed, and from which they poured a most destructive fire – I deemed it expedient to withdraw the boats, and accordingly made the signal for the general recall.

I did not, however, accomplish this without the loss of the paddle-box boat of this ship, which was destroyed by the enemy's fire; and it is with sorrow I contemplate the severe loss of officers and men we have sustained. Lieutenant Carrington, of the Odin, fell while in the act of carrying out my orders. His boat, a cutter, was the object of the enemy's first fire, by which she had eleven struck down, and gave us first notice of their proximity. Mr. N.J. Morphy, mate, in charge of the Vulture's paddle-box boat, I observed encouraging his crew with great gallantry. Mr. C.F.H. Montague (mate), Odin, I am sorry to say fell mortally wounded while most gallantly doing his duty in the paddle-box boat of that ship. I have to add that the conduct of every officer and man was most exemplary. I cannot close this report without mentioning my approbation of the cool and praiseworthy conduct of Lieutenants Madden and Fellowes, who commanded the other two boats with guns.

I am, &c..
(Signed) CHAS. A. WISE,
Senior Lieutenant H.M.S. Vulture.

Captain F.H.H. Glasse,
H.M.S. Vulture.

* *Centre –*

	Vulture's 1st gig.
Vulture. –	Starboard Division
	Pinnace.
	2nd paddle-box boat.
	1st cutter.
	2nd cutter.
Odin. –	Port Division
	1st paddle-box boat.
	Pinnace.
	1st cutter.
	2nd cutter.

Return of the Boats of Her Majesty's ships Vulture and Odin, employed in the attack on Gamla Carleby, the night of the 7th and 8th June, 1854.

Vulture's Boats.

Pinnace –   Edward Madden, lieutenant; 22 men.

2nd Paddle-box boat –	Nathl. J. Morphy, mate; 27 men.
1st Cutter –	George P. Chapman, 2nd master; George Duncan, M.D., assistant-surgeon; 14 men.
2nd Cutter –	J.V.D. Butler, naval cadet; 11 men.
1st Gig –	Charles A. Wise, lieutenant; Wm. P. Burton, 1st lieutenant, R.M.A.; 5 men.

Total –   **Officers 7; men 79.**

Reserve:

1st Paddle-box boat –	Charles F. Hill, mate; 22 men.
Vulture's whole total –	Officers 8; men 101.

Odin's Boats.

Pinnace –	Thomas H.B. Fellowes, lieutenant; Henry Magrath, midshipman; Henry Salmund,

naval cadet; 29 men.

1st Paddle-box boat –	Edward M.W. Carrington, lieutenant; Charles F. Montague, mate; Arthur Lewis, lieutenant R.M.; Ernest Rice, naval cadet; 40 men.
1st Cutter –	William Long, acting 2nd master; John E. Hamilton, assistant-surgeon; 16 men.
2nd Cutter –	Henry Athorpe. midshipman; 16 men.

Total –   **Officers 10; men 101.**

Reserve:

2nd Paddle-box boat –	William Mould, lieutenant; Charles Leigh, master's assistant; 22 men.
1st Gig –	Francis Scott, Esq., captain; 7 men.
Odin's whole total –	Officers 13; men 130.
Whole force, 252; viz.: –	Officers 21; men 231.

(Signed) FREDERICK GLASSE,
Captain.

Sub-Enclosure No. 3,* in Sir Charles Napier's Letter No. 152.

THE undersigned Commanding Officer of Her Britannic Majesty's ships at anchor off the port, presents his compliments to his Excellency the Governor of Gamla Carleby, and trusting to the high and honourable feeling that should always exist between civilized nations, to alleviate, when possible, the horrors of war, has sent in to request his consideration for the wounded and prisoners who have fallen into his hands, that the former may be permitted the aid of surgical attendance in mitigation of their sufferings.

His Excellency will confer a favour on the undersigned by informing him of the number of killed and wounded of the party captured in last night's attack.

(Signed) FREDERICK H.H. GLASSE,
Captain.

* This letter was sent in charge of Lieutenant Wise, of the Vulture, but was not delivered; the flag of truce not being acknowledged. F.H.H.G.

FREDERICK GLASSE,
Captain.

THE English Admiral will not molest or injure private persons or their property.

He only intends to destroy the castles and defences, shipping, and the property of the Emperor of Russia.

So long as the inhabitants continue peaceable within their houses, they will be protected, but should they offer assistance to the Russian troops, they will be treated as enemies.

The English Admiral desires that the women and children should be sent out of the town.

Enclosure No. 4 in Sir Charles Napier's Letter, No. 152.

Her Majesty's ship Odin, at Sea,
June 10, 1854.

SIR,

I HAVE the honour to request that you will be pleased to move Rear-Admiral James Hanway Plumridge to bring under the notice of the Commander-in-Chief the extremely gallant conduct of Mr. Henry Hugh Monk Magrath, midshipman, in the pinnace of this ship on the occasion of an attack on Gamla Carleby, on the night of the 7th instant, who, whilst loading the 12-pounder for the fifteenth time, was struck down by a severe wound from a musket-ball, and removed to the stern sheets, where it was bound up, and he was then only prevented from attempting to resume his former duty by the express order of Lieutenant Fellowes, commanding the boat.

I am, &c.
(Signed) F. SCOTT,
Captain.

Captain F.H.H. Glasse,
H.M.S. Vulture.
Admiralty, 29th June, 1854.

With reference to the above Despatches, Lieutenant Benjamin Pentland Priest has this day been promoted to the rank of Commander.

No. 6. *Camp before Bomarsund,*

MY LORD DUKE, *August* 19, 1854.

I HAVE the honour to report, that on the morning of the 16th the fire from the fleet was resumed, and after about two hours' firing, the white flag was hoisted on the large fort of Bomarsund, and the garrison* surrendered unconditionally, and were embarked in two hours afterwards.

The interior of the fort showed that the fire from the ships had been excellent; nevertheless the injury to the works was trifling, and ought not to have induced the Governor, with such a strong garrison, no breach, and a well casemated work, to have surrendered. The cause may be considered that, finding two of his principal advanced works taken, a breaching battery ready to open, and no prospect of relief, it would be a sacrifice of life to hold out any longer: thus has been lost to Russia a most important military post, and, judging from the nature of the works existing, those partly erected, and the foundations of others which have been laid, it was evidently the intention of the Russian Government to have created a first-rate fortress; the position of Bomarsund at the entrance of the Gulfs of Finland and Bothnia, with a beautiful and extensive anchorage well sheltered, points it out as a position of the most favourable nature, and no expence apparently has been spared in the construction of the works already built, and the walls of those partly erected are of the same substantial nature.

The position of Bomarsund is naturally very strong, and favourable for defence; bold and rocky, with a fine command of the ground in its immediate front, and when occupied with suitable advanced works would make its capture a very long operation, and if fully garrisoned would require a very large force for its reduction: the Admiral has sent home his report accompanied by a joint report from the French General Niel and myself, upon the practicability of holding Bomarsund in its present state; that report will have reached London before this despatch, it is therefore needless for me to recapitulate the substance of that report, as your Grace will have been acquainted with it; in fact I have no copy, as it was called for in great haste, and no time was allowed me to do so before the departure of Lieutenant Nugent, Royal Engineers, the bearer of the Admiral's despatches.

This the first operation of the combined forces having been brought to a successful termination, I may be permitted to state that the utmost cordiality and good feeling have pervaded every branch of the service employed, English as well as French; and in making these observations I should not do justice to the officers of the Royal Navy, the seamen and marines of the fleet who were employed under my orders on shore, if I did not notice the great order and regularity as well as the great zeal with which every duty was performed, and the strict discipline which was observed in camp; not a single complaint has been made to me of any irregularity on their part.

From Captain Ramsay, R N., in charge of the seamen, and from Colonel Graham, in command of the Royal Marines, I have received the most ready assistance, for which my acknowledgments are due; Captain Ord, my Brigade-Major, has been most active and zealous, and in addition to his staff duties he offered his services, and took his tour of duty, as an engineer, during the period our works were erecting. I have also to express how much indebted I am to my naval aide-de-camp, the Hon. Edward Cochrane, for the assistance he has afforded me throughout our operations, and since I have been deprived of the services of Lieut. Cowell, he has performed that officer's duty, so far as a naval man could perform military duties.

I have, &c.,
(Signed) HARRY D. JONES,
Brigadier-General.

P.S. – I have omitted to mention the services of Captain King, Royal Engineers, who laid out with great judgment the road up the hill leading to the breaching battery. My thanks are due to him and Lieut. Nugent for the able and zealous manner in which they performed the harassing duties which fell to their lot. The Royal Sappers and Miners have distinguished themselves by their good conduct and in the construction of the batteries.

(Signed) H. D. J.

His Grace the Duke of Newcastle,
&c. &c. &c.

* *Prisoners, 2,300; 139 pieces of artillery taken in the different forts.*

TUESDAY, AUGUST 22, 1854.
Admiralty, August 21, 1854.

DESPATCHES, of which the following are copies, have been received from Vice-Admiral Sir Charles Napier, K.C.B., Commander-in-Chief of Her Majesty's Ships and Vessels in the Baltic:

CAPTURE OF TWO TOWERS OF BOMARSUND.

No. 354. Bulldog, off Bomarsund,
August 16, 1854.

SIR,

1. AT four o'clock in the morning of the 13th instant the French battery, of four 16-pounders and four mortars, opened a splendid fire on the western tower, which commands the fortress of Bomarsund and the anchorage: a white flag was displayed in the afternoon, which led to nothing; but on the morning of the 14th the tower was surprised by the Chasseurs. General Jones's battery of 32-pounders was finished in the night and ready to open; but, not being wanted, was turned against the eastern tower, and on the morning of the 15th he opened his fire: the battery was manned by seamen and marine artillery from the four ships named in the margin,* under the direction of Captain Ramsay, of the Hogue, assisted by Commander Preedy, Lieutenant Somerset, of the Duke of Wellington, and the officers named in the margin;† their fire was beautiful.

2. At six P.M. one side was knocked in, and the tower surrendered.

In the attack on the western tower the Chasseurs, with Minnié rifles, were employed so successfully, that it was difficult for the enemy to load their guns; in the attack on the eastern tower we had no Chasseurs, and they were enabled to load their guns with more facility.

3. Our loss has been trifling, one man killed and one wounded, but I have to lament the death of the Honourable Lieutenant Cameron Wrottesley, R.E., who was mortally wounded by a cannonball, and died twenty minutes after he had been sent to the Belleisle.

4. The enemy had 6 men killed; 7 wounded, and 125 were taken prisoners. I have sent the latter to the Termagant.

5. The loss of the French at the western tower was also trifling.

6. Both batteries were admirably constructed and admirably fought, which accounts for the small loss. General Jones speaks in high terms of the conduct of the seamen and marine artillery, and the precision of their fire.

7. During the time the operations were going on, General Daraguay d'Hilliers was employed in establishing his breaching batteries against the great fortress, and the French and English steamers, as per margin,‡ supported by Trident (bearing the flag of Rear-Admiral Penau), Duperré, Edinburgh, and Ajax, kept up a well-directed fire from their shell guns, and very much damaged the fortress, whilst Captain The Honourable F.T. Pelham, of the Blenheim, kept up a beautiful fire from a 10-inch gun, landed in the battery we had driven the enemy out of a few days before. His position was one of great danger, but the battery was put in such good order by Captain Pelham, that the men were well covered, and he had no loss.

8. The General's breaching batteries will be ready by to-morrow, and they shall be well supported by the ships-of-the-line of both nations, and the steamers. The

narrowness of the ground on which the General has established his breaching battery, very much circumscribes the space; the greatest caution will be necessary to prevent firing on his troops, and the little space in the anchorage before Bomarsund, and the intricacy of the navigation, will prevent ships approaching the main fortress so near as could be wished; but when the batteries are established acting in the rear of the fort, and supported by the shell guns in front, it cannot hold out more than a few hours.

9. I have put off to the last moment the departure of the mail, but I shall send an extra courier the moment the fort surrenders.

10. The western tower was fired either by accident or design, I do not know which, and blew up at 11 A.M. yesterday.

11. I am sorry to add that Lieutenant Cowell, Royal Engineers, Aide-de-Camp to Brigadier-General Jones, was unfortunately wounded in the leg by the accidental discharge of his pistol; he is now on board the Belleisle, doing well, but the loss of his services is much to be regretted.

I have, &c.,

(Signed) CHAS. NAPIER,

Vice-Admiral and Commander-in-Chief.

The Secretary of the Admiralty.

* *Edinburgh; Hogue; Ajax; Blenheim.*

† *H. M. S. Blenheim—*   *Lt. F.A. Close.*
                             J.J. Ball, Master.
                             L. Wildman, Acting Mate.
                             Lieut. T.L. Ward.
                             David Orr, Acting Mate.
                             P.B. Nolloth, Brevet-Major, R.M.
                             Wm. Sanders, First Lt. R.M.
                             S. Wade, Asst. Surgeon.
H. M.S. Ajax—   *W.L. Sayer, Capt. R.M.*
                             Thos. Bent, First Lieut., R.M.
                             H.L.C. Robinson, Mate.
H.M.S. Hogue—   *Chas. Smith. Mate.*
                             M. Singer, Lt. R.M.
                             Capt. Fosbroke, R.M.
                             A.R. Bradford, Surgeon.
H, M. S. Edinburgh—   *Lieut. G.F. Burgess.*
                             Capt. Delacombe, R.M.
                             A. Tait, Lt. R.M.
                             E.J. Giles, Passed Clerk.

‡ *Asmodée, Phlegeton, Darien; Arrogant, Amphion, Valorous, Driver, Bulldog, Hecla.*

SURRENDER OF BOMARSUND.

No. 355. Bulldog, off Bomarsund,
August 16, 1854.

SIR,

IN continuation of my despatch of this date, I beg you will inform their Lordships that, after sending away the mail, the fortress opened a heavy fire on Captain Pelham's battery, which had annoyed them much, and which he maintained all yesterday and to day, and it is wonderful how he and his men escaped. He had with him Lieutenant Close and Mr. Wildman, Mate, of whom he speaks highly. Seeing his position, I immediately ordered the ships and steamers named in the margin,* who were within range with their 10-inch guns, as well as the French mortars on shore, which had been playing on them some time, to give them a shot and shell every five minutes; and their fire was so well directed that the enemy held out a flag of truce.

2. I sent Captain Hall (of the Bulldog) onshore, who was shortly joined by Admiral Parseval's Aide-de-Camp, and two of General Baraguay d'Hillier's Staff, and the troops in the fortress agreed to lay down their arms and march out.

3. After I had landed I was joined by the French Admiral and the Commander-in-Chief of the Army; the prisoners (about 2,000 I believe) were marched out and embarked in steamers, and proceeded to Led Sund, to Commodore The Honourable Frederick Grey, who will conduct them to the Downs to await for further orders.

4. I beg to congratulate their Lordships on the fall of this important fortress, which will be followed by the submission of the Garden of Islands, with so small a loss; and I am happy to say the greatest cordiality has subsisted between the French General and Admiral and myself, as well as between the soldiers and sailors of the two nations.

5. As soon as I can collect a list of the stores captured, it shall be forwarded to their Lordships, and a Commissary has been named for that purpose.

6. This despatch will be delivered by my Flag Lieutenant (Lieutenant John de Courcy Agnew),whom I beg to recommend to their Lordships for promotion.

I have, &c.,
(Signed) CHARLES NAPIER,
Vice-Admiral and Commander-in-Chief.
The Secretary of the Admiralty.

* *Edinburgh; Ajax; Arrogant; Amphion; Valorous; Sphynx; Driver.*

TUESDAY, AUGUST 29, 1854
Admiralty, August 28, 1854.

DESPATCHES, of which the following are copies or extracts, have been received from Vice-Admiral Sir Charles Napier, K.C.B., Commander-in-Chief of Her Majesty's Ships and Vessels in the Baltic:

No. 380. Bulldog, off Bomarsund,
August 19, 1854.

SIR,

I BEG to inclose a letter from Rear-Admiral Plumridge, who was stationed, with the Hecla and the French steamer Cocyte (commanded by Lieutenant de Vaisseau A. Georgette du Buisson),on the north side of Bomarsund.

2. I had intended to have brought his squadron through the Presto Channel to have shelled the north side of Bomarsund, but when the breaching batteries were placed he could not take that station without endangering the men in the French batteries; he therefore very wisely took up a position so that he had the Presto Tower and Bomarsund in a line, and did good service against the Presto Tower, which I afterwards examined. He was rather too close, being within range of the enemy's fire, and received some damage, but no one was hurt.

3. The ships I stationed to the southward were out of range of the enemy's guns, and received no damage; but the shot and shells from the 10-inch guns, together with the fire from the four French mortars, which never missed, and the excellent fire from Captain Pelham's battery, together with the preparations the enemy saw in progress, I presume expedited the surrender.

4. Had the enemy held out till the following morning, when the breaching battery, judiciously placed by the French Engineer (General Niel) within 400 yards of the rear of the fort, and the ships the French and English Admirals intended to place in their flank, the fortress would have been reduced to ashes.

5. I have the honour of enclosing lists of the whole British Force landed, and of casualties, together with a list of prisoners and guns captured, being no less than 112 mounted, 3 mortars,7 field pieces, and 79 not mounted.

6. The Commissioners are now taking an account of the stores, and they are preparing plans not only of the batteries in existence but of those in progress, which I shall send home as soon as possible.

7. This has been a most arduous and laborious service, and I have great reason to be satisfied with the great exertions of all the officers, seamen, and marines, and their orderly conduct.

8. General Jones speaks in the highest terms of the conduct of Colonel Graham and his marines. The firing of the seamen and marines and marine artillery, under Captain Ramsay, was most precise; he himself was slightly wounded.

9. The shells thrown by the ships were most destructive, and had the fortress

resisted till the following day when all was ready on shore, they would have been irresistible.

I have, &c.,
CHAS. NAPIER.
Vice-Admiral and Commander-in-Chief.
The Secretary of the Admiralty.

No. 10.
RESPECTING OPERATIONS AT BOMARSUND.

Her Majesty's ship Blenheim, Bomarsund,
August 17, 1854.

IT is with great pleasure that I have to report to you, for the information of the Commander-in-Chief, the exceeding good conduct and gallantry displayed by the officers and men under my command on shore at Blenheim Battery, during the attack on Bomarsund, on the 15th and 16th instant, when under a very heavy fire of shell and shot during the greater part of this period.

All deserve the highest praise, and I name in the margin* the two officers and captain of gun.

I have, &c.,
FREDK. PELHAM,
Captain.
Rear-Admiral Henry D. Chads, C. B.

* *Fras. A. Close, Lieutenant; Leveson Wildman, Acting Mate; John Farrell, Chief Boats Mate and Captain of Gun.*

Edinburgh off Bomarsund,
August 18, 1854.

Submitted for the consideration of the Commander-in-Chief.

H. D. CHADS,
Rear-Admiral.
Vice-Admiral Sir Charles Napier, K. C.B.

Leopard, at Bomarsund.
August 17, 1854.

SIR,

OBSERVING on the 16th instant the Presto Tower's fire was harassing the constructors of General Jones' battery, I moved (in obedience to your orders) the Leopard, Hecla, and French steamer Cocyte into a delightful sequestered position, screened from observation by the trees on the neck of land to the eastward of the tower, having the great Bomarsund Fort and it in one, so that our over shot and shell should fall to the lot of Bomarsund.

The simultaneous opening fire from the three broadsides was the first intimation the tower inmates had of our movements, and I had the satisfaction of seeing (at times from aloft) the steadiness and precision with which the shot and shell were delivered from each vessel. I only regret that the trees alluded to obscured us all from your view, as I feel almost assured this bit of service would have been deemed worthy of better notice than it becomes me to give at so short a distance from your flag. It is however, Sir, my most gratifying duty to state, on behalf of the whole of the officers and ships' companies, that I entertain the most lively admiration of their exertions, as well as of the exemplary animation exhibited by Captains Hall and Giffard, and Lieutenant de Vaisseau A. Georgette du Buisson, of His Imperial Majesty's steam-vessel Cocyte.

I have, &c.
HANWAY PLUMRIDGE,
Rear-Admiral of the White.
Vice-Admiral Sir Charles Napier, K.C.B.,
Commander-in-Chief, &c. &c. &c.

In Camp, Bomarsund, Aland Islands,
August 18, 1854.

SIR,

I HAVE the honour to acquaint you that in compliance with your directions, I landed at Bomarsund on the 8th instant, in command of a battalion of Royal Marines, and placed myself under the orders of Brigadier-General Jones, R.E., the general officer commanding the brigade.

The brigadier-general having by a brigade order of yesterday's date, thanked the officers, non-commissioned officers and men of the Royal Marines under my command for their good conduct during the period they have been employed on shore, as also for the cheerful and willing manner in which they have performed the very laborious duties they were called upon to perform, and which has contributed so greatly to the successful results which have been obtained, I have only to bear my testimony to their zeal and steadiness in the performance of every duty allotted to them.

The artillery companies of the corps under the direction of Captain Ramsay, R.N., with Lieutenants Mawbey, Poore, and Hewett, R.M.A., performed their part well. The exactness and precision of their fire from the battery reflected great credit on the officers in command of the several guns.

The divisional companies were repeatedly exposed to a heavy fire of round and grape as well as from the Minnié rifle, the casualties have been few, for which we have to be thankful to a divine providence.

I beg to bring to your favourable notice the zeal and energetic conduct of the two officers appointed by brigade orders of the 9th instant, to perform the duties of field officers, viz.; Major Nolloth and Captain Heriot, R.M., of my brigade, Major Captain W.C.P. Elliott, whose exertions in support of my orders call forth my warmest thanks.

I beg also to assure you that the captains of companies, subalterns, non-commissioned officers and men, did their duties in a manner highly satisfactory to me.

Lieutenant Fraser, R.M., acted as the adjutant, and Lieutenant Lennox as my orderly officer, and I have great pleasure in bringing them both under your favourable consideration as deserving officers, together with Assistant-Surgeon Daniel John Duigan, and the other medical officers employed under my orders, who evinced the greatest willingness and promptitude in the execution of their duties.

I have, &c.,
F. GRAHAM,
Colonel, Royal Marines, A.D.C., in
command of Brigade in Camp.
Vice-Admiral Sir Charles Napier, K.C.B.,
&c. &c. Commander-in-Chief.

Head-Quarters, Bomarsund,
August 19, 1854.

SIR,

I BEG leave to enclose a copy of a Brigade Order which I directed to be issued previous to the seamen and marines, who have been employed on shore, returning to their respective ships, and it affords me great satisfaction to state that the discipline observed merits my warmest approbation; not a single complaint has been addressed to me on the part of the inhabitants against any individual of the force employed on shore under my orders.

I beg leave to bring to your notice the valuable assistance I have received from my naval aide-de-camp the Honourable Ernest Cochrane, who has been most zealous and active in the discharge of the duties required of him, many of which have, in consequence of Lieut. Cowell's absence, from his wounds, partaken more of the military character.

Mr. Cochrane is a young officer of great intelligence, and I beg leave to recommend him most strongly to your favourable notice, and to express a hope, should a force be again employed on shore, that I may have the benefit of his assistance.

I have, &c.,
HARRY D. JONES,
Brigadier-General.
Vice-Admiral Sir Charles Napier,
&c. &c. &c.

No. 396. *Bulldog, off Bomarsund.*
August, 22, 1854.

SIR,

I BEG to transmit their Lordships the enclosed letter I have received from General Baraguay d'Hilliers, expressing his satisfaction at the zealous manner in which Commander the Hon. Arthur Cochrane performed his duties during the time he was attached to the General's Staff.

Commander Cochrane was in the batteries throughout the operations of the siege of Bomarsund, and General Baraguay d'Hilliers has spoken to me in the highest terms of his conduct.

I have, &c.,
CHARLES NAPIER,
Vice- Admiral and Commander-in-Chief.
The Secretary of the Admiralty.

No. 380. *Brigade Orders.*
Camp, Bomarsund, August 17, 1854.

THE Brigadier-General cannot allow the force which he has had the honour to command, during the operations against the forts of Bomarsund, to re-embark without requesting the officers, seamen, non-commissioned officers and privates of the Royal Sappers and Miners and Royal Marines, to accept his thanks for their good conduct during the period they have been employed on shore, as also for the cheerful and willing manner in which they performed the very laborious duties which they were called upon to perform, and which has contributed so greatly to the successful results which have been obtained.

The excellence and precision of the fire from the two batteries was the admiration of every one who witnessed it, and reflects great credit upon the officers in command of the several guns.

Captain Ramsay, R.N., and Colonel Graham, Royal Marines, are requested to accept the Brigadier-General's thanks for the very able assistance they have afforded him during the period he has had the honour to have them under his command.

(Signed) H. ST. GEORGE ORD,
Major of Brigade.

No. 381. Bulldog, off Bomarsund
August 19, 1854.

SIR,

I HAVE received their Lordships' letter of the 7th instant, approving of all my proceedings and their satisfaction at Admiral Plumridge's activity and judiciousness.

2. I owe much to Admiral Plumridge for the manner he placed his squadron to prevent reinforcements being thrown in; and I am informed two Russian Admirals were sent among the islands to see if it were possible to pass the blockading squadron, and returned in despair.

Rear-Admiral Plumridge, as second in command, I have removed into the Neptune; Rear-Admiral Martin will hoist his flag on board the Leopard, and take charge of the Gulf of Bothnia, during the rest of the season, which will not be long.

I have, &c.,
CHAS. NAPIER,
Vice-Admiral and Commander-in-Chief.
The Secretary of the Admiralty.

No. 397. Bulldog, Led Sund,
August 22, 1854.

SIR,

I AM happy to inform their Lordships, that Rear-Admiral Chads has conducted three of his line of battle ships in perfect safety through all the intricate navigation of the channels from Bomarsund to this anchorage.

I have, &c.,
CHAS. NAPIER,
Vice-Admiral and Commander-in-Chief.
The Secretary of the Admiralty.

Admiralty, September 6, 1854.

DESPATCHES, of which the following are copies or extracts, have been received from Vice-Admiral Sir Charles Napier, K.C.B., Commander-in-Chief of Her Majesty's Ships and Vessels in the Baltic:

RECONNAISSANCE OF THE ENEMY'S GUN BOATS AND STEAMERS AT ABO.

No. 410. Duke of Wellington, Led Sund,
August 27, 1854.

SIR,

HAVING received information that Russian troops and gun boats were amongst the islands, I sent Captain Scott with a small squadron, as per margin,* to find them out, and I beg to enclose his very able report.

2. Captain Scott threaded his way through the islands in a most persevering manner, as their Lordships will see by the chart I send; his ships were repeatedly on shore, and the Odin no less than nine times, before they discovered the enemy's gun boats and steamers lying behind a floating boom, supported on each side by batteries and a number of troops, covering the town of Abo, where they have collected a large force.

3. I take this opportunity of bringing under their Lordships' notice the very great exertions of the surveying officers, Captain Sulivan, assisted by Mr. Evans, Master of the Lightning, and Commander Otter, of the Alban; and I have no hesitation in saying, that it is owing to their exertions this fleet have found their way, with comparatively little damage, into creeks and corners, never intended for ships-of-the-line; day and night have they worked, and worked successfully; Commander Otter is an old officer, and well worthy of promotion, and Captain Sulivan and his assisting surveyor, deserve the protection of their Lordships.

I have, &c.,
CHAS. NAPIER,
Vice-Admiral and Commander-in-Chief.
The Secretary of the Admiralty,

* *Odin, Alban, Gorgon, Driver.*

Enclosure No. 1 in Sir Charles Napier's Letter No. 410.

Her Majesty's ship Odin, Led Sund,
August 25, 1854.

SIR,

I HAVE the honour to state that in pursuance of your orders, dated the 18th of August, I proceeded with Her Majesty's ships Odin, Alban, Gorgon, and Driver, under my command, towards Kumblinge, and the islands east of it.

2. Having procured a pilot at Dagerby, we felt our way on with boats and leads through a most difficult and intricate navigation, in the course of which every ship has been on shore (Gorgon and Odin frequently), but we hope with no further injury than that done to the copper in various places.

3. At Kumblinge and the adjacent islands I was unable to obtain any information of troops or gun boats, but learnt on Sunday, at Asterholm, that a small fast steamboat from Abo was in our immediate vicinity.

4. Rather than return to your flag without intelligence, I resolved to attempt a passage to Abo, and on Monday at daylight, leaving the larger ships at anchor, I took all the masters in the Alban, surveyed and buoyed off a passage for ten miles to Bergham, and then returned for the other ships, but the Gorgon grounding, delayed us for that night.

5. On Tuesday we made our way in safety into the comparatively main open track to Abo, beyond Bergham; at two P.M., observed a small steamer watching us, and at three P.M., several gun boats moving a body of troops from the point (one and a half miles to the north-west) up to the chain across the narrow entrance to the harbour.

6. Having approached to within 3,000 yards the Alban stood in to sound. The entrance of the harbour was closed by two impediments, the one in front appeared to be a chain laid on a floating platform, the other of stakes and booms, between which the gun boats were stationed at regular intervals, and the steam vessels (four in number) were under the shelter of the points.

7. About 4 P.M. the Alban fired the first shell which burst over one of the gun boats. I then commenced firing and was followed at intervals by Gorgon and Driver, but with little or no effect that we could discover, except that of fully answering my purpose in drawing a return from the masked batteries and gun boats. Only one of the former at the end of the boom mounted a gun or guns of large calibre and long range, but which was concealed from our view by a point of land. The others, three in number, about one mile to the west of the boom, as far as we could judge, did not

in any one case mount more than five, or less than three small guns. A fort, of apparently eight or nine large guns, at a distance, constructed to enfilade both passages, fired repeatedly, but the shot invariably fell a very short distance beyond the south end of Little Beckholm.

8. As my object was not to attack Abo, but to examine its defences, I contented myself with firing a shot occasionally at the gun boats, or whatever looked like a masked battery. In the meantime Commander Otter, in the most zealous and gallant manner, after going as close as it was prudent in the Alban, pulled in with his gig, sounding just within range of the gun boats and batteries, which were all the time keeping up a constant fire.

9. The sum of the information I have been able to obtain with his assistance, and that of Commanders Cracroft and Hobart, amounts to this – seventeen row boats, two guns each, and about twenty oars on each side, four steam vessels (all small),two having the flag with cross anchors in it, and another was observed steaming away through the Channel to the eastward of Beckholm. Three (if not four) masked batteries, and another I think in course of construction, for the position of which I refer you to the very clear delineation executed by Commander Otter.

10. The Channel appears to be very narrow, and the thick woods were evidently full of soldiers. We learnt that our arrival had been anticipated (as we expected, knowing that we had been watched by a steamer for some days), and that four thousand additional troops had been sent on the previous day, and five thousand more were expected to arrive on the following day; that there were six steamers, five small and one large (the latter we did not see), and eighteen boats and two guns, and eighty men, besides soldiers in each.

The weather was so bad on Thursday, that I was detained under Bergo, and went into Bomarsund this morning; when, having communicated with Captain Warden, and received his despatches, I proceeded to join your flag.

I have only to add my very anxious hope that my proceedings may meet with the approbation of the Commander-in-Chief.

I have, &c,,
Captain.
Vice-Admiral Sir Charles Napier, K.C.B.,
Commander-in-Chief, &c., &c., &c.

Enclosure No. 2 in Sir Charles Napier's Letter, No. 410.

Her Majesty's ship Odin, Led Sund,
August 25, 1854.

SIR,

IN returning to your flag from detached service with the squadron you did me the honour to place under my orders, it is my gratifying duty to express to you how well and ably I have been supported by Commanders Otter, Cracroft, and Hobart, in their respective ships, during my late examination of Abo and its defences, and engagement with the batteries and gun-boats at that place; and I beg to offer my humble testimony to their ability, zeal, and great exertions during a week of very difficult and harrassing duties.

I desire most particularly to call your attention to the services performed by Commander Otter during that time. Nothing but the most unceasing and laborious efforts of a clever, indefatigable, and zealous officer could have performed the duties I required of him, and which alone enabled me to obtain the information herewith enclosed, and to examine a place so difficult of access and so little known as Abo, in the limited time to which I was restricted by you.

Under the above circumstances, upon public grounds, and for the advantage of the naval service, which I know you have so much at heart, I beg to urge your recommendation of that officer and Lieutenant William Mould, senior and gunnery lieutenant of this ship, to the Lords Commissioners of the Admiralty for that promotion their constant and valuable services have so long entitled them to expect and hope for.

I have, &c.,
FRANCIS SCOTT,
Captain.
Vice-Admiral Sir Charles Napier, K.C.B.
&c. &c. &c.

CHAPTER 2

PRELIMINARY OPERATIONS IN THE BLACK SEA AND CRIMEA, THE BATTLE OF THE ALMA

Admiralty, July 27, 1854.

DESPATCHES, of which the following are copies, have been received from Vice-Admiral Dundas, C.B., Commander-in-Chief of Her Majesty's Ships and Vessels in the Mediterranean and Black Sea:

Destruction of Batteries, &c., at the Sulina. Death of Captain Hyde Parker, of the Firebrand. No. 330. Britannia, off Baljik, July 11, 1854.

SIR,

I HAVE the honour to enclose for the information of the Lords Commissioners of the Admiralty, copies of the reports of Commander Powell and other officers, who, on the 8th instant, attacked and completely destroyed the inner batteries, stockades and buildings, at the Sulina Mouth of the Danube.

2. The satisfaction I feel at the perfect success of this gallant exploit, is much diminished by the death of Captain Hyde Parker, who fell when leading his men.

The service has lost in him a most promising young officer, who was always zealous to do his duty, and never made a difficulty.

3. Acting Lieutenant Lyons, after the fall of his gallant captain, commanded the Firebrand's boats, and most admirably did his duty, suffering a loss in his own boat of five men wounded.

I have, &c.

J.W.D. DUNDAS, Vice-Admiral.
The Secretary of the Admiralty.

Enclosure No. 1, in Mediterranean Letter No. 333.
Her Majesty's ship Vesuvius, off Sulina,
July 8, 1854.

SIR,

IT is with great grief that I have to report to you that Captain Hyde Parker, of Her Majesty's steam-frigate Firebrand, has been this day killed whilst in the act of leading his men to take a stockade battery on the Danube.

The loss of this gallant Officer is but ill compensated by the complete success with which his attack was attended.

The circumstances are as follows: Captain Hyde Parke directed a strong party of boats from the Firebrand and Vesuvius to accompany him up the Danube for the purpose of destroying some works which were occupied by the Russians. At 2 P.M. the boats entered the Danube, Captain Parker's gig in advance; at a bend of the river, opposite a number of houses on the right bank and a large stockade on the left, a sharp fire was opened upon him, and his boat was nearly riddled, some of his men were wounded.

The heavy boats were coming up and Captain Parker at once pulled back to them, hailing me to land the marines and be ready to storm. This order was executed by the marines and a detachment of seamen in the same gallant spirit with which it was given. Captain Parker then dashed on shore, in his gig, and at once advanced with a few men, he was in front and greatly exposed; a tremendous fire was soon opened by the enemy upon them, and a few minutes after landing a bullet passed through their leader's heart, and in a moment this gallant sailor ceased to live. Thus died an officer whose merits, sir, are well known to yourself. His conduct on this occasion leaves an example of valour that never can be erased from the memory of those who were present.

The command of the force then devolved upon myself. I directed the gun-boats, and rocket-boat at once to be brought to the front; the storming party was formed by Lieutenant Jull, R.M.A., the gun-boats commenced a most effective fire upon the houses and battery, and in a short time the enemy's fire was silenced.

I directed the storming party to advance, and the place was entered at a run by a detachment of marines and sailors, headed by Lieutenant Jull, R.M.A., and Lieutenant Hawkey, R.M.

We found that the enemy had already retreated at the rear, and so thick was the cover, that pursuit was in vain.

The work that we had taken was a gabion battery, the guns of which had been taken away and the embrasures filled up. It consisted of a front along the river raised about 15 feet high, and 400 yards in extent; in the rear was a morass, and the two flanks, which were not 30 yards in length, were defended as in front; this work enclosed about fifty Government houses, stables, store-houses, and a magazine. The works have been entirely demolished, the houses destroyed, and nothing now marks the spot but a heap of ruins. Part of the town of Sulina, from whence the enemy had opened fire, has been burnt; the principal street I have thought it proper to spare.

There was no means of computing the enemy's loss, although they were seen to fall inside the intrenchments. I am disposed to think that they were assisted in carrying off their wounded, and even defending the place, by some Greeks, as men in the dress of that country were seen intermixed with the Russian troops.

From the heavy fire that was opened upon us, and from the number that were seen afterwards collected at a distance, the enemy must have been in great force before they retreated.

It becomes my duty to report to you the extreme good conduct of all employed on this occasion. The gun-boats were most skilfully managed under circumstances of great difficulty. They were commanded by Lieutenant Sullivan, Acting-Lieutenant Lyons, and Messrs. Goolden and Kerby, mates.

Mr. Carey, second master, has, I regret to say, been badly wounded; he behaved most creditably.

It fell to Lieutenant Jull's lot to have an opportunity of particularly distinguishing himself by his coolness and gallantry whilst in command of the marines, and he speaks most highly of Lieutenant Hawkey, the non-commissioned officers and men that were with him.

The medical officers have merited our best thanks. Dr. O'Hagan, in the execution of his duty, was in the midst of the fire, and his clothes were pierced with bullets.

I must claim your indulgence for the hasty manner in which this Dispatch has been written, as I wish the Firebrand to join your flag immediately, with the body of the late well-loved and gallant Captain Hyde Parker.

I have. &c.
(Signed) RICHARD A. POWELL,
Commander.
Vice-Admiral J.W.D. Dundas, C.B.

Enclosure No. 2, in Mediterranean Letter No. 333.
Her Majesty's steam-frigate Firebrand,
off Sulina, July 8, 1854.

SIR,

I BEG leave to enclose the accompanying letter from Mr. Lyons (Acting-Lieutenant), who commanded the boats of this ship in the attack and destruction of the stockaded battery at the Sulina Mouth of the Danube. He speaks highly of the conduct of the officers and men under his command, especially James Shade, able seaman; but as you were personally present, it only remains for me to state, that Mr. Lyons has displayed much courage and ability, on more than this occasion, since joining the ship.

The death, ever and deeply to be lamented, of our much loved Captain Hyde Parker, has thrown a deep gloom on all who had the fortune to serve under him; but he died leaving an example to all who survive him, of heroic gallantry and ability.

I have, &c.,
(Signed) WM. GORE JONES,
Senior Lieutenant Commanding Her
Majesty's Ship Firebrand.

To Commander R. Powell, R.N.,
H.M.'s Steam-sloop Vesuvius.
Sub-Enclosure No. 1, in Enclosure No. 2, in the Mediterranean Letter, No. 330.
Her Majesty's steam-frigate Firebrand,
off Sulina, July 8, 1854.

SIR,

I HAVE the honour to forward the returns of the boats employed and the number of men killed and wounded at the attack and capture, this day, of a stockade on the left bank of the Danube.

The command of one division of the boats, after the lamented death of Captain Hyde Parker, devolved on me; the pinnace under my immediate command being in advance of the other boats, caused the principal part of the enemy's fire to be directed upon her, and I regret to say that five men in that boat were wounded (three severely).

I have, sir, to speak in the highest terms of the good conduct and steadiness of the whole of the officers and men under my command under the galling fire of the enemy, and I would beg to bring them strongly before your notice. Where all behaved so well it is almost invidious to particularize, but I beg particularly to mention James Shade, able seaman, who, I regret to say, after much distinguishing himself, was severely wounded.

Lieutenant Jull, R.M.A., speaks in equally high terms of the conduct of the marines under his
command.

As you have already been made acquainted with the circumstances under which his country has to mourn the death of Captain Hyde Parker, and the total defeat of the enemy and destruction of their works, which followed, yet scarcely avenged it, it will not be necessary for me to enter into any details of the engagement.

I have, &c.
(Signed) ALGERNON LYONS,
Acting Lieutenant.

To Lieutenant W.G. Jones, R.N.
H.M.S. Firebrand.
Downing-Street, September 30, 1854.

TWO Dispatches, of which the following are an extract and a copy, have been received by the Duke of Newcastle from General Lord Raglan, G.C.B.:

Extract of a Dispatch from General Lord Raglan, G.C.B., to the Duke of
Newcastle. Varna, August 29, 1854.

SIR,

THE embarkation is proceeding rapidly and successfully, thanks to the able arrangements of Rear-Admiral Sir Edmund Lyons, and the unceasing exertions of the officers and men under his orders. It is impossible for me to express in adequate terms my sense of the value of the assistance the Army under my command derives from the Royal Navy.

The same feeling prevails from the highest to the lowest; from Vice-Admiral Dundas to the youngest sailor, an ardent desire to co-operate by every possible means is manifest throughout; and I am proud of being associated with men who are animated by such a spirit, and are so entirely devoted to the service of their country.

Camp above Old Fort Bay,
MY LORD DUKE, September 18, 1854.

SIR,

I DO myself the honour to acquaint your Grace, that the combined Fleets and their convoys appeared in the Bay of Eupatoria on the 13th instant, and in the course of the following night proceeded some miles to the southward, where the Allied Armies commenced disembarking early in the morning of the 14th, – the French in the Bay below Old Fort, the English in the next Bay nearer to Eupatoria, – and before dark the whole of the British Infantry, and some Artillery, and most of the French Troops, were on shore.

Shortly before dark, the weather unfortunately changed, and it became hazardous to attempt to continue landing either troops or guns.

The surf on the beach impeded the operation the following morning; and since, on more than one occasion; but thanks to the great exertions of the Navy, under the able and active superintendence of Rear-Admiral Sir Edmund Lyons, who was charged with the whole arrangement, every obstacle has been overcome, and I am now enabled to report to your Grace that the disembarkations have been completed.

I should not do justice to my own feelings, or to those of the troops I have the honour to command, if I did not prominently bring to the knowledge of your Grace, the deep sense entertained by all, of the invaluable services rendered by Her Majesty's Navy.

The spirit by which both officers and men were animated, made them regardless of danger, of fatigue, and indeed of every consideration but that of performing an arduous and important duty; and that duty they discharged to the admiration of all who had the good fortune to witness their unceasing efforts to land horses and carriages, with the utmost expedition and safety, under frequently the most trying circumstances.

I have, &c.,

(Signed) RAGLAN.

His Grace the Duke of Newcastle,

&c. &c. &c.

War Department, October 1, 1854.

THE Duke of Newcastle has this day received Telegraphic Despatch from General Lord Raglan, G.C.B., of which the following is a translation:

Copy of a Telegraphic Despatch from General Lord Raglan to the Duke of Newcastle, - transmitted through Belgrade, - (not dated, but evidently written from the Crimea on 21st September.)

"THE Allied Armies yesterday attacked the position of the enemy on the heights above the Alma, and carried it after a desperate battle, about an hour and a half before sunset. Nothing could surpass the bravery and excellent conduct of the troops. The position was very formidable and defended by a numerous artillery of heavy calibre; our loss, I regret to add, is very considerable, but no General Officer has been wounded. The main body of the army of the enemy was estimated from 45,000 to 50,000 infantry. A few prisoners, amongst whom are 2 General Officers, and 2 guns, have been taken by the English Army.

(Signed) RAGLAN."

Translation of the Exact Copy of a Telegraphic Despatch, Received October 5, 10 A.M., and transmitted by the Agent of England, in Wallachia, at Bucharest, the 30th of September,

1854, 3½ P.M.

Lord Stratford, Constantinople, to Lord Clarendon,

Minister of Foreign Affairs, London.

September 30, 1854, at 9½ p.m.

SIR,

THE Allied Armies established their basis of operations at Bala Clava on the morning of the 28th, and were preparing to march without delay upon Sevastopol. The Agamemnon and other vessels-of-war of the Allies, were in the Port of Bala Clava. There were facilities there for disembarking the battering train.

It is stated that Prince Menchikoff was in the field at the head of 20,000 men, expecting reinforcements; that the fortified place of Anapa has been burnt by the Russians; that its garrison was marching to the scene of action; and that a Convoy of Ammunition, escorted by Cossacks, had been taken and destroyed by an English detachment.

The Banshee, bearer of this news, left the Crimea on the evening of the day before yesterday.

STRATFORD DE REDCLIFFE.

Admiralty, October 8, 1854.

THE Lords Commissioners of the Admiralty have this day received Despatches from Vice-Admiral Dundas, containing intelligence as to the proceedings of Her Majesty's Fleet in the Black Sea, of which the following are copies:-

ATTACK OF THE RUSSIAN ENTRENCHMENTS ON THE ALMA BY THE ALLIED ARMIES.

No. 485. Britannia, off the Alma,
September 21, 1854.

SIR,

IN my letter of the 18th instant (No. 480), I reported to you, for the information of the Lords Commissioners of the Admiralty, that the Allied Armies were ready to move, and I now beg you will acquaint their Lordships that, on the morning of the 19th, they marched to a position about two miles north of the Alma River, where they halted for the night; the French and Turks on the right, close to the sea, and the English to the left, about four miles inland.

The Russians, with some 5,000 or 6,000 cavalry and artillery, and 15,000 infantry, made a demonstration north of the river, but returned on the approach of the armies, and recrossed the river at sunset.

About noon, on the 20th, the Allies advanced in the same order to force the Russian position and entrenchments south of the Alma. This was effected by 4 o'clock, the Russians retreating apparently to the eastward of the main road to Sevastopol.

The Russian left fell back before the French very rapidly, and their batteries on the right were carried by the bayonet by the English.

Our loss has necessarily been severe, and is estimated at about 1200 killed and wounded; that of the French about 900.

The Russian loss has also been great, two general officers and 3 guns were captured by our men, but we have few prisoners beyond the wounded, in consequence it is believed of our deficiency of cavalry.

Lieutenant Derriman, of the Caradoc accompanied the Staff of General Lord Raglan, during the action and I also sent Lieutenant Glynn of this ship to convey any message to me from his lordship.

All the medical officers of the fleet (excepting one in each ship), 600 seamen and marines, and all the boats have been assisting the wounded, and conveying them to the transports, that will sail for the Bosphorus as soon as possible.

I believe it is the intention of the Allied Forces to move to-morrow, and the Sampson which I detached last night with the Terrible off Sevastopol, has signalized that the Russians were retreating on Sevastopol, and that they have burnt the villages on the Katscha.

I have, &c.,

(Signed) J.W.D. DUNDAS,

Vice-Admiral.

The Secretary of the Admiralty.

MOVEMENTS OF THE FLEETS AND ARMIES.

No. 487. Britannia, off the Katscha,

Sept. 23, 1854.

SIR,

I BEG you will inform the Lords Commissioners of the Admiralty, that since my letter to you of the 21st instant (No. 485), the men and boats of the fleet have been employed in bringing from the field (about four miles distant), and carrying on board the transports, the English and Russian officers and men wounded in the battle of the Alma, as well as the sick of the Army.

2. All the medical officers of the different ships have been zealously and usefully occupied in attending them, and I have been obliged to send several assistant-surgeons in the vessels with the wounded to Constantinople.

3. The Vulcan and Andes, with 800 wounded and sick, sailed for Constantinople yesterday, and to day the Orinoco and Colombo, with 900, including some sixty or seventy Russians will follow.

Another vessel (by the request of Lord Raglan), with about 500 wounded Russians, will also proceed, under charge of the Fury, to land them at Odessa.

4. On the night of the 21st instant the Russians made a very great alteration in the

position of their fleet in Sevastopol. I enclose a report made by Captain Jones, of the Sampson; and I propose attacking the outer line the first favourable opportunity.

5. Captain Jones also reports that great exertions appear to be making to strengthen the land defences, as well as those by sea.

New batteries on both sides of the port have been erected, defending the entrances and line of coast. One, to the north, has heavy guns, of a range of 4000 yards, two shots having passed over the Sampson when nearly at that distance.

6. Provisions for the Army have been landed; and the Forces move on to-day towards Sevastopol, accompanied by the Fleets, which have anchored off the Katscha.

I have, &c.,
(Signed) J.W.D. DUNDAS,
Vice-Admiral.
The Secretary of the Admiralty.

OBSERVATIONS ON THE FLEET IN SEVASTOPOL, MADE ON SEPTEMBER 22, 1854, BY CAPTAIN L.T. JONES, C.B., H.M.S. SAMPSON.

Moored across the entrance of the Harbour.

From north to south are the following vessels:-

1st – A frigate, at northern extreme.
2nd – A two-decker.
3rd – A three-decker, with round stern.
4th – A two-decker.
5th – A two-decker.
6th – A two-decker, without masts, quite light, and appears to be newly coppered.
7th – A large frigate.

Artillery Creek.

The top-gallant masts of these are on deck and sails unbent.

The ship without masts is lying across Artillery Creek; inside is a two-decker ready for sea, and bearing an Admiral's flag at the mizen.

Head of Harbour.

The ships at the head of the harbour, which had hitherto been lying with their broadsides to the entrance are now lying with their heads out:

No. 1 – On the north a two-decker.
   2 – A two-decker.

3 – A two-decker.
4 – A two-decker.
5 – A two-decker.
6 – A three-decker at the entrance of the Dockyard Creek.
7 – A three-decker bearing an Admiral's flag at the fore.

Above these are two ships, one appears to be a line-of-battle ship and the other a frigate.

Steamers.

Five steamers under the northern shore. Three small steamers at the head of the harbour, and four in Careening Bay.

General Observations.

Dockyard Creek shuts in with Northern Fort, bearing S.E. ½ E. Observed about 500 infantry marching towards the town, from the direction of Balaklava.

Noticed about 60 men employed on brow of signal hill, carrying mould from brink of cliff to Square Fort.

3 45 P.M. – Cape Constantine and ships in one bearing, S. ¾ W.

(Copy.)

SINKING OF THE RUSSIAN SHIPS AT THE ENTRANCE OF THE HARBOUR OF SEVASTOPOL.

No. 489. Britannia, off the Katscha,
September 24, 1854.

SIR,

IN my letter of yesterday, No. 487, I reported the extraordinary change that had taken place in the position hitherto maintained by the enemy's fleet in the harbour of Sevastopol, and I now beg you will acquaint the Lords Commissioners of the Admiralty, that the same afternoon, on the appearance of the Allied Fleets in sight of Sevastopol, the whole of the vessels moored across the harbour were sunk by the Russians, leaving their masts more or less above water, and I went last evening to the mouth of the harbour to assure myself of this singular event.

Captain Drummond has examined the harbour this morning, and reports that the lower mast heads of the ships are generally above water; that the passage is closed, except perhaps a small space near the shoal off the North Battery, and the double booms inside are thus rendered more secure.

Eight sail of the line are moored east and west, inside of the booms, and three of the ships are heeled over to give their guns more elevation to sweep over the land to the northward.

2. An intelligent seaman, a deserter, who escaped from Sevastopol on the 22nd, had partly prepared me for some extraordinary movement. He had informed me that the crews of the ships moored across the harbour (to one of which he had been attached) had been landed, with the exception of a very few in each ship; that the vessels were plugged ready for sinking; that the guns and stores were all on board; and that the other ships were moored under the south side to defend the harbour from attack from the northward. He reported that the Battle of Alma had greatly dispirited the Russians; that the troops had retreated on Sevastopol without a halt; that he believes the whole Russian force not to exceed 40,000. The man's statements were clear, and on points that came under his own observation were mostly corroborated, and I consider reliance may be placed on his information generally, considering the means his station in life afforded of enabling him to obtain it. At the request of Lord Raglan I have sent him on shore to act as a guide to the Army on their approach to the environs of Sevastopol.

3. The Allied Armies moved this afternoon to take up a position to the south of the port of Sevastopol, and the fleet will move so as to meet their arrival there.

I have, &c,,

J.W.D. DUNDAS,

Vice-Admiral.

To the Secretary of the Admiralty.

BATTLE OF THE ALMA.

War Department, October 8, 1854, 8½ *o'clock a.m.*

MAJOR the Lord Burghersh arrived this morning with a Despatch from General the Lord Raglan, G.C.B., to His Grace the Duke of Newcastle, of which the following is a copy:

Head Quarters, Katscha River,
September 23, 1854.

MY LORD DUKE,

I HAVE the honour to inform your Grace, that the Allied Troops attacked the position occupied by the Russian Army, behind the Alma, on the 20th instant; and I have great satisfaction in adding, that they succeeded, in less than three hours, in driving the enemy from every part of the ground which they had held in the morning, and in establishing themselves upon it.

The English and French Armies moved out of their first encampment in the Crimea on the 19th, and bivouacked for the night on the left bank of the Bulganac, the former having previously supported the advance of a part of the Earl of Cardigan's brigade of Light Cavalry, which had the effect of inducing the enemy to move up a large body of Dragoons and Cosaques, with artillery.

On this, the first occasion of the English encountering the Russian force, it was impossible for any troops to exhibit more steadiness, than did this portion of Her Majesty's cavalry.

It fell back upon its supports with the most perfect regularity under the fire of the Artillery, which was quickly silenced by that of the batteries I caused to be brought into action.

Our loss amounted to only four men wounded.

The day's march had been most wearisome and, under a burning sun, the absence of water, until we reached the insignificant but welcome stream of the Bulganac, made it to be severely felt.

Both Armies moved towards the Alma the following morning, and it was arranged that Marshal St. Arnaud should assail the enemy's left by crossing the river at its junction with the sea, and immediately above it, and that the remainder of the French divisions should move up the heights in their front, whilst the English Army should attack the right and centre of the enemy's position.

In order that the gallantry exhibited by Her Majesty's troops, and the difficulties they had to meet may be fairly estimated, I deem it right, even at the risk of being considered tedious, to endeavour to make your Grace acquainted with the position the Russians had taken up.

It crossed the great road about 2½ miles from the sea, and is very strong by nature.

The bold and almost precipitous range of heights, of from 350 to 400 feet, that from the sea closely border the left bank of the river here ceases and formed their left, and turning thence round a great amphitheatre or wide valley, terminates at a salient pinnacle where their right rested, and whence the descent to the plain was more gradual. The front was about two miles in extent.

Across the mouth of this great opening is a lower ridge at different heights, varying from 60 to 150 feet, parallel to the river, and at distances from it of from 600 to 800 yards.

The river itself is generally fordable for troops, but its banks are extremely rugged, and in most parts steep; the willows along it had been cut down, in order to prevent them from affording cover to the attacking party, and in fact everything had been done to deprive an assailant of any species of shelter.

In front of the position on the right bank, at about 200 yards from the Alma, is the village of Bouliouk, and near it a timber bridge, which had been partly destroyed by the enemy.

The high pinnacle and ridge before alluded to was the key of the position, and consequently, there the greatest preparations had been made for defence.

Halfway down the height, and across its front was a trench of the extent of some hundred yards, to afford cover against an advance up the even steep slope of the hill. On the right, and a little retired, was a powerful covered battery, armed with heavy guns, which flanked the whole of the right of the position.

Artillery, at the same time, was posted at the points that best commanded the passage of the river and its approaches generally.

On the slopes of these hills (forming a sort of table land) were placed dense masses of the enemy's infantry, whilst on the heights above was his great reserve, the whole amounting, it is supposed, to between 45,000 and 50,000 men, The combined Armies advanced on the same alignement, Her Majesty's troops in contiguous double columns, with the front of two divisions covered by light infantry and a troop of horse artillery, the 2nd Division, under Lieutenant-General Sir De Lacy Evans, forming the right, and touching the left of the 3rd Division of the French Army, under His Imperial Highness Prince Napoleon, and the Light Division, under Lieutenant-General Sir George Brown, the left; the first being supported by the 3rd Division, under Lieutenant-General Sir Richard England, and the last by the 1st Division, commanded by Lieutenant-General His Royal Highness the Duke of Cambridge.

The 4th Division, under Lieutenant-General Sir George Cathcart, and the cavalry under Major-General the Earl of Lucan, were held in reserve to protect the left flank and rear against large bodies of the enemy's cavalry, which had been seen in those directions.

On approaching to near the fire of the guns, which soon became extremely formidable, the two leading divisions deployed into line, and advanced to attack the front, and the supporting divisions followed the movement. Hardly had this taken place, when the village of Bouliouk, immediately opposite the centre, was fired by the enemy at all points, creating a continuous blaze for three hundred yards, obscuring their position and rendering a passage through it impracticable. Two regiments of Brigadier-General Adams' brigade, part of Sir De Lacy Evans' division, had, in consequence, to pass the river at a deep and difficult ford to the right under a sharp fire, whilst his first brigade, under Major-General Pennefather, and the remaining regiment of Brigadier-General Adams crossed to the left of the conflagration, opposed by the enemy's artillery from the heights above, and pressed on towards the left of their position, with the utmost gallantry and steadiness.

In the meanwhile, the Light Division, under Sir George Brown, effected the passage of the Alma in his immediate front. The banks of the river itself were, from their rugged and broken nature, most serious obstacles, and the vineyards, through which the troops had to pass, and the trees which the enemy had felled, created additional impediments, rendering every species of formation, under a galling fire, nearly an impossibility. Lieutenant-General Sir George Brown advanced against the enemy under great disadvantages.

In this difficult operation he nevertheless persevered, and the 1st Brigade, under Major-General Codrington, succeeded in carrying a redoubt, materially aided by the judicious and steady manner in which Brigadier-General Buller moved on the left flank, and by the advance of four companies of the Rifle Brigade, under Major Norcott, who promises to be a distinguished officer of light troops.

The heavy fire of grape and musketry, however to which the troops were exposed, and the losses consequently sustained by the 7th, 23rd, and 33rd Regiments, obliged this brigade partially to relinquish its hold.

By this time, however, the Duke of Cambridge had succeeded in crossing the river, and had moved up in support, and a brilliant advance of the brigade of Foot Guards, under Major-General Bentinck, drove the enemy back, and secured the final possession of the work.

The Highland Brigade, under Major-General Sir Colin Campbell, advanced in admirable order and steadiness up the high ground to the left, an in co-operation with the Guards; and Major-General Pennefather's Brigade, which had been connected with the right of the Light Division, forced the enemy completely to abandon the position they had taken such pains to defend and secure.

The 95th Regiment, immediately on the right of the Royal Fusiliers in the advance, suffered equally with that corps an immense loss.

The aid of the Royal Artillery in all these operations was most effectual. The exertions of the Field Officers and the Captains of troops and batteries to get the guns into action were unceasing, and the precision of their fire materially contributed to the great results of the day. Lieutenant-General Sir Richard England brought his division to the immediate support of the troops in advance, and Lieutenant-General the Honourable Sir George Cathcart was actively engaged in watching the left flank.

The nature of the ground did not admit of the employment of the cavalry under the Earl of Lucan; but they succeeded in taking some prisoners at the close of the battle.

In the detail of these operations, which I have gone into as far as the space of a dispatch would allow, your Grace will perceive that the services in which the General and other Officers of the Army were engaged, were of no ordinary character; and I have great pleasure in submitting them for your Grace's most favourable consideration.

The mode in which Lieutenant-General Sir George Brown conducted his division under the most trying circumstances, demands the expression of my warmest approbation. The fire to which his division was subjected, and the difficulties he had to contend against, afford no small proof that his best energies were applied to the successful discharge of his duty.

I must speak in corresponding terms of Lieutenant-General Sir De Lacy Evans, who likewise conducted his division to my perfect satisfaction, and exhibited equal coolness and judgment in carrying out a most difficult operation.

His Royal Highness the Duke of Cambridge brought his division into action in support of the Light Division with great ability, and had for the first time an opportunity of showing the enemy his devotion to Her Majesty, and to the profession of which he is so distinguished a member.

My best thanks are due to Lieutenant-General Sir R. England, Lieutenant-General the Honourable Sir George Cathcart, and Lieutenant-General the Earl of Lucan, for their cordial assistance wherever it could be afforded, and I feel it my duty especially to recommend to your Grace's notice the distinguished conduct of Major-General Bentinck, Major-General Sir Colin Campbell, Major-General Pennefather, Major-General Codrington, Brigadier-General Adams, and Brigadier-General Buller.

In the affair of the previous day, Major-General the Earl of Cardigan exhibited the utmost spirit and coolness, and kept his brigade under perfect command.

The manner in which Brigadier-General Strangways directed the Artillery, and exerted himself to bring it forward, met my entire satisfaction.

Lieutenant-General Sir John Burgoyne was constantly by my side; and rendered me, by his counsel and advice, the most valuable assistance; and the Commanding Royal Engineer, Brigadier-General Tylden, was always at hand to carry out any service I might direct him to undertake.

I deeply regret to say that he has since fallen a victim to cholera, as has Major Wellesley, who was present in the affair of the previous day, notwithstanding that he was then suffering from serious illness. He had, during the illness of Major-General Lord de Ros, acted for him in the most efficient manner. I cannot speak too highly of Brigadier-General Estcourt, Adjutant-General, or of Brigadier-General Airey, who, in the short time he has conducted the duties of the Quartermaster-General, has displayed the greatest ability, as well as aptitude for the office.

I am much indebted to my Military Secretary, Lieutenant-Colonel Steele, Major Lord Burghersh, and the officers of my personal Staff, for the zeal, intelligence, and gallantry, they all, without exception, displayed.

Lieutenant Derriman, R.N., the Commander of the Caradoc, accompanied me during the whole of the operation, and rendered me an essential service, by a close observation of the enemy's movements, which his practised eye enabled him accurately to watch.

I lament to say that Lieutenant-Colonel Lagondie, who was attached to my head quarters, by the Emperor of the French, fell into the enemy's hands on the 19th, on his return from Prince Napoleon's division, where he had obligingly gone at my request, with a communication to his Imperial Highness.

This misfortune is deeply regretted, both by myself and the officers of my personal Staff.

The other officer placed with me under similar circumstances, Major Vico, afforded me all the assistance in his power, sparing no exertion to be of use.

I cannot omit to make known to your Grace the cheerfulness with which the regimental officers of the Army have submitted to most unusual privations.

My anxiety to bring into the country every cavalry and infantry soldier who was available, prevented me from embarking their baggage animals, and these officers have with them at this moment nothing but what they can carry, and they, equally with the men, are without tents or covering of any kind.

I have not heard a single murmur. All seem impressed with the necessity of the arrangement; and they feel, I trust, satisfied that I shall bring up their bât horses at the earliest moment.

The conduct of the troops has been admirable. When it is considered that they have suffered severely from sickness during the last two months; that, since they landed in the Crimea, they have been exposed to the extremes of wet, cold, and heat; that the daily toil to provide themselves with water has been excessive, and that they have been pursued by Cholera to the very battle field, I do not go beyond the truth in declaring that they merit the highest commendation.

In the ardour of attack they forgot all they had endured, and displayed that high courage, that gallant spirit, for which the British soldier is ever distinguished; and under the heaviest fire they maintained the same determination to conquer, as they had exhibited before they went into action. I should be wanting in my duty, my Lord Duke, if I did not express to your Grace, in the most earnest mannner, my deep feeling of gratitude to the officers and men of the Royal Navy for the invaluable assistance they afforded the Army upon this as on every occasion, where it could be brought to bear upon our operations.

They watched the progress of the day with the most intense anxiety; and as the best way of evincing their participation in our success, and their sympathy in the sufferings of the wounded, they never ceased, from the close of the battle till we left the ground this morning, to provide for the sick and wounded, and to carry them down to the beach, a labour in which some of the officers even volunteered to participate, an act which I shall never cease to recollect with the warmest thankfulness.

I mention no names, fearing I might omit some who ought to be spoken of; but none who were associated with us, spared any exertion they could apply to so sacred a duty.

Sir Edmond Lyons, who had charge of the whole, was, as always, most prominent in rendering assistance, and providing for emergencies.

I enclose the return of killed and wounded. It is, I lament to say, very large; but I hope, all circumstances considered, that it will be felt that no life was unnecessarily exposed, and that such an advantage could not be achieved without a considerable sacrifice.

I cannot venture to estimate the amount of the Russian loss. I believe it to have been great, and such is the report in the country.

The number of prisoners who are not hurt is small; but the wounded amount to 800 or 900.

Two General Officers, Major Generals Karganoff and Shokanoff fell into our hands. The former is very badly wounded.

I will not attempt to describe the movements of the French Army; that will be done by an abler hand; but it is due to them to say that their operations were eminently successful, and that under the guidance of their distinguished commander, Marshal St. Arnaud, they manifested the utmost gallantry, the greatest ardour for the attack, and the high military qualities for which they are so famed.

This despatch will be delivered to your Grace by Major Lord Burghersh, who is capable of affording you the fullest information, and whom I beg to recommend to your especial notice.

I have, &c.,
RAGLAN.

CHAPTER 3

BALAKLAVA AND THE OPENING OF THE SIEGE OF SEVASTOPOL

War Department, October 10, 1854.

HIS Grace the Duke of Newcastle has this day received two Despatches, of which the following are copies, addressed to his Grace by General the Lord Raglan, G.C.B.:

Balaklava, September 28, 1854.

MY LORD DUKE,

IN continuation of my Despatch of the 23rd instant, I beg leave to lay before your Grace the names of the officers whose names have been brought to my notice by the Generals of Division, and the Heads of Departments.

Lieutenant-General Sir George Brown speaks in the highest terms of Lieutenant-Colonel Yea, of the Royal Fusiliers; Lieutenant-Colonel Chester, of the 23rd, who was unfortunately killed, and of Captain Bell, who succeeded to the command, and brought the regiment out of action, and Lieutenant-Colonel Blake, of the 33rd. Lieutenant-Colonel Saunders, of the 19th, who was severely wounded; Lieutenant-Colonel Egerton, of the 77th Regiment, and Lieutenant-Colonel Shirley, of the 88th; also of Lieutenant-Colonel Lawrence and Major Norcott, of the Rifle Brigade, each commanding a wing of that corps; Lieutenant-Colonel Lake, commanding the Artillery, of Captain Brandling, commanding a 9-pounder troop of Horse Artillery, and Captain Anderson, commanding a Field Battery, and Captain Gordon, of the Royal Engineers; likewise of Lieutenant-Colonel Sullivan, and Lieutenant-Colonel Airey, of the Adjutant and Quartermaster-General's Department, and Captain Hallowell of the latter, and Captain Whitmore and the other officers of his personal Staff; and Captains Glyn and Mackenzie, the Brigade-Majors serving with the division.

Lieutenant-General His Royal Highness the Duke of Cambridge recommends

Colonel the Honourable Francis Hood, of the Grenadier Guards, Colonel the Honourable George Upton, of the Coldstream Guards, and Colonel Sir Charles Hamilton, of the Scots Fusilier Guards; Lieutenant-Colonel Cameron, of the 42nd, Lieutenant-Colonel Douglas, of the 79th, and Lieutenant-Colonel Ainslie, of the 93d; Lieutenant-Colonel the Honourable Alexander Gordon, and Lieutenant-Colonel Cunynghame, the Assistant-Adjutant and Quartermaster-General, Captain Butler and the Honourable Arthur Hardinge, the Deputy Assistant-Adjutant and Quartermaster-General of the Division, and Major the Honourable James Macdonald, and the other officers of his personal Staff; also Lieutenant-Colonel Dacres commanding, and Captains Paynter and Woodhouse of the Royal Artillery, and Captain Chapman of the Royal Engineers; and Lieutenant-Colonel Stirling, and Captain the Honourable Percy Fielding, the Brigade-Major of the division.

Lieutenant-General Sir De Lacy Evans eulogizes the conduct of Lieutenant-Colonel the Honourable Percy Herbert of the Quartermaster-General's Department, who was wounded, I hope not severely; Major Lysons of the 23rd, acting as Assistant-Adjutant-General in the absence from sickness of Lieutenant-Colonel Wilbraham, Captain Lane Fox and Captain Thompson, Deputy-Assistant-Adjutant and Quartermaster-General, and Captain Allix and the other officers of his personal Staff. He also praises the exertions of Lieutenant-Colonels Hoey, of the 30th, Lieutenant-Colonel Warren, of the 55th, and Lieutenant-Colonel Webber Smith, of the 95th, who was severely wounded; Lieutenant-Colonel Carpenter, of the 41st, Lieutenant-Colonel Haly, of the 47th, and Major Dalton, of the 49th, Lieutenant Colonels Fitzmayer and Dupuis, and Captains Turner and Swinton, of the Royal Artillery, and to these I may add Captain Lovell, of the Royal Engineers, Brevet-Majors Thackwell and Armstrong, the Brigade-Majors of the division.

I consider it my duty especially to recommend Captain Adye, of the Royal Artillery, the principal Staff officer of that branch of the Service, and Captain the Honourable Edward Gage, Brigade-Major of Artillery, and Major Tylden, Brigade-Major of the Royal Engineers, and Major the Honourable Edward Pakenham, and Captain Weare, who was wounded, of the Adjutant-General's, and of Captains Wetherall, Woodford, Sankey, and Hamilton, of the Quartermaster-General's Department.

Mr. Commissary-General Filder and Dr. Hall, the. principal Medical Officer, were in the field the whole time, and merit my approbation for their exertions in discharging their onerous duties.

I have, &c.,
(Signed) RAGLAN.
:His Grace the Duke of Newcastle,
&c. &c. &c.

Balaklava, September 28, 1854.

MY LORD DUKE,

I HAVE the greatest satisfaction in acquainting your Grace, that the Army under my command obtained possession of this important place on the 26th instant, and thus established a new and secure base for our future operations.

The Allied Armies quitted their position above the Alma on the morning of the 23rd, and moved across the Katscha, where they halted for the night, and on the following day passed the Belbeck.

It then appeared that the enemy had established a work, which commanded the entrance of the river, and debarred its use for the disembarkation of troops, provisions, and material; and it became expedient to consider whether the line of attack upon the north side should not be abandoned, and another course of operation adopted.

It having, after due deliberation, been determined by Marshal St. Arnaud and myself, that we should relinquish our communication with the Katscha, and the hope of establishing it by the Belbeck, and endeavour, by a flank march to the left to go round Sevastopol and seize Balaklava, the movement was commenced on the 25th, and completed on the following day by the capture of this place by Her Majesty's troops, which led the advance. The march was attended with great difficulties. On leaving the high road from the Belbeck to Sevastopol, the Army had to traverse a dense wood, in which there was but one road that led in the direction it was necessary to take. That road was left in the first instance to the Cavalry and Artillery; and the divisions were ordered to march by compass and make a way for themselves as well as they could; and, indeed, the Artillery of the Light Division pursued the same course as long as it was found to be possible, but, as the wood became more impracticable, the batteries could not proceed otherwise than by getting into the road above mentioned.

The Head Quarters of the Army, followed by several batteries of Artillery, were the first to clear the forest, near what is called, in Major Jarvis' map, Mackenzie's Farm, and at once found themselves on the flank and rear of a Russian division, on the march to Baské-Serai. This was attacked as soon as the cavalry, which had diverged a little into a bye and intricate path, could be brought up. A vast quantity of ammunition and much valuable baggage fell into our hands, and the pursuit was discontinued after about a mile and a half, it being a great object to reach the Tschernaya that evening.

The Russians lost a few men, and some prisoners were taken, amongst whom was a Captain of Artillery.

The march was then resumed by the descent of a steep and difficult defile into the plains, through which runs the Tschernaya River, and this the cavalry succeeded in reaching shortly before dark, followed in the course of the night by the Light, First, Second, and Third Divisions; the Fourth Division having been left on the heights above the Belbeck till the following day, to maintain our communication with the Katscha.

This march, which took the enemy quite by surprise, was a very long and toilsome one, and, except at Mackenzie's Farm, where two wells, yielding a scanty supply, were found, the troops were without water, but they supported their fatigues and privations with the utmost cheerfulness, and resumed their march to this place on the morning of the 26th.

As they approached Balaklava nothing indicated that it was held in force; but as resistance was offered to the advance of the Rifle Brigade, and guns were opened from an old castle, as the head of the column shewed itself on the road leading into the town, I deemed it prudent to occupy the two flanking heights by the Light Division and a portion of Captain Brandling's troop of Horse Artillery on the left; movements terminated by the surrender of the place, which had been occupied by very inconsiderable numbers of the enemy.

Shortly after we had taken possession we were greeted by Captain Mends, of the Agamemnon, and soon after by Sir Edmund Lyons himself.

His co-operation was secured to us by the activity and enterprize of Lieutenant Maxse, of Her Majesty's Ship Agamemnon, who reached my camp on the Tschernaya, on the night of the 25th with despatches, and who volunteered immediately to retrace his steps through the forest, and to communicate to Sir Edmund the importance I attached to his presence at the mouth of the harbour of Balaklava the next morning, which difficult service (from the intricacy of the country infested by Cossacks) he accomplished so effectually that the Admiral was enabled to appear off this harbour at the very moment that our troops shewed themselves upon the heights.

Nothing could be more opportune than his arrival, and yesterday the magnificent ship that bears his flag entered this beautiful harbour; and the Admiral, as has been his invariable practice, co-operated with the Army in every way possible.

We are busily engaged in disembarking our siege train and provisions, and we are most desirous of undertaking the attack of Sevastopol without the loss of a day. I moved up two divisions yesterday to its immediate neighbourhood, when I was enabled to have a good view of the place; and Lieutenant-General Sir John Burgoyne and General Bisot, the French Chef de Génie are occupied in reconnoitering it closely to-day.

The march of the French Army on the 25th was still more fatiguing and prolonged than ours.

Being behind our columns they could not reach Tschernaya till the next day, and I fear must have suffered sadly from want of water.

I regret to have to acquaint your Grace, that Marshal St. Arnaud has been compelled, by severe illness, to relinquish the command of the Army. I saw him on the 25th, when he was suffering very much, and he felt it his duty to resign the next morning. I view his retirement with deep concern, having always found in him every disposition to act in concert with me. He has since become much worse, and is I fear in a very precarious state.

Fortunately he is succeeded by an officer of high reputation, General Canrobert, with whom I am satisfied I shall have great pleasure in acting, and who is equally desirous of maintaining the most friendly relations with me.

I have, &c.,
(Signed) RAGLAN.
His Grace the Duke of Newcastle.
&c. &c. &c.
Admiralty, November 5, 1854.

THE following Despatches from Vice-Admiral Dundas have this day been received at the Admiralty:-

No. 523. Britannia, off the Katscha,
October 13, 1854.

SIR,

1. I BEG you will acquaint the Lords Commissioners of the Admiralty that the Allied Armies are employed in erecting batteries to the south of Sebastopol, but I hear are much retarded by the rocky nature of the ground; the Russian fire of shot and shell by day and night has produced little or no effect. The Naval and Marine battalions are healthy, and there is less sickness in the Army.

2. Sir Edmund Lyons, in the Agamemnon, with the Diamond, and a squadron of steamers, is at Balaklava, assisting the troops. A French squadron, under Vice-Admiral Bruat, is anchored between the lighthouse and the harbour, in communication with the left of the French Army. A division of steam-vessels watches the mouth of the port constantly, where four or five Russian steam-vessels always have their steam up, and the large sailing vessels are with Admiral Hamelin and myself anchored off the Katscha River, the weather hitherto having permitted our remaining in those positions.

3. The Sidon and Inflexible, with Cacique and Caton, are still in Odessa Bay, to prevent any communication by sea with the Crimea, and I have sent a transport to them with coals and fresh provisions, which I have drawn from Sinope.

4. On the 11th, an Austrian vessel, laden with hay for the Commissariat, got within range of the batteries, and was deserted by her crew at the second shot; she ran on shore about 1500 yards south of the harbour mouth, and was got off that evening and towed to Balaklava. I enclose the report of Captain Jones, of the Sampson, who, with Captain Stewart, of the Firebrand, and Mr. Boxer, Second Master in charge of the Beagle, assisted by the French launches, of the inshore squadron, got the Austrian to sea from under the batteries in a very successful and creditable manner. The Firebrand has four shots in her hull, but fortunately no casualties.

5. I learnt from Captain King, of the Leander, of the approach to Eupatoria of a large Russian force near the town. I have sent the Firebrand and Vesuvius to assist in the defence, should it be attacked, and shall send two other vessels to-day.

6. The French and Turkish troops sent for from Varna and Constantinople by the Simoom, Vulcan, Cyclops, and our transports, are hourly expected; they have been kept back and detained by the late strong north-east gales.

I have, &c.,
(Signed) J.W.D. DUNDAS,
Vice-Admiral.
To the Secretary of the Admiralty. &c. &c. &c.

No. 527. Britannia, off the Katscha,
October 18, 1854.

SIR,

1. I BEG you will acquaint the Lords Commissioners of the Admiralty that the siege batteries of the Allied Armies opened fire upon the Russian works south of Sebastapol about half past 6 o'clock yesterday morning, with great effect, and small loss.

2. In consequence of the most urgent request of Lord Raglan and General Canrobert, it was agreed by the Admirals of the Allied Fleets that the whole of the ships should assist the land attack by engaging the sea batteries north and south of the harbour, on a line across the port, as shown in the accompanying plan, but various circumstances rendered a change in the position of the ships necessary and unavoidable.

3. The Agamemnon, Sanspareil, Sampson, Tribune, Terrible, Sphinx, and Lynx, and Albion, London, and Arethusa, towed by the Firebrand, Niger, and Triton, engaged Fort Constantine and the batteries to the northward; while the Queen, Britannia, Trafalgar, Vengeance, Rodney, Bellerophon, with Vesuvius, Furious, Retribution, Highflyer, Spitfire, Spiteful and Cyclops, lashed on the port side of the several ships, gradually took up their positions, as nearly as possible as marked on the plan.

4. The action lasted from about half-past one to half-past six, P.M., when being quite dark, the ships hauled off.

5. The loss, sustained by the Russians, and the damage done to Fort Constantine and Batteries cannot, of course, as yet be correctly ascertained.

6. An action of this duration against such formidable and well armed works, could not be maintained without serious injury, and I have to regret the loss of 44 killed and 266 wounded, as detailed in the accompanying lists. The ships, masts, yards, and rigging are more or less damaged, principally by shells and hot shot. The Albion has suffered much in hull and masts, the Rodney in her masts, she having tailed on the reef, from which she was got off by the great exertions of Commander Kynaston, of the Spiteful, whose crew and vessel were necessarily exposed in performing this service; but with the exception of the Albion and Arethusa, which ships I send to Constantinople to be repaired, I hope to be able to make my squadron serviceable in twenty-four hours. Foreseeing from the nature of the attack that we should be likely to lose spars, I left the spare topmasts and yards on board Her Majesty's Ship Vulcan at this anchorage, where I had placed her with all the sick and prisoners.

7. I have now the pleasure of recording my very great satisfaction with the ability and zeal displayed by Rear Admirals Sir Edmund Lyons and the Honourable Montagu Stopford, and all the captains under my command, as well as my sincere thanks to them, and to the officers, seamen, and marines employed for their unremitting exertions and the rapidity of their fire, in the absence of a large number of the crews of each ship, who were landed to assist in working the siege batteries, &c., on shore, and to this circumstance I attribute the small loss of killed and wounded.

8. The gallant and skilful conduct of our French Allies in this action was witnessed

by me with admiration, and I hear with regret that they have also suffered considerable loss.

9. I beg to express my gratitude at the manner in which Ahmed Pasha, the Turkish Admiral, did his duty.

I have, &c.,
(Signed) J.W.D. DUNDAS,
Vice-Admiral.
Secretary of the Admiralty,
&c., &c., &c.

War Department, 11.55 a.m.,
November 11, 1854.

HIS Grace the Duke of Newcastle has this day received a Despatch of which the following is a copy, addressed to His Grace by General the Lord Raglan, G.C.B.

(This Despatch was lost in its passage through France, and was received at the above hour, by His Grace, to whom it was transmitted by His Excellency the Lord Cowley, G.C.B.)

Before Sebastopol, October 18, 1854.

MY LORD DUKE,

IT was arranged between General Canrobert and myself, that the batteries of the two armies should open immediately after daylight on the morning of the 17th, and we invited Admiral Dundas and Admiral Hamelin to attack the enemy's works at the mouth of the harbour with the combined fleets, as nearly simultaneously as circumstances might permit.

Accordingly, upon a signal being given from the centre of the French lines, the batteries of the two armies commenced their fire about a quarter before seven yesterday morning.

On this occasion we employed about 60 guns of different calibres, the lightest being 24 pounders.

It may here be proper to observe that the character of the position which the enemy occupy on the south side of Sebastopol is not that of a fortress, but rather of an army in an entrenched camp on very strong ground, where an apparently unlimited number of heavy guns, amply provided with gunners and ammunition, are mounted.

The guns having opened as above stated, a continuous and well directed fire was carried on from the works of the two armies until about ten o'clock A.M., when, unfortunately, a magazine in the midst of one of the French Batteries exploded and occasioned considerable damage to the works, and I fear many casualties, and almost paralyzed the efforts of the French Artillery for the day.

The British Batteries, however, manned by sailors from the fleet, under the command of Captain Lushington and Captain Peel, and by the Royal Artillery, under the superintendence of Lieutenant-Colonel Gambier, kept up their fire with unremitting energy throughout the day to my own and the general satisfaction, as well as to the admiration of the French Army, who were witnesses of their gallant and persevering exertions, materially injuring the enemy's works, and silencing the heavy guns on the top of the loop-holed tower, to which I adverted in my despatch of the 13th instant, and many of the guns at its base, and causing an extensive explosion in the rear of a strong redoubt in our immediate front, the enemy notwithstanding, answered to the last from a number of guns along their more extended line.

The fire was resumed this morning at daylight by the British sailors and artillery, and responded to, though in a somewhat less degree, by the Russians; but the French troops, being occupied in the repair of their batteries, and in the formation of others, have not contributed to the renewal of the attack, except from a work on their extreme left; they expect, however, to be able to do so tomorrow morning.

I beg to lay before your Grace a return of the loss sustained by the Royal Navy, and the Army under my command, between the 13th and the 17th instant, and to this I am deeply concerned to add that of Colonel the Honourable Francis Hood, commanding the 3rd battalion Grenadier guards, an excellent officer, whose death in the trenches this morning has just been reported to me.

The English, French, and Turkish fleets moved towards the mouth of the harbour about noon, and kept up a heavy fire upon the enemy's forts for several hours.

I am not fully acquainted with the details of the attack, or its result, but I understand that Rear-Admiral Sir Edmund Lyons, with the Agamemnon and Sanspareil, assisted occasionally by the London, Queen, and Albion, gallantly approached to within six hundred yards of Fort Constantine, the great work at the northern entrance, where he maintained himself till late in the afternoon, and succeeded in exploding a magazine, and causing considerable injury to the face of the fort.

Since I wrote to your Grace on the 18th, six battalions of Turkish infantry and 300 Turkish artillery have been added to the force in front of Balaklava.

These troops have been sent from Constantinople, and placed under my command by the government of the Porte, and I feel greatly indebted to Her Majesty's ambassador, Viscount Stratford de Redcliffe, for the ability and energy with which he brought under the notice of the Sultan the importance I attached to an immediate reinforcement of the Imperial troops.

I have, &c.,
RAGLAN.
His Grace the Duke of Newcastle,
&c. &c. &c.

Portman-Square, Midnight,
November 6, 1854.

HIS Grace the Duke of Newcastle has this evening received a Despatch, of which the following is a copy, addressed to his Grace by General Lord Raglan, G.C.B.

Before Sebastopol, October 23, 1854,

MY LORD DUKE,

THE operations of the siege have been carried on unremittingly since I addressed your Grace on the 18th instant.

On that afternoon, the French batteries not having been able to re-open, the enemy directed their guns almost exclusively on the British entrenchments, and maintained a very heavy fire upon them till the day closed, with less damage, I am happy to say, to the works, and with fewer casualties than might have been anticipated.

On the following morning, shortly after daylight, General Canrobert not only resumed his fire from the batteries which had been injured, but materially added to the weight of his attack by the fire of batteries which he had caused to be constructed the previous day; and these have continued ever since; and he has had it in his power to push his approaches forward, and like the English, materially to injure the defences of the place; but these are as yet far from being subdued, neither is a serious diminution of their fire perceivable.

Our fire has also been constant and effective; but the enemy having at their disposal large bodies of men, and the resources of the fleet and arsenal at their command, have been enabled by unceasing exertion to repair their redoubts to a certain extent, and to replace many of the guns that have been destroyed in a very short space of time; and to resume their fire from works which we had succeeded in silencing.

This facility of repairing and re-arming the defences naturally renders the progress of the assailants slower than could be wished; and I have it not in my power to inform your Grace, with anything like certainty, when it may be expected that ulterior measures may be undertaken.

I have the honour to transmit to your Grace the Return of killed and wounded between the 18th and 20th instant inclusive.

In my last I announced to your Grace the death which had just been reported to me of that deeply lamented officer the Honourable Colonel Hood of the Grenadier Guards. No other military officer has since fallen; but Major Prince Edward of Saxe Weimar was slightly wounded on the 19th. His Serene Highness insisted, however upon remaining in the trenches until the detachment to which he was attached was relieved at the usual hour, and he has now resumed his duty.

Captain Lord Dunkellin of the Coldstream Guards was unfortunately taken prisoner yesterday morning before daylight in front of the trenches.

The naval batteries have continued their exertions without intermission, and I regret to have to report the death of two gallant officers of the Royal Navy; the

Honourable Lieutenant Ruthven who has died of his wounds, and Lieutenant Greathed of Her Majesty's ship Britannia. Both are universally regretted. The latter received a mortal wound while laying a gun, after having, to use the language of Brigadier-General Eyre, who was then in charge of the trenches, "performed his duty in the batteries in a manner that excited the admiration of all."

A considerable body of Russians appeared two days ago in the vicinity of Balaklava, but they have since withdrawn, and are no longer to be seen in in our front.

I have reason to believe that Prince Menschikoff is not in Sebastopol. He is stated to have placed himself with the main body of the army in the field, which is represented to be stationed in the plains south of Bacshi Serai.

Admiral Cernilof, the chief of the staff, and temporarily in command of Sebastopol, is reported to have died of his wounds the day before yesterday.

I have, &c.,
RAGLAN.
His Grace the Duke of Newcastle,
&c. &c. &c.

Admiralty, Midnight, November 6, 1854.

A DESPATCH, of which the following is a copy, has this night been received at the Admiralty:

No. 534. Britannia, off the Katscha,
23rd October, 1854.

SIR,

I BEG to acquaint you, for the information of the Lords Commissioners of the Admiralty, that since my letter of the 18th instant, the siege batteries have continued their fire against the Russian works, which appear to have suffered much, and the fire slackened, although it is still considerable.

2. The Naval Brigade are doing good service, and, up to the 20th, had a loss of 12 killed and 53 wounded, as per annexed list. By the desire of Lord Raglan, I have reinforced them by 410 officers and seamen, and placed Lord John Hay in the Wasp, under the orders of Captain Lushington.

3. Captain Brock, at Eupatoria, supported by the Leander and Megaera, has maintained his position well, although threatened and attacked by heavy bodies of Cavalry, with guns; we have drawn large supplies from there, but as the Russians are destroying all the villages, I fear they will in future become very scanty and uncertain.

4. Since the action of the 17th, the enemy have been working incessantly in repairing their batteries, and in constructing new works on the north side of the harbour, commanding the approaches by sea and land.

5. I have sent the Albion and Arethusa to Constantinople to repair; the other ships of the fleet have fished their masts, &c., and are ready for service.

6. The Lynx, Sphinx, Stromboli, and Viper, have arrived.

7. The weather hitherto has been very favourable, and the crews of the ships are generally healthy.

8. The English and French Steam Division still continue in the Bay of Odessa, actively employed in preventing communication with the Crimea.

I have, &c.,

(Signed) J.W.D. DUNDAS,

Vice-Admiral.

To the Secretary of the Admiralty,

&c. &c. &c.

War Department, November 12, 1854.

4 o'clock p.m.

HIS Grace the Duke of Newcastle has this day received two Despatches, with Enclosures, of which the following are copies, addressed to His Grace by General the Lord Raglan, G.C.B.

No. 85. Before Sevastopol,

October 28, 1854.

MY LORD DUKE,

I HAVE the honour to acquaint your Grace that the Enemy attacked the position in the front of Balaklava at an early hour on the morning of the 25th instant.

The low range of heights that runs across the plain at the bottom of which the town is placed, was protected by four small redoubts hastily constructed. Three of these had guns in them, and on a higher hill, in front of the village of Camara, in advance of our right flank, was established a work of somewhat more importance.

These several redoubts were garrisoned by Turkish troops, no other force being at my disposal for their occupation.

The 93rd Highlanders was the only British Regiment in the plain, with the exception of a part of a battalion of detachments composed of weakly men, and a battery of Artillery belonging to the Third Division; and on the heights behind our right were placed the Marines, obligingly landed from the Fleet by Vice-Admiral Dundas. All these, including the Turkish troops, were under the immediate orders of Major-General Sir Colin Campbell, whom I had taken from the First Division with the 93rd.

As soon as I was apprised of this movement of the Enemy, I felt compelled to withdraw from before Sevastopol, the First and Fourth Divisions, commanded by Lieutenant-Generals His Royal Highness the Duke of Cambridge and the Honourable

Sir George Cathcart, and bring them down into the plain; and General Canrobert subsequently reinforced these troops with the First Division of French Infantry and the Chasseurs d'Afrique.

The Enemy commenced their operation by attacking the work on our side of the village of Camara, and, after very little resistance, carried it.

They likewise got possession of the three others in contiguity to it, being opposed only in one, and that but for a very short space of time.

The farthest of the three they did not retain, but the immediate abandonment of the others enabled them to take possession of the guns in them, amounting in the whole to seven. Those in the three lesser forts were spiked by the one English artilleryman who was in each.

The Russian cavalry at once advanced, supported by artillery, in very great strength. One portion of them assailed the front and right flank of the 93rd, and were instantly driven back by the vigorous and steady fire of that distinguished regiment, under Lieutenant-Colonel Ainslie.

The other and larger mass turned towards Her Majesty's heavy cavalry, and afforded Brigadier-General Scarlett, under the guidance of Lieutenant-General the Earl of Lucan, the opportunity of inflicting upon them a most signal defeat. The ground was very unfavourable for the attack of our Dragoons, but no obstacle was sufficient to check their advance, and they charged into the Russian column, which soon sought safety in flight, although far superior in numbers.

The charge of this brigade was one of the most successful I ever witnessed, was never for a moment doubtful, and is in the highest degree creditable to Brigadier-General Scarlett and the officers and men engaged in it.

As the enemy withdrew from the ground which they had momentarily occupied, I directed the cavalry, supported by the Fourth Division, under Lieutenant-General Sir George Cathcart, to move forward, and take advantage of any opportunity to regain the heights; and, not having been able to accomplish this immediately, and it appearing that an attempt was making to remove the captured guns, the Earl of Lucan was desired to advance rapidly, follow the enemy in their retreat, and try to prevent them from effecting their objects.

In the meanwhile the Russians had time to reform on their own ground, with artillery in front and upon their flanks.

From some misconception of the instruction, to advance, the Lieutenant-General considered that he was bound to attack at all hazards, and he accordingly ordered Major-General the Earl of Cardigan to move forward with the Light Brigade.

This order was obeyed in the most spirited and gallant manner. Lord Cardigan charged with the utmost vigour; attacked a battery which was firing upon the advancing squadrons and, having passed beyond it, engaged the Russian Cavalry in its rear; but there his troops were assailed by artillery and infantry, as well as cavalry, and necessarily retired, after having committed much havoc upon the enemy.

They effected this movement without haste or confusion; but the loss they have sustained has, I deeply lament, been very severe, in officers, men, and horses, only counterbalanced by the brilliancy of the attack, and the gallantry, order, and discipline which distinguished it, forming a striking contrast to the conduct of the enemy's cavalry, which had previously been engaged with the heavy brigade.

The Chasseurs d'Afrique advanced on our left, and gallantly charged a Russian battery, which checked its fire for a time, and thus rendered the British cavalry an essential service.

I have the honour to inclose copies of Sir Colin Campbell's and the Earl of Lucan's reports.

I beg to draw your Grace's attention to the terms in which Sir Colin Campbell speaks of Lieutenant-Colonel Ainslie, of the 93rd, and Captain Barker, of the Royal Artillery; and also to the praise bestowed by the Earl of Lucan on Major-General the Earl of Cardigan, and Brigadier-General Scarlett, which they most fully deserve.

The Earl of Lucan not having sent me the names of the other officers who distinguished themselves, I propose to forward them by the next opportunity.

The enemy made no further movement in advance, and at the close of the day the brigade of Guards of the 1st Division, and the 4th Division returned to their original encampment, as did the French troops with the exception of one brigade of the 1st Division, which General Canrobert was so good as to leave in support of Sir Colin Campbell.

The remaining regiments of the Highland Brigade also remained in the valley.

The 4th Division had advanced close to the heights, and Sir George Cathcart caused one of the redoubts to be reoccupied by the Turks, affording them his support, and he availed himself of the opportunity to assist with his riflemen in silencing two of the enemy's guns.

The means of defending the extensive position which had been occupied by the Turkish troops in the morning having proved wholly inadequate, I deemed it necessary, in concurrence with General Canrobert, to withdraw from the lower range of heights, and to concentrate our force, which will be increased by a considerable body of seamen, to be landed from the ships under the authority of Admiral Dundas, immediately in front of the narrow valley leading, into Balaklava, and upon the precipitous heights on our right, thus affording a narrower line of defence.

I have, &c.,
RAGLAN.
His. Grace the Duke of Newcastle,
&c. &c. &c.
Enclosures.

Balaklava,
October 27th, 1854.

MY LORD,

I HAVE the honour to report that the Cavalry Division under my command was seriously engaged with the enemy on the 25th instant, during the greater part of which day it was under a heavy fire; that it made a most triumphant charge against a very superior number of the enemy's cavalry, and an attack upon batteries which for daring and gallantry could not be exceeded. The loss, however, in officers, men, and horses, has been most severe.

From half-past six in the morning, when the Horse Artillery first opened fire, till the enemy had possessed itself of all the different forts, the cavalry, constantly changing their positions, continued giving all the support they could to the Turkish troops, though much exposed to the fire of heavy guns and riflemen, when they took post on the left of the second line of redoubts, by an order from your lordship.

The Heavy Brigade had soon to return to the support of the troops defending Balaklava. And was fortunate enough in being at hand when a large force of Russian cavalry was descending the hill. I immediately ordered Brigadier-General Scarlett to attack with the Scots Greys and, Enniskillen Dragoons, and had his attack supported in second line by the Fifth Dragoon Guards, and by a flank attack of the Fourth Dragoon Guards.

Under every disadvantage of ground, these eight small squadrons succeeded in defeating and dispersing a body of cavalry estimated at three times their number and more.

The Heavy Brigade having now joined the Light Brigade, the division took up a position with a view of supporting an attack upon the heights, when being instructed to make a rapid advance to our front, to prevent the enemy carrying the guns lost by the Turkish troops in the morning, I ordered the Light Brigade to advance in two lines, and supported them with the Heavy Brigade. This attack of the Light Cavalry was very brilliant and daring; exposed to a fire from heavy batteries on their front and two flanks, they advanced unchecked until they reached the batteries of the enemy, and cleared them of their gunners, and only retired when they found themselves engaged with a very superior force of cavalry in the rear. Major-General the Earl of Cardigan led this attack in the most gallant and intrepid manner; and his lordship, has expressed himself to me as admiring in the highest degree the courage and zeal of every officer, non-commissioned officer and man that assisted.

The Heavy Brigade advanced to the support of the attack under a very galling fire from the batteries and infantry in a redoubt, and acted with most perfect steadiness, and in a manner to deserve all praise.

The losses, my Lord, it grieves me to state, have been very great indeed, and, I fear, will be much felt by your Lordship.

I cannot too strongly recommend to your Lordship the two General Officers commanding the Brigades, all the officers in command of regiments, as also the Divisional and Brigade Staffs; indeed, the conduct of every individual, of every rank, I feel to be deserving of my entire praise, and, I hope, of your Lordship's approbation.

The conduct of the Royal Horse Artillery Troop, first under the command of Captain Maude, and, after that officer was severely wounded, of Captain Shakespear, was most meritorious and praiseworthy. I received from those officers every possible assistance during the time they respectively commanded.

I have, &c.,
LUCAN,
Lieutenant-General Commanding
Cavalry Division.
His Excellency the Commander of the Forces,
&c. &c. &c.

Camp Battery No. 4, Balaklava,
October 27, 1854.

SIR,

I HAVE the honour to inform you that on the morning of the 25th instant, about 7 o'clock, the Russian force which has been, as I already reported for some time amongst the hills on our right front, debouched into the open ground in front of the redoubts Nos. 1, 2 and 3, which were occupied by Turkish Infantry and Artillery, and armed with 7 12-pounders (iron). The enemy's force consisted of 18 or 19 battalions of infantry, from 30 to 40 guns and a large body of cavalry. The attack was made against No. 1 redoubt by a cloud of skirmishers supported by 8 battalions of infantry and 16 guns. The Turkish troops in No. 1, persisted as long as they could and then retired, and they suffered considerable loss in their retreat. This attack was followed by the successive abandonment of Nos. 2, 3 and 4 redoubts by the Turks as well as of the other posts held by them in our front. The guns however in Nos. 2, 3 and 4 were spiked. The garrisons of these redoubts retired, and some of them formed on the right, and some on the left flank of the 93rd Highlanders which was posted in front of No. 4 battery and the village of Katichioi. When the enemy had taken possession of these redoubts, their artillery advanced with a large mass of cavalry, and their guns ranged to the 93rd Highlanders, which with 10 invalids under Lieut.-Col. Daveney in support, occupied very insufficiently from the smallness of their numbers, the slightly rising ground in front of No. 4 battery. As I found that round shot and shell began to cause some casualties among the 93rd Highlanders and the Turkish battalions on their right and left flank, I made them retire a few paces behind the crest of the hill. During this period our batteries on the hills, manned by the Royal Marine Artillery and the Royal Marines, made most excellent practice on the enemy's cavalry, which came over the hill ground in front. One body of them, amounting to about 400 men, turned to their left, separating themselves from those who attacked Lord Lucan's Division, and charged the 93rd Highlanders, who immediately advanced to the crest of the hill and opened their fire, which forced the Russian cavalry to give way and turn to their left, after which they made an attempt to turn the right flank of the 93rd, having observed the flight of the Turks who were placed there, upon which the Grenadiers of the 93rd, under Captain Ross, were wheeled up to their right and fired on the enemy, which manoeuvre completely discomfited them.

During the rest of the day the troops under my command received no further molestation from the Russians. I beg to call Lord Raglan's attention to the gallantry and eagerness of the 93rd Highlanders under Lieut.-Col. Ainslie, of which probably his Lordship was an eye-witness; as well as the admirable conduct of Captain Barker, and the officers of the Field Battery under his orders, who made most excellent practice against the Russian cavalry and artillery while within range.

I have, &c.,
(Signed) COLIN CAMPBELL,
Major-General.
To Brigadier-General Estcourt,
Adjutant-General.

2nd Division, Heights of the Tchernay,
October 27, 1854.

MY LORD,

YESTERDAY the enemy attacked this division with several columns of infantry supported by artillery. Their cavalry did not come to the front. Their masses, covered by large bodies of skirmishers, advanced with much apparent confidence. The division immediately formed line in advance of our camp, the left under Major-General Pennefather, the right under Brigadier-General Adams. Lieutenant-Colonel Fitzmayer and the Captains of batteries (Turner and Yates) promptly posted their guns and opened fire upon the enemy.

Immediately on the cannonade being heard, the Duke of Cambridge brought up to our support the brigade of Guards under Major-General Bentinck, with a battery under Lieutenant-Colonel Dacres. His Royal Highness took post in advance of our right to secure that flank, and rendered me throughout the most effective and important assistance. General Bosquet with similar promptitude and from a greater distance, approached our position with five French battalions. Sir G. Cathcart hastened to us with a regiment of Rifles, and Sir G. Brown pushed forward two guns in co-operation by our left.

The enemy came on at first rapidly, assisted by their guns on the Mound-hill. Our piquets, then chiefly of the 49th and 30th regiments, resisted them with very remarkable determination and firmness. Lieutenant Conolly of the 49th greatly distinguished himself, as did Captain Bayley of the 30th, and Captain Atcherley, all of whom, I regret to say, were severely wounded. Serjeant Sullivan also displayed at this point great bravery.

In the mean time, our 18 guns in position, including those of the First Division, were served with the utmost energy. In half an hour they forced the enemy's artillery to abandon the field. Our batteries were then directed with equal accuracy and vigour upon the enemy's columns, which (exposed also to the close fire of our advanced infantry) soon fell into complete disorder and flight. They were then literally chased by the 30th and 95th regiments over the ridges and down towards the head of the bay. So eager was the pursuit that it was with difficulty Major-General Pennefather eventually effected the recall of our men. These regiments and the piquets were led gallantly by Major Mauleverer, Major Champion, Major Eman, and Major Hume. They were similarly pursued further towards our right, by four companies of the 41st, led gallantly by Lieutenant-Colonel the Honourable P. Herbert, A.Q.M.G. The 47th also contributed. The 55th were held in reserve.

Above 80 prisoners fell into our hands, and about 130 of the enemy's dead were left within or near our position. It is computed that their total loss could scarcely be less than 600.

Our loss, I am sorry to say, has been above 80, of whom 12 killed, 5 officers wounded. I am happy to say, hopes are entertained that Lieutenant Conolly will recover, but his wound is dangerous.

I will have the honour of transmitting to your Lordship a list of officers, non-commissioned officers, and privates, whose conduct attracted special notice. That of the piquets excited general admiration.

To Major-General Pennefather and Brigadier-General Adams I was, as usual, greatly indebted. Of Lieutenant-Colonel Dacres, Lieutenant-Colonel Fitzmayer, Captains Turner, Tates, Woodham, and Hemlin, and the whole of the Royal Artillery, we are under the greatest obligation.

Lieutenant-Colonel Herbert, A.Q.M.G., rendered the division, as he always does, highly distinguished and energetic services. Lieutenant-Colonel Wilbraham, A. A. G., while serving most actively, I regret to say, had a very severe fall from his horse. I beg leave also to recommend to your Lordship's favourable consideration, the excellent services of Captains Glasbrook and Thompson, of the Quartermaster-General's department, the Brigade-Majors Captains Armstrong and Thackwell, and my personal staff, Captains Allix, Gubbins, and the Hon. W. Boyle.

I have, &c.

DE LACY EVANS.

Lieutenant-General.

To General the Right Hon. Lord Raglan, G.C.B.

&c. &c. &c.

No. 86. Before Sevastopol,

October 28, 1854.

MY LORD DUKE,

I HAVE nothing particular to report to your Grace respecting the operations of the siege, since I wrote to you on the 23rd instant. The fire has been somewhat less constant, and our casualties have been fewer, though I regret to say that Captain Childers, a very promising officer of the Royal Artillery, was killed on the evening of the 23rd, and I have just heard that Major Dalton of the 49th, of whom Lieutenant-General Sir De Lacy Evans entertained a very high opinion, was killed in the trenches last night.

The enemy moved out of Sevastopol on the 26th with a large force of infantry, cavalry, and artillery, amounting, it is said, to 6000 or 7000 men, and attacked the left of the 2nd Division, commanded by Lieutenant-General Sir De Lacy Evans, who speedily and energetically repulsed them, assisted by one of the batteries of the 1st Division, and some guns of the Light Division, and supported by the brigade of Guards and by several regiments of the 4th Division, and in rear by the French Division commanded by General Bosquet, who was most eager in his desire to give him every aid.

I have the honour to transmit a copy of Sir De Lacy Evans' report, which I am sure your Grace will read with the highest satisfaction, and I beg to recommend the officers whom he particularly mentions to your protection.

Captain Bayly of the 30th, and Captain Atcherley of the same Regiment, and Lieutenant Conolly of the 49th, all of whom are severely wounded, appear to have greatly distinguished themselves.

I cannot speak in too high terms of the manner in which Lieutenant-General Sir De Lacy Evans met this very serious attack. I had not the good fortune to witness it myself, being occupied in front of Balaklava at the time it commenced, and having only reached his position as the affair ceased, but I am certain I speak the sentiments of all who witnessed the operation, in saying that nothing could have been better managed, and that the greatest credit is due to the Lieutenant-General, whose services and conduct I have before had to bring under your Grace's notice

I have, &c.
RAGLAN.
His Grace the Duke of Newcastle,
&c. &c. &c.

CHAPTER 4

THE BATTLE OF INKERMAN

War Department, November 17, 1854,
12¾ o'clock Afternoon.

HIS Grace the Duke of Newcastle has this day received three Despatches and Enclosures, of which the following are copies, addressed to his Grace by General the Lord Raglan, G.C.B.

No. 93.
Before Sebastopol, October 31, 1854.

MY LORD DUKE,

ADVERTING to that part of your Grace's Despatch of the 10th instant, No. 116, in which it is stated that Her Majesty will be most anxious to receive such further accounts from me as may tend to relieve the affectionate anxiety of the friends of the wounded, I have the honour to acquaint your Grace that the Inspector-General of Hospitals has reported, from personal observation, that the majority of the wounded are making satisfactory progress, although there is too much reason to apprehend that among such a number of severe and dangerous injuries, a certain proportion of casualties must occur.

I have, &c.,
RAGLAN.
His Grace the Duke of Newcastle,
&c. &c. &c.

No. 94. Before Sebastopol,
October 31, 1854.

MY LORD DUKE,

WHEN I wrote to your Grace on the 28th instant, I was not in possession of the names of the officers of the Cavalry Division who had distinguished themselves in the action of the 25th.

I have now the honour to inclose a letter from Lieut.-General the Earl of Lucan, containing the list of those whose services entitle them to be specially mentioned, and I beg leave to recommend them to your Grace's notice.

In the Despatch to which I above refer, I had the honour to draw your Grace's attention to the conduct of Major-General the Earl of Cardigan and the Honourable Brigadier-General Scarlett.

I omitted in my Despatch of the 28th September, to state, that when, in the battle of the Alma, Lieutenant-Colonel Webber Smith was obliged, in consequence of being severely wounded, to leave the field, Major Champion assumed the charge of the 95th, which your Grace will recollect was one of the regiments, that suffered the most; and he gained great credit, by the way in which he conducted the command.

I am glad of the opportunity to repair this omission.

I stated to your Grace on the 28th instant, that Major Dalton, of the 49th, had been killed in the trenches; this was an error, the officer whose loss the service has to deplore is Major Powell, of the same regiment. I deeply regret that this mistake should have occurred.

I have, &c.,
RAGLAN.
His Grace the Duke of Newcastle,
&c. &c. &c.

No. 95.
Before Sebastopol, November 3, 1854.

MY LORD DUKE,

SINCE I wrote to your Grace, on the 28th ultimo, the enemy have considerably increased their force in the Valley of the Tschernaya, both in artillery, cavalry, and infantry, and have extended to their left, not only occupying the village of Camara, but the heights beyond it, and pushing forward pickets and even guns towards our extreme right; and these yesterday fired a few shots, apparently to try the range, which fell somewhat short.

These movements have induced me to place as strong a force as I can dispose of on the precipitous ridge in that direction, in order to prevent any attempt to get round to Balaklava by the sea; and the whole line is strengthened by a breastwork, which has been thrown up by the Highland Brigade, the Royal Marines and the Turkish

Troops, thus circumscribing that part of the position; whilst immediately in front of the gorge leading into the town a strong redoubt is in course of being completed, which is to be garrisoned by the 93rd Regiment, and armed with several guns; and on high ground behind, and to the left, is a battery manned by seamen, which terminates the position to be defended by the troops under the command of Major-General Sir Colin Campbell.

Further to the left, and in a more elevated position, is the Brigade of the 1st French Division, commanded by General Vinois, ready to move to the assistance of any of the British Force that may be assailed, and maintaining the connexion between the troops in the valley and those on the ridge on which the main armies are posted.

The harbour of Balaklava is under the charge of Captain Dacres of the Sanspareil, and Rear- Admiral Sir Edmund Lyons is in the roadstead, outside, and is in daily communication with me.

Thus every possible step has been taken, to secure this important point, but I will not conceal from your Grace, that I should be more satisfied if I could have occupied the position in considerably greater strength.

With reference to the operations of the combined Armies, engaged in the attack on Sebastopol, I have the honour to state, that, there is no material diminution in the enemy's fire, and yesterday morning, two hours before daylight, the cannonade from all parts of the south front was heavy in the extreme, both on the French and British lines, and it occasioned, I deeply regret to say, some loss, but less than might have been expected under the circumstances.

In the meanwhile the French, who have before them the town and real body of the place, have taken advantage of the more favourable ground, and are carrying on approaches systematically on the most salient and commanding part of the enemy's lines; and they have constructed and opened batteries, the precision of the fire from which has most materially damaged the Russian works, although as yet they have not succeeded in silencing their guns.

The weather is still fine, but it has become extremely cold, and there was a severe frost last night.

I beg to submit to your Grace the nominal returns of casualties amongst the non-commissioned officers and rank and file from the 22nd October to the 1st November, both days inclusive, and a list of officers killed and wounded between the 27th October and 1st November.

Captain Maude, of the Horse Artillery, an excellent officer, is I am assured doing well.

I likewise enclose the naval return of casualties.

I have, &c.
RAGLAN.
His Grace the Duke of Newcastle,
&c. &c. &c.

Portman Square, November 16, 1854.
12.30 a.m.

THE Duke of Newcastle has to-night received a Telegraphic Despatch, of which the following is a translation, from General Lord Raglan, G.C.B.

The Despatch was delayed between Bucharest and Vienna by an interruption of the telegraph from injuries received during a violent storm.

Translation of a Telegraphic Despatch received by
the Duke of Newcastle, on 16th November, 12.30 a.m., from Lord Raglan.
November 6, 1854.

THE Enemy, with immense forces, attacked yesterday, in the dawn of morning, the right of the English position before Sevastopol, which was defended by the Second Division and the Brigade of Guards of the First Light Division, the Fourth Division, and part of the third, and subsequently by the division of General Bosquet and other corps of the French Army, which by their gallant conduct contributed essentially to the decided success of the day. General Canrobert immediately came to the spot, and gave me the support of his assistance and of his excellent counsel. The battle was extremely obstinate, and it was not till past noon that the enemy was definitively repulsed and forced to retreat, leaving the field of battle covered with his dead and several hundreds of prisoners. The number of the Enemy much exceeded that which was opposed to us at Alma, and the losses of the Russians have been enormous. Our losses have also been very great. General Sir George Brown, Major-General Bentinck, Brigadier-Generals Adams, Buller, and Torrens, have been wounded. They are all doing well.

The conduct of the troops in the face of an enemy so superior in numbers has been excellent.

(Signed) RAGLAN.

Received at Bucharest, Friday the 10th November at 4½ p.m., and forwarded to Kronstadt at 6 p.m.

THE BRITISH AGENT.
BATTLE OF INKERMAN.

War Department,
November 22, 1854, 9½ a.m.

HIS Grace the Duke of Newcastle has this day received a Despatch, of which the following is a copy, addressed to his Grace by Field-Marshal the Lord Raglan, G.C.B.

No. 96.
Before Sebastopol, November 8, 1854.

MY LORD DUKE,

I HAVE the honour to report to your Grace that the army under my command, powerfully aided by the corps of observation of the French Army, under the command of that distinguished officer, General Bosquet, effectually repulsed and defeated a most vigorous and determined attack of the enemy on our position overlooking the ruins of Inkerman, on the morning of the 5th instant.

In my letter to your Grace of the 3rd, I informed you that the enemy had considerably increased their force in the valley of the Tschernaya. The following day this augmentation was still further apparent, and large masses of troops had evidently arrived from the northward, and on two several occasions persons of distinguished rank were observed to have joined the Russian Camp.

I have subsequently learnt that the 4th corps d'armée, conveyed in carriages of the country, and in the lightest possible order, had been brought from Moldavia, and were to be immediately followed by the 3rd corps.

It was therefore to be expected that an extensive movement would not be long deferred. Accordingly, shortly before daylight, on the 5th, strong columns of the Enemy came upon the advanced picquets covering the right of the position. These picquets behaved with admirable gallantry, defending the ground foot by foot against the overwhelming numbers of the enemy, until the 2nd Division, under Major-General Pennefather, with its field guns, which had immediately been got under arms, was placed in position.

The Light Division, under Lieutenant-General Sir George Brown, was also brought to the front without loss of time; the 1st Brigade, under Major-General Codrington, occupying the long slopes to the left towards Sebastopol, and protecting our right battery, and guarding against attack on that side, and the 2nd Brigade, under Brigadier-General Buller, forming on the left of the 2nd Division, with the 88th Regiment, under Lieutenant-Colonel Jeffreys, thrown in advance.

The Brigade of Guards under His Royal Highness the Duke of Cambridge and Major-General Bentinck, proceeded likewise to the front, and took up most important ground to the extreme right on the alignment of the 2nd Division, but separated from it by a deep and precipitous ravine, and posting its guns with those of the 2nd Division.

The 4th Division, under Lieutenant-General Sir George Cathcart, having been brought from their encampment, advanced to the front and right of the attack, the 1st Brigade, under Brigadier-General Goldie, proceeded to the left of the Inkerman road; the 2nd Brigade, under Brigadier-General Torrens, to the right of it, and on the ridge overhanging the valley of the Tschernaya.

The 3rd Division, under Lieutenant-General Sir Richard England, occupied in part the ground vacated by the 4th Division, and supported the Light Division by two regiments under Brigadier-General Sir John Campbell, while Brigadier-General Eyre held the command of the troops in the trenches.

The morning was extremely dark with a drizzling rain, rendering it almost impossible to discover anything beyond the flash and smoke of artillery and heavy musketry fire.

It, however, soon became evident that the enemy under cover of a vast cloud of skirmishers, supported by dense columns of infantry, had advanced numerous batteries of large calibre to the high ground to the left and front of the 2nd Division, while powerful columns of infantry attacked with great vigour the Brigade of Guards.

Additional batteries of heavy artillery were also placed by the enemy on the slopes to our left; the guns in the field, amounting in the whole to 90 pieces, independently however of the ship guns and those in the works of Sebastopol.

Protected by a tremendous fire of shot, shell, and grape, the Russian columns advanced in great force, requiring every effort of gallantry on the part of our troops to resist them.

At this time two battalions of French infantry, which had on the first notice been sent by General Bosquet, joined our right, and very materially contributed to the successful resistance to the attack, cheering with our men, and charging the enemy down the hill with great loss.

About the same time a determined assault was made on our extreme left, and for a moment the enemy possessed themselves of four of our guns, three of which were retaken by the 88th, while the 4th was speedily recaptured by the 77th Regiment, under Lieutenant-Colonel Egerton.

In the opposite direction the Brigade of Guards under His Royal Highness the Duke of Cambridge, was engaged in a severe conflict.

The enemy, under the cover of thick brushwood, advanced in two heavy bodies, and assaulted with great determination a small redoubt which had been constructed for two guns but was not armed. The combat was most arduous, and the Brigade, after displaying the utmost steadiness and gallantry was obliged to retire before very superior numbers, until supported by a wing of the 20th Regiment of the 4th Division, when they again advanced and retook the redoubt.

This ground was afterwards occupied in gallant style by French troops, and the Guards speedily reformed in rear of the right flank of the Second Division.

In the meanwhile, Lieutenant-General, the Honourable Sir George Cathcart, with a few companies of the 68th Regiment, considering that he might make a strong impression by descending into the valley, and taking the enemy in flank, moved rapidly forward, but finding the heights above him in full occupation of the Russians, he suddenly discovered that he was entangled with a superior force, and while attempting to withdraw his men, he received a mortal wound, shortly previously to which Brigadier-General Torrens, when leading the 68th, was likewise severely wounded.

Subsequently to this, the battle continued with unabated vigour and with no positive result, the enemy bringing upon our line not only the fire of all their field-batteries, but those in front of the works of the place, and the ship guns, till the afternoon, when the symptoms of giving way first become apparent; and shortly after, although the fire did not cease, the retreat became general, and heavy masses were observed retiring over the bridge of the Inkerman, and ascending the opposite heights, abandoning on the field of battle five or six thousand dead and wounded, multitudes of the latter having already been carried off by them. I never before witnessed such a spectacle as the field presented, but upon this I will not dwell.

Having submitted to your Grace this imperfect description of this most severe battle, I have still two duties to discharge, the one most gratifying, the last most painful to my feelings.

I have the greatest satisfaction in drawing your Grace's attention to the brilliant conduct of the Allied Troops. French and English vied with each other in displaying their gallantry and manifesting their zealous devotion to duty, notwithstanding that they had to contend against an infinitely superior force, and were exposed for many hours to a most galling fire.

It should be borne in mind that they have daily for several weeks undergone the most constant labour, and that many of them passed the previous night in the trenches.

I will not attempt to enter into the detail of the movements of the French, troops, lest I should not state them correctly, but I am proud of the opportunity of bearing testimony to their valour and energetic services, and of paying a tribute of admiration to the distinguished conduct of their immediate Commander General Bosquet, while it is in the highest degree pleasing to me to place upon record my deep sense of the valuable assistance I received from the Commander-in-Chief, General Canrobert, who was himself on the ground and in constant communication with me, and whose cordial co-operation on all occasions I cannot too highly extol.

Your Grace will recollect that he was wounded at the Alma. He was again wounded on the 5th, but I should hope that he will not long feel the effects of it.

I will in a subsequent despatch lay before your Grace the names of the officers whose services have been brought to my notice. I will not detain the mail for that purpose now, but I cannot delay to report the admirable behaviour of Lieutenant-General Sir George Brown, who was unfortunately shot through the arm, but is doing well; of Lieutenant-General His Royal Highness the Duke of Cambridge, who particularly distinguished himself; and of Major-General Pennefather in command of the Second Division, which received the first attack, and gallantly maintained itself under the greatest difficulties throughout this protracted conflict; of Major-General Bentinck, who is severely wounded; Major-General Codrington. Brigadier-General Adams, and Brigadier-General Torrens, who are severely wounded; and Brigadier-General Buller, who is also wounded, but not so seriously.

I must likewise express my obligations to Lieutenant-General Sir Richard England for the excellent disposition he made of his division, and the assistance he rendered to the left of the Light Division, where Brigadier-General Sir John Campbell was judiciously placed, and effectively supported Major-General Codrington; and I have great pleasure in stating that Brigadier-General Eyre was employed in the important duty of guarding the trenches from any assault from the town.

Lieutenant-General Sir De Lacy Evans, who had been obliged by severe indisposition to go on board ship a few days previously, left his bed as soon as he received intelligence of the attack, and was promptly at his post, and though he did not feel well enough to take the command of the Division out of the hands of Major-General Pennefather, he did not fail to give him his best advice and assistance.

It is deeply distressing to me to have to submit to your Grace the list of the killed, wounded, and missing on this memorable occasion. It is indeed heavy, and very many valuable officers and men have been lost to Her Majesty's service.

Among the killed your Grace will find the names of Lieutenant-General the Honourable Sir G. Cathcart, Brigadier-General Strangways, and Brigadier-General Goldie.

Of the services of the first it is almost unnecessary to speak. They are known throughout the British empire, and have within a short space of time been brought conspicuously before the country by his achievements at the Cape of Good Hope, whence he had only just returned when he was ordered to this army.

By his death Her Majesty has been deprived of a most devoted servant, an officer of the highest merit, while I personally have to deplore the less of an attached and faithful friend.

Brigadier-General Strangways was known to have distinguished himself in early life, and in mature age throughout a long service, he maintained the same character.

The mode in which he had conducted the command of the Artillery, since it was placed in his hands by the departure through illness of Major-General Cator, is entitled to my entire approbation, and was equally agreeable to those who were confided to his care.

Brigadier-General Goldie was an officer of considerable promise, and gave great satisfaction to all under whom he has served.

It is difficult to arrive at any positive conclusion as to the actual numbers brought into the field by the enemy. The configuration of the ground did not admit of any great development of their force, the attack, consisting of a system of repeated assaults in heavy masses of columns; but judging from the numbers that were seen in the plains after they had withdrawn in retreat, I am led to suppose that they could not have been less than sixty thousand men. Their loss was excessive, and it is calculated that they left on the field near five thousand dead, and that their casualties amount in the whole, in killed, wounded, and prisoners, to not less than 15,000.

Your Grace will be surprised to learn that the number of British Troops actually engaged little exceeded 8,000 men, whilst those of General Bosquet's division only amounted to 6,000, the remaining available French troops on the spot having been kept in reserve.

I ought to mention, that while the enemy was attacking our right, they assailed the left of the French trenches, and actually got into two of their batteries; but they were quickly driven out in the most gallant manner with considerable loss, and hotly pursued to the very walls of Sebastopol.

I have, &c.
RAGLAN.
His Grace the Duke of Newcastle,
&c. &c. &c.

War Department,
December 2, 1854, 1 p.m.

HIS Grace the Duke of Newcastle has this day received a Despatch, of which the following is a copy, addressed to his Grace by Field-Marshal the Lord Raglan, G.C.B.

No. 98. Before Sebastopol,
November 11, 1854.

MY LORD DUKE,

WHEN, on the 8th instant, I reported the gallant and successful repulse of the very formidable attack made upon the position occupied our troops above the ruins of Inkerman, I stated that I would in a subsequent Despatch lay before your Grace the names of the officers whose conduct upon the occasion had been brought to my notice. I now proceed to discharge that duty.

His Royal Highness the Duke of Cambridge reports most favourably of the exertions of Colonel the Honourable George Upton, of the Coldstream Guards, Lieutenant-Colonel Reynardson, of the Grenadier Guards, and Colonel Walker, of the Scots Fusilier Guards, as well as of Colonel Cunynghame, Assistant-Quarter-Master-General, and Lieutenant-Colonel Brownrigg, Assistant-Adjutant-General; Captain the Honourable Percy Fielding, Acting Deputy-Assistant-Quartermaster-General, who was severely wounded; and of Captain Butler, Deputy-Assistant-Adjutant-General, who was unfortunately killed; and here I may pause to mention that he was the brother of Captain Butler, who so distinguished himself at Silistria, and fell just before the siege was raised.

The Duke of Cambridge likewise recommends Lieutenant-Colonel Dacres, of the Royal Artillery, who commanded the field batteries of the 1st Division, which were admirably served by Captains Paynter and Woodhouse, Captain Hamley of the Royal Artillery acting as Staff Officer to that branch of the service; Captain Ellison, the Brigade Major to the Guards, and Major the Honourable James Macdonald (whose conduct particularly attracted my attention), and the other Officers of his personal Staff.

His Royal Highness speaks also in the highest terms of the spirited exertions of Assistant-Surgeon Wilson, of the 7th Hussars, who at a critical moment rallied a few men which enabled them to hold the ground till reinforced.

In the 2nd Division, which, as I have already informed your Grace, received the first attack, and was engaged throughout the day, the Officers whose names I have to bring forward are very numerous.

Those who commanded the regiments of which it is composed were, without exception, either killed or wounded; and, in many instances, those who succeeded were wounded. Major-General Pennefather commends them highly. Colonel Warren, of the 55th, in command of the 1st Brigade, and Lieutenant-Colonel Daubeney, 55th, who succeeded to it on the former being wounded, and was himself wounded afterwards; Lieutenant-Colonel Mauleverer, 30th, and Major Patullo, of the same regiment, who took the command of the regiment when the Lieutenant-Colonel was wounded; Major Champion, 95th Regiment, and Major Hume, of the same corps, who were both wounded, the latter having succeeded the former in the command, and being himself relieved by Captain Davis when he was obliged to leave the field.

Lieutenant-Colonel Carpenter, of the 41st, who was mortally wounded, and succeeded in the command by Major Eman; Lieutenant-Colonel Haly, of the 47th, who was obliged, when wounded, to relinquish his command to Major Farren; Major Dalton, of the 49th, who fell at the head of his corps, and was replaced by Major Grant; Lieutenant-Colonel Fitzmayer, commanding the batteries of the 2nd Division, under the able direction of Captains Pennycuick and Turner; Lieutenant-Colonel Wilbraham, and Lieutenant-Colonel the Honourable Percy Herbert, the Assistant-Adjutant, and Assistant-Quartermaster-General, and Captain Thompson, 10th Hussars, and Captain Glazbrook, 49th Regiment, the Deputy-Assistant-Adjutant, and Deputy-Assistant-Quartermaster-General of the Division; Captains Thackwell and Armstrong, the Brigade-Majors; Captain Harding, Aide-de-Camp, and the other officers attached to the Major-General's personal Staff, one of whom, Captain Allix, the First Aide-de-Camp of Lieutenant-General Sir De Lacy Evans, and a most promising officer, was unfortunately killed.

The 3rd Division was only partially engaged; but having been actively employed in all the siege operations, Lieutenant-General Sir Richard England avails himself of the opportunity to mention, in terms of high approbation, the Staff Officers and the officers in command of regiments, and has drawn my attention to the services of Major Wood, Assistant-Adjutant-General, the Honourable Major Colborne, Assistant-Quarter-Master-General, Captain Wortley, Deputy-Assistant-Quartermaster-General, and Colonel Bell, of the Royal Regiment;

Colonel Cobbe, of the 4th Regiment; Colonel the Honourable A. Spencer, of the 44th; Lieutenant-Colonel Lowth, of the 38th; Lieutenant-Colonel Adams, of the 28th; and Lieutenant-Colonel Waddy, of the 50th Regiments; Major the Honourable A. Hope, of the 60th Regiment, Captain Daniell, of the 38th, Brigade Majors; and Captain Edward Neville, Scots Fusilier Guards, his Aide-de-Camp.

The superior officers of the 4th Division, Lieutenant-General the Honourable Sir George Cathcart, and Brigadier-General Goldie, having fallen, and the survivor, Brigadier-General Torrens, having been severely wounded, I take upon myself to recommend the surviving officers of the Staff, viz.: Colonel Wyndham, Assistant-Quartermaster-General, and Captain Hugh Smith, 3rd Foot, Deputy-Assistant-Quartermaster-General; Major Maitland, Deputy-Assistant-Adjutant-General, who is wounded; and Captain Street, 57th Regiment, and Lieutenant Torrens, 23rd Regiment, Brigade Majors; and I may here express my deep regret that Lieutenant-Colonel Charles Seymour, Scots Fusilier Guards should have fallen. He had served on the Staff with the lamented Sir George Cathcart at the Cape, and had accompanied him to this country in the capacity of Assistant-Adjutant-General; and he was remarkable for his intelligence, gallantly, and zeal.

I would likewise beg to solicit your Grace's attention to the services of Colonel

Horn, who commanded the 20th, and came out of action the senior officer of the division; Captain Inglis, commanding 57th, and Lieutenant-Colonel Smyth commanding the 68th Regiment, who was severely wounded; and Captain Dallas, commanding detachment of the 46th; of Lieutenant-Colonel Ainslie of the 21st, who was wounded; of Lieutenant-Colonel Swyny, who unfortunately fell at the head of the 63rd, and was succeeded in the command by Major the Honourable Robert Dalzell; and Lieutenant-Colonel Horsford, of the Rifle Brigade; of Lieutenant-Colonel D. Wood the senior officer of the Artillery of the Division; and Major Townsend, of the Artillery, who was unfortunately killed. He was considered a most valuable officer, and was ably succeeded by Captain Hoste. Lieutenant-Colonel Powell would have commanded the 57th, but he was on duty in the trenches.

The officers of the Light Division, whose services have been brought to my notice by Lieutenant-General Sir George Brown, who was obliged by a wound in his arm to quit the field before the action terminated, and by Major-General Codrington, who succeeded him in the command, are Lieutenant-Colonel Yea, of the Royal Fusiliers; Major Sir Thomas Troubridge, of the same regiment, who was commanding in a battery, and though desperately wounded, behaved with the utmost gallantry and composure; Major Bunbury, of the 23rd, who replaced him in command; Brevet-Major Mundy, commanding the 33rd; Lieutenant-Colonel Shirley, of the 88th, who was employed in the trenches; Lieutenant-Colonel Jefferies, commanding the portion of that regiment which was in the field; Lieutenant-Colonel Egerton, commanding the 77th; Majors Straton and Dixon, of the same regiment; Lieutenant-Colonel Unett, of the 19th, on duty in the trenches; Lieutenant-Colonel Lawrence and Captain Ebrington, of the Rifle Brigade; and Captain Hopkins, commanding a detachment of Royal Marines, which had been brought up to replace a wing of the Rifle Brigade that had been sent down to Balaklava, and fully maintained the reputation of that distinguished corps; Lieutenant-Colonel Lake, of the Royal Horse Artillery; and Captain Morris, commanding the battery attached to the division, Colonel Sullivan, Assistant-Adjutant-General; Lieutenant-Colonel Airey, Assistant-Quartermaster-General; Captain Hallewell, Deputy Assistant-Quartermaster-General; Captain Macdonell and the other officers of the Lieutenant-General's personal Staff; Lieutenant the Honourable H. Campbell, Aide-de-Camp to Major-General Codrington; and Brigadier-General Buller's Aide-de-Camp, Lieutenant the Honourable H. Clifford, whose conduct is represented to have been peculiarly conspicuous; Captains Mackenzie and Glyn, the Brigade-Majors of the division.

It is due to the principal Medical Officers of the several divisions, Doctors Alexander, Cruickshank, Forest, Linton, and Humfrey, to report that their able exertions have been strongly represented to me, and deserve to be most honourably mentioned, and the arrangements of the Inspector-General of Hospitals, Dr. Hall, for the care of the wounded, merit the expression of my entire approbation.

Lieutenant-Colonel Gambier, of the Royal Artillery, who had the command of the Artillery in the trenches during the siege, a duty which he discharged to my perfect satisfaction, was I regret to say unfortunately wounded, when moving up with the two 18-pounders, which I had ordered to be brought to the right of the 2nd Division;

and I have great pleasure in speaking in terms of high panegyric of Lieutenant-Colonel Dickson, who had charge of those guns, Captain D'Aguilar, and the officers and men who worked them; they performed under Lieutenant-Colonel Dickson's directions the most effective service, notwithstanding that they had a very heavy fire upon them, and that their loss in consequence was very severe, seventeen men having been either killed or wounded, and one officer wounded.

I derived, as upon every other occasion, the most able and effective assistance from the Adjutant and Quartermaster-General, Brigadier-General Estcourt, and Brigadier-General Airey, and their Assistants, Major the Honourable W. Pakenham, and Lieutenant-Colonel the Honourable A. Gordon, and the officers of their departments; and from the Military Secretary, Lieutenant-Colonel Steele, Lieutenant-Colonel Poulett Somerset, and the officers of my personal Staff; and I feel deeply indebted to Lieutenant-General Sir John Burgoyne, for the constancy with which he applies himself to the discharge of his arduous duties, and the benefit I derive from his advice and assistance, as well as to Captain Gordon, Commanding Royal Engineer, Captain Chapman, and. the officers of that corps; and to Major Adye, the Honourable Captain Gage, and Captain Fortescue, the Staff Officers of the Royal Artillery, to the command of which Lieutenant-Colonel Dacres has succeeded by the lamented death of Brigadier-General Strangways, whose Aide-de-Camp Captain Gordon, I would also bring to your Grace's notice.

I profit by this opportunity to render justice to two officers whom I omitted to mention in my Despatch of the 28th September.

The one, Captain Maude, of the Royal Horse Artillery, who has since been badly wounded, distinguished himself at the battle of the Alma, as I myself observed; the other, Captain W. Pitcairn Campbell, became the Senior Officer of the 23rd Regiment, when Lieutenant-Colonel Chester was killed, and, though severely wounded, could hardly be persuaded to quit the field.

I have, &c.

RAGLAN.

His Grace the Duke of Newcastle,

&c. &c. &c.

CHAPTER 5

SEVASTOPOL, THE FIRST WINTER

War-Department, 10 a.m., December 11, 1854.

HIS Grace the Duke of Newcastle has this day received Despatches and Enclosures, of which the following are copies, addressed to his Grace by Field-Marshal the Lord Raglan, G.C.B.

No. 110. Before Sebastopol,
November 23, 1854.

MY LORD DUKE,

THE Russian advanced posts in front of our left attack having taken up a position which in-commoded our troops in the trenches, and occasioned not a few casualties, and at the same time took in reverse the French troops working in their lines, a representation of which was made to me both by our own officers and by General Canrobert, a detachment of the 1st Battalion Rifle Brigade, under Lieutenant Tryon, was directed on the night of the 20th to dislodge the enemy; and this service was performed most gallantly and effectively, but at some loss both in killed and wounded, and at the cost of the life of Lieutenant Tryon, who rendered himself conspicuous on the occasion, was considered a most promising officer, and held in the highest estimation by all.

The Russians attempted several times to re-establish themselves on the ground before daylight on the 21st, but they were instantly repulsed by Lieutenant Bourchier, the senior surviving officer of the party, and it now remains in our possession.

Brigadier-General Sir John Campbell speaks highly of the conduct of the detachment, and of Lieutenant Bourchier and Lieutenant Cuninghame, and he laments the death of Lieutenant Tryon, who so ably led them in the first instance.

This little exploit was so highly prized by General Canrobert that he instantly published an "Ordre Général," announcing it to the French Army, and combining, with a just tribute to the gallantry of the troops, the expression of his deep sympathy in the regret felt for the loss of a young officer of so much distinction.

Nothing else has occurred since I had last the honour to address your Grace.

The weather is again very bad, and steady rain is constantly falling.

I have, &c.,

RAGLAN.

His Grace the Duke of Newcastle,

&c. &c. &c.

No. 112. Near Sebastopol,

November 28, 1854.

MY LORD DUKE,

IN the despatch which I addressed to your Grace on the 23rd instant, I reported the gallant conduct of a detachment of the 1st battalion Rifle Brigade, and its occupation of an advanced position which it continued to retain, notwithstanding the repeated efforts of the enemy to re-establish themselves upon it.

On the night of the 22nd and on the following morning, shortly before daylight, the Russians renewed their endeavours to get possession of the ground they had been driven from, but they were repulsed on each occasion in the most spirited manner, in the first instance by a detachment of the 4th Foot, under Lieutenant Patric Robertson, and a working party belonging to the 57th Regiment, in the last instance by the detachment of the 4th Foot alone.

Brigadier-General Eyre speaks in the highest terms of the conduct of these troops, and particularly that of Lieutenant Robertson, whose former distinguished service at the Cape, coupled with that he displayed in the present affair, fully entitle him to be considered an officer of much promise.

There has been no movement of importance on the part of the enemy. The weather has been very bad, and the camp and the country are in consequence of the rain in a most unsatisfactory state.

The men are, however, endeavouring, and with some success, to shelter themselves with the stones that are found in the vicinity of the encampment, and every effort is making to provide them with the materials for hutting themselves, but the condition of the roads render this a matter of extreme difficulty.

It is gratifying to me to be able to assure you, that, notwithstanding their privations, their exposure to the weather, and the constant labour required of them, they exhibit the same cheerfulness, the same ardour in the discharge of their duty as they have manifested throughout the extensive operations in which they have been engaged.

The defences of the Inkerman position, notwithstanding the frequent interruptions from the weather are making considerable progress.

I have, &c.,

RAGLAN.

War-Department,
December 30, 1854, 10½ o'clock a.m.

HIS Grace the Duke of Newcastle has this day received a Despatch, of which the following is a copy, addressed to his Grace by Field-Marshal the Lord Raglan, G.C.

Before Sevastopol,
December 13, 1854.

MY LORD DUKE,

YOUR Grace will be happy to hear that the weather has continued fine, since I had the honour to address your Grace on the 8th instant.

The enemy has made no movement of importance, and nothing of any material consequence has taken place before Sevastopol.

The Russians moved upon our advanced pickets, in front of our left attack, the night before last, in some force; but they were instantly driven back by a detachment of the 1st Battalion Rifle Brigade, on the right, and by one of the 46th on the left. The firing, however, was kept up for some time, and the 3rd and 4th Divisions were held in readiness to support, in case their assistance should have been required.

I have, &c.,
RAGLAN.
His Grace the Duke of Newcastle,
&c. &c. &c.

War Department, January 8, 1855.

HIS Grace the Duke of Newcastle has this day received a Despatch, of which the following is a copy, addressed to His Grace by Field-Marshal the Lord Raglan, G.C.B.

Before Sevastopol,
December 18, 1854.

MY LORD DUKE,

NOTHING has occurred since I had the honour to address your Grace on the 13th instant. The weather, which was then fine, changed on the following afternoon, and, from that time to the evening of the 16th, it hardly ceased either to rain, hail, or snow.

The night of the 16th was particularly severe; but it cleared up yesterday, and to-day it is again dry.

The bad days above mentioned have, however, rendered the communications more difficult, and materially retarded the movement of supplies and stores.

The 89th and 17th Regiments have arrived from Gibraltar, and will take their place in the 3rd and 4th Divisions this day.

A considerable portion of the warm clothing has been received, and is in course of issue; and the men are most grateful to Her Majesty's Government for having provided for them what conduces so essentially to their comfort.

I have, &c.,

RAGLAN.

His Grace the Duke of Newcastle,

&c. &c. &c.

War-Department, January 9, 1855.

HIS Grace the Duke of Newcastle has this day received two Despatches, of which the following are copies, addressed to his Grace by Field-Marshal the Lord Raglan, G.C.B.

Before Sevastopol,
December 23, 1854.

MY LORD DUKE,

A GREAT deal of rain has fallen in the last forty-eight hours, and the weather has again become very inclement.

The only occurrence in the siege operations has been a sortie made by the enemy on both our right and left attack, during the night of the 20th, the one being conducted silently, the other with drums beating, and shouting; the first being probably the real object of the advance, as nearer to the Inkerman heights.

Owing to the extreme darkness of the night the enemy were enabled to come very near the right attack without being perceived, and having made a sudden rush upon the most forward parallel, they compelled the men occupying it to withdraw, until reinforced by a party under Major Welsford, of the 97th Regiment, when it was regained possession of, and the Russians retired, not however without occasioning some loss in both killed, wounded, and missing, Lieutenant Byron, of the 34th Regiment, being amongst the latter.

On the left attack, the enemy were met with great gallantry by Lieutenant Gordon, of the 38th Regiment, who, when supported by the covering party of the trenches, under Lieutenant-Colonel Waddy of the 50th, succeeded in at once driving them back. But here too I regret to say, the loss was still more severe, Major Möller, of the 50th, fell mortally wounded, and I am concerned to add is since dead, and Captain Frampton, and Lieutenant Clarke, both of the 50th Regiment, are missing. Sir Richard England speaks in high terms of the gallantry and vigilance of these troops, and of the distinguished conduct of Lieutenant-Colonel Waddy.

I enclose the return of casualties to the 20th inclusive.

Two regiments of French cavalry under General D'Allonville, made a reconnoissance on the 20th, towards the ground recently occupied by the enemy in front of Balaklava, while the 42nd Regiment, a detachment of the Rifle Brigade under Colonel Cameron, 42nd Regiment, and a battalion of Zouaves, made a corresponding movement on the extreme right. The latter saw only a picket of Cosaques, which retired upon their approach, the former exchanged shots with the enemy, and ascertained that they had scarcely any troops on the left bank of the Tchernaya.

I have, &c.,
RAGLAN.
His Grace the Duke of Newcastle,
&c. &c. &c.

Before Sevastopol,
December 26, 1854.

MY LORD DUKE,

I HAVE nothing to report to your Grace to-day.

The rain which prevailed on Saturday was succeeded by snow on Sunday, and it was almost the worst day I ever saw. At night it froze, and the frost has continued ever since, without being severe; but it has not as yet tended to dry the ground, still in a lamentable state.

Every effort is making, that the state of the roads will permit, to bring up ammunition and the materials of siege, and General Canrobert is in this respect affording us every possible assistance.

The garrison keeps up a heavy fire upon our trenches, particularly at night, and your Grace will regret to see by the returns which I inclose, that we daily sustain some casualties.

I have, &c.,
RAGLAN
His Grace the Duke of Newcastle,
&c. &c. &c.

War Department, January 12, 1855.

HIS Grace the Duke of Newcastle has this day received a Despatch, of which the following is a copy, addressed to His Grace by Field-Marshal the Lord Raglan, G.C.B.

Before Sevastopol,
December 30, 1854.

MY LORD DUKE,

SINCE I wrote to your Grace on the 26th, the weather has been somewhat more propitious; but the state of the ground is hardly more satisfactory.

The 18th Regiment has arrived; and I have likewise the honour to inform you that we are daily receiving vast supplies of ammunition, warm clothing, and huts for the Army. The utmost efforts will be made to disembark all those stores; but the difficulty of effecting this desirable object is very great, owing to the very limited extent of the harbour, its crowded state, and the narrow entrance to the town, and want of space on the beach, the rocks on the north side rising directly out of the water, and there being, consequently, no accommodation but on one side.

The Russians continue to withdraw from the Valley of the Tchernaya, whilst they have constructed defensive works on the heights above, which would imply a difficulty of maintaining their troops in the field.

A reconnoissance was sent out this morning by General Canrobert towards the river, in co-operation with a portion of Major-General Sir Colin Campbell's force on the extreme right of Balaklava, the result of which is not yet known.

I have, &c.,
RAGLAN.
His Grace the Duke of Newcastle,
&c. &c. &c.

War-Department, January 27, 1855.

HIS Grace the Duke of Newcastle has received a Despatch, of which the following is a copy, addressed to his Grace by Field-Marshal the Lord Raglan, G.C.B.

Before Sevastopol,
January 13, 1855.

MY LORD DUKE,

THE weather continues very severe, and to-day it blows a gale of wind, with drifting snow.

Although I have not received the official report from the officer commanding the 4th Division, the officer of the Quartermaster-General's department, whose duty it is to visit the advanced posts at daylight, has brought in an account of a sortie made by the Russians in the course of last night upon our right and left attack, the enemy advancing, under protection of a heavy cannonade, along the Woronzow road and the ravine on our extreme left.

The enemy succeeded in driving in the troops in the advanced trench, which was not reoccupied until the reserves were brought forward from the second parallel.

A party in pits on the right of the advanced trench, consisting of 1 serjeant and 13 rank and file, are missing, and 1 officer and 36 privates are stated to be wounded.

The time for the despatch of the mail being at hand, I am very sorry that I shall not be able to send your Grace to-day a more accurate statement of this affair.

Great progress is making in disembarking and issuing to the troops vast quantities of warm clothing of all descriptions, and I believe I may assert that every man in this army has received a second blanket, a jersey frock, flannel drawers, and socks, and some kind of winter coat, in addition to the ordinary great coat.

The provision of fuel is still a great difficulty.

Every effort is making, and with tolerable success, in landing and putting up the huts; their great weight (2½ tons each) is a serious obstacle to their conveyance to the camp, with our limited transport. Each hut requires three stripped artillery waggons, with from 8 to 10 horses each, or 180 men.

Much sickness continues to prevail.

> I have, &c.
> RAGLAN.
> *His Grace the Duke of Newcastle,*
> *&c. &c. &c.*

.

War-Department, February 2, 1855.

HIS Grace the Duke of Newcastle has received a Despatch, of which the following is a copy, addressed to His Grace by Field-Marshal the Lord Raglan, G.C.B.

Before Sevastopol,
January 15, 1855.

MY LORD DUKE,

THE fall of snow has been very great for the last three days, and it is now fully a foot deep; which, I am assured, is a very unusual occurrence in this part of the Crimea.

This circumstance adds materially to our difficulties in obtaining fuel; but detachments of Turks are posted near the coast to bring up wood, which has been cut by parties of our own in the neighbourhood of the Monastery of St. George, to the nearest divisions.

I am happy to say that the number of wounded in the sortie of the Russians, on the night of the 12th instant, was only six instead of thirty-six, as I erroneously stated to your Grace in my Despatch of the 13th, and that it was altogether a less serious affair than was at first reported.

Last night the enemy attacked the French advanced trench in considerable force, but were repulsed after a sharp contest and some loss on both sides.

I have, &c.,
RAGLAN.
His Grace the Duke of Newcastle,
&c. &c. &c.

War-Department, February 7, 1855.

HIS Grace the Duke of Newcastle received last night a Despatch, of which the following is a copy, addressed to His Grace by Field-Marshal the Lord Raglan, G.C.B.

Before Sevastopol,
January 23, 1855.

MY LORD DUKE,

NOTHING has occurred of importance in our front; but the enemy has occasionally opened a fire upon our left attack, and Mr. Spalding, a fine young man, an Acting Mate of Her Majesty's ship London, and in charge of the battery, was unfortunately killed by a round shot the day before yesterday.

His loss is deeply deplored.

The weather has become milder; but the country is still in a dreadful state from melted snow.

The Army is well supplied with warm clothing, and if the Commissariat were adequately provided with transport, and the huts could be at once brought up, there would be no other cause of suffering than the severity of a Crimean winter, and the duties imposed of carrying on a siege in such a climate at this season of the year.

I have, &c.,
RAGLAN.
His Grace the Duke of Newcastle,
&c. &c. &c.

War-Department, February 12, 1855.

LORD PANMURE has this day received a Despatch and its Enclosures, of which the following are copies, addressed to His Grace the Duke of Newcastle, by Field-Marshal the Lord Raglan, G.C.B.

Before Sevastopol,
January 27, 1855,

MY LORD DUKE,

I HAVE the satisfaction to acquaint your Grace that the weather continues fine. There are severe frosts at night; but the sun shines brightly through the day, and there is an absence of wind, which, whilst it continued, added considerably to the sufferings of the troops.

Every exertion is making by public transport, and individually, in getting huts up; but this is a most difficult operation, and the ground is still so rotten that it is a most arduous labour to pass along it.

The extremely confined space of Balaklava, and the vast accumulation of stores, has obliged me to erect huts at some distance outside the town for their reception.

I have, &c.,
RAGLAN.
His Grace the Duke of Newcastle,
&c. &c. &c.

War-Department, February 16, 1855.

LORD PANMURE has this day received a Despatch, of which the following is a copy, addressed to His Grace the Duke of Newcastle, by Field-Marshal the Lord Raglan, G.C.B.

Before Sevastopol,
February 3, 1855.

MY LORD DUKE,

NOTHING has occurred in front of the British lines since I wrote to your Grace on the 27th January.

Before daylight, on the morning of the 1st, the enemy made a vigorous sortie on the most advanced works of the French right: they were repulsed, after a sharp contest, in the most gallant manner by our Ally, who however sustained some loss.

The weather, which had latterly been fine, broke yesterday; and, after a rainy evening, there was a fall of snow during the night, and there is again a frost, with an exceedingly cold wind.

The materials for the railway continue to arrive, but I fear it will not be possible for me to supply the amount of military labour which Mr. Beatty would seem to require.

Nearly two hundred Croatians, who were hired at Constantinople, have arrived, and been handed over to him, and more are expected, and, as a matter of experiment, I have obtained four hundred Tartars from Eupatoria.

I have, &c.,
(Signed) RAGLAN.
His Grace the Duke of Newcastle,
&c. &c. &c.

War-Department, February 20, 1855.

LORD PANMURE has this day received a Despatch and its Enclosures, of which the following are copies, addressed to His Grace the Duke of Newcastle, by Field-Marshal the Lord Raglan, G.C.B.

Before Sevastopol,
February 6, 1855.

MY LORD DUKE,

I MENTIONED to your Grace on Saturday that the weather had broken. The frost was very severe on that night, and the thermometer down at thirteen, and the wind was very high and piercingly cold.

Sunday was rather milder, and yesterday was fine. To-day the glass has fallen, and there is every appearance of rain.

I am happy to state that the Medical Officers consider that the general condition of the men has improved, although apparently there is no diminution in the number of the sick.

The enemy has made no movement of importance, but great convoys of waggons have been observed to go into Sevastopol laden either with ammunition or provisions.

Lieutenant-Colonel Collingwood Dickson, of the Royal Artillery, an excellent officer, whom I have before had occasion to bring to your notice, was slightly wounded on the 4th instant, when making a reconnaissance in company with some French officers.

I have, &c.,
RAGLAN.
His Grace the Duke of Newcastle,
&c. &c. &c.

War-Department, February 23, 1855.

LORD PANMURE has this day received a Despatch and its Enclosures, of which the following are copies, addressed to His Grace the Duke of Newcastle, by Field-Marshal the Lord Raglan, G.C.B.

Before Sevastopol,
February 10, 1855.

MY LORD DUKE,

I HAVE nothing material or important to report to your Grace since I addressed you on the 6th.

There was rain yesterday and the day before, and in the course of last night there was a considerable fall of snow, which remains on the ground; but it does not freeze, and the country is again saturated with wet.

It is reported from the front that great activity prevails in the town and harbour of Sevastopol.

Large convoys of apparently sick men were observed to be moving out of the place, and numerous carts, with one horse, to be coming in.

The enemy appear to be breaking up hulks in the Arsenal Creek, and to be using the material for platforms and chevaux de frise at the battery "du Mat."

We are proceeding with the armament of the works on the right.

The health of the troops continues to improve in some slight degree. They are amply supplied with warm clothing and with provisions.

Forage is our only want, and this arises chiefly from the Commissary-General not receiving from England the supplies of hay upon which he has reckoned.

I have, &c.,
RAGLAN.
His Grace the Duke of Newcastle,
&c. &c. &c.

War-Department, February 27, 1855.

LORD PANMURE has this day received a Despatch and its Enclosures, of which the following are copies, addressed to His Grace the Duke of Newcastle, by Field-Marshal the Lord Raglan, G.C.B.

Before Sevastopol,
February 13, 1855.

MY LORD DUKE,

I MENTIONED to your Grace in my Despatch of the 10th instant, that there had been a return of bad weather, and that the country was again saturated with wet.

On Sunday it rained or snowed from morning till night, and the wind was very high, and though it was fine yesterday, still the ground was in a worse state than I had seen it for some time.

The Enemy has made no movement.

Major-General Jones, Royal Engineers, arrived a few days ago, and is busily engaged in making himself acquainted with the position occupied by both Armies.

Lieutenant-General Sir George Brown has also returned, and I have great satisfaction in adding, in excellent health. His wound is healed, and, with the exception of not having entirely regained the full use of his elbow, he no longer suffers any inconvenience from it.

He will resume the command of his division without loss of time.

I have, &c.,
RAGLAN.
His Grace the Duke of Newcastle,
&c. &c. &c.

War-Department, March 2, 1855.

LORD PANMURE yesterday received a Despatch and its Enclosures, of which the following are copies, addressed to His Grace the Duke of Newcastle, by Field-Marshal the Lord Raglan, G.C.B.

Before Sevastopol,
February 17, 1855.

MY LORD DUKE,

I HAVE the satisfaction to acquaint your Grace that the weather has improved since I last addressed you, and the country is becoming drier.

Two days ago the thermometer was up at 60. It was somewhat lower yesterday, and early this morning it was down below freezing point, and at this moment it is snowing.

I mention these particulars in order to show your Grace how variable this climate is.

No movement has been made upon the part of the enemy. The garrison of Sevastopol is engaged in deepening the ditches, and improving the defences of the south front, and in constructing works on the north side of the harbour.

I have received information that the Russian Army, in the neighbourhood of Backshi Serai and Simpheropol, is suffering much from the want of provisions, and from privations of all kinds.

I am happy to be able to say that the railway is making considerable progress, and that every hope is entertained that in the course of a very short time it will be available for transit as far as Kadikoi, which will accelerate the conveyance of stores up to the camp.

I have great pleasure in stating that Colonel Bell, of the Royal Regiment, who received a slight wound in the side from a musket-ball, when commanding in the trenches on the night of the 14th instant, experiences very little inconvenience from it, and has felt well enough to continue to discharge his duty with his accustomed zeal.

I have, &c.,
RAGLAN.
His Grace the Duke of Newcastle,
&c. &c. &c.

OCCURRENCES IN NAVAL BRIGADE.

Royal Albert, off Sevastopol.
February 20, 1855.

SIR,

IN continuation of my letter of the 7th instant, No. 103, I enclose, for the information of the Lords Commissioners of the Admiralty two letters from Captain Lushington, detailing the proceedings of the Naval Brigade since that date, and reporting their extraordinary good health.

I have, &c.,
ED. LYONS,
Rear-Admiral and Commander-in-Chief.

To the Secretary of the Admiralty,
London.
Enclosure No. 1.
Camp, Naval Brigade,
February 11, 1855.

SIR,

IN continuation of our proceedings, I have the honour to inform you that we have been employed this week in carrying shot into the batteries. The enemy continues augmenting his defences and firing on our working parties during the day. Several ineffectual sorties have been made on the French during the past week.

I have also been getting up slops and provisions, and have a supply for seven days of the latter in our store tents.

I have much pleasure in informing you of the healthy state of the brigade, having only 44 in the sick list, no serious cases, and victualling 998.

I have, &c.,
(Signed) S. LUSHINGTON,
Captain Commanding Naval Brigade.
Rear-Admiral Sir Edmd. Lyons, G.C.B.,
Commander-in- Chief.

Enclosure No. 2.

Camp, Naval Brigade,
February 18, 1855.

SIR,

I HAVE the honour to inform you that the enemy still continues strengthening his works.

I am happy to say that there have been no casualties this week, and that the brigade is remarkably healthy. We have only 27 men in the sick list, victualling 999 men and officers. All symptoms of scurvy have disappeared; and I am informed by the medical officers in charge, that he considers this as principally owing to the liberal supply of oranges issued to the brigade.

I have, &c.,
(Signed) S. LUSHINGTON,
Captain, Commanding Naval Brigade.
Rear-Admiral Sir Edmund
Lyons, Bart., G.C.B..
&c. &c. &c.

War-Department, March 8, 1855.

LORD PANMURE has this day received Despatches and Enclosures, of which the following are copies, addressed to His Grace the Duke of Newcastle, and to His Lordship, by Field-Marshal the Lord Raglan, G.C.B.

Before Sevastopol,
February 20, 1855.

MY LORD DUKE,

YOUR Grace will have learnt, by my telegraphic despatch of the 18th inst., that the enemy had on the previous morning, at daylight, attacked Eupatoria with a very large force, and a powerful body of artillery, and had been repulsed, after an engagement which terminated with their retirement at 10 A.M.

I have now the honour to lay before your Grace copies of two letters which I have received from Colonel Simmons, who is attached to the head-quarters of Omer Pasha, containing the details of the action; and, whilst your Grace will rejoice to see that the Turkish troops which have been landed at Eupatoria have availed themselves of the earliest opportunity to show that the character they acquired on the Danube was well merited and remained unimpaired, you will join in the regret which I feel that they have suffered so considerable a loss, and that among the killed is numbered the General of Division, Selim Pasha (an Egyptian), and among the wounded a General of Brigade, also an Egyptian.

This loss, however, and particularly that sustained by a battery of artillery, afford ample proof of the gallant and determined conduct of the troops, and of the serious nature of the attack made upon them, as well as of their being worthy of their illustrious chief.

I have great satisfaction in drawing your Grace's attention to that part of Lieutenant Colonel Simmons' dispatch, in which he bears testimony to the efficient assistance rendered to the Ottoman army by Her Majesty's ships in the bay, under the command of the Honourable Captain Hastings, of the Curaçoa.

I have, &c.,
RAGLAN.
His Grace the Duke of Newcastle,
&c. &c. &c.

Eupatoria, February 17, 1855,
1 P.M.

MY LORD,

I HAVE the honour to inform your Lordship that on the 15th instant, several large convoys and arrivals of troops were seen moving along the north shore of the Sasik Putrid Lake, from the eastward.

This movement on the part of the enemy caused Omer Pasha to place the garrison on the alert. No further movement, however, was seen yesterday on the part of the enemy; but this morning, at daylight, they advanced in great force, and opened with artillery upon the entrenchments which inclose the town. The advanced line of works, which I informed your Lordship it was his Highness's intention to erect, were not yet commenced.

The enemy's artillery opened their fire about twelve hundred yards from the place, covered by skirmishers, and supported by heavy masses of infantry in their rear, and cavalry on their flanks. The artillery subsequently took up a second position more in advance, about four hundred yards from a small crown work which is being erected in front of the mills to the north-east of the town, and after continuing their fire for some time, the infantry advanced to the attack, having formed under the cover of a wall about six hundred yards from the right of the town. They were repulsed at this point, leaving from 150 to 200 dead on the field. On other points of the field a number of horses were left dead, but the killed men were removed. At length, about 10 A.M., the whole force retired, covered by the artillery and cavalry.

I am not able as yet to ascertain the number of men engaged, but I should think there were not less than 40,000 of all arms, with a very powerful artillery.

As many as sixty of the enemy's guns must have been firing at one time, amongst them some 32-pounders. Prisoners report that they were accompanied by 100 guns. As yet all the particulars I have been able positively to ascertain is that Liprandi's division (the 12th) was present.

At present I understand that they are in position about five miles north from this, their left leaning on the Sasik Putrid Lake.

It is with much pleasure I have to inform your Lordship that the portion of Her Majesty's Fleet, under the Honourable Captain Hastings, have rendered most efficient assistance. The Valorous threw some well directed shells and completely covered our left, whilst the Viper gun-boat, which was at first stationed on the left with the Valorous, by Captain Hastings' directions moved and took up a flanking position on the right near the mills.

I cannot at present give your Lordship any details of the killed and wounded on the side of the Turks; I regret to say, however, that Selim Pasha, commanding the Egyptian Brigade here, is amongst the former.

One battery of Turkish artillery was completely disabled, every gun having been struck and a great number (nearly one-third) of the horses killed.

I am desirous your Lordship should receive a report of the action, with as little delay as possible, by the Queen of the South; so I must beg your Lordship to excuse further details, which shall be sent by a future occasion.

I am, &c.
(Signed) JOHN SIMMONS,
Captain Royal Engineers, Brevet-Major.
Field-Marshal Lord Raglan, G.C.B.,
&c. &c. &c.

P.S. A prisoner informs us that a prince commanded, but he could not remember his name.

I am happy to say there are no casualties among the English or French officers. Two French sous-officers are among the killed, and two privates wounded.

(Signed) JOHN S.

War-Department, March 17, 1855.

LORD PANMURE has this day received a Despatch and its Enclosures, of which the following are copies, addressed to His Lordship, by Field-Marshal the Lord Raglan, G.C.B.

Before Sevastopol,
February 27, 1855.

MY LORD,

IT appears that on Saturday night the enemy sunk three or four more ships of war in the harbour, as far within the booms as the first sunken ships were outside of them; and, according to the most accurate examination yesterday, there are now four barriers or impediments to the entrance of the harbour, viz.: two of sunken ships, and two booms.

The only movement on the part of the enemy, since I last wrote to your Lordship, is the march of some infantry and artillery from the neighbourhood of Bakchi-Sarai towards the Tchernaya, upon which river, near Chagouna, they have at present five guns and several hundred men.

The weather has been fine for the last three days, the snow is gradually disappearing, and the country is becoming drier.

The enemy have re-occupied the ground which was the scene of contest between the French and Russians on Saturday morning before daylight; and they are making great progress in a work they are establishing upon that point.

I have, &c.,
RAGLAN.
The Lord Panmure, &c. &c.

Before Sevastopol,
March 20, 1855.

MY LORD,

IN my despatch of the 17th instant, I reported to your Lordship the progress made in forming the parallel constructed to unite the right of our right attack with the left of the French on the Inkerman heights.

The contest of the latter with the enemy for the possession of the Rifle pits in their immediate front was renewed after dark on that night, and was continued for several hours, the fire being excessively heavy, particularly of musketry, and considerable loss must have been sustained by our allies I fear, as well as by the enemy, who continue to hold the ambuscades; but the French persevere, notwithstanding, in working forward, and are approaching the mamelon, on which the Russians are busily engaged in building a formidable work, though frequently interrupted by our batteries and those of the French.

On the night of the 17th the English parallels were not attacked, but the fire to which I have above alluded was so continuous, that the whole force was either under arms or ready to turn out.

It was currently reported yesterday that Prince Menchikoff had died on his way to Moscow. I have not been able to ascertain if this report be founded; but it was so fully credited as to have been despatched to Constantinople.

Prince Gortchakoff is stated to have arrived at Bachshi Sarai, and to have assumed the command of the army.

Reinforcements are reported to be on their way from Russia, and the 9th Division to have reached the neighbourhood of Eupatoria. The position of the Russian troops in the vicinity of the Tchernaya remains unaltered.

The progress of the railway continues to be satisfactory, and we are already enabled to use it with considerable advantage, both for the conveyance of supplies and hutting, so far as the high ground some way on this side of Kadikoi.

Mr. Beattie's exertions deserve every commendation.

I have, &c.,
RAGLAN.

War-Department, March 22, 1855.

LORD PANMURE has this day received a Despatch and its Enclosures, of which the following are copies, addressed to His Lordship, by Field-Marshal the Lord Raglan, G.C.B.

Before Sevastopol,
March 8, 1855.

MY LORD,

THE enemy continue to manifest great activity in preparing the work which I mentioned to your Lordship in my despatch (No. 187), and are now bringing up platform timber and guns for the equipment and armament of it.

Vast convoys are daily observed arriving on the north side of the town; and I learn, from information entitled to credit, that the road leading from Simpheropol is covered with waggons laden with provisions and munitions of war.

This morning three British guns, placed in a battery overhanging the Tchernaya, opened upon two small steamers anchored at the head of the harbour, and, after a fire of about an hour, obliged them to take refuge behind a point. One of them appeared to have sustained considerable damage, and is supposed to have been deserted by her crew.

The weather was fine yesterday, and is particularly so to day, and the country is becoming quite dry.

I have reason to hope that the sick are deriving material benefit from this change.

I have established a convalescent hospital on the heights immediately above Balaklava, near a fine spring of water.

The Inspector-General of Hospitals entertains great expectations of the advantages that will result from placing the huts in so healthy a locality.

Lieutenant-General Pennefather has resumed the command of the 2nd Division; and is, I am happy to be able to report, looking remarkably well.

I have, &c.,
RAGLAN.
The Lord Panmure, &c. &c. &c.

CHAPTER 6

THE SECOND BOMBARDMENT OF SEVASTOPOL

War-Department, March 24, 1855.

LORD PANMURE has this day received a Despatch and its Enclosures, of which the following are copies, addressed to His Lordship, by Field-Marshal the Lord Raglan, G.C.B.

Before Sevastopol,
March 10, 1855.

MY LORD,

I HAVE really nothing to report to your Lordship this day.

I am happy however to be able to inform you that the weather is exceedingly fine; and that I entertain great hopes, derived from the reports of the Principal Medical Officer, that the sick will materially benefit by the improvement in the temperature.

Our advanced batteries are making considerable progress.

Every effort is directed to the maintenance of the camps in a healthy state, which, as the warm weather approaches, becomes daily more important

I received on the evening of the 6th instant, a telegraphic despatch from Lord John Russell, dated Berlin, the 2nd, announcing the death of the Emperor of Russia at twelve o'clock on that day.

According to the information of deserters, the event has not been promulgated at Sevastopol.

I have, &c.,
RAGLAN.
The Lord Panmure, &c. &c.

War-Department, March 28, 1855.

LORD PANMURE has this day received two Despatches and their Enclosures, of which the following are copies, addressed to His Lordship by Field-Marshal the Lord Raglan, G.C.B.

Before Sevastopol,
March 13, 1855.

MY LORD,

THE enemy commenced working upon the mamelon in front of the tower of Malakoff in the night of Friday; but the nature of the work, from the thickness of the atmosphere, could not be distinguished.

Great progress, however, had been perceived on Sunday, and that night a strong working party of the British troops was occupied in commencing a parallel from the advanced point of our right attack, with a view to form a junction with the corresponding parallel to be made on their side by the French, who began it on the following evening; and much was done to forward the operation before daylight this morning, and it is hoped that the object will be completed to-night.

The weather is generally fine in the early part of the day, but towards evening heavy sea fogs come rolling in, and wholly obscure the view of the place.

The enemy have shewn a battalion and some Cosaques on the heights above Balaklava, and towards Kamara, probably with the view to interrupt the French and English wood-cutting parties, for the construction of gabions, in the immediate neighbourhood, but the allied detachments have not been obliged to discontinue their work.

I have, &c.,
RAGLAN.
The Lord Panmure, &c. &c.

Before Sevastopol,
March 17, 1855.

MY LORD,

THE progress of the parallel, which I reported to your Lordship in my despatch of the 13th instant (No. 205), has not been as rapid as was anticipated, the ground being extremely rocky, and the difficulty of procuring cover consequently excessive, and rendering it almost impossible to carry on the operation during the day.

Both the English and the French have now, however, succeeded in establishing the communication between them. Her Majesty's troops have not been assailed; but our Allies have been kept constantly in action, and they have succeeded in driving the enemy from the rifle pits, in which they had established themselves in their immediate front, with distinguished gallantry and great perseverance. They, however, have sustained some loss, though not equal to that which they have inflicted upon their opponents.

A steady fire has been maintained upon the mamelon in the occupation of the enemy, from the guns in our right attack; and the practice of both the navy and the artillery has been conspicuously good, and reflects the highest credit on those branches of Her Majesty's service.

Although no positive attack had been directed against our works, our approaches are carried so close to the enemy, that the casualties are greater than they have lately been, as your Lordship will be concerned to remark in examining the returns I have the honour to enclose; and it is my painful duty to announce to your Lordship the death of Captain Craigie, of the Royal Engineers, whose zeal and devotion to the service could not be surpassed, and who was killed on the 13th, after he had been relieved from the trenches, and was on his way to the Engineer Park, by a splinter from a shell, which burst close to him.

I have the honour to report the arrival of Lieutenant-General Simpson, who joined my Head Quarters yesterday, and that of Sir John McNeill and Colonel Tulloch, who reached Balaklava a few days before.

I have, &c.,
RAGLAN.
The Lord Panmure, &c. &c. &c.

War-Department, April 3, 1855.

LORD PANMURE has this day received a Despatch and its Enclosure, of which the following are copies, addressed to His Lordship, by Field-Marshal the Lord Raglan, G.C.B.

Before Sevastopol,
March 20, 1855.

MY LORD,

IT is with deep concern that I transmit for your Lordship's information the copy of a letter, which I received on the 18th instant, from General Canrobert, announcing, with every expression of concern, the death of a British officer, who appears to have wandered into the French camp, and not answering the challenge that was repeated three times was shot dead by the French sentry, whose post he had approached.

This officer, Surgeon Le Blanc, of the 9th Foot, occupied a tent near the hospital huts of his regiment, situated at some distance from the encampment of the regiment itself. He was a gentleman of most temperate habits, and was occupied in reading, when suddenly, upon the alarm sounding, he rose from his seat, leaving his candle lighted and his book open, and walked out, he was never seen alive afterwards.

It should be explained that, shortly after the close of day on the 17th, there was a very heavy fire on the left of the French right, which was maintained for several hours. None of the English posts were attacked, but it was considered prudent to get the greater portion of our troops under arms. Mr. Le Blanc was shortsighted, and probably mistook his way from the first, the night being excessively dark, for he was found far distant to the left, and must have wandered from our position without knowing the direction in which he was going.

Being anxious to ascertain the facts of this unfortunate case, as correctly as possible, I have set on foot an enquiry to be conducted by English and French officers, in association with each other; and I propose to do myself the honour to send you their report.

I have addressed a similar letter to the General Commanding-in-Chief.

I have, &c.,

RAGLAN

The Lord Panmure, &c. &c.

War-Department, April 6, 1855.

LORD PANMURE has this day received a Despatch and its Enclosures, of which the following are copies, addressed to His Lordship, by Field-Marshal the Lord Raglan, G.C.B.

Before Sevastopol,
March 24, 1855.

MY LORD,

ON the morning of the 22nd the French troops in the advanced parallel moved forward, and drove the enemy out of the rifle pits in their immediate front, but nothing of any importance occurred during the day.

Early in the night, however, a serious attack was made upon the works of our Allies in front of the Victoria redoubt, opposite the Malakof tower.

The night was very dark, and the wind so high, that the firing which took place, and which was very heavy, could scarcely be heard in the British camp; it is therefore difficult to speak with certainty of what occurred from any thing that could be heard or observed at the moment.

It appears, however, that the Russians, after attacking the head of the sap which the French are carrying on towards the Mamelon, fell with two heavy masses on their new parallel, to the rear of which they succeeded in penetrating and momentarily possessing themselves of, after a gallant resistance on the part of our Allies.

Having broken through, they passed along the parallel and in rear of it, until they came in contact with the troops stationed in our advanced parallel extending into the ravine, from the right of our advance, where it connects with the French trench.

The enemy was here met by detachments of the 77th and 97th Regiments, forming part of the guard of the trenches, who, although thus taken suddenly both in flank and rear, behaved with the utmost gallantry and coolness.

The detachments of the 97th, which was on the extreme right, and which consequently first came in contact with the enemy, repulsed the attack at the point of the bayonet.

They were led by Captain Vicars, who, unfortunately, lost his life on the occasion; and I am assured that nothing could be more distinguished than the gallantry and good example which he set to the detachment under his command.

The conduct of the detachment of the 77th was equally distinguished; and the firmness and promptitude with which the attack, in this part of our works, was met, were in the highest degree creditable to that regiment.

These troops were under the direction of Major Gordon, of the Royal Engineers, who was wounded on the occasion so severely, as for some time I fear, to deprive the Army of the benefit of his valuable services.

The attention of the troops in our advanced works having been by these transactions drawn to the right, the enemy took occasion to move upon, and succeeded in penetrating into, the left front of our right attack, near the battery where two 10-inch mortars have recently been placed. They advanced along the works until they were met by a detachment of the 7th and 34th regiments, which had been at work in the neighbourhood, under the direction of Lieutenant-Colonel Tylden, of the Royal Engineers, who promptly made them stand to their arms, and led them with the greatest determination and steadiness against the enemy, who were speedily ejected from the works and fairly pitched over the parapet, with but little or no firing on our part.

Lieutenant-Colonel Tylden speaks in the highest terms of the conduct of the troops on this occasion, and particularly of that of Lieutenant Marsh, Acting-Adjutant of the 33rd Regiment, whose services and activity throughout the night were very useful to him.

Captain the Honourable Cavendish Browne, of the 7th, and Lieutenant Jordan of the 34th Regiment, were unfortunately killed in this attack after displaying the most distinguished gallantry and Lieutenant McHenry of the former Regiment was wounded, but I hope not very severely. Lieutenant-Colonel Kelly, of the 34th Regiment, who commanded in the trenches, is, I regret to have to add, missing.

The French, in retiring from their advanced parallel upon their supports, speedily rallied, and fell upon the enemy, whom they repulsed with great loss, and followed so far up towards the Mamelon, that they were enabled to level and destroy nearly all the "ambuscades" or "rifle concealments" erected along their front.

I fear, however, that this success has not been accomplished without considerable loss on their part, although that of the enemy is much greater.

Yesterday the whole of the ground between the posts of the two armies was covered with their dead, amounting to several hundreds, besides those which they had undoubtedly carried off before daylight.

In the meanwhile the enemy in great numbers found their way into the advanced batteries on our extreme left, which are not yet armed, and momentarily got possession of them.

The working parties were, however, speedily collected and reformed by Captain Chapman, of the 20th Regiment, Acting-Engineer, and they at once drove the enemy out of the trenches with the utmost gallantry.

Captain Montagu, of the Royal Engineers, who was superintending the works, unfortunately fell into the hands of the enemy.

The wind is excessively high, but the weather is in other respects fine.

I have, &c.,
RAGLAN.
The Lord Panmure, &c. &c.

War-Department, April 12, 1855.

LORD PANMURE has this day received a Despatch and its Enclosures, of which the following are copies, addressed to His Lordship by Field-Marshal the Lord Raglan, G.C.B.

Before Sevastopol,
March 27, 1855.

MY LORD,

ADVERTING to my despatch of the 24th instant, I do myself the honour to state that the following officers have been brought to my notice as having distinguished themselves on the night of the 22nd and morning of the 23rd, in addition to those whose names I have already submitted to your Lordship; Major The Hon. James Lyon Browne of the 21st Regiment, brother of The Hon. Captain Browne of the Royal Fusiliers, who, it has already been my painful duty to report, fell upon this occasion; Captain Butler of the 20th and Captain Rickman of the 77th.

I am happy to say that Captain Montagu of the Royal Engineers, who was taken prisoner, was not wounded, and that Lieutenant-Colonel Kelly, of the 34th Regiment, who also fell into the enemy's hands, is not severely wounded, though he received some injury both in his head and hand.

Major-General Eyre the General Officer of the Trenches, highly eulogizes the dispositions of Lt.-Colonel Kelly and laments the loss of his services.

The Major-General also speaks in the warmest terms of the conduct of Lieut.-Colonel Tylden, Royal Engineers, who received a contusion, which however I am glad to be able to assure your Lordship does not incapacitate him from continuing those exertions and displaying those qualities which render him so valuable an officer.

There was a suspension of hostilities for about three hours on Saturday for the purpose of burying those who had fallen in the late encounters; and it was evident from the numbers of bodies of the Enemy, and of the French, to whom the last sad offices had to be paid, that the loss sustained both by the French and the Russians had been very severe, particularly that of the latter. Some French, too, were found lying close to the Mamelon, a proof that their gallant spirit had carried them up to the Enemy's intrenchments.

Nothing of importance has since occurred. The siege operations continue to progress, and during the last two nights the interruption from the fire of the Enemy has been inconsiderable.

The Enemy are very assiduous in the improvement of their defences, and in the establishment of a trench in the front of the Mamelon, towards which our ally is advancing by serpentine sap.

The weather continues very fine, and the appearance and health of the troops are manifestly improving.

Dr. Gavin, of the Sanitary Commission and Mr. Rawlinson, Civil Engineer, have arrived, and are earnestly applying themselves to the discharge of the duties they have undertaken to perform; and I will take care that they receive every assistance it may be in my power to afford them.

The Himalaya has arrived, and has been disembarking her horses yesterday and this day in Kasatch Bay.

Since writing the above, I have received the official report that Captain A.E. Hill of the 89th Regiment was severely wounded, and taken prisoner last night whilst posting his sentries in front of the advanced trench on our extreme left.

I have, &c.,
RAGLAN.
The Lord Panmure, &c. &c.

War-Department, April 14, 1855.

LORD PANMURE has this day received a Despatch and its Enclosures, of which the following are copies, addressed to His Lordship by Field-Marshal the Lord Raglan, G.C.B.

Before Sevastopol,
March 31, 1855.

MY LORD,

SINCE I wrote to your Lordship, on the 27th instant, the operations of the siege have been continued, without any material interruption from the enemy beyond occasional shots from guns and mortars, and the more constant firing of musketry from rifle-pits, which have occasioned, I regret to say, the casualties which your Lordship will see in the returns I inclose.

Captain A.E. Hill, of the 89th Regiment, whom I mentioned in my despatch, No. 222, as having been severely wounded and taken prisoner, died, I regret to say, of his wounds, before he reached the Russian ambulance, as I learnt last night from General Osten-Sacken, to whom I had written for information on the subject.

He had gone forward with a view to place the sentries in front of our advanced works, as I stated to your Lordship on Tuesday, and he, unfortunately, mistook a Russian for a French picquet, and, having challenged it in French, he was immediately fired upon, and brought to the ground.

Early yesterday morning a fire was observed in the town of Sevastopol, which raged with violence for a considerable time, but how it originated I have not been able to ascertain.

The enemy has made no movement on the side of the Tchernaya.

The railway continues to progress in the most satisfactory manner, and last night had nearly reached the top of the hill, usually called the Col de Balaklava, and advantage has been taken of it to bring up large quantities of ammunition and stores.

I have, &c.,

RAGLAN.

The Lord Panmure, &c. &c.

Before Sevastopol,
April 7, 1855.

MY LORD,

SOME interchange of troops has taken place since I addressed your Lordship on the 31st ultimo.

Battalions and considerable convoys have entered the town, and other bodies of troops have been seen to leave the north side. The garrison has been constantly engaged in adding to the works, and particularly in connecting the rifle pits in the immediate front of our right attack; and as we have pushed forward, the fire upon our advance has occasioned more loss, I deeply regret to say, than we have sustained since the sortie of the 23rd March.

Lieutenant Bainbrigge, of the Royal Engineers, was, I lament to have to add, killed on the morning of the 4th April, whilst in the execution of his duty, by the bursting of a shell.

He was a young officer of much promise, and though he had not long been here, he had acquired the esteem and good opinion of his brother officers, and his loss is greatly deplored by all.

I have, &c.,

RAGLAN.

The Lord Panmure, &c. &c. &c.

Before Sevastopol,
April 17, 1855.

MY LORD,

THE fire of both the French and English armies has been continued upon Sevastopol since I addressed your Lordship on the 14th instant, and though superior to that of the enemy, it has not produced that permanent effect which might have been anticipated from its constancy, power, and accuracy.

The guns of the Russians have been turned upon some of our advanced works in vast numbers, and in one particular instance the injury sustained by a battery was so great that the unremitting exertions of Captains Henry and Walcot, and the gallantry and determination of the artillerymen under their orders, alone enabled them to keep up the fire and to maintain themselves in it.

In another battery yesterday a shell burst close to the magazine, which in consequence exploded, killing I am much concerned to say, one man, wounding two most severely, and seven in a less degree.

Both the batteries I have mentioned have been repaired and restored to their original condition.

I have to lament the loss of two young and promising officers who had only lately joined the army, Lieutenant Preston, of the 88th Regiment, and Lieutenant Mitchell, of the Artillery; and I regret to add that two others have been severely wounded, Captain Green, of the East India Company's Service, who has been employed throughout the siege as an Assistant Engineer, with great credit to himself and every advantage to the service, and Captain Donovan, of the 33rd, who has most zealously served from the commencement of the campaign.

The French blew up several small mines in front of the Bastion du Mât after sunset on Sunday evening, with a view to establish a parallel on the spot. This operation greatly alarmed the enemy, who at once commenced a heavy fire of cannon and musketry in every direction from that part of the town, which they kept up for a considerable time. It occasioned no harm on our left attack, upon which a part of it was directed, and I hope did little injury to our allies.

Several hundreds of the Russian Cavalry and a small body of Cossacks appeared on the low range of heights in front of Balaklava this morning, and remained about an hour, when they retired, the greater portion by the bridge of Tractea. The object of this movement was probably a reconnaissance.

I have, &c.,
RAGLAN.
The Lord Panmure, &c. &c. &c.

War-Department, April 20, 1855.

LORD PANMURE has this day received two Despatches and their Enclosures, of which the following are copies, addressed to His Lordship by Field-Marshal the Lord Raglan, G.C.B.

Before Sevastopol,
April 3, 1855.

MY LORD,

I HAVE the honour to transmit to your Lordship a letter of this date, from Dr. Hall, enclosing a weekly return of the sick of the Army, up to the 31st ultimo.[*not enclosed*]

Your Lordship will see, with satisfaction, that the general health of the Army continues steadily to improve.

I have also to submit to your Lordship, with reference to your despatch, No. 22, of the 26th February, the copy of a letter from the same officer, on the question of accommodation for wounded men, on the event of any sudden emergency occurring.

As the ships referred to by Dr. Hall arc constantly on passage, and might all be so at the time they might be wanted for the wounded, I proposed to Sir Edmund Lyons to have some sailing vessels got ready for their reception, and accordingly, with his sanction, the following transports are under preparation; – Orient, Sir George Pollock, St. Hilder, William Jackson, and Poictiers; – and it is calculated that they will hold from 100 to 150 men each.

I have, &c.,
RAGLAN.
The Lord Panmure, &c. &c.

War-Department, April 24, 1855.

LORD PANMURE has this day received a Despatch and its Enclosures, of which the following are copies, addressed to His Lordship by Field-Marshal the Lord Raglan, G.C.B.

Before Sevastopol,
April 10, 1855.

MY LORD,

IN accordance with the arrangement made between General Canrobert and myself, the batteries of the French and English armies opened upon Sevastopol soon after daylight yesterday morning.

The weather was extremely unpropitious. Much rain had fallen in the course of the night, and it continued during the day, accompanied by a tempestuous wind and a heavy mist, which obscured everything, and rendered it impossible to ascertain with any degree of accuracy the effect of the fire, which has been continued with little or no interruption from the commencement, and has been superior to that of the enemy, who were evidently taken by surprise, and, except upon the extreme left, did not respond to the attack for nearly half an hour.

This morning has been hazy, and for some time there was a drizzling rain; but it is clearing this afternoon, and there is again a prospect of fine weather.

The country yesterday was covered with water, and the ground was again very deep. The trenches were likewise extremely muddy, and their condition added greatly to the labours of the men employed in the batteries, who consisted chiefly of sailors, artillerymen, and sappers. They conducted their duties admirably, and I am sorry to say that the two former, particularly the Navy, sustained considerable loss.

I have not yet received the returns of the casualties beyond the 9th instant, which are herewith inclosed; but the death of Lieutenant Twyford, of the Royal Navy, a most promising officer, and greatly respected by all, has been notified to me; and Captain Lord John Hay, who has taken a most active part in the gallant and distinguished services of the Naval Brigade, was wounded almost at the very moment, I believe by the same shot. I hope the injury he has received is not very serious, but the loss of his assistance even for a time is much to be regretted.

The Russians have not shown themselves in any force in front of Balaklava.

I have, &c.,
RAGLAN.
The Lord Panmure, &c. &c. &c.

War-Department, April 26, 1855.

LORD PANMURE has this day received a Despatch and its Enclosures, of which the following are copies, addressed to His Lordship by Field-Marshal the Lord Raglan, G.C.B.

Before Sevastopol,
April 14, 1855.

MY LORD,

SINCE I wrote to your Lordship on the 10th instant, a steady and heavy fire upon the works of the enemy has been maintained from all the batteries of the Allies.

The fire of the British artillery, chiefly directed against the Garden Batteries, the Barrack Battery, the Redan, the Malakoff Tower, and the Mamelon, has been most effective, and the enemy's works have suffered very considerably, although they have as usual made a good use of the night to repair damages, notwithstanding that the vertical fire has been continued throughout the twenty-four hours.

The practice both of the Naval Brigade and the Artillery has been excellent.

The casualties have not been very numerous, but the loss has fallen heavily upon the sailors, as your Lordship will see by the accompanying returns, and the Royal Navy has to deplore the death of Lieutenant Douglas, who had served with great ability and zeal from the commencement of the siege.

Lieutenants Urmston and D'Aeth, Royal Navy, and Steele, Royal Marine Artillery, all valuable officers, have been wounded.

The Royal Artillery has also to lament the death of Lieutenant Luce, who was an officer of much promise; and Lieutenants Sinclair and L'Estrange are among the wounded. The former has sustained several severe injuries, but I am happy to add that there is every hope of his recovery. They are both highly meritorious officers.

Captain Crofton, of the Royal Engineers, who had in the course of the protracted operations before Sevastopol rendered most essential service, has also received a wound, which will, I fear, detain him from duty for a very considerable time.

Our batteries and parapets continue to stand remarkably well, notwithstanding the very unfavourable state of the weather.

The enemy's fire has been comparatively slack, but the practice good, and owing to their having ascertained the range of our batteries with great nicety, several guns have been disabled in both the right and left attacks.

Towards the Tchernaya nothing important has been observed, but small bodies of men, from 150 to 500, have been seen, with a heavy gun and some ordnance carriages, moving along the Inkerman heights towards Mackenzie's Farm-road, near which it has been placed in position.

Although the duties have been unusually severe and arduous both by day and night during the week, they have been carried out with the utmost cheerfulness and zeal, reflecting much credit both on officers and men.

The submarine telegraph has been safely brought to the Monastery from Cape Kelegra, and as soon as it is established at the former place, the engineers will proceed to convey it from the latter to the immediate neighbourhood of Varna, where I hope it may be in a state to act in a week or ten days from this time.

The first division of the 10th Hussars, arrived this day at Balaklava.

I have, &c.,
RAGLAN.
The Lord Panmure, &c. &c.

Admiralty, April 26, 1855.

A DESPATCH, of which the following is a copy, has been received from Rear-Admiral Sir Edmund Lyons, Bart., G.C.B., Commander-in-Chief of Her Majesty's Ships and Vessels in the Mediterranean and Black Sea.

PROCEEDINGS OF NAVAL BRIGADE.

Royal Albert, off Sevastopol,
April 13, 1855.

SIR,

MY letter of the 10th instant, No. 284, will have informed the Lords Commissioners of the Admiralty that the siege batteries before Sevastopol re-opened their fire on the 9th instant.

I grieve to say that the casualties have been severe, though not, perhaps, more than might have been expected, considering the number of guns which are manned by seamen. Lists of the casualties on each day are enclosed for the information of their Lordships; and I have to lament the fall of two gallant and promising young officers, Lieutenant Samuel Twyford, of the London, and Lieutenant W.H. Douglas, of the Queen. Captain Lord John Hay and Lieutenant Urmston, of the Queen, have been wounded, though not severely.

The services of the officers and seamen of the Naval Brigade have been invaluable.

I have, &c.,
ED. LYONS,
Rear-Admiral and Commander-in-Chief.
To the Secretary of the Admiralty,
London.

War-Department, May 7, 1855.

LORD PANMURE has this day received a Despatch and its Enclosures, of which the following are copies, addressed to His Lordship by Field-Marshal the Lord Raglan, G.C.B.

Before Sevastopol,
April 24, 1855.

MY LORD,

NOTHING material has occurred since I made my report to your Lordship on the 21st instant.

The Russian rifle pit, immediately in front of that which was taken on the night of the 19th, was destroyed by a party of volunteers on the morning of the 21st instant. These were headed by Lieutenant and Adjutant Walker, of the 30th Regiment, who is stated to be an excellent officer, and to have conducted himself on the occasion in the most spirited manner.

The pit was found to be empty, and being useless was immediately levelled and filled in. The enemy did not interrupt the work.

I inclose the list of casualties, which, I regret to say, is heavy.[*not enclosed*] The nearer we approach the place the more loss is to be apprehended. Hitherto it has been less than might have been expected.

I have, &c.,

RAGLAN.

The Lord Panmure, &c. &c. &c.

War-Department, May 16, 1855.

LORD PANMURE has this day received a Despatch and its Enclosures, of which the following are copies, addressed to His Lordship by Field-Marshal the Lord Raglan, G.C.B.

Before Sevastopol,
May 1, 1855.

MY LORD,

I HAVE little to report to your Lordship to-day.

The Russians continue actively engaged in covering their advanced works, and they have constructed a new battery on their left of the Mamelon; troops are constantly in motion on the north side, and there is every appearance of the establishment of a very large camp on the plateau above the Balbek, extending towards Mackenzie's Farm.

No movement has been perceived on the Tchernaya.

I have the satisfaction to acquaint your Lordship, that the 3rd Regiment or Buffs has arrived at Balaklava, and that the Alma, having the draft of the Guards on board, reached Kazutch Bay yesterday; she has proceeded to Balaklava to-day.

I have, &c.,

RAGLAN.

The Lord Panmure, &c. &c. &c.

War-Department, May 18, 1855.

LORD PANMURE has this day received a Despatch and its Enclosures, of which the following are copies, addressed to His Lordship by Field-Marshal the Lord Raglan, G.C.B.

Before Sevastopol,
May 5, 1855.

MY LORD,

SINCE I wrote to your Lordship on the 1st instant, nothing of importance has arisen; the enemy still appear to be collecting troops upon the high ground on the opposite side of the Tchernaya, in the neighbourhood of Sevastopol, and convoys are constantly seen moving in that direction.

The fire from the place upon our trenches has not been heavy; but, notwithstanding, I have some casualties to report to you, as shewn in the accompanying returns; and I have to lament the death of three promising young officers, Lieutenants Carter of the Royal Engineers, Curtis of the 46th, and White of the 62nd Regiments.

On the night of the 1st instant the French attacked a kind of counterguard which the Russians had established in front of the central bastion.

The operation was quite successful, and the enemy were driven out with great loss, leaving behind them nine small mortars. Our Allies have remained in the work, notwithstanding the heavy fire to which they have been exposed, and have established themselves therein, frustrating the efforts made by their adversaries to dispossess them of it on the following day, when a vigorous sortie was repulsed, and the Russians were again great sufferers.

The conduct of the French troops was very brilliant.

I have, &c.,
RAGLAN.
The Lord Panmure, &c. &c. &c.

War-Department, May 21, 1855.

LORD PANMURE has this day received a Despatch and its Enclosures, of which the following are copies, addressed to His Lordship by Field-Marshal the Lord Raglan, G.C.B.

Before Sevastopol,
May 8, 1855.

MY LORD,

THE enemy assaulted our advanced parallel on the right attack on the night of the 5th instant, and some actually got into the trench; but they were speedily driven out and repulsed with the utmost gallantry by the detachments occupying it, of the 30th and 49th Regiments, under Captain Williamson and Lieutenant Gubbins, of the former, and Lieutenant Rochfort, of the latter, who, unfortunately, was severely wounded; and I regret to have to add that several valuable non-commissioned officers and men were killed and wounded on the occasion.

On the same night Captain Arnold,* of the 4th Foot, was wounded and taken prisoner, whilst posting the advanced sentries on the left attack. The loss of the services of this Officer is greatly to be lamented. He had done his duty unremittingly, and in the most spirited manner, throughout the operations of the siege.

I have heard that six ships, having on board Sardinian troops, have arrived in the Bosphorus.

I have, &c.,
RAGLAN.

P.S. I have the satisfaction to announce to you the arrival of the first detachment of the 12th Lancers.

The Lord Panmure, &c. &c.

War-Department, May 7, 1855.

LORD PANMURE has this day received a Despatch and its Enclosures, of which the following are copies, addressed to His Lordship by Field-Marshal the Lord Raglan, G.C.B.

Before Sevastopol,
April 24, 1855.

MY LORD,

NOTHING material has occurred since I made my report to your Lordship on the 21st instant.

The Russian rifle pit, immediately in front of that which was taken on the night of the 19th, was destroyed by a party of volunteers on the morning of the 21st instant. These were headed by Lieutenant and Adjutant Walker, of the 30th Regiment, who is stated to be an excellent officer, and to have conducted himself on the occasion in the most spirited manner.

The pit was found to be empty, and being useless was immediately levelled and filled in. The enemy did not interrupt the work.

I inclose the list of casualties, which, I regret to say, is heavy. The nearer we approach the place the more loss is to be apprehended. Hitherto it has been less than might have been expected.

I have, &c.,
RAGLAN.
The Lord Panmure, &c. &c. &c.

War-Department, May 16, 1855.

LORD PANMURE has this day received a Despatch and its Enclosures, of which the following are copies, addressed to His Lordship by Field-Marshal the Lord Raglan, G.C.B.

Before Sevastopol,
May 1, 1855.

MY LORD,

I HAVE little to report to your Lordship to-day.

The Russians continue actively engaged in covering their advanced works, and they have constructed a new battery on their left of the Mamelon; troops are constantly in motion on the north side, and there is every appearance of the establishment of a very large camp on the plateau above the Balbek, extending towards Mackenzie's Farm.

No movement has been perceived on the Tchernaya.

I have the satisfaction to acquaint your Lordship, that the 3rd Regiment or Buffs has arrived at Balaklava, and that the Alma, having the draft of the Guards on board, reached Kazutch Bay yesterday; she has proceeded to Balaklava to-day.

I have, &c.,
RAGLAN.
The Lord Panmure, &c. &c. &c.

FRIDAY, MAY 18, 1855.

War-Department, May 18, 1855.

LORD PANMURE has this day received a Despatch and its Enclosures, of which the following are copies, addressed to His Lordship by Field-Marshal the Lord Raglan, G.C.B.

Before Sevastopol,
May 5, 1855.

MY LORD,

SINCE I wrote to your Lordship on the 1st instant, nothing of importance has arisen; the enemy still appear to be collecting troops upon the high ground on the opposite side of the Tchernaya, in the neighbourhood of Sevastopol, and convoys are constantly seen moving in that direction.

The fire from the place upon our trenches has not been heavy; but, notwithstanding, I have some casualties to report to you, as shewn in the accompanying returns; and I have to lament the death of three promising young officers, Lieutenants Carter of the Royal Engineers, Curtis of the 46th, and White of the 62nd Regiments.

On the night of the 1st instant the French attacked a kind of counterguard which the Russians had established in front of the central bastion.

The operation was quite successful, and the enemy were driven out with great loss, leaving behind them nine small mortars. Our Allies have remained in the work, notwithstanding the heavy fire to which they have been exposed, and have established themselves therein, frustrating the efforts made by their adversaries to dispossess them of it on the following day, when a vigorous sortie was repulsed, and the Russians were again great sufferers.

The conduct of the French troops was very brilliant.

I have, &c.,
RAGLAN.
The Lord Panmure, &c. &c. &c.

War-Department, May 21, 1855.

LORD PANMURE has this day received a Despatch and its Enclosures, of which the following are copies, addressed to His Lordship by Field-Marshal the Lord Raglan, G.C.B.

Before Sevastopol,
May 8, 1855.

MY LORD,

THE enemy assaulted our advanced parallel on the right attack on the night of the 5th instant, and some actually got into the trench; but they were speedily driven out and repulsed with the utmost gallantry by the detachments occupying it, of the 30th and 49th Regiments, under Captain Williamson and Lieutenant Gubbins, of the former, and Lieutenant Rochfort, of the latter, who, unfortunately, was severely wounded; and I regret to have to add that several valuable non-commissioned officers and men were killed and wounded on the occasion.

On the same night Captain Arnold,* of the 4th Foot, was wounded and taken prisoner, whilst posting the advanced sentries on the left attack. The loss of the services of this Officer is greatly to be lamented. He had done his duty unremittingly, and in the most spirited manner, throughout the operations of the siege.

I have heard that six ships, having on board Sardinian troops, have arrived in the Bosphorus.

I have, &c.,
RAGLAN.

P.S. I have the satisfaction to announce to you the arrival of the first detachment of the 12th Lancers.

The Lord Panmure, &c. &c.
*Intelligence has since been received of the death of Captain Arnold.

War-Department, May 24, 1855.

LORD PANMURE has this day received a Despatch and its Enclosures, of which the following are copies, addressed to His Lordship by Field-Marshal the Lord Raglan, G.C.B.

Before Sevastopol,
May 12, 1855.

MY LORD,

I DO myself the honour to acquaint your Lordship that General de la Marmora, with a portion of the Sardinian Contingent, arrived off Balaklava on the night of the 8th instant, and he came up to head-quarters the following morning.

The very unfavourable state of the weather since the 9th has prevented any material part of the force being landed; and it has been found necessary to send the vessels that brought it, and which could not be got into the harbour, to Kazatch Bay, until it should moderate.

Five troops of the 12th Lancers landed on the 9th from the Himalaya, which performed the voyage from Alexandria to Balaklava in ninety-four hours.

The enemy made two serious assaults upon our most advanced parallel of the right attack on the night of the 9th, but were on each occasion most nobly met and repulsed with considerable loss.

The arrangements of Colonel Trollope, who had charge of the right attack, and Lieutenant-Colonel Mundy, the Field Officer of the trenches, were most judicious; and Captain Turner, of the Royal Fusiliers, and Captain Jordan, of the 34th Regiment, are reported to have done their duty in the most gallant manner.

They opened a powerful fire on our trenches on the following night, and exposed their columns to a heavy musketry fire from the troops on duty. They did not however reach the parapets, nor indeed come very near them.

Last night a very determined sortie was made upon the advance of our left attack. The enemy moved forward in two columns from the Woronzow road. Our advanced sentries having slowly retired, the guard of the trenches was prepared to receive them, and consequently drove them back in the most determined manner. A few Russians only got into the parallel, and five were left dead close outside.

The conduct of both officers and men was admirable, and it is with deep concern that I have to report the death of Captain Edwards, of the 68th Foot, and that of five men.

I have also the pain of saying, that the wounded amount to thirty.

Owing to the great quantity of rain which has fallen during the last few days, the service in the trenches has again been most arduous and severe upon our men, who deserve all praise for their energy and untiring perseverance.

I have, &c.,
RAGLAN.
The Lord Panmure, &c. &c. &c.

War-Department, May 28, 1855.

LORD PANMURE has this day received two Despatches and their Enclosures, of which the following are copies, addressed to His Lordship by Field-Marshal the Lord Raglan, G.C.B.

Before Sevastopol,
May 15, 1855.

MY LORD,

SINCE my despatch of the 12th instant, nothing has occurred worthy of being reported to your Lordship.

The fire has been very slack, and that of the enemy has been directed towards the French works rather than against the English trenches.

The remainder of the 12th Lancers has arrived and will be disembarked to day.

All our means are devoted to the landing of the Sardinian troops, which the bad weather had prevented on the arrival of the first ships.

I have found it necessary, in some instances, to land artillery horses at Kazatch Bay, to avoid further crowding the harbour of Balaklava.

I have, &c.,
RAGLAN.
The Lord Panmure, &c. &c. &c.

War-Department, June 6, 1855.

LORD PANMURE has this day received two Despatches and their Enclosures, of which the following are copies, addressed to His Lordship by Field-Marshal the Lord Raglan, G.C.B.

Before Sevastopol,
May 26, 1855.

MY LORD,

I HAVE the honour to report to your Lordship that a portion of the Allied Armies took up a position yesterday on this side of the Tchernaya, the left of the French resting under a redoubt established upon the edge of this ridge overhanging the valley, and opposite the Inkerman heights; the right extending beyond Tractir; and the ground more to the right, behind Chorgouna, being occupied by the Sardinian troops, aided in their advance by the 10th Hussars and 12th Lancers and the Horse Artillery, under Colonel Parlby.

Omer Pasha at the same time moved forward to the low heights in front of Balaklava, and thus afforded support to the French Divisions before him. These were commanded by General Canrobert, who pushed forward across the bridge of Tractir, and drove the enemy, who were not in great numbers, off, and having cleared his front, he withdrew to this side of the river, where he now remains.

Sir Colin Campbell advanced the Royal Marines from the high ridge on our extreme right to a point commanding the old Baidar-road; and Colonel Parlby, with the regiments I have mentioned, reconnoitred the country on the immediate right of General La Marmora's position, and patrolled along the Woronzow-road, in the direction of Baidar.

The appearance and bearing of the Sardinian troops are highly satisfactory, and I anticipate the greatest advantage from their addition to this army under their distinguished leader General La Marmora, whose zeal for the service and ardent desire to co-operate with us, I am happy to have so early an opportunity of acknowledging and recording. Nothing of importance has occurred in the British trenches since I wrote to your Lordship on the 19th instant.

The death of Colonel Egerton, of the 77th, on the night of the 19th ultimo, as already announced to your Lordship, prevented my receiving in due course the official report of the conduct of the officers serving immediately under him, and it is only a few days ago that I learnt that Captain Gilby was the next in seniority to him, of the 77th, on the occasion, and that he had highly distinguished himself.

I deem it an act of justice to a most deserving officer to bring his conduct under the notice of your Lordship.

I enclose the returns of casualties to the 24th instant. Your Lordship will regret to see that Lieutenant Williams, of the 17th, has been severely wounded.

I have the greatest pleasure in announcing to your Lordship the brilliant success which attended an attack by the French Army, of some ambuscades at the head of the Quarantine Bay, and in front of a cemetery near it. The attack was made on the night of the 22nd, and the operation was completed on the following evening. The enemy had collected a very large force on the first occasion to resist our Allies; but, notwithstanding, the French were enabled by their brilliant gallantry and determined resolution to maintain themselves in the pits at the head of the bay on the 22nd, and on the 23rd to occupy the whole with less resistance on the part of the Russians, who are stated to have sustained a very severe loss.

The French were necessarily exposed to a very heavy fire, and were assailed by vastly superior numbers. The achievement they accomplished redounds therefore highly to their renown, and is hailed with satisfaction by their Allies.

An expedition, composed of British, French, and Turkish troops, sailed for Kertch on Tuesday evening and Wednesday morning, and I hope soon to be able to announce the landing of the corps, and the result of its first operations. It is commanded by Lieutenant-General Sir George Brown, and has been conveyed in English and French ships, under the command of Admiral Sir E. Lyons and Admiral Bruat, whose exertions to carry out this important service have been most conspicuous.

The 31st Regiment has arrived from Corfu.

I am much concerned to have to report that Major-General Buller has been obliged by the failure of his health to leave the army. He has been constant in the discharge of his duty since he joined this army, distinguished himself both at Alma and Inkerman, and persevered in taking his turn in the trenches until driven by illness to withdraw.

I regret the loss of his services exceedingly.

I have, &c.
RAGLAN.
The Lord Panmure, &c. &c. &c.

Before Sevastopol,
June 2, 1855.

MY LORD,

THE reports which have been received from Kertch since I had the honour of writing to your Lordship on the 29th May, are of the most satisfactory character.

Five vessels, laden with corn, had come into Kertch in ignorance of the capture of the place, and had fallen into the hands of the Allies.

The French and English squadron had appeared before Berdiansk, and the enemy in consequence destroyed four of their war-steamers, and considerable depôts of corn.

They then exchanged a cannonade with the Russian forts at Arabat, and were so fortunate as to blow up a magazine with shells; and since, Captain Lyons, R.N., of the Miranda, has performed a most successful operation upon Genitschi. The Russian authorities of the town having refused to deliver up the Government depôt of corn, and ninety vessels, having on board supplies for their army in the Crimea, Captain Lyons bombarded the place with his squadron, and having driven the troops out of it, he landed the Sailors and Marines, and destroyed all the stores and the shipping.

This brilliant and decisive success marks the resolution and daring of Captain Lyons, and fortunately was accomplished with no other loss than that of one man wounded.

Admiral Sir Edmund Lyons states, that in no longer a period than four days the squadron has destroyed 241 vessels, employed exclusively in transporting provisions to the Crimea, besides four war steamers, and six millions of rations of flour and corn.

I beg leave to offer your Lordship my warmest congratulations on these important occurrences.

I have nothing of interest to report to your Lordship from hence, except that some more detachments of Sardinian troops have arrived.

A battery has arrived off the harbour.

I have, &c.,
RAGLAN.
The Lord Panmure, &c. &c.

CHAPTER 7

FURTHER OPERATIONS IN THE BLACK SEA AND KERTCH

Admiralty, March 29, 1855.

THE following Despatch and Enclosure were received at the Admiralty on the 15th January last.

GALLANT REPULSE OF THE ENEMY FROM EUPATORIA, IN NOVEMBER LAST.

Britannia, in the Archipelago,
December 30, 1854.

SIR,

I BEG you will lay before the Lords Commissioners of the Admiralty the accompanying letter, sent to me some time since, by Captain Brock, from Eupatoria, detailing the gallant repulse of a large body of the enemy by the force under his orders.

I have, &c.,
J.W.D. DUNDAS,
Vice-Admiral.
To the Secretary of the Admiralty,
&c. &c. &c.

Enclosure.

Eupatoria, November 15, 1854.

I HAVE the honour to inform you, that, encouraged by the catastrophe* mentioned in my other letter of this day's date, and our rockets having been blown down, a large body of the enemy's cavalry, between seven and eight thousand, supported by sixteen guns of horse artillery, made an attack on us at 3.45 P.M.

They planted their guns (under cover of the mills) at about a thousand yards, in front of our upper rocket battery, where we had two rockets, one 12-pounder howitzer, and an 18-pounder iron carronade, procured from a merchant ship.

They commenced a heavy fire of shot and shell, and with sufficiently good practice to fall very thick around us, and many shot lodged, and several shell exploded, in the parapet of the redoubt. Their fire was returned with great spirit on our side, by the two rocket batteries, the upper one commanded by Lieutenant Lambert, of the Spiteful, and Mr. Lake, midshipman of the Leander; Lieutenant Hood, of the Arethusa, attended the lower battery, with Mr. Mitchell mate of the Leander, where were two 12-pounder howitzers, and one 18-pounder merchant ship's guns, and three rockets, one 24-pounder, and two 12-pounders.

Having no marines and but few seamen, I reinforced both batteries with fifty Arab troops, who, however, as the enemy did not approach within musket shot, had no opportunity of doing anything, though, from their behaviour under fire, they seemed to promise well. The fire was kept up with animation on both sides for nearly an hour, without any casualties amongst us, except one man's thumb slightly wounded; although it seemed wonderful that no one was struck by the shot and shell, which flew pretty thickly. The enemy's cavalry was drawn up in dense masses in the rear and on each flank of their artillery, and, though an occasional shot or rocket fell amongst them and disturbed their formation, they seemed to be in excellent order. Both our officers and men seemed animated with the highest spirit, and, considering the immensely superior force on the enemy's side, their firmness merited my warmest approbation. My attention was devoted to the upper battery, being nearest the enemy, and whence I could best observe his movements. Some of our rockets were beautifully directed by Lamb,† gunner's mate of the Arethusa, and Ball, quartermaster of the Leander, and appeared to fall amongst the horse artillery, and I have no doubt contributed to hasten their retreat, which they did at about 4.40.

I may add that the officers and men did their duty with alacrity, and seemed anxious to have an opportunity of meeting the enemy. I have particularly to call your attention to the steady and cool conduct of Lieutenant Hood, who rode over the field this morning, after the action, and ascertained that our shot and rockets were well directed, and appeared to fall exactly in the right place; he has recovered many of our shot at a time when we most need them. I have likewise great satisfaction in bringing before your notice the zeal and intelligence of Mr. Brine, mate of the Leander, in charge of two 18-pounder merchant ship's guns, at the Hospital post, and he has reported to me the good conduct of James Mongomery, leading seaman of Her Majesty's ship Leander; I beg to recommend him to your favourable consideration. The Tartars say the Russians lost many men, as they saw many saddles vacant.

I have great pleasure in particularizing the conduct of Mr. Hamilton, senior lieutenant of the Leander, from whom I have received the most efficient assistance throughout these trying times to both officers and men, as well as that of Messrs. Irvine, mate of the Megaera, Dupuis, midshipman of the Leander, Phillips, master's-assistant of the Megaera, who has acted as my aide-de-camp, Doctor Blake, assistant-surgeon of the Leander, and the Rev. S. Robson, of the same ship, whose manifold services in the field, as well as his own duties, have merited great praise. Assistant-Commissary-General Gardiner I have found a most able assistant in everything connected with his duty. I respectfully trust that in the defence of this town that you have done me the honour to entrust me with, I have, as far as my limited means will allow, carried your wishes into effect.

I have, &c.,

SAUMAREZ BROCK,

Captain, R.N., Commanding the Forces.

Vice-Admiral J.W.D. Dundas, C.B.,

Commander-in- Chief.

*Damages done by gale of November 14.
†Lamb promoted in vacancy caused by death of Gunner of Banshee.

Royal Albert, off Sevastopol,
February 24, 1855.

SIR,

I HAVE the honour to report, for the information of the Lords Commissioners of the Admiralty, that no attack has taken place at Eupatoria since that of the 17th inst., which, as their Lordships will perceive by the enclosed copy of a letter from Colonel Simmons to me, was more serious than was at first supposed. Her Majesty's ships are in eligible positions for assisting in the repulse of any future attack.

The weather, which for the last few days has been very severe, is now remarkably fine.

I am, &c.

(Signed) E. LYONS,

Rear-Admiral and Commander-in-Chief.

The Secretary of the Admiralty,

London.

Enclosure No. 1.

Eupatoria, February 20, 1855.
9 P.M.

SIR,

THE bearer is an Aide-de-Camp of the Seraskier, bearing despatches from Omar Pasha to his Government.

His Highness would be much obliged to you if you would kindly order him a passage to Constantinople by the first opportunity.

The position is much stronger here than it was; in fact, I should say doubly so, and nearly twice as many guns mounted as on the 17th.

That affair was pretty sharp, and the Russians lost a great many men: we have interred 453, and there can be no doubt they carried off and buried many more who were killed at long ranges by our artillery.

They also left nearly 300 dead horses on the field.

Our loss was 87 killed, 277 wounded, Turks; 4 killed and 9 wounded; French; and 13 killed, 11 wounded, of the population; besides 79 horses killed and 18 wounded. Our field battery had 19 men (Turks) killed, and every gun (6) disabled.

The Turks behaved very well. Selim Pasha, the Egyptian, who was killed, was a great loss, but his place is well supplied by Suliman Pasha, who was wounded.

Omar Pasha is most gratified for the promptitude with which you sent up ships after hearing of the attack. The exertions of the officers and men of your fleet in disembarking troops, &c., here are beyond all praise; but, unfortunately the weather during the last week or ten days has not been propitious and consequently transports have been detained longer than they otherwise would.

I am, &c.,
(Signed) J.N.SIMMONS,
Royal Engineers,
attached to Omar Pasha's Staff.
Rear-Admiral Sir Edmund Lyons, G.C.B.,
&c. &c. &c.

Admiralty, March 19, 1855.

A DESPATCH, of which the following is a copy, has been received from Rear-Admiral Sir Edmund Lyons, Bart., G.C.B., Commander-in-Chief of Her Majesty's Ships and Vessels in the Mediterranean and Black Sea.

PROCEEDINGS AT KERTCH.

Royal Albert, off Sevastopol,
February 27, 1855.

SIR,

WITH reference to my letter of the 20th instant (No. 135), reporting the highly creditable proceedings of the blockading squadron off Kertch, under the command of Captain Giffard, of Her Majesty's ship Leopard.

2. I have now the honour to enclose copies of two letters which I have received from that active and intelligent officer, reporting his further proceedings, and of his having, in conjunction with His Imperial Majesty's steamer Fulton, captured and destroyed ten 50 cwt. 6-inch guns, and burnt seven large boats, two ranges of barrack buildings, also a quantity of military stores and provisions, near the Boghaz of the Kouban Lake, on the 22nd instant; and I beg leave to call their Lordships' particular attention to the fact that this gallant service was performed during weather which must have rendered its accomplishment exceedingly difficult, and that Vice-Admiral Bruat and I consider that it reflects the highest credit on Captain Giffard, Captain Lebris, of the Fulton, and the officers and men of both nations employed on the occasion.

3. The enemy appears to have lost a considerable number of men on the occasion, whereas no casualties have occurred on our side.

I am, &c.,
ED. LYONS,
Rear-Admiral and Commander-in-Chief.
To the Secretary of the Admiralty,
London.

Enclosure.

Her Majesty's steam-frigate Leopard,
off Kertch, February 25, 1855.

REPORTING THE CAPTURE OF ENEMY'S GUNS, AND DESTRUCTION OF MILITARY STORES.

SIR,

I HAVE the honour to inform you that on the 22nd instant, His Imperial French

Majesty's ship Fulton having gone to Kaffa to reconnoitre, I proceeded towards Anapa in Her Majesty's ship Leopard, but on passing the Boghaz of the Kouban Lake, we observed numbers of troops crossing the passage in boats, from Anapa to Taman, so I ran in and anchored off the passage in 4½ fathoms.

The troops had landed, but we opened fire on them and drove them to the hills.

I sent a division of boats, under Lieutenant Graham, to examine the buildings on the points, which proved to be guard-houses, barracks, storehouses, and stables, some of which were burnt, but a heavy snow-storm coming on I recalled the boats.

Lieutenant Graham reporting he had seen some guns and other military stores, which he had not time to destroy, and which the enemy were transporting from Anapa to Kertch, I again proceeded there on the 24th instant, in company with the Fulton.

A few rounds of shot and shell drove the Cossacks and other troops, 400 or 500 in number, to the hills; when the boats under Lieutenant Graham landed, and Monsieur de Bris, in the Fulton took up a position, to the north-west, to check the advance of the enemy, who soon after brought some field batteries on the hills and opened a heavy fire of shot and shell upon the ships and boats.

The very accurate fire of the Fulton drove them from two positions, and the Leopard's shell from a third, after which they retreated behind the hills.

After three hours' work the boats returned, having captured and destroyed ten new and handsome 50 cwt. 6-inch guns and burnt seven large boats, two ranges of barracks and buildings, also a quantity of military stores and provisions.

The Fulton received one shot in her hull, but I am happy to say no casualties occurred.

The loss of the enemy must have been considerable.

I have, &c.,
(Signed) GEO. GIFFARD, Captain.
Rear-Admiral Sir Edmund
Lyons, Bart., G.C.B.,
&c. &c. &c.

Admiralty, March 8, 1855.

DESPATCHES, of which the following are copies, have been received from Rear-Admiral Sir Edmund Lyons, Bart., G.C.B., Commander-in-Chief of Her Majesty's Ships and Vessels in the Mediterranean and Black Sea.

UNSUCCESSFUL ATTACK BY THE RUSSIAN ON EUPATORIA.

Royal Albert, off Sevastopol,
February 20, 1855.

SIR,

I HAVE the honour to enclose, for the information of the Lords Commissioners of the Admiralty, copies of two letters which I have received from Captain Hastings, of the Curaçoa, Senior Officer at Eupatoria, reporting an unsuccessful attack made upon that place, at daybreak, on the 17th instant, by a large Russian force of cavalry, artillery, and infantry, and enclosing a letter from Omar Pasha, expressing warm acknowledgments for the great services rendered by Her Majesty's ships Curaçoa, Valorous, Furious, and Viper, as well as his Highness' thanks for the reinforcements of steamers which I had sent to him on hearing that the enemy was still in force in his neighbourhood.

2. Captain Hastings appears to have conducted his share of the defence with his accustomed zeal and ability, and to have been well and effectively seconded by Captains Buckle and Loring and Lieutenant Brock, and the officers, seamen, and marines of all Her Majesty's ships present on that occasion.

3. Colonel Simmons, of the Royal Engineers, who is attached to Omar Pasha's Staff, estimates the attacking force at 40,000 of all arms, and he states that as many as sixty guns, some of them 32-pounders, played upon the place at one time.

4. I understand that at nine o'clock the enemy's infantry formed under the shelter of a wall, at 350 yards from the place, and advanced to the attack, but were repulsed with considerable loss, and soon afterwards retired, leaving nearly two hundred dead on the nearest spot, and removing the rest of their dead from the more distant parts of the field.

5. Omar Pasha's army appears, from the latest and most authentic accounts, to have had nearly a hundred men killed and about two hundred and fifty wounded, and to have had eighty artillery horses killed, and some guns much damaged.

6. The Banshee has brought me a report from Captain Hastings up to noon yesterday, at which time the enemy remained encamped about five miles from Eupatoria, with his left leaning on the Putrid Lake Sasik; whilst Omar Pasha, with the garrison, having been reinforced after the battle by further Turkish troops, brought over from Varna in British transports, as well as by the Dauntless, Curlew, Arrow, and Lynx, sent by me from hence, and by two French steamers sent by Admiral Bruat, awaited an attack with confidence in a favourable result.

I am, &c.,
ED. LYONS,
Rear-Admiral and Commander-in-Chief.
To the Secretary of the Admiralty,
London.

Enclosure No. 1.

Her Majesty's ship Curaçoa, Eupatoria,
February 17, 1855.

SIR,

I HAVE the honour to acquaint your Excellency that, this, morning about 6.30 A.M., the Russians in considerable force attacked the Turkish troops which are encamped at this place under the command of his Highness Omar Pasha.

The ships under my command at this anchorage, which are named in the margin,* immediately proceeded under steam to close the flanking position of the Turkish entrenchments, – Valorous and Viper taking the left flank, and Curaçoa and Furious the right. About half an hour after the commencement of the attack, I received from his Highness Omar Pasha, a request to strengthen as much as possible the right flank, as the enemy were pressing their attack upon that point.

The Viper was immediately recalled, and from her light draught of water was enabled to effect good service, as also the three other ships in their respective positions.

The conduct of the captains, officers, seamen, and marines under my command on this occasion, deserves your Excellency's approbation.

I have, &c.,
(Signed) G.F. HASTINGS,
Captain.

P.S. – The French and Turkish vessels also did good service in their respective positions which they took up.

His Excellency Rear Admiral Sir
Edmund Lyons, Bart., G.C.B.,
K.C.H., &c., &c., &c.

Enclosure No. 2.

Her Majesty's ship Curaçoa,
Eupatoria, February 18, 1855.

SIR,

I HAVE the honour to acknowledge the receipt of your memorandum of yesterday's date, relative to my report of the Russians having attacked this place on the 17th instant, as communicated by the steam transport Queen of the South, and beg to inform you that the reinforcement of vessels mentioned therein have duly arrived here; and that I immediately informed his Highness Omar Pasha of the reinforcement being sent to his support, who begged me to offer to your Excellency his warmest thanks.

In the late attack the Turks suffered a loss of 88 men killed, 250 wounded, and 78 horses killed: the loss on the part of the Russians cannot be ascertained.

No further attack has been made; but the Russians still remain in force about five miles from Eupatoria, and large reinforcements, both of men and waggons, are daily arriving from the road to Simferopol. If the Arrow's services could be spared she would be of great assistance here.

I have, &c.,
(Signed) G.F. HASTINGS,
Captain
His Excellency Rear Admiral Sir
Edmund Lyons, Bart., G.C.B.,
K.C.H., &c., &c.

*Her Majesty's ships Valorous, Furious, and Viper.

Her Majesty's steam-vessel Viper,
off Kertch, March 8, 1855.

SIR,

I HAVE the honour to report, that in obedience to your instructions, I left this anchorage at 5.30 this morning, for the purpose of examining the mouth of the Kuban Lake. I arrived off there at nine, and observing a small force of Cossacks on the north spit, opened fire and dispersed them, then examined the lake in the whale-boat of this ship, but observing nothing of consequence, proceeded along the coast to the south-eastward.

I had just previously taken possession of a small vessel laden with charcoal and other goods, which I have brought in with me, with three prisoners on board. I enclose you her papers, &c., as they may be useful to His Excellency, the Commander-in-Chief, and request your directions in reference to the prisoners.

At 1.50 P.M. I arrived off the Martello Tower, at Djimiteia, anchoring bow and stern at a distance of 500 yards from the beach, and at 2 P.M. opened fire upon the fort, dispersing the few Cossacks that remained.

It is now my pleasing duty to inform you that I have effectually destroyed the fort, barracks, and granaries (having set fire to the latter), spiked and disabled the two guns, destroying the ammunition; and all, I am happy to say, without any casualty on board the Viper.

I beg to bring under your notice the conduct of Mr. James Roche, Second Master, who commanded the landing parties; and Mr. John R. Moss, Master's Assistant, who aided him in destroying the guns; both having performed their duty much to my satisfaction.

I have, &c.
(Signed) WM. ARMYTAGE, Lieutenant
and Commander.
Captain George Giffard, H.M.S. Leopard,
Senior Officer.

Royal Albert, off Sevastopol,
March 17, 1855.

SIR,

I HAVE the honour to enclose, for the information of the Lords Commissioners of the Admiralty, a letter which has been addressed to me by Captain Giffard, stating, that while making a reconnaissance near Soujak-Kalé, with Her Majesty's ship Leopard, under his command, and accompanied by Her Majesty's ships Highflyer, Swallow, and Viper, and also by H.I.M.'s steam-ship-of-war Fulton, he was informed by the Circassians in the neighbourhood, that the enemy had so reduced the strength of that fortress by the removal of men and guns to Anapa, that they were ready to attack it by land if he would do so by sea; and that he, wishing to encourage the natives and to embarrass the Russians, had assented to the proposal, and moved the ships to within 1000 yards of the south face of the fort, where he performed his part, but that on finding the Circassians did not perform theirs, he withdrew, after having driven all the garrison out of the place, with the exception of a few gunners in the earthern batteries, and having also dismounted several guns, and done considerable damage to the arsenal and public works; leaving the garrison, about a mile from the place, surrounded by Circassians, who were collecting reinforcements.

The ships appear to have been well placed, and to have fired with great effect: and Captain Giffard expresses his thanks to Captain Le Bris, his able coadjutor on former occasions, as well as to Captain Moore, Commander Craufurd, and Lieutenant Armytage, and their respective officers and ships' companies, for their support.

Of Captain Giffard himself, I may perhaps be permitted to observe that this is not the first time that his zeal and gallantry have been conspicuous since he has been under my command.

I am, &c.,
(Signed) ED. LYONS,
Rear-Admiral and Commander-in-Chief.
To the Secretary of the Admiralty,
London.

REPORTING AN ATTACK UPON SOUJAK.

Her Majesty's ship Leopard, Soujak Bay,
March 13, 1855.

SIR,

I HAVE the honour to acquaint you, that from the information I had received from the Circassians, at Ghelenjik, and also from the observations of Monsieur Le Bris of His Imperial Majesty's steam-vessel Fulton, as well as my own on the 6th instant in Soujak Bay, I was led to believe the Russians had sent many guns, stores, &c. away from that fort, and would probably leave if a force appeared off it.

Wishing to have more certain information for you, on my return to your flag, I, on the evening of the 11th instant, when the Highflyer joined me, proceeded with the vessels named in the margin* to Soujak Bay, where we anchored on the morning of the 12th; but a fresh gale, with heavy swell, prevented our closing the batteries. I therefore threw some shells into the place; and the Circassians, who soon appeared in numbers, at the same time attacked the small fort at the head of the bay, opposite the town, drove out the garrison, and burnt it, at 8 A.M. This morning the Circassians informed me they had a sufficient force, and would attack Soujak Kalé by land if I would do so by sea, and wishing to encourage them and embarrass the enemy, I immediately moved the squadron to within 1000 yards of the South Face and opened fire on it. From this point the enemy only had ten guns to bear on the ships, but the light wind and damp weather made the smoke hang over and conceal them from our fire, while our masts above were conspicuous to them.

We soon drove all the inhabitants and troops out of the place, except those in the earthen batteries, but I was much disappointed to find that the Circassians did not advance to attack them when out of the town, as they had promised. I, therefore, moved out again, as, with our small force of men, it would have been too great a risk to land, the main body of the garrison being close at hand.

The arsenal and public buildings are much injured, and several of the guns were silenced and dismounted. Our loss, I am happy to say, has been small; and some injury has been done to the masts and hulls of the ships.

I was much pleased with the able way in which all the ships took up their assigned positions, and have to thank Monsieur le Bris, of the Fulton, Captain Moore, Commander Craufurd and Lieutenant Armytage, commanding the Viper, for their able support as well as all the officers and men.

The Russian force, apparently 1500 or 2000 men, and the other inhabitants are now encamped about a mile north of the town, having left a few men in the batteries; they will have great difficulty in communicating with Anapa, being surrounded by the Circassians (who were collecting reinforcements), and should they return to the town, a small naval force can at any time drive them out again.

I enclose list of casualties among the ships.

I have, &c.,
(Signed) GEORGE GIFFARD,
Captain.
Rear-Admiral Sir Edmund Lyons,
Bart., G.C.B.

*Leopard, Highflyer, Swallow, Viper, and Fulton, French steamer.

War-Department, March 8, 1855.

LORD PANMURE has this day received Despatches and Enclosures, of which the following are copies, addressed to His Grace the Duke of Newcastle, and to His Lordship, by Field-Marshal the Lord Raglan, G.C.B.

Before Sevastopol,
February 20, 1855.

MY LORD DUKE,

YOUR Grace will have learnt, by my telegraphic despatch of the 18th inst., that the enemy had on the previous morning, at daylight, attacked Eupatoria with a very large force, and a powerful body of artillery, and had been repulsed, after an engagement which terminated with their retirement at 10 A.M.

I have now the honour to lay before your Grace copies of two letters which I have received from Colonel Simmons, who is attached to the head-quarters of Omer Pasha, containing the details of the action; and, whilst your Grace will rejoice to see that the Turkish troops which have been landed at Eupatoria have availed themselves of the earliest opportunity to show that the character they acquired on the Danube was well merited and remained unimpaired, you will join in the regret which I feel that they have suffered so considerable a loss, and that among the killed is numbered the General of Division, Selim Pasha (an Egyptian), and among the wounded a General of Brigade, also an Egyptian.

This loss, however, and particularly that sustained by a battery of artillery, afford ample proof of the gallant and determined conduct of the troops, and of the serious nature of the attack made upon them, as well as of their being worthy of their illustrious chief.

I have great satisfaction in drawing your Grace's attention to that part of Lieutenant Colonel Simmons' dispatch, in which he bears testimony to the efficient assistance rendered to the Ottoman army by Her Majesty's ships in the bay, under the command of the Honourable Captain Hastings, of the Curaçoa.

I have, &c.,
RAGLAN.
His Grace the Duke of Newcastle,
&c. &c. &c.

Eupatoria, February 17, 1855,
1 P.M.

MY LORD,

I HAVE the honour to inform your Lordship that on the 15th instant, several large convoys and arrivals of troops were seen moving along the north shore of the Sasik Putrid Lake, from the eastward.

This movement on the part of the enemy caused Omer Pasha to place the garrison on the alert. No further movement, however, was seen yesterday on the part of the enemy; but this morning, at daylight, they advanced in great force, and opened with artillery upon the entrenchments which inclose the town. The advanced line of works, which I informed your Lordship it was his Highness's intention to erect, were not yet commenced.

The enemy's artillery opened their fire about twelve hundred yards from the place, covered by skirmishers, and supported by heavy masses of infantry in their rear, and cavalry on their flanks. The artillery subsequently took up a second position more in advance, about four hundred yards from a small crown work which is being erected in front of the mills to the north-east of the town, and after continuing their fire for some time, the infantry advanced to the attack, having formed under the cover of a wall about six hundred yards from the right of the town. They were repulsed at this point, leaving from 150 to 200 dead on the field. On other points of the field a number of horses were left dead, but the killed men were removed. At length, about 10 A.M., the whole force retired, covered by the artillery and cavalry.

I am not able as yet to ascertain the number of men engaged, but I should think there were not less than 40,000 of all arms, with a very powerful artillery.

As many as sixty of the enemy's guns must have been firing at one time, amongst them some 32-pounders. Prisoners report that they were accompanied by 100 guns. As yet all the particulars I have been able positively to ascertain is that Liprandi's division (the 12th) was present.

At present I understand that they are in position about five miles north from this, their left leaning on the Sasik Putrid Lake.

It is with much pleasure I have to inform your Lordship that the portion of Her Majesty's Fleet, under the Honourable Captain Hastings, have rendered most efficient assistance. The Valorous threw some well directed shells and completely covered our left, whilst the Viper gun-boat, which was at first stationed on the left with the Valorous, by Captain Hastings' directions moved and took up a flanking position on the right near the mills.

I cannot at present give your Lordship any details of the killed and wounded on the side of the Turks; I regret to say, however, that Selim Pasha, commanding the Egyptian Brigade here, is amongst the former.

One battery of Turkish artillery was completely disabled, every gun having been struck and a great number (nearly one-third) of the horses killed.

I am desirous your Lordship should receive a report of the action, with as little delay as possible, by the Queen of the South; so I must beg your Lordship to excuse further details, which shall be sent by a future occasion.

I am, &c.
(Signed) JOHN SIMMONS,
Captain Royal Engineers, Brevet-Major.
Field-Marshal Lord Raglan, G.C.B.,
&c. &c. &c.

P.S. A prisoner informs us that a prince commanded, but he could not remember his name.

I am happy to say there are no casualties among the English or French officers. Two French sous-officers are among the killed, and two privates wounded.

(Signed) JOHN S.

Admiralty, March 19, 1855.

A DESPATCH, of which the following is a copy, has been received from Rear-Admiral Sir Edmund Lyons, Bart., G.C.B., Commander-in-Chief of Her Majesty's Ships and Vessels in the Mediterranean and Black Sea.

PROCEEDINGS AT KERTCH.

Royal Albert, off Sevastopol,
February 27, 1855.

SIR

WITH reference to my letter of the 20th instant (No. 135), reporting the highly creditable proceedings of the blockading squadron off Kertch, under the command of Captain Giffard, of Her Majesty's ship Leopard.

2. I have now the honour to enclose copies of two letters which I have received from that active and intelligent officer, reporting his further proceedings, and of his having, in conjunction with His Imperial Majesty's steamer Fulton, captured and destroyed ten 50 cwt. 6-inch guns, and burnt seven large boats, two ranges of barrack buildings, also a quantity of military stores and provisions, near the Boghaz of the Kouban Lake, on the 22nd instant; and I beg leave to call their Lordships' particular attention to the fact that this gallant service was performed during weather which must have rendered its accomplishment exceedingly difficult, and that Vice-Admiral Bruat and I consider that it reflects the highest credit on Captain Giffard, Captain Lebris, of the Fulton, and the officers and men of both nations employed on the occasion.

3. The enemy appears to have lost a considerable number of men on the occasion, whereas no casualties have occurred on our side.

I am, &c.,
ED. LYONS,
Rear-Admiral and Commander-in-Chief.
To the Secretary of the Admiralty,
London.

Enclosure.

Her Majesty's steam-frigate Leopard,
off Kertch, February 25, 1855.

REPORTING THE CAPTURE OF ENEMY'S GUNS, AND DESTRUCTION OF MILITARY STORES.

SIR,

I HAVE the honour to inform you that on the 22nd instant, His Imperial French Majesty's ship Fulton having gone to Kaffa to reconnoitre, I proceeded towards Anapa in Her Majesty's ship Leopard, but on passing the Boghaz of the Kouban Lake, we observed numbers of troops crossing the passage in boats, from Anapa to Taman, so I ran in and anchored off the passage in 4½ fathoms.

The troops had landed, but we opened fire on them and drove them to the hills.

I sent a division of boats, under Lieutenant Graham, to examine the buildings on the points, which proved to be guard-houses, barracks, storehouses, and stables, some of which were burnt, but a heavy snow-storm coming on I recalled the boats.

Lieutenant Graham reporting he had seen some guns and other military stores, which he had not time to destroy, and which the enemy were transporting from Anapa to Kertch, I again proceeded there on the 24th instant, in company with the Fulton.

A few rounds of shot and shell drove the Cossacks and other troops, 400 or 500 in number, to the hills; when the boats under Lieutenant Graham landed, and Monsieur de Bris, in the Fulton took up a position, to the north-west, to check the advance of the enemy, who soon after brought some field batteries on the hills and opened a heavy fire of shot and shell upon the ships and boats.

The very accurate fire of the Fulton drove them from two positions, and the Leopard's shell from a third, after which they retreated behind the hills.

After three hours' work the boats returned, having captured and destroyed ten new and handsome 50 cwt. 6-inch guns and burnt seven large boats, two ranges of barracks and buildings, also a quantity of military stores and provisions.

The Fulton received one shot in her hull, but I am happy to say no casualties occurred.

The loss of the enemy must have been considerable.

I have, &c.,
(Signed) GEO. GIFFARD, Captain.
Rear-Admiral Sir Edmund
Lyons, Bart., G.C.B.,
&c. &c. &c.

Admiralty, March 28, 1855.

DESPATCHES, of which the following are copies, have been received from Rear-Admiral Sir Edmund Lyons, Bart., G.C.B., Commander-in-Chief of Her Majesty's Ships and Vessels in the Mediterranean and Black Sea.

DESTRUCTION OF THE TOWER OF DJIMITEIA BY HER MAJESTY'S STEAM-VESSEL VIPER.

Royal Albert, off Sevastopol,
March 17, 1855.

SIR,

I HAVE the honour to enclose, for the information of the Lords Commissioners of the Admiralty, a copy of a letter that I have received from Captain Giffard, of Her Majesty's ship Leopard, enclosing one from Lieutenant Armytage, reporting his having destroyed in Her Majesty's steam-vessel Viper, under his command, the Martello Tower and Barracks of Djimiteia, which had been recently erected for the defence of the direct communication between Anapa and Kertch.

This very useful service has been performed by Lieutenant Armytage in the manner that might have been expected from an officer of his acknowledged merit.

I am, &c.,
(Signed) EDMUND LYONS,
Rear-Admiral and Commander-in-Chief.
To the Secretary of the Admiralty.

The Commander-in-Chief of the British force was the 66-year-old General FitzRoy James Henry
Somerset, 1st Baron Raglan, seen here in this portrait by William Salter.

General FitzRoy James Henry Somerset, 1st Baron Raglan. Lord Raglan was a highly experienced soldier, his career having begun in 1804 when he was commissioned into the 4th Light Dragoons, later joining the staff of Sir Arthur Wellesley, the future Duke of Wellington, at the Battle of Copenhagen. He continued to serve with Wellesley throughout the Peninsular War as his principle aide-de-camp and then his Military Secretary. He also fought with Wellington in the Waterloo campaign where he was severely wounded, losing his right hand. When Wellington became Commander-in-Chief of the Army, Somerset continued as his Military Secretary. In 1854 he was promoted to full General and given command of the Eastern Army. Raglan became a Field Marshal following the Battle of Inkerman in November 1855. On 29 June 1855 he died due to complications brought on by a bout of dysentery. Though well-liked by some, Raglan proved to be indecisive and his orders inexplicit, as exemplified by his instructions to the Light Brigade at Balaklava. According to one Guards officer, Colonel Henry Percy, Raglan, 'never shows himself not even after an action, to the men ... [he] has thrown away his opportunities of being known to the troops, he is a myth to half of them.' Fanny Duberly gave this assessment of Raglan following his death: 'We are almost tempted to lose sight of the inefficient General, in the recollection of the kind-hearted, gentlemanly man, who had so hard a task, which he fulfilled so well, of keeping together and in check the head of so many armies.'

rtrait of the British admiral Sir Charles Napier, by Henry Valentin.

HMS *Duke of Wellington*, Flagship of the Baltic Fleet, which was used by Sir Charles Napier during the Crimean War.

The 33rd (or The Duke of Wellington's) Regiment at the Battle of the Alma.
(Courtesy of David Rowlands; www.davidrowlands.co.uk)

photograph of warships at Balaklava, more specifically 'Cossack Bay'. At its widest point the harbour was less than 300 yards across and from the harbour entrance to the head of the harbour was about three-quarters of a mile. 'The stench along the waterside is very bad,' wrote Fenton shortly after his arrival at Balaklava. 'All the dead oxen and horses floating about the harbour have been towed out to sea. Do what they will, there is an immense quantity of putrefying matter which cannot be got rid of. The ground is everywhere thickly strewn with barley, the harbour is crammed with ships lying closer than in any docks, many of them empty, doing nothing themselves and keeping others from discharging their cargo.'

The Cavalry camp near Balaklava. The photograph shows the South Valley and beyond the Causeway Heights. It is easy to understand why the Causeway Heights were considered to be of supreme importance to both sides. If the Russians were able to establish themselves on the heights they would be able to dominate the British positions around Balaklava. The Battle of Balaklava wa effectively a battle for control of the Causeway Heights.

Charge of the Heavy Brigade.

Maréchal Aimable Jean Jacques Pélissier was chief of staff for the province of Oran in Algiera and as still in North Afriaca when the French forces were shipped to the Crimea but after the death of Arnaud he was sent out to the Crimea to take over command of the army from *Maréchal* anrobert on 16 May 1855. His successful storming of Sevastopol's Malakoff Tower on 8 September inched victory for the Allies and resulted in him being created *duc de Malakoff* by Napoleon III.

Situated between the Fedioukine Heights and the Causeway, was the North Valley, and thanks to Tennyson's poem it became known as 'The Valley of Death'. Fenton took two photographs here, or of which was without the cannonballs dispersed along the road, leading to speculation that he arranged for them to be placed there to create a more dramatic effect. However, when Fenton visited there on 4 April 1855, he wrote in a private letter, 'the sight passed all imagination: round shot and shell lay like a stream at the bottom of the hollow all the way down, you could not walk without treading upon them'.

Edmund Lyons, from an 1857 engraving by D.J. Pound, after a photograph by Kilburn.

J.W.D. Dundas.

A tinted lithograph captioned as 'showing soldiers transporting winter clothing, lumber for huts, and other supplies through a snow-covered landscape, with partially buried dead horses along the roadside, to the British camps; huts under construction in the background'.

The 20th Regiment of Foot at the Battle of Inkerman, 5 November 1854.
(Courtesy of David Rowlands; www.davidrowlands.co.uk)

Raglan's Adjutant-General was Sir James Estcourt. In his thirty-four years of service in the Army, James Bucknall Bucknall Estcourt had never seen action, yet on 21 February 1854 he was made a Brigadier-General and was appointed Adjutant-General to the expeditionary force in the Crimea. He was regarded as being quite incapable of fulfilling his new role and it is said that Raglan did not even 'pay him the compliment of attempting to transact business with him'. Nevertheless, he was a friend of Raglan and he was promoted to Major-General on 12 December 1854. It soon became apparent that Estcourt was out of his depth and the Secretary of State for War, the Duke of Newcastle, demanded that both Estcourt and Richard Airey (see below) should be recalled. Estcourt however, was struck down by cholera during the siege of Sevastopol and he died on the morning of 24 June 1855.

Scottish-born Lieutenant General Sir George Brown began his military career with the 43rd Regiment in 1806. He was involved in the Battle of Copenhagen in 1807 and in the Peninsular War, his battalion forming part of the famous Light Division. After serving in America Brown received a staff appointment at Horse Guards, becoming a Lieutenant General and Adjutant-General to the Forces. Brown relinquished the latter post in 1853. When the force was assembled for the Crimea, Brown was given command of the Light Division, and was nominally Raglan's second in command. Though he was said to be the most unpopular general in the army he led a successful subsidiary expedition against the port of Kertch in May 1855 to cut off supplies reaching the Russians from there. He was invalided home on 29 June 1855, the same day that Lord Raglan died. This photograph shows Brown with officers of his staff: Major Hallewell, Colonel Brownrigg, an orderly, Colonel Airey, Captain Pearson, Captain Markham, and Captain Ponsonby.

As a young officer with the 1st Regiment of Foot Guards (later the Grenadier Guards) Sir James Simpson served in the Peninsular War and the Waterloo campaign. He later commanded the 29th Regiment in Mauritius and India. In February 1855, as a full General, he was sent out to the Crimea to act as Raglan's chief of staff. When Raglan died in June, Simpson reluctantly took command of the army in the Crimea. He resigned that post on 10 November, 'mortified and disgusted' at his treatment in the British press, which continuously criticized his handling of the army. 'He deserves recall,' ran *The Times* after the British failure to capture the Sevastopol Redan on 8 September 1855. 'The British army had been beaten, and beaten, it was reasonable to suppose, through the incapacity of the General ... It cannot be too often that our army requires a younger man ... not [a man] of the age of the British Commander-in-Chief who sits in a ditch muffled up in a cloak when a whole army rushes to the assault.' Command of the army devolved upon William Codrington.

vo views of the Siege of Sevastopol 1855. (Courtesy of Valentin Ramirez)

Though he was the son of an admiral, General Sir William John Codrington GCB, chose a career in the Army, joining the 88th Regiment in 1821. In September 1854 he was appointed to the command of the 1st Brigade of the Light Division. Codrington took command of the division after Sir George Brown was wounded. After the resignation of General James Simpson in November 1855, though still only a substantive major-general, he became Commander-in-Chief of the British Army in the Crimea. So the man that had set off for the Crimea as a regimental major ended the war as a Lieutenant General. Codrington owed his promotion, according to Captain Earle, to being part of the influential 'Guards set' in the Crimea, 'and their influence built the nest which is now filled wi₥ their protégés.'

(*Opposite*) Following the storming of Sevastopol, Robertson was able to photograph inside the Russian defensive works. The above is a view of the Barracks Battery and below is a photograph o₋ the interior of the Redan. Fanny Duberly described the nature of the Russian works: 'The Redan is succession of little batteries, each containing two or three guns, with traverses behind each divisio⌐ and hidden away under gabions, sand-bags, and earth, are little huts in which the officers and me᷉ used to live … The centre, the open space between the Redan and the second line of defence, was completely ploughed by our thirteen-inch shells, fragments of which, together with round shot, quite paved the ground.'

Memorial in the Balaklava valley to the British personnel who fell in the Crimean War. (Courtesy of George Chernilevsky)

Enclosure.

Her Majesty's ship, Leopard,
off Kertch, March 8, 1855.

SIR,

THE wind being off shore this morning, I sent Her Majesty's ship Viper to examine the Boghaz of the Kouban Lake, and also the coast as far as the Tower of Djimiteia, and have the honour to enclose a letter from Lieutenant Armytage, reporting his having, in the latter place, destroyed the new tower, with two guns, also the barracks and other buildings.

Lieutenant Armytage deserves great credit for the able manner in which he has performed this service with his small vessel.

I have, &c.,
(Signed) GEO. GIFFARD, Captain.
Rear-Admiral Sir Edmund
Lyons, Bart., G.C.B.,
Commander-in-Chief.

CHAPTER 8

THE BALTIC CAMPAIGN 1855

Admiralty, July 2, 1855.

DESPATCHES, of which the following are copies, have been received from Rear-Admiral the Honourable R.S. Dundas, Commander-in-Chief of Her Majesty's ships and vessels on the Baltic Station.

PROCEEDINGS OF ADMIRAL SEYMOUR IN NARVA BAY.

Duke of Wellington, at anchor,
Tolboukin Lighthouse W.S.W., 5 miles,
June 21, 1855.

SIR,

IN my letter of the 18th instant, No. 196, I reported, for the information of the Lords Commissioners of the Admiralty, that I had directed Rear-Admiral Seymour to proceed with Her Majesty's ships Exmouth and Blenheim, and with the gunboats Pincher and Snap, to examine the coast in the Bay of Narva; and I have now the honour to transmit the enclosed letter which I have received from the Rear-Admiral, reporting his proceedings.

I have much pleasure in expressing my satisfaction at the spirited and judicious manner in which he took occasion to occupy the attention of the troops which were strongly posted in the neighbourhood, and my sense of the zealous efforts of the officers and men under his orders, particularly those in the two gun-boats, which appear to have been well handled under a smart fire from the enemy's batteries.

I have, &c.
(Signed) R.S. DUNDAS,
Rear-Admiral and Commander-in-Chief.

To the Secretary of the Admiralty.
No. 1 Enclosure.

Report of Proceedings at Narva.
Her Majesty's ship Exmouth,
Off Seskar, June 19, 1855.

SIR,

IN obedience to your directions of the 15th instant, I quitted Seskar anchorage at 8 A.M. on Saturday the 16th, anchoring at 7 P.M. under East Tyters Island, off a village situate on its S.S.E. extremity, with a view of obtaining information respecting the River Narva; but only succeeded in learning that a considerable body of troops were about Narva and its vicinity.

Quitting East Tyters, on the evening of Sunday the 17th, Narva Lighthouse was made out yesterday, at 2.30 A.M., with the broad extent of sandy beach that borders the bay.

On nearing the entrance of the river, which is narrow, and has a bar on which the breaking shoal water was visible, a considerable number of troops, including a party of cavalry, were seen in active movement and a large caisson or construction of timber was floated and sunk in the entrance of the river, and became the means of communication with either side: a few wood vessels and river craft only were visible inside the river, the banks of which are of sand, thickly timbered and well adapted for defence by troops. An earth battery of 12 guns lies on the east side of the river's entrance and one of 10 guns near the lighthouse, with another in its rear, seen from the mast-head, apparently to command the river; and 2 other guns were placed in position on the right extremity of the Lighthouse Battery.

An opportunity was afforded to try the practical efficiency of the gun boats, Pincher and Snap, under the immediate charge of Captain Hall, of the Blenheim, who, with good judgment, added one of his main-deck 68-pounders to the armament of the former, and until rain and squally weather interfered, their practice was good, and their constant change of position, rendered them difficult objects to hit, though the fort guns were well served, using hot shot, which frequently passed near and over them.

On the weather clearing the gun-boats opened fire, and the Blenheim and Exmouth likewise took an opportunity of a couple of hours' practice, covering the gun-boats with good effect, which were ably manoeuvred by Lieutenant C.A.C. De Crespigny, in command of the Snap, and Lieutenant Steward, in command of the Pincher, in the former of which I had placed Lieutenant Travers, R.M., with ten gunners of the Royal Marine Artillery of the Exmouth, who did good service. Mr. Harper, Assistant-Surgeon of this ship, was likewise on board the Snap, he having volunteered for that service.

As it was evident, from the first, that no serious attempt could be made on the enemy's position, and as a large expenditure of ammunition would have been useless,

I considered that enough had now been done to occupy the attention of the troops in the neighbourhood and no advantage appearing to offer itself for a longer continuance in Narva Bay, the signal was made to discontinue firing and I proceeded, in compliance with your orders, to rejoin your flag.

I enclose a return of a casualty which, I regret to learn, occurred to Captain Searle, R.M., of the Blenheim, the effects of which, I trust, will not prove serious.

I have, &c.,
(Signed) M. SEYMOUR,
Rear-Admiral.
Rear-Admiral the Hon. R.S. Dundas, C.B.

Admiralty, July 10, 1855.

DESPATCHES, of which the following are copies or extracts, have been received at this Office from Rear-Admiral the Honourable R.S. Dundas, Commander-in-Chief of Her Majesty's ships and vessels on the Baltic Station.

Duke of Wellington, at anchor off Tolboukin
Lighthouse, July 2, 1855.

"THE Arrogant arrived here from the neighbourhood of Biorko on the 28th ultimo, and returns to-day to the same station. I have directed Captain Yelverton to extend his examination of the coast as far westward as Lovisa; and I beg leave to direct their Lordships' attention to a report, herewith transmitted, which I have this day received from Captain Vansittart, of the Magicienne, through whose activity and zeal, with the aid of the Ruby gun-boat, a large number of vessels, laden with granite blocks, have been successfully destroyed in Werolax Bay."

Her Majesty's ship Magicienne,
Off Nerva Beacon, July 1, 1855.

SIR,

I HAVE the honour to report that, in obedience to orders received from Captain Yelverton, I left the anchorage of Biorko on the 28th of last month, with Her Majesty' ship Magicienne under my command, and Ruby gun-boat, in search of a number of vessels said to be freighted by the Russian Government to carry blocks of granite, and in the neighbourhood of the Island of Lukar.

Having arrived off the Island of Kyskykyla the same evening, early on the 29th I proceeded in Her Majesty's gun-boat Ruby, and boats of Her Majesty's ship Magicienne, under the First Lieutenant H.B. King, to the very end of the bay, looking well in about the Island of Lukar, and in boats ascending some little distance up the

River of Kyskykyla, finding only four vessels, which, being both new and empty, I left unhurt.

The following morning, the 30th, I proceeded with Her Majesty's ship Magicienne and Ruby gun-boat, to the next large Bay of Werolax, where anchoring Her Majesty's ship Magicienne at the entrance, I proceeded to the very end of Werolax Bay, a distance of about nine miles, where I found a large granite quarry with near two hundred men at work, who at our approach went off.

Anchoring the Ruby, so as to command the whole place with the boats, I had the various vessels at anchor, consisting of thirty large galiots, boarded.

Twenty-nine being laden with granite blocks, I had them destroyed by fire.

With the exception of three or four rifle shots being fired upon us, which were quickly returned by rockets and rifles, we met with no resistance.

The head of Werolax Bay was evidently the rendezvous for the granite vessels, as, with the exception of one, all their sails were unbent, colours and papers secured, and most of their vessels were slung and buoyed, so as to be ready for scuttling if discovered, which many had commenced doing on the present occasion.

I have, &c.,
(Signed) NICHOLAS VANSITTART,
Captain.
Rear-Admiral the Hon. R.S. Dundas, C.B.

Her Majesty's Ship Arrogant,
off Biorka, June 25, 1855.

SIR,

I HAVE the honour to acquaint you with my proceedings since the 18th instant.

On the 20th I anchored at Rotsinshalm, and took immediate steps for blowing up the fort, which was accomplished on the following day.

On the afternoon of the 20th I made a careful reconnoissance of Kotka, in the Ruby, and discovered at the back of the island, where I had not been before, large government buildings, with barracks fit to contain about 5000 men, stables, storehouses, and hospital, all of which I destroyed. The buildings had evidently been very recently occupied. I met no troops except a few Cossacks, who retired on our approach.

I have, &c.
(Signed) H.R. YELVERTON,
Captain.

Admiralty, July 16, 1855.

DESPATCHES, of which the following are copies or extracts, have been this day received from Rear-Admiral the Honourable R.S. Dundas, Commander-in-Chief of Her Majesty's ships and vessels in the Baltic.

Duke of Wellington,
Tolboukin Lighthouse, July 7, 1855.

"THE Magicienne returned this morning from Lovisa, and I annex a report which I have received from Captain Yelverton, of Her Majesty's ship Arrogant, who has been again successful in destroying a well constructed fort at Svartholm, in the entrance of the Bay of Lovisa, but their Lordships will observe, with regret, that, notwithstanding the humane desire of that officer, the town of Lovisa was unfortunately destroyed by fire, which occurred accidentally, on the night following the visit of Her Majesty's ships. Captain Vansittart informs me that the authorities of the town have themselves admitted and explained the accidental origin of the fire."

Her Majesty's ship Arrogant,
off Hogland, July 8, 1855.

SIR,

I HAVE the honour to inform you, that I reached Lovisa on the afternoon of the 4th instant, and anchored the vessels close to Fort Svartholm.

The enemy must have had intelligence of our movements and quitted the fort on our approach, for they had been at work but a few hours before unroofing the barracks and taking away stores. The guns and ammunition had been previously removed.

Svartholm was in good condition, and a work of great strength, entirely commanding the approaches to Lovisa; it has had important additions of late years, can mount 122 guns, and had accommodation in casemated barracks for about 1000 men, with governor's house and garden, and excellent officers' quarters. I made immediate arrangements for blowing up the fort and completely destroying the barracks; these have since been fully carried out.

On the 5th, I made a reconnaissance of the town of Lovisa, in the Ruby, accompanied by the boats of the Arrogant and Magicienne. A strong detachment of Cossacks made their appearance at one time, but they were dispersed by the fire from the boats, the rockets particularly throwing them into great confusion. On landing at Lovisa, sent for the authorities and explained the object of my visit; some demur was caused by our not having a flag of truce. I told them they had no right to such a guarantee, as the respect due to it had been so grossly violated at Hangö. I then proceeded to the barracks and Government stores within the town, which I destroyed, but did not set fire to them, as by so doing the whole town must have been burnt.

This precaution was not destined to save Lovisa, for during the night an accidental fire occurred in a portion of the town where we had not been, and before morning the whole place was reduced to ashes.

I have, &c.
(Signed) H.E. YELVERTON,
Captain.
Rear-Admiral the Hon. R.S. Dundas,
Commander-in- Chief.

Extract of a letter from Rear-Admiral Honourable R.S. Dundas, to the Secretary of the Admiralty, dated-

Duke of Wellington,
Tolboukin Lighthouse, July 7, 1855.

I CANNOT conclude this letter without calling the particular attention of their Lordships to the active exertions of Captain Storey, of Her Majesty's ship Harrier, which led a few days later to the destruction of a large amount of shipping, discovered afterwards in another anchorage near Nystad, as detailed in the enclosure to Captain Warden's report of the 2nd instant.

Harrier, off Little Wahas,
June 24, 1855.

SIR,

I HAVE the honour to inform you that the boats of this ship destroyed 47 ships belonging to the enemy, varying from 700 tons to 200 tons, on the nights of the 23rd and 24th instant.

On the first night the ships destroyed were one mile from the town of Nystad, and about three miles from the ship, and we were enabled to bring one barque, the Victoria, of about 450 tons, off with us.

On the following morning the steam was got up and we proceeded to sea to anchor the prize off Enskov Lighthouse.

At 5 P.M., however, we steamed towards the land and anchored at about 7.30 P.M., and at 8 P.M. the boats were again despatched.

During the night and following day we discovered 42 ships, the whole of which we either burned or scuttled.

I have the greatest pleasure in being able to state that these proceeding were so successfully carried out without any casualty.

Owing to the distance we got away from the ship (10 or 11 miles) and the blowing weather, accompanied with rain, that came on during the morning, we were prevented from bringing any vessel out with us.

We did not get back to the ship until after 6 P.M. this afternoon, the men having been on their oars twenty-two hours.

I think, Sir, I am only doing common justice to the men when I state how pleased I was to see the zeal and perseverance with which they worked for so many hours, neither can I omit stating my belief that this arose in a great measure from the good example of the officers, especially the senior Lieutenant, Mr. Annesley, from whom I have ever received the most active assistance.

Having then, in two following nights and one day, destroyed the whole of the Nystad shipping (probably upwards of 20,000 tons) I trust these proceedings will meet with your approval.

I have, &c.,
(Signed) HENRY STOREY,
Commander.
Captain Warden, Senior Officer,
Her Majesty's Ship Ajax.

Admiralty, July 23, 1855.

DESPATCHES, of which the following are copies, have been received at the Admiralty from Rear-Admiral the Honourable R.S. Dundas, Commander-in-Chief of Her Majesty's ships and vessels in the Baltic.

Duke of Wellington,
at Nargen, July 17, 1855.

SIR,

I TRANSMIT herewith, to be laid before my Lords Commissioners of the Admiralty, a report of proceedings during the past week from Captain Yelverton, who rejoined me yesterday at this anchorage in Her Majesty's ship Arrogant, and who, with the Magicienne and Ruby gunboats in company, visited the south coast of the Gulf of Finland, and attacked some military posts of the enemy at Kounda Bay and in the River Portsoiki.

Returning afterwards to his former station in the Bay of Viborg, he proceeded with boats towards the town, and engaged with a superior force of the enemy defended by batteries.

I request you will express to their Lordships my approbation of the conduct of this enterprising officer upon all occasions; and I would beg to recommend to their favourable notice the conduct of Captain Vansittart, of the Magicienne, and of Lieutenant Haggard, of the Arrogant, and Lieutenant Dowell, of the Royal Marine Artillery, and the excellent behaviour of all the officers and men.

Captain Yelverton has spoken favourably also of the conduct of Mr. Hale, mate, in command of the Ruby.

I regret much to have to report the loss of Mr. Story, midshipman, of the Arrogant, with nine others wounded in the boats of the two ships, of whom one is since dead.

I have, &c.

To the Secretary of the Admiralty.

Enclosure in Admiral Dundas's Letter.

Her Majesty's ship, Arrogant,
off Viborg, July 14, 1855.

SIR,

I HAVE the honour to acquaint you with my proceedings during the week.

The Magicienne rejoined me on Wednesday, and I proceeded direct to Kounda Bay, on the South Coast, where I had reason to think that troops were concentrated. It turned out to be a large Cossack encampment, on a most commanding position, from whence I dislodged them, with shell and rockets from the Ruby and ship's boats. Some opposition was made to our landing, and shots fired from behind hedges, &c.; but I succeeded in examining the place, which I did not injure, as it only contained private property.

The following morning I anchored at the mouth of the River Portsoiki, and landing on its right bank, destroyed a Cossack barrack and stables, driving the soldiers into the country. I then came on here.

Having anchored the ships as close as I could to the Island of Stralsund, I proceeded in the Ruby, accompanied by Captain Vansittart, of the Magicienne, and Captain Lowder, R.M., of this ship, the latter officer having under his command a strong detachment of marines; we towed with us the boats of this ship, under the command of Lieutenants Haggard and Woolcombe, and those of the Magicienne, under the command of Lieutenants King and Loady.

Having opened the bay, called Trangsund, we saw a Russian man-of-war steamer with two large gun-boats in tow, not far off; this most novel and unexpected sight of a Russian man-of-war for once clear of a stone wall, and to all appearance inclined to give us a fair and honest fight, create the greatest enthusiasm amongst the men and officers.

I directed Mr. Hale, commanding the Ruby, to open fire on her at once, but she very soon retired out of range, having, I think, received some damage. We had now reached the entrance of the sound; Viborg was in sight, and a fair prospect of attacking three large gun-boats, lying with another steamer under an island about one mile off. We were here brought up by a barrier, impeding the passage of the gun-boat and launches.

At this moment, a masked battery on the left bank, not more than 350 yards off, opened on us a heavy fire of musketry, round, and grape; this was instantly returned and kept in check by a rapid and well directed fire from the Ruby and all the boats. The enemy's steamer and gun-boats then came from under the island and also opened fire on us.

As it was impossible to get the Ruby through the barrier, I returned towards Stralsund, the enemy's riflemen following us along the banks, but driven from their positions as fast as they took them by the fire from the Ruby and boats.

An explosion took place in one of the Arrogant's cutters, which swamped the boat; the men were saved, but I regret to say that Mr. Story, the midshipman in command of her, was killed. In endeavouring to save the crew, the boat drifted close to the battery, and would have fallen into the hands of the enemy, had not Lieutenant Haggard, of this ship, and Lieutenant Dowell, R.M. A., of the Magicienne, in the Ruby's gig, with a volunteer crew, towed her out under a very heavy fire.

I cannot sufficiently praise the conduct of all the officers and men who were engaged in this affair, where their cool and determined courage enabled them to handle most severely, and keep in check for upwards of one hour, the enemy far superior in number, with the advantage of local knowledge and a good position.

I beg to enclose a list of the casualties, and also a list of the officers in the boat.

I have, &c.,

(Signed) H.R. YELVERTON,

Captain.

Rear-Admiral the Hon. R.S. Dundas,

&c. &c. &c.

Admiralty, July 30, 1855.

A DESPATCH, of which the following is an extract, has been received at the Admiralty from Rear-Admiral the Honourable R.S. Dundas, Commander-in-Chief of Her Majesty's Ships and Vessels in the Baltic.

Extract of a Letter from Rear-Admiral Honourable R.S. Dundas to the Secretary of the Admiralty, dated Duke of Wellington, at Nargen, 23rd July, 1855.

I HAVE the satisfaction of transmitting a copy of a report which I have received from Captain Yelverton, detailing the circumstances under which, with the Cossack, Magicienne, and Ruby in company, he has again availed himself of an opportunity to attack, with good effect, a position occupied by troops of the enemy, assembled in considerable force, for the defence of Fredericksham; and I have much pleasure in submitting to their Lordships this additional proof of the zeal and gallantry of the officers and men under his orders, and of their good conduct, especially of Mr. H.G. Hale, Mate, and the crew of the Ruby gun-boat.

I have, &c.,

(Signed) R.S. DUNDAS.

Enclosure in Admiral Dundas's Letter.

Her Majesty's ship, Arrogant,
off the Crops Islands, July 22, 1855.

SIR,

I HAVE the honour to inform you that, on leaving the Fleet, I proceeded off the Island of Hogland, where I was joined by the Cossack, Magicienne, and Ruby gun-boat.

Information having reached me that the enemy had sent 3000 troops to Fredericksham, and were making every possible exertion to put the place in a state of defence, I lost no time in getting there.

I arrived on the afternoon of the 20th, and would have attacked them that evening, but that the Ruby got on shore in examining the intricate channel leading to the town, and it was too late to take the ships in by the time she was off.

Early the following morning I succeeded in getting the ships up to the town, and at 9.40 we opened fire. After an engagement of one hour, the enemy ceased fire, and abandoned their guns, some of which were dismounted.

If I judge by the number of men we saw them carrying away on stretchers, they must have suffered severely.

I am happy to say the injury on our side has been trifling, though our hull bears evidence of the precision with which they fired, but generally speaking their shot fell short.

I regret to say that one man belonging to the Ruby was dangerously wounded by a round shot.

I must not allow this opportunity to pass without mentioning Mr. Hale, Mate, Commanding the Ruby gun-boat, who, together with his gallant crew, deserve the highest praise for the way in which they worked and fought their long gun, so close to this, that I had an opportunity of observing the precision of their fire.

One portion of a suburb caught fire and was destroyed, but I am happy to say the town remained uninjured, owing to the strict observance of an order I gave to fire on the fort only.

I have, &c.,
H.R. YELVERTON,
Captain.
Rear-Admiral the Hon. R.S. Dundas,
&c. &c. &c.

Admiralty, August 6, 1855.

A DESPATCH, of which the enclosed is a copy, has this day been received from Rear-

Admiral the Honourable R.S. Dundas, C.B., the Commander-in-Chief of Her Majesty's Ships and Vessels in the Baltic.

Duke of Wellington,
at Nargen, July 30, 1855.

SIR,

I BEG you will be pleased to acquaint the Lords Commissioners of the Admiralty, that having received, on the 24th instant, from Captain Yelverton, of Her Majesty's ship Arrogant, information which appeared to render it desirable that he should again examine the south-western shores of the Island of Kotka, I took immediate measures to strengthen the squadron under his orders by the addition of four gun-boats, to be detached from off Cronstadt by Rear-Admiral Baynes, together with the further addition of four mortar-vessels from hence, which he had hoped to be able to employ.

I have much satisfaction in transmitting for their Lordships' information the enclosed report of proceedings of Captain Yelverton, who, with the squadron under his orders, has again succeeded in completing the destruction of buildings and military stores to a considerable extent on the Island of Kotka; and I beg once more to express my entire approbation of the manner in which he has executed the service entrusted to him, and of the conduct of the officers and men employed on the occasion.

I am happy in having this opportunity to recommend to the favourable notice of their Lordships the conduct of Mr. George Giles, Master of the Arrogant, and Mr. Macfarlane, the Master of the Magicienne, who have now been constantly employed in those ships on the various services which I have recently had occasion to report.

I have, &c.
(Signed) R.S. DUNDAS,
Rear-Admiral and Commander-in-Chief.
The Secretary of the Admiralty.

Enclosure in Admiral Dundas's Letter.

Her Majesty's ship, Arrogant,
off the Mouth of the Kymene,
July 28, 1855.

SIR,

I HAVE the honour to inform you that very early on the morning of the 26th I was joined, off the Island of Hogland, by the Cossack and Magicienne bringing with them the mortar vessels Prompt, Pickle, Rocket, and Blazer. I stood immediately to the northward, leaving the Ruby to bring on the gun-boats, which wore not then in sight. They joined at noon, and at 2 P.M. we all anchored off Fort Rotsensholm.

As the safety of our expedition rested chiefly on our investing and holding the entire possession of the fortified Island of Kotka, I determined upon taking it at once. Accordingly I anchored the mortar vessels out of range, and leaving two gun-boats to look after them, I proceeded with the rest of the vessels to the westward of Kotka, for the purpose of destroying the bridge, so as to cut off the retreat of the garrison, and prevent their receiving reinforcements from the mainland. Captain Vansittart of the Magicienne, with his accustomed zeal and activity, threaded his way at once through the shoals, and destroyed the bridge. As soon as all the vessels had anchored, so as to command the great military road leading from the fort of Hogfors Holm, and also the channel dividing the island from the main, I landed all the Marines under command of Captain S.N. Lowder, R.M. with Lieutenant Geo. D. Dowell, R.M.A. and Lieutenants H.C. Mudge and P.R. Holmes, R.M., who took possession without being opposed, as the garrison (no doubt apprised of our coming by the telegraphs along the coast) had very recently evacuated, leaving behind them a large amount of military stores, which have since been burnt.

I beg to enclose a list of all the Crown property destroyed by Captain Lowder, including barracks, magazines, ordnance stores, storehouses, stables, guard-houses, and other Government buildings, with an immense amount of timber intended for building and other military purposes.

The following morning I weighed, leaving Captain Fanshawe with the Cossack in charge of this most important point, which required the utmost care and attention, as the enemy on several occasions threw out reconnoitring parties, as if inclined to attempt the recovery of the island.

I feel it due to Mr. George Giles, Master of this ship, and Mr. Geo. A. Macfarlane, Master of the Magicienne, to mention the zeal and attention with which they have sounded and buoyed, night and day, the intricate channels of this coast, enabling me (without the assistance of pilots) to got into many places, where our presence was least expected.

I have, &c.,
(Signed) H.R. YELVERTON,
Captain.

P.S. Owing to a change of wind to the east-ward, I regret to say that the village unfortunately caught fire from some Government buildings, and I fear much injury was done to it.

It is, however, a source of congratulation to be able to add that the fine Church sustained no damage whatever, owing to the precautions that were immediately taken to save it.

H.R. YELVERTON,
Captain.
Rear-Admiral the Hon. R.S. Dundas, C.B.
Commander-in-Chief.

Admiralty, August 20, 1855.

DESPATCHES, of which the following are copies, have been received at the Admiralty from Rear-Admiral the Honourable R.S. Dundas, Commander-in-Chief of Her Majesty's Ships and Vessels in the Baltic.

Duke of Wellington,
before Sweaborg, August, 13, 1855.

SIR,

I HAVE the honour to report, for the information of the Lords Commissioners of the Admiralty, that, after my arrival here on the 6th instant, with the squadron under my orders, I was joined the same evening by Rear-Admiral Pénaud, in the Tourville, and on the following day by the remainder of the French squadron, including, in addition to the ships of the line, five mortar-vessels and five gun-boats, with store ships and steam vessels.

On the 7th instant, the Amphion arrived from Nargen, completing the British squadron, to the ships and vessels named in the margin,* and the intention of Rear-Admiral Pénaud and myself being to commence operations against the Fortress and Arsenal of Sweaborg, no time was lost in making the necessary preparations.

My former reports will have informed their Lordships, that during the past year, and in the course of the last five months, the enemy has been actively employed in strengthening the defences of the place and completing the sea defences, by erecting batteries on every advantageous position and commanding every practicable approach to the harbour in this intricate navigation.

It has therefore formed no part of my plan to attempt a general attack by the ships on the defences; and the operations contemplated by the Rear-Admiral and myself were limited to such destruction of the fortress and arsenal as could be accomplished by means of mortars.

The intricate nature of the ground, from rocks a-wash and reefs under water, rendered it difficult to select positions for the mortar vessels at proper range. In completing the arrangements for this purpose, I have derived the greatest advantage from the abilities of Captain Sulivan, of Her Majesty's ship Merlin, and the positions ultimately chosen were in a curved line on either side of the Islet of Oterhall, with space in the centre reserved for the mortar vessels of the French squadron, as concerted with Rear-Admiral Pénaud.

The extremes of the line were limited, with reference to the extent of the range and the distance from the heavily armed batteries of Bak-Holmen to the eastward, and of Stora Rantan to the westward of Sweaborg; and a most effective addition to the force of the Allied squadrons consisted in a battery of 4 lighter mortars established by Admiral Pénaud on an islet in advance of Oterhall.

To carry these arrangements into effect I directed Captain Ramsay, of Her Majesty's ship Euryalus, with Captain Glasse, of the Vulture, Captain Vansittart, of the Magicienne, and Captain Stewart, of the Dragon, to anchor to the southward of Oterhall, and the mortar vessels, under the charge of Lieutenant the Hon. Augustus C. Hobart, of the Duke of Wellington, being distributed to the care of those officers, the whole were anchored on the evening of the 7th instant in position, in readiness to warp into action, and hawsers for that purpose were laid out before daylight. Much assistance in towing was rendered by the officers of the gun boats, and great praise is due to all concerned for their active exertions.

In the course of the same night Rear-Admiral Pénaud had commenced the establishment of his battery with sand bags, on the rocks within Oterhall, but the active arrangements could not be completed before the morning of the 9th instant.

During the whole of the previous day the royal standard of Russia was flying upon the citadel of Gustafsvard, but was not afterwards observed.

The success of our operations being dependent entirely on the state of the weather and the rapidity with which shells could be thrown, no time was lost in trying the ranges of the mortars which proved to be accurate, and general firing commenced soon after 7 o'clock. The direction of this service was confided to Captain T.M. Wemyss, of the Royal Marine Artillery, assisted by Captain Lawrence and Captain Schomberg, and every exertion was used by these officers to press the fire of the mortars to the fullest extent which could be deemed proper.

The gunboats, having been previously armed with additional guns of heavy calibre, removed temporarily from ships of the line, and the Stork and Snapper gunboats, being armed with Lancaster guns, I availed myself of the experience of Captain Hewlett to direct the fire of the two latter vessels to the greatest advantage, and his attention was specially directed to a three-decked ship of the line moored to block the passage between Gustafsvard and Bak Holmen.

Commander Preedy, of the ship bearing my flag, was directed to take the Starling and four other gun-boats under his orders, and to manoeuvre and attack the batteries in front of the mortar-vessels towards the west extremity of the line.

The remainder were distributed in a similar manner to stations assigned to them, with orders to engage the batteries and protect the mortar-vessels under the general direction of Captain Ramsay, assisted by Captains Glasse, Vansittart, and Stewart.

On the evening of the 8th instant, I had despatched Captain Key in Her Majesty's ship Amphion, to proceed off Stora Miölö, and to place himself under the orders of Captain Wellesley of Her Majesty's ship Cornwallis; and I instructed the latter officer to employ the Hastings and the Amphion, and to take advantage of any proper opportunity to engage the enemy at the east end of the Island of Sandhamn.

Captain Yelverton, in Her Majesty's ship Arrogant, was detached to the westward with the Cossack and Cruiser under his orders, and was directed to occupy the attention of troops which were observed to be posted on the Island of Drumsio, and to watch the movements of small vessels which had been noticed occasionally in creeks in that direction.

Early in the day I observed that the detached squadrons in both directions had opened fire upon the enemy, and the action was general upon all points. A rapid fire of shot and shells was kept up from the fortress for the first few hours upon the gun boats, and the range of the heavy batteries extended completely beyond the mortar vessels; but the continued motion of the gun boats, and the able manner in which they were conducted by the officers who commanded them, enabled them to return the fire with great spirit, and almost with impunity throughout the day.

About ten o'clock in the forenoon fires began first to be observed in the different buildings, and a heavy explosion took place on the Island of Vargon, which was followed by a second about an hour afterwards; a third, and far more important explosion, occurred about noon on the Island of Gustafsvard, inflicting much damage upon the defences of the enemy, and tending greatly to slacken the fire from the guns in that direction.

The advantage of the rapidity with which the fire from the mortars had been directed, was apparent in the continued fresh conflagrations, which spread extensively on the Island of Vargon.

The intricate nature of the reefs on which the gun-boats had occasionally grounded, compelled me also to recall them before sunset, and the fire of the enemy was slack. The boats of the fleet were then ordered to be assembled with rockets before dark, and under the direction of Captain Caldwell, in command of the ship bearing my flag, they maintained a continuous fire for upwards of three hours, which was attended with considerable success, causing fresh fires, and adding much to the general conflagration.

At daylight on the morning of the 10th instant, the positions of several of the mortar vessels had been advanced within easier range, and the gun-boats were again directed to engage.

The three-decked ship, which had been moored by the enemy to block and defend the channel between Gustafsvard and Bak Holmen, had been withdrawn during the night to a more secure position, but the fire from the batteries was increased, and the engagement was renewed with activity on both sides; fires continued to burn without intermission within the fortress, and about noon a column of smoke, heavier and darker than any which had yet been observed, and succeeded by bright flames, gave signs that the shells had reached combustible materials in the direction of the arsenal, the exact situation was at first concealed from our view, but the flames continuing to spread, it was soon evident that they extended beyond the Island of Vargon, and that many buildings on the Island of Svarto, were already in progess of destruction.

By the judicious management of the officers of artillery, a steady fire was kept up during the whole of the following night.

The rocket-boats in the evening were again assembled, when the gun-boats were recalled, and proceeded successively in separate divisions. The first, under the direction of Captain Seymour, of the Pembroke, made excellent practice, at a distance of about 2000 yards from the fortress; the second, under the direction of Captain Caldwell, at a later period of the night, succeeded also in adding to the fires already burning; but the glare of the flames exposing the boats to the view of the enemy, they maintained their ground, under a smart fire of bursting shells, with steady gallantry.

Considering the extent of injury which had now been inflicted upon the enemy, and reflecting that few buildings of importance remained to be destroyed on the Island of Vargon, and that those still standing upon Svarto were at the extreme extent of our range, and in positions where no shells had yet reached them, I was of opinion that no proportionate advantage was to be gained by continuing the fire during another day.

I accordingly despatched Captain Seymour, of Her Majesty's ship Pembroke, to communicate with Rear-Admiral Pénaud, and with the cordiality and ready concord which I have invariably experienced from that officer, arrangements were immediately concerted, and orders given to cease firing after daylight. Little fire, except at the rocket boats, had been returned by the enemy during the night, and it ceased almost entirely on his side before daylight, although the sea defences in general were little injured.

It remains for me to transmit now for their Lordships' information the enclosed reports of the proceedings of Captain Wellesley, of Her Majesty's ship Cornwallis, with the detached squadron to the eastward, on the 9th instant; and I beg you will inform their Lordships that the troops on Drumsio having offered no resistance to the ships under the orders of Captain Yelverton, he returned.to his former anchorage the same evening.

Enclosed are the lists of casualties which have occurred in execution of the service which I have had the honour to detail; and I am thankful to say that they have been fewer than could possibly have been expected under the fire to which those who were engaged were repeatedly exposed. Some of the most severe injuries are those which unfortunately occurred from explosions of the rockets, in the boats of the Hastings and Vulture.

Their Lordships will observe that I abstain entirely from reports on the proceedings of the squadron under the command of Rear-Admiral Pénaud, which will, no doubt, be fully and ably explained to his own Government; but I may be permitted to acknowledge my deep sense of the valuable co-operation they have afforded, and to express my admiration of the gallant conduct of those under his orders, and my warmest thanks for the cordial support which I have received.

I have much satisfaction in reporting in the most favourable manner on the conduct of the officers, seamen, and marines under my command; and I transmit, for their Lordships' information, the lists of the officers and others who were employed on the various detached services which occurred during the operations.

My best thanks are due to Rear-Admiral Sir Michael Seymour, who has at all times afforded me the most ready assistance.

From Commodore the Honourable Frederick Pelham, Captain of the Fleet, I have received the most valuable support, and the energy and ability with which he has performed the important duties of his station have tended greatly to further the execution of the service, and demand my warmest thanks.

I am much indebted to Captain Ramsay of Her Majesty's ship Euryalus, for his active and useful exertions, as well as to Captain Glasse, of the Vulture, and Captain Vansittart, of the Magicienne, and to none more than to Captain Stewart, of Her Majesty's ship Dragon, whose zeal and ready resource attracted my particular attention.

The services allotted to Captain Wellesley, as well as those assigned to Captains Seymour, Hewlett and Caldwell, were executed to my entire satisfaction; and my best thanks are due for the assistance rendered by Captain Hall, of Her Majesty's ship Exmouth, on several occasions.

Late on the evening of the 10th instant, Her Majesty's ship Merlin, under the command of Captain Sulivan, struck upon an unknown rock on ground, which he had himself repeatedly examined while conducting me along the line of the mortar vessels.

No blame whatever can attach to this officer on the occasion, and I gladly avail myself of the opportunity which is thus afforded me of calling the especial attention of their Lordships to the unwearied activity of this valuable officer. It is to the singular ability and zeal with which his arduous duties have been performed that much of the success of the operations of the fleet may be attributed; and I trust that I may be permitted on this occasion to recommend to the especial notice of their Lordships the services of Lieutenant R.B. Creyke, of that ship, whose conduct has been most favourably reported.

My especial thanks are due to the officers and men of the Royal Marine Artillery for the manner in which their important duties have been performed. The cool and steady courage with which they continued to conduct the duties of their stations deserves the highest praise; and I have much pleasure in calling their Lordship's attention to the services of Captain Wemyss, as well as to those of Captains Lawrence and Schomberg, of that distinguished corps.

Great praise is also due to the officers and crews of the mortar-vessels, on the occasion.

The admirable manner in which the officers in charge of gun-boats maintained their stations under fire, and the general activity of the crews of those vessels upon all occasions is deserving of the favourable notice of their Lordships; but in referring to the enclosed list of the Officers employed, I am unwilling to particularize any, when all have been highly deserving of their Lordships' favour; and the gallant conduct of the crews has been conspicuous.

I have, &c.,

(Signed) R.S. DUNDAS, Rear-Admiral

and Commander-in-Chief.

The Secretary of the Admiralty.

Duke of Wellington (bearing my flag), Exmouth (bearing the flag of Rear-Admiral Sir Michael Seymour), Euryalus, Arrogant, Pembroke, Cornwallis, Cossack, Merlin, Vulture, Hastings, Edinburgh, Amphion, Magicienne, Dragon, Belleisle, Cruizer, Geyser, Locust, Lightning, Eolus, Princess Alice, Volcano (arrived on the 10th).

Gun-Boats. – Starling, Lark, Thistle, Redwing, Magpie, Badger, Pelter, Snap, Dapper, Weazel, Stork, Pincher, Gleaner, Biter, Skylark, Snapper.

Mortar Vessels. – Rocket, Surly, Pickle, Blazer, Mastiff, Manly, Drake, Porpoise, Prompt, Sinbad, Carron, Redbreast, Beacon, Grappler, Havock, Growler.

Her Majesty's ship Cornwallis,
off Stora Miolo, August 9, 1855.

SIR,

I HAVE the honour to acquaint you that, in compliance with your memorandum of the 8th instant, on observing the mortar-vessels open fire this morning, I immediately weighed in Her Majesty's ship under my command, in company with the Hastings and Amphion, and proceeded to attack the forts at the south-east end of Sandhamn.

Our attack was more particularly directed against the battery on the south-eastern entrance, and another on Storholm; but, on arriving within long range, a general fire was opened from the whole of the batteries on the south side of Sandhamn.

A very brisk and extremely well-directed fire was kept up from the ships, which did considerable damage to one of the batteries on Sandhamn, and one or two of the guns were silenced for a short period, but no permanent effect was produced.

At 10.50, therefore, considering that the object contemplated in your memorandum had been attained, I made signal to discontinue the engagement, and anchored the ships in the positions they left this morning.

I deem it my duty to represent to you the effective co-operation I received from Captains Caffin and Key, as well as the steadiness and activity of the officers and crews of the ships engaged.

I have, &c.,
(Signed) GEORGE WELLESLEY,
Captain.
Rear-Admiral the Hon. R.S. Dundas, C.B.
Commander-in-Chief.

Her Majesty's ship Cornwallis,
off Stora Miolo, August 10, 1855.

SIR,

I HAVE the honour to inform you, that in further prosecution of your orders of the 8th instant, I despatched last night after dark, under the direction of Lieutenant Tattnall, senior of the Cornwallis, the barges and pinnaces of this ship, Hastings, and Amphion, each armed with rockets, to endeavour with them, if possible, to set fire to a frigate moored head and stern in Kung's Sound.

Moored as she was down under the land with only her lower masts in she was quite invisible, but the boats maintained a very well directed fire in her direction, which, although not effecting the object of setting her on fire, drew the attention of the enemy, whose batteries, as well as the frigate, opened fire on the boats, without, I am happy to say, any casualty to them.

I regret, however to add that in the pinnace of the Hastings two men were wounded, one severely, by the rocket bursting in the tube.

I beg to enclose a list of the officers employed on this occasion, and to express to you how much pleased I was with the manner in which Lieutenant Tattnall carried out my orders, and of the zeal and activity of the other officers and men employed.

I have, &c.,
(Signed) GEORGE G. WELLESLEY,
Captain.

Admiralty, September 4, 1855.

DESPATCHES, of which the following are copies, have been received at the Admiralty from Rear-Admiral the Honourable R.S. Dundas, Commander-in-Chief of Her Majesty's Ships and Vessels in the Baltic.

No. 431. Duke of Wellington,
in Nargen August, 27, 1855.

SIR,

I HAVE the honour to transmit, for the information of the Lords Commissioners of the Admiralty, a letter from Captain Warden, of Her Majesty's ship Ajax, enclosing a report, detailing the proceedings of Captain Henry C. Otter, in Her Majesty's ship Firefly, before Brandon, the sea-port of Wasa, in the Gulf of Bothnia, which are highly creditable to that officer, and to the officers and crew under his command; and I beg leave to recommend to the favourable notice of their Lordships the gallant conduct of Lieutenants Edward Burstal and John Ward, as well as that of Mr. John A. Bull, Second Master, and Mr. James W. Salter, the Gunner, on the occasion.

I have, &c.,
(Signed) R.S. DUNDAS, Rear-Admiral
and Commander-in-Chief.
The Secretary of the Admiralty.

No. 34. Ajax, in Fogle Fiord,
August, 22, 1855.

SIR,

I HAVE the honour to lay before you the accompanying report of Captain Otter, of the Firefly, of his proceedings between the 27th July, and 11th instant, at Brandon, in the neighbourhood of Wasa, whilst temporarily occupying that part of the station, together with a list of vessels taken, and property and vessels otherwise destroyed; and I desire to draw your favorable notice to this report, as it bears witness to the zeal and energy of Captain Otter in the performance of this service.

I have, &c.,
(Signed) FRED. WARDEN.
Rear-Admiral
The Hon. R.S. Dundas, C.B.,
&c. &c. &c.

Her Majesty's Ship Firefly,
Korsoren Beacon, August 11, 1855.

SIR,

I BEG to acquaint you that after leaving Fogle Fiord on the 27th ultimo, I communicated with Her Majesty's ship Harrier, and His Imperial Majesty's corvette D'Assas, on their stations, and on the evening of the 31st, despatched Her Majesty's ship Driver to you from Noorskar Light. At 10 A.M. on 1st August, I anchored Her Majesty's ship Firefly half a mile outside of Korsoren Beacon, and with the two paddle-box boats and the gig, accompanied by Lieutenant Ward and Mr. Bull, pushed on to the south-east; on our way we got information of a large barque at anchor to the eastward of Wasklöt, and also that there was a military force in the neighbourhood.

On arriving within two miles from Brandon, a telegraph was observed on a small island in Korsharn Fiord, signalizing with three large balls, and on pulling in towards it, two men in a boat pushed off from the land with a flag of truce; fortunately I did not fire, for the flag was so large I mistook it for the boat's mainsail, and concluded they were trying to escape.

This very improper opportunity of using a flag of truce could not be recognised, and I ordered the telegraph to be cut down, but released the men and their boat.

No time was now to be lost as the signal had been answered from the main; I therefore pushed on with all expedition, and on rounding the E. point of Wasklöt observed the object of our search in the mud, which with little difficulty was got off, and towed out of range of any guns that could be brought to bear. The prize proved to be the Vides of 300 tons, with from 200 to 300 casks of tar on board.

At midnight two Russian deserters came on board, and stated the troops have moved off to Wasa, on seeing the boats approaching, thinking an attack was contemplated on that place.

At 8.30 A.M., 2nd August, I returned to the Firefly, and immediately got under weigh for Korsoran Fiord, but the navigation was so difficult that it was not until 5.30 P.M., I came along side the prize. At 8.30 P.M., I weighed and proceeded towards Brandon, the seaport of Wasa, and a great ship-building place; it had immense magazines on an island, separated by a very narrow deep water channel from the town, with a custom-house and barracks.

At midnight, anchored within 400 yards of the town, and sprung the broadside to enfilade the channel and protect the boats, which were sent under Lieutenant Ward to examine the magazines. Some of them were opened, and found to be empty; others contained coal, tar, resin, salt, spars, anchors and cables, boats, salt fish, hawsers, and numerous piles of 3-inch deals, but no sails or rigging, as we were led to expect. On a few of the principal inhabitants joining us on the island, they were told that the sails of the barque must be given up, and they immediately sent to Wasa to Mr. Wolf a wealthy merchant and ship owner, but he refused. I therefore determined to burn the magazines; but as the wind was blowing directly on the town, I agreed to wait a reasonable time until a change took place, and gave the inhabitants notice that they were at liberty to remove anything from the island that belonged to them, except ship's stores; for this forbearance they expressed themselves very grateful.

Towards the afternoon, Lieutenant Burstal brought in a schooner, and reported having discovered two fine barques and two brigs, in a creek a mile and a half distant.

As the wind was still on the shore, and the destruction of the town inevitable had the magazines been fired, I directed the schooner to be hauled close into the island, and a working party to put some casks of tar and deals into her. Everything had the appearance of security; ladies were walking about the beach, parties of pleasure sailing round the ship, and the people employed taking their property from the island.

At 8 P.M., I landed to communicate with the First Lieutenant, and had just visited the sentry placed on a building platform, when a heavy fire of musketry, from different parts of the town, was opened upon the working party and the ship, and was immediately replied to by the latter, with shot and shell, which appears to have done great execution.

The deck of the schooner was so enfiladed, that it was impossible to get on board for the arms, and had it been practicable to do so not a man could be seen from her to fire at. Providentially all escaped on board uninjured, and Mr. Bull having returned in the paddle-box boats, with a fine barque in tow, a fire from the four guns and rifles was kept up, so hot, that in about an hour and a half the fusillade from the shore nearly ceased.

At midnight, I moved the ship into a better position for sinking the schooner, and the bows being nearly driven in by the shot, I proceeded to the destruction of the barque and two brigs, before the enemy could rescue them ; this was successfully performed with the assistance of the Second Master, Mr. Bull, and Mr. Salter, Gunner.

It was ascertained afterwards, from two different sources, that the enemy had 25 killed and from 4 to 18 wounded; the injury appears to have been inflicted chiefly by the first three shots, whilst the troops were drawn up abreast of the ship.

On our side I am thankful to report that no more serious casualties occurred than a man and a boy being struck with spent balls.

During the 6th and 7th the weather was so wet and boisterous that it was impossible to act against the enemy, but I ascertained during the night, that reinforcements had arrived to the amount of 200 or 300 sharpshooters and cossacks, with several guns.

On the morning of the 8th, the weather being moderate, I took up a position 1500 yards from the magazine, and the same distance from a battery of four guns, and opened fire upon the latter, which not being returned I commenced firing red-hot shot at the magazines.

At 2.30 P.M. smoke began to issue from the houses, and Lieutenant Ward, having volunteered to try and cut out the schooner, pushed in with paddle-box boat, and with great gallantry drove the soldiers three times out of the woods, but ultimately was obliged to retire before an overwhelming force secreted in the Custom-house; the boat was struck in many places, but I am thankful to say not a man hurt.

At 8 P.M., the principal magazines being all in a blaze and their destruction inevitable, I closed the battery to 1000 yards, but still receiving no return (though both guns and soldiers could be seen), and the ammunition nearly expended, I was backing out, when suddenly several heavy guns, from an elevated position masked by trees, opened fire, chiefly with shells, and at the same time the whole force of Riflemen, – and the power of these weapons may be imagined, when I mention that a ball cut through a spar on the bridge, two inches thick at a distance of 1,500 yards.

It is with the greatest pleasure I have to speak of the coolness of the officers and men at this trying juncture; the narrowness of the channel and shoalness of the water (at the most 2¾ fathoms), rendered it injudicious to attempt turning the Firefly round, and she was slowly backed astern, 1¼ miles, before she was out of range, an evolution which, from the lightness of the wind, was not performed under 40 minutes.

I cannot conclude without mentioning how much I am indebted to the First Lieutenant, Mr. Edw. Burstal, who so materially assisted in inflicting this serious blow on the enemy's property.

I have, &c.

(Signed) HENRY C. OTTER,

Captain.

Capt. Fred. Warden, C.B., H.M.S. Ajax.

CHAPTER 9

THE KERTCH EXPEDITION

Admiralty, June 6, 1855.

A DESPATCH, of which the following is a copy, has been received from Rear-Admiral Sir Edmund Lyons, Bart., G.C.B., Commander-in-Chief of Her Majesty's Ships and Vessels in the Mediterranean and Black Sea.

Royal Albert, Straits of Kertch,
May 26, 1855.

SIR,

I HAVE great pleasure in requesting you to inform the Lords Commissioners of the Admiralty that the Allied Forces are masters of the Straits of Kertch, and that they have in the Sea of Azof a powerful steam flotilla, of light draught of water, capable of cutting off the enemy's supplies, and harassing him at all points; and moreover, that the means are at hand for sending in a vast number of gun-boats of the lighter draught, if it should be found desirable to do so.

My letter of the 22nd instant, No. 396, will have informed their Lordships that an Allied Expedition, consisting of 15,000 men of all arms, and five batteries of artillery, were then on the point of leaving the anchorage off Sevastopol, for Kertch, and my message by electric telegraph will have announced the complete success of that expedition; but it now remains for me to give an account of our proceedings for their Lordships' information:

The Fleet, which consisted of Her Majesty's ships named in the margin,* and a French Fleet of nearly equal force, under the command of my very gallant and energetic colleague, Vice-Admiral Bruat, assembled off the Straits of Kertch at early dawn on the birthday of Her Most Gracious Majesty the Queen, and both armies and navies confidently anticipated a successful celebration of that auspicious day. The Fleets steamed rapidly up to Kameish, where the army landed under cover of the guns of the steam-frigates, and immediately ascended the heights without opposition, whilst the steamers of light draught of water pushed on towards Kertch and Enikalé; and the enemy, apparently taken by surprise at the rapidity of these movements, and at the imposing appearance of the expedition, blew up his fortifications on both sides of the straits, mounting not less than fifty guns (new and of heavy calibre), which have fallen into our possession, and retired after having destroyed 3 steamers and several other heavily armed vessels, as well as large quantities of provisions, ammunition and stores, thus leaving us masters of the entrance into the Sea of Azof, without our having sustained any loss whatever.

4. As the disembarkation was unopposed, in consequence of the fire of the steam frigates having arrested the advance of the enemy, there was no field for the gallantry that animated every one in the expedition; but the duties they had to perform were very arduous, and I should be doing injustice to them and to my own feelings if I were not to say that no Commander-in-Chief was ever more ably assisted than I am by the captains and those under their command – one and all follow the admirable example of the zealous and talented second in command, Rear-Admiral Stewart, and they could not possibly do better. There was, however, an incident during the day that called forth the admiration of both fleets, and which deserves to be particularly noticed, Lieutenant McKillop, whose gun-vessel, the Snake, was not employed like the others in landing troops, dashed past the forts after an enemy's steamer, and although he soon found himself engaged not only with her but also with two others who came to her support, he persevered, and by the cleverness and extreme rapidity of his manoeuvres, prevented the escape of all three, and they were consequently destroyed by the enemy, and the Snake had not a man hurt, though shot passed though the vessel.

5. Yesterday Admiral Bruat and I accompanied the combined steam flotilla, named in the margin,† into the Sea of Azof, and despatched them, under the orders of Captain Lyons, of the Miranda, on the interesting and important service they have before them.

6. Had this expedition been deferred but a short time longer, there would have been many and great difficulties to overcome, for the enemy was actively employed in strengthening the sea defences, and in replacing the sunken vessels which had been carried away by the current during the winter months.

Of the 40 vessels sunk last year some still remain, and a French steamer touched upon one of them yesterday. It appears that the enemy did not succeed in destroying the coals, either at Kertch or Enikalé, so that about 17,000 tons remain, which will be available for our steamers.

7. It will be evident to their Lordships, that the rapid operations which I have had the honour and happiness to describe to them, could not have been brought to so satisfactory a conclusion, if the most perfect understanding, and the most hearty good will towards each other, had not prevailed throughout the allied fleets and armies.

I am, &c.

(Signed) EDMUND LYONS,

Rear-Admiral and Commander-in-Chief.

The Secretary of the Admiralty,

London.

Royal Albert, Hannibal, Algiers, Agamemnon, St. Jean d'Acre, Princess Royal, Sidon, Valorous, Leopard, Tribune, Simoom, Furious, Highflyer, Terrible, Miranda, Sphinx, Spitfire, Gladiator, Vesuvius, Curlew, Swallow, Caradoc, Stromboli, Ardent, Medina, Wrangler, Viper, Lynx, Recruit, Arrow, Banshee, Snake, Beagle.

†*Miranda, Vesuvius, Curlew, Swallow, Stromboli, Ardent, Medina, Wrangler, Viper, Lynx, Recruit, Arrow, Snake, Beagle, and five French steam-vessels.*

War-Department June 13, 1855.

LORD PANMURE has this day received four Despatches and their Enclosures, of which the following are copies, addressed to His Lordship by Field-Marshal the Lord Raglan, G.C.B.

Before Sevastopol,
May 29, 1855.

MY LORD,

SIR EDMUND LYONS'S telegraphic despatch of the 25th, which was forwarded from hence on the morning of the 27th, and one from me that immediately followed, will have informed your Lordship that the Allied Expedition to Kertch reached its destination on the morning of the 24th, and the troops having landed without delay, and the war steamers drawing little water having pushed on towards Kertch and Euikali, that all the objects in contemplation were accomplished in twenty-four hours without any resistance on the part of the enemy, who blew up the fortifications on both sides of the passage and retired, thus leaving us masters of the Sea of Azov, to be speedily occupied by a French and English flotilla.

I have now the honour to lay before you a copy of the report of Lieutenant-General Sir G. Brown, commanding the allied troops; and in congratulating your Lordship, which I do most cordially, on the complete success of the operation, I have the greatest satisfaction in drawing your attention to the promptitude with which the disembarkation was effected, to the efficient measures taken by the Lieutenant-General to ensure his position and attain the objects in view, and to the just tribute which he pays in his interesting narrative to the judicious arrangements of Admirals Bruat and Sir E. Lyons, and to the zeal and energy displayed by the officers and men of the allied fleets in carrying them out under their vigilant superintendence, as well as to the cordial co-operation and assistance of General Dantemarre, commanding the French Division, and Reschid Pasha, commanding the Turkish troops.

I have not received any further advices from Sir G. Brown or Sir E. Lyons.

Nothing material has occurred in front of the new position taken up by the Allies on the morning of the 25th. The enemy have made no movement from the high ground towards the advance, but they have displayed a considerable force to-day on the Inkerman heights.

Convoys continue to arrive on the north side of Sevastopol.

A further portion of the Sardinian Contingent has arrived, under General La Marmora's brother, the details of which I have not yet received.

I have, &c.,

RAGLAN.

The Lord Panmure, &c. &c. &c.

Enclosure 1.

Yeni Kali, May 25, 1855.

MY DEAR LORD RAGLAN,

THE Expedition to this place so far has proved entirely successful, and we have got possession of all we proposed without striking a blow, and almost without firing a shot.

On leaving the anchorage off Sevastopol, on the 22nd, the night became so foggy that the fleet made but little progress towards its destination, but the whole of the ships and steamers reached the rendezvous, four leagues off Cape Takli, soon after daylight on the morning of the 24th, when it was speedily determined to run at once in for the spot at which, as your Lordship is aware, it was originally proposed to disembark, and which is a fine smooth bay, round a low point running out immediately under the village of Kazatch Bouroun.

The water in the straits is so shallow that large ships cannot ascend higher than about three miles from this spot, but the steamers and vessels in which the whole of the British infantry and artillery were embarked, could get at least a mile nearer to it.

All the vessels got as high up as the depth of water would permit, and came to an anchor about eleven, when the English and French troops began to get into the boats, and small steamers, which were assigned to them, towed them to the shore, and the gun-boats and smaller war-steamers were stationed to scour the beach, and protect the disembarkation.

Although we had observed some six or eight pieces of light artillery following us along the shore, no opposition was made to the disembarkation, and the first of the troops reached the shore at ten o'clock, which, as soon as they were formed, were pushed on to occupy the village on the rising ground bordering the marshy plain, on which they landed for the purpose of covering the remainder of the disembarkation. As they were the most numerous, and as your Lordship had done so on a former occasion, I placed the French on the right, and the British troops on the left, intending to hold the Turkish Contingent in reserve.

Soon after the disembarkation had commenced, several loud explosions were heard, and it was soon discovered that the enemy had blown up the magazines of all his batteries on Cape St. Paul, and was retiring by the road leading to Theodosia or Kaffa. It therefore became exceedingly desirable that I should advance to occupy the ridge of which the cape is the continuation; but as only a few of the Turkish troops had got landed, and but little of the artillery, I contented myself by requesting General Dantemarre to patrol to the cape and towards Kertsch, and took up the best position I could find for the security of the troops, and the protection of the disembarkation of all the necessary material and horses during the night, just before dark – which, in an open steppe, where we were exposed to the attacks of cavalry, was an operation of some difficulty.

In the course of the evening, several more loud explosions were heard, and it was soon discovered that he had also blown up and abandoned the whole of his works here, and along the coast between this and Kertch, and spiked all the guns. He had also set fire to and destroyed some large corn magazines in Kertch, as well as two steamers in the harbour; and the Cossacks, as usual, burnt all the forage and farm-houses in their way.

As soon as the batteries on Cape St. Paul were abandoned, or soon before, some of the smaller war-steamers were enabled to round Cape Ackbouroun, and enter the Bay of Kertch, when they engaged and endeavoured to cut off some of the enemy's steamers attempting to escape into the Sea of Azof. They succeeded, I believe, in capturing a small one; but the other two managed to get through.

The disembarkation of horses, guns, and materiel went on during the whole night, under the zealous and active superintendence of Rear-Admiral Houston Stewart and Captain Sir Thomas Pasley; but, with all this, there was a good deal to be done at daylight this morning, and I was ultimately compelled to proceed with only three of the guns of the Turkish Contingent, and without any of their officers' horses.

Under the circumstances, however, I considered it imperative to proceed, and the whole force marched off their ground at six this morning, – the French in contiguous columns, followed by their artillery; the British in echelons of columns, covering their flank, and their own artillery and baggage; and the Turkish troops in contiguous columns of battalions, covering the rear of the whole, until they approached the precincts of Kertch, when the whole of the troops broke into an ordinary column of route. The town of Kertch is clean, and remarkably well built, and the troops passed through it with the greatest regularity and without the slightest disorder; subsequently the day became excessively hot, and the march being a long one, the men suffered greatly from fatigue and want of water, which was only to be found at occasional wells. We managed to get in here, however, by one o'clock, where we were soon after visited by the three Admirals, and found a large squadron of small steamers and gun-boats, ready to proceed into the Sea of Azof, under the command of Captain Lyons, of the Miranda.

The result of these operations, besides the opening of the passage into that sea, and the destruction of the enemy's works, has been the capture of upwards of fifty of his guns, many of them of the largest calibre and the best construction; and if the enterprize has from circumstances not added greatly to the glory of Her Majesty's arms, it has, as already stated, so far been attended by complete success.

That success, however, is mainly to be attributed to the judicious arrangements of Admirals Bruat and Sir E. Lyons, and to their indefatigable attention in carrying them out, as well as to the able and willing assistance they have received from the Captains and other officers of the French and British navy under their respective commands; nor must I omit to mention the invariable and willing assistance I have on all occasions received in the course of this service from General Dantemarre, commanding the French Division, and from Reschid Pasha, commanding the Sultan's troops.

I omitted to state, that in passing through Kertch this morning, observing that an iron foundry there had been employed in the manufacture of shot and shells, as well as in casting Minié bullets, I caused it to be destroyed, with all its new and expensive machinery.

Yours, &c.,
G. BROWN.
F.M. the Lord Raglan, G.C.B.,
&c., &c., &c.

Admiralty, June 13, 1855.

DESPATCHES, of which the following are copies, have been received from Rear-Admiral Sir Edmund Lyons, Bart., G.C.B., Commander-in-Chief of Her Majesty's Ships and Vessels in the Mediterranean and Black Sea.

SNAKE'S ENGAGEMENT WITH RUSSIAN STEAMERS.

Royal Albert, Straits of Kertch,
June 2, 1855.

SIR,

IN my letter of the 26th ult., No. 398, I had the pleasure of bringing under the notice of the Lords Commissioners of the Admiralty the gallant, able, and successful way in which Lieutenant Henry F. McKillop had conducted Her Majesty's steam gun-vessel Snake, under his command, on the day the Allied Forces obtained possession of the Straits of Kertch.

2. I have now to request you to lay before their Lordships the enclosed copy of a letter which I have received from Lieutenant McKillop, reporting his proceedings on that day; and their Lordships will observe that he speaks in high terms of his officers

and ship's company, and particularly so of Mr. Nathaniel B. Herbert, Second Master, and Mr. Sydney E. Wright, Assistant-Paymaster in charge.

I am, &c.
(Signed) EDMUND LYONS,
Rear-Admiral and Commander-in-Chief.
The Secretary of the Admiralty,
London.

(REPORTING ENGAGEMENT.)

Her Majesty's ship Snake, off Enikale,
24th May, 1855.

SIR,

I HAVE the honour to inform you that in obedience to your signal granting me permission to intercept a Russian war steamer, that I proceeded into Kertch Bay, exchanging shots with the batteries at Akbourno in passing.

I succeeded in cutting off the steamer and engaging her, but not until she had placed herself under the protection of the forts of Enikale; after a sharp fire on both sides, for three-quarters of an hour, I was fortunate in succeeding in setting her on fire with Lancaster shells, from which she blew up – the crew with difficulty getting away. She had apparently soldiers on board. During this engagement the forts at Enikale hulled the ship, and kept up a well-directed and continuous fire the whole time, which was returned with apparent good effect with our heavy shell.

Three steamers also came down from the entrance (to the Sea of Azoff) and opened fire on us with very long range guns, their shot frequently passing over us at about 4000 yards. I continued to engage the batteries and steamers after the arrival of the ships sent up to my assistance, until recalled by signal from the Miranda.

The whole of the sailing vessels standing towards the Sea of Azov were intercepted, and afterwards captured; two steamers, also intercepted in Kertch Bay, were blown up by their own crews, and a gun-boat sunk.

The batteries along the coast, which fired upon us whilst chasing the steamer, also were blown up.

I should feel I was neglecting my duty unless I mentioned the zealous and creditable manner in which the officers and crew performed their duties; being very short handed rendered working the guns for so many hours a work of great labour.

I beg to recommend for your favourable consideration Mr. N.B. Herbert (Second Master in charge), who with much skill conducted the ship through the intricate and comparatively unknown passage, under the guns of Akbourno, and inside the shoal of Enikale, without any accident.

I am equally indebted to Mr. Sydney E. Wright, Assistant-Paymaster (an officer of long and meritorious service), for his assistance as a volunteer executive, who, with Dr. Roche and Mr. George Wilson (Senior Engineer), manned and worked the 12-pounder howitzer, sinking a gun-boat.

I am happy that no casualties occurred, and the Snake received but little damage, one shot through the mizen rigging, carrying it away, and one through the hull at the water-line.

I am, &c.,
(Signed) H.F. McKILLOP.
Lieutenant and Commander.
Rear-Admiral Sir Edmund
Lyons, Bart., G.C.B.,
Commander-in-Chief.

OPERATIONS IN THE SEA OF AZOF.

Royal Albert, Straits of Kertch,
June 2, 1855,

SIR,

I HAVE the honour to transmit to you here-with, copies of two letters that have been addressed to me by Captain Edmund M. Lyons, of the Miranda, in which he reports the proceedings of the Allied Steam-squadrons, under his orders, during the first four days of their appearance in the Sea of Azof.

In that short space of time the squadrons forced the enemy to run on shore, burn to the water's edge and abandon four steamers of war, under the command of Rear-Admiral Wolff; they bombarded Arabat and blew up the powder magazine, and they destroyed 246 merchant vessels, which were employed in the conveyance of supplies to the Russian Army in the Crimea, as well as immense magazines of corn and flour at Berdiansk and Genitchesk, containing at least two months' rations for an army of one hundred thousand men.

Captain Lyons is justly and deeply sensible of what he owes to the cordial and efficient co-operation of Captain Sédaiges, and our Allies, acting under the orders of that distinguished officer; nor is he less sensible of, or less grateful for, the able support he has received from every one in the British squadron under his own immediate orders.

4. I beg leave to recommend to their Lordships' particular notice the mention which Captain Lyons makes of the very important services rendered by the boats of the squadron on several occasions, under the command of that active, zealous, and excellent officer, Lieutenant J.F.C. Mackenzie, of the Miranda, as well as of the gallant and successful exploit of Lieutenant Cecil W. Buckley, of the Miranda,

Lieutenant Hugh T. Burgoyne, of the Swallow, and Mr. John Roberts, Gunner, of the Ardent, which was productive of the most important results.

I am, &c.,
(Signed) EDMD. LYONS,
Rear-Admiral and Commander-in-Chief.

Her Majesty's ship, Miranda,
off Arabat, Sea of Azoff,
May 28, 1855.

SIR,

I HAVE the honour to inform you that on hauling down your flag on the afternoon of the 25th, I proceeded with the steam vessels under my orders named in the margin,* and the French steamer, Lucifer, towards Berdiansk; at dark, we stopped for the French steamers, Megere, Brandon and Fulton. These having joined, at 3 A.M. on the 26th, we all went on in company; at 3.30 P.M. on that day, we anchored off the lighthouse, on the spit at Berdiansk, in such a position as to command the harbour and beach and a large number of merchant vessels; I then sent the boats of the squadrons under Commander Sherard Osborn, accompanied by the boats of the French ships to destroy these vessels, as well as some lying about 4 miles off, and a storehouse; all this was completed by dark; during this time steamers of the two squadrons were chasing and destroying vessels in other directions.

At daylight of the 27th I weighed with the ships under my orders, accompanied by the four French steamers, and anchored off the town of Berdiansk, the Miranda in 15 feet, and the gun boats in proportionally less water, in a position which effectually commanded the town and beach. Here we found run on shore and burnt to the water's edge, and abandoned, the four steamers of war which had escaped from Kertch, under the command of Rear-Admiral Wolff, whose flag was flying in the Moloditz. I now landed the small-arm men and marines of the squadron under Commander Lambert of the Curlew, accompanied by those of the French ships, with orders to destroy all shipping and Government stores, but to respect private property. This was done without molestation, although we had information that 800 Cossacks with guns were at Petioskoi, five miles off. Many vessels were destroyed, and corn stores to the estimated value of £50,000. An 8-inch 62-cwt. gun was also recovered from the wreck of one of the Russian steamers, and is now on board the Miranda.

Immediately the boats returned, the squadrons weighed for Arabat; I at the same time detached the Swallow and Wrangler to Genitchesk, to command the entrance to the Putrid Sea, and the Curlew to cruize between Krivaia Spit and Sand Island, and thus prevent vessels escaping us by getting up the Don.

3. On the morning of the 28th we arrived off Arabat, and engaged the fort (mounting 30 guns), for an hour and a half, at the end of which time a shell blew up the enemy's magazine; the ships having been ordered to keep at shell range, and being

well-handled, had only one casualty, the chief engineer of the Medina being slightly wounded by a splinter; the French senior officer's ship received two shots in the hull, but fortunately no one was hurt. The enemy must have lost many men, from the precision with which the shells burst in his works, independently of that caused by the explosion.

The Commanders of the vessels employed† deserve every credit for the skilful manner in which they manoeuvred their vessels in a very strong breeze and shoal water, without a single accident; and I may be permitted to say none were more distinguished than our gallant Allies. The large garrison at Arabat rendering any attempt at landing out of the question, I now proceeded for Genitchesk, parting, with a regret, from Captain de Sédaiges and his squadron, who left at the same time for Kertch. I take this opportunity of mentioning the efficient, cordial, and hearty co-operation I received on every occasion from M. de Sédaiges and the ships under his orders, and my hope that it may again be my good fortune to have him for my colleague.

4. The allied squadrons have destroyed upwards of 100 vessels during the three days they have been in this sea, principally laden with provisions for the Russian army in the Crimea; had we sent these vessels in as prizes, we should have lost much valuable time, and not been able to effect so many captures. The active and zealous way in which the officers and ships' companies perform their duties, and the cheerful manner in which they suffer this pecuniary loss, for the benefit of the service, will I trust meet with your approbation.

I have, &c.,
(Signed) E.M. LYONS,
Captain.

Sub-Inclosure to No. 1.

Name of Officer slightly wounded off Arabat on the 28th May, 1855, belonging to Her Majesty's steam-vessel Medina.

Mr. W.H. Houghton, Assistant Engineer, First Class.

(Signed) E.M. LYONS,
Captain and Senior Officer.

Her Majesty's ship Miranda, off the town of Genitchesk, May 29, 1855.

SIR,

I HAVE the honour to inform you, that I arrived here shortly after dark last night, with Her Majesty's ships under my orders, and joined the Swallow and Wrangler, which ships had already destroyed or captured all the vessels in this neighbourhood outside the Straits of Genitchesk; but a very great number had passed the straits, which are only fifty yards wide, and are commanded by the low cliffs on which the town is built, and were moored inside under the cliff.

At six o'clock this morning, I sent Commander Craufurd with a flag of truce, to demand the immediate surrender of all these vessels, and of the immense corn stores for the supply of the army in the Crimea, and of all Government property of every description; stating that if these terms were complied with I would spare the town and respect private property, but that if not the inhabitants were immediately to leave the town.

Commander Craufurd was met by an officer, of apparently high rank, who refused to accede to these terms, saying that any attempt to land or to destroy the vessels would be resisted.

The enemy at this time had six field-pieces in position, and with about 200 men with them, and, visible from the mast-head drawn up behind the town, a battalion of infantry, besides Cossacks.

Having allowed till 9 A.M., for the reconsideration of the refusal to deliver up the vessels and stores, and receiving no answer, I at that time hauled down the flag of truce, and placed the steamers as near to the town and the passage into the Putrid Sea, as the depth of the water would allow, but they were only able to approach within long range. Seeing that if the enemy, who had removed his guns from their former position, could place them in the town, so as to command the passage, and that if he could place his infantry in a similar manner, it would be impossible for the boats to pass the channel and destroy the vessels and stores, I directed the ships to shell the town, which they did so effectually, that the boats, as per enclosure, under the command of Lieutenant J.F.C. Mackenzie, got safely through the passage, and set fire to the shipping (73 in number), and the corn stores. This service was ably performed by Lieutenant Mackenzie, and the boats returned without accident.

4. The wind having shifted about two hours after the boats came off, some of the corn stores did not catch fire; conceiving the destruction of this corn, as well as of some more distant vessels in so favourable a position for supplying the Russian armies in the Crimea, to be of the utmost importance, I sent the boats again, commanded and officered as before, although I was aware that from the enemy having had time to make preparations, it would be a hazardous enterprize. The ships accordingly resumed their fire upon the town, and the boats proceeded. Lieutenant Cecil W. Buckley of this ship; Lieutenant Hugh T. Burgoyne, of the Swallow; and Mr. John Roberts, gunner of the Ardent, volunteered to land alone and fire the stores; this offer I accepted, knowing the imminent risk there would be in landing a party in presence of such a superior force, and out of gun-shot of the ships. This very dangerous service they most gallantly performed, narrowly escaping the Cossacks, who all but cut them off from their boat; at the same time Lieutenant Mackenzie pushed on and burned the remaining vessels, the enemy opening a fire from four field-guns and musketry, placed almost within point blank range of the boats.

Everything being now effectually accomplished, the boats returned. Although several of them were struck by grape and case shot, most fortunately only one man was slightly wounded. Lieutenant Mackenzie speaks in high terms of the coolness and excellent behaviour of all employed under his orders; and I trust I may be allowed to bring to your notice the conspicuous merit of Lieutenant Mackenzie himself on this occasion, when more than ninety vessels, and also corn for the Russian army of the value of £100,000 were destroyed, owing to his gallantry and ability, with so trifling a loss as one man slightly wounded.

Since the squadron entered the Sea of Azoff, four days ago, the enemy has lost four steamers of war, 246 merchant vessels, also corn and flour magazines to the value of at least £150,000.

I have, &c.,
(Signed) E.M. LYONS,
Captain.

A List of Boats under the command of Lieutenant J.F.C. Mackenzie, at Genitchesk,
on the 29th day of May, 1855.

Miranda.-
Pinnace – One 12-pounder howitzer, with small arms for boat's crew.
Cecil W. Buckley, Lieutenant.
Benjamin Crabbe, Assistant-Surgeon.

1st Cutter –
Wm. H. Lilley, additional Boatswain.
2nd Cutter – Small arms for boat's crew.
John Liddell, Midshipman.
Henry Cooper, additional Boatswain.

Vesuvius.-
Two Paddle-box Boats – One 24-pounder howitzer in each boat,
    with small arms.
Herbert Campion, Senior Lieutenant.
John H. Patterson, Surgeon.
Shuldham Hill, Assistant Clerk.
William Kirk, Boatswain.

Stromboli.-
Starboard Paddle-box Boat – One 24-pounder howitzer, with small arms
    for boat's crew.
John F. Ross, Lieutenant.
John S. Adams, Assistant-Surgeon.
Arthur K. Forde, Mate.

Port Paddle-box Boat – One 24-pounder rocket tube, with rockets and
small arms.
Augustus H. Webb, Acting-Mate.

Ardent.-
1st Cutter – Small arms for crew.
E.P. Bedwell, Acting 2nd Master, only employed in second attack. One
man slightly wounded.
2nd Cutter – One 12-pounder rocket tube, with rockets and small arms.
J. Roberts, Gunner.

Swallow.-
Gig – One 12-pounder rocket tube, and small arms for boat's crew.
T. Burgoyne, Lieutenant.

(Signed) E.M. LYONS,
Captain and Senior Officer.

*Name of one man Wounded at Genitchesk, on the 29th day of May, 1855, belonging
to Her Majesty's Steam-vessel Ardent.*

William Walker, Captain maintop, received a contusion on left knee by a shrapnell
shell.

(Signed) E.M. LYONS.
Captain and Junior Officer.

NAVAL OPERATIONS IN THE STRAITS OF KERTCH.

Royal Albert, Straits of Kertch,
May 30, 1855.

SIR,

I HAVE the honour to transmit to you, for the information of the Lords
Commissioners of the Admiralty, a copy of a letter that has been addressed to me by
Captain Lyons, of the Miranda, recounting the measures he took for obliging the
enemy to abandon his last hold in these straits, and reporting his having entered the
Sea of Azof with the squadron I had placed under his orders.

I am, &c.,
(Signed) EDMUND LYONS,
Rear-Admiral and Commander-in-Chief.
To the Secretary of the Admiralty.

Her Majesty's ship, Miranda, at anchor
above Yenikale, May 25, 1855.

SIR,

I HAVE the honour to inform you that having yesterday afternoon taken under my orders the ships named in the margin,‡ I, in pursuance of your orders passed the Straits of Kertch, and anchored for the night just out of gun shot of the batteries of Yenikale. At 7 P.M. the enemy blew up the magazines and these batteries with a tremendous explosion.

At 4 o'clock this morning I sent Mr. George Williams, Master of this ship, to find and buoy a channel through the straits on the Yenikale side; and I desired Lieutenant Armytage in the Viper to follow as near as possible, and endeavour to pass the straits and get into a position to threaten the retreat of the Russian garrison of the forts on the Chesura Spit side of the strait, by commanding the neck of the spit; at the same time I sent Lieutenant Aynsley, in the Lynx, to pass round by the Taman Lake and take up a position to command the rear of the Russian forts. This service was ably performed by these officers, and on their obtaining the assigned positions the enemy, as I had anticipated, exploded his magazines, abandoned his works, and made a precipitate retreat under the fire of the Viper's guns. Mr. Williams now returned having found and buoyed a 16 feet channel, and I immediately weighed and, with the vessels under my orders, proceeded through the Straits of Yenikale; thus we became complete masters of the Sea of Azof.

I have, &c.,
(Signed) E.M. LYONS, Captain.
Rear-Admiral Sir Edmund Lyons,
Bart., G.C.B.

OPERATIONS IN THE STRAITS

Royal Albert, Straits,
June 2, 1855.

SIR,

IN my letter, No. 398, of the 26th ult. I stated that we had captured fifty of the enemy's guns. It now appears that more than a hundred guns have fallen into our hands in the different sea defences, many of them of heavy calibre, and remarkably well cast. Those which may not be required for the land defences which the Allied Armies are now constructing, will be shipped and sent to England and France.

It has been ascertained from the Custom House returns, that the enemy on evacuating Kertch, on the 24th ultimo, destroyed 4,166,000 lbs. of corn and 508,000 lbs. of flour. This quantity, taken together with what has been destroyed by the Allied Squadrons in the Sea of Azof, comprises nearly four months' rations for an army of a hundred thousand men; and it seems that shortly before our arrival the enemy had commenced sending towards Sevastopol daily convoys of about fifteen hundred waggons, each containing half a ton weight of grain or flour.

4. Sir George Brown confidently expects that by the 7th instant Enikalé will be in such a state of defence as fully to justify his leaving it in charge of the Ottoman troops now here, under the command of Hadji Reschid Pacha, and that the British and French forces will be at liberty to proceed to the attack of Anapa and Soujak Kaleh, in order to drive the enemy out of his last holds on the coast of Circassia.

I am, &c.,

E. LYONS,

Rear-Admiral.

To the Secretary of the Admiralty.

*Vesuvius, Curlew, Swallow, Stromboli, Medina, Wrangler, Viper, Lynx, Recruit, Arrow, Snake, Beagle.

†Vesuvius, Commander S. Osborne; Stromboli, Commander C.P. Coles; Ardent, Lieutenant W. Horton; Medina, Lieutenant H.B. Beresford; Viper, Lieutenant W. Armytage; Lynx, Lieutenant C.M. Aynsley; Recruit, Lieutenant G.F. Day; Arrow, Lieutenant W.K. Jolliffe; Snake, Lieutenant H. McKillop; Beagle, Lieutenant W.N.W. Hewett.

‡Vesuvius, Curlew, Swallow, Stromboli, Ardent, Medina, Wrangler, Lynx, Recruit, Arrow, Viper, Snake, Beagle.

Rear-Admiral Sir Edmund
Lyons, Bart., G.C.B.,
Commander-in-Chief.
Admiralty, June 28, 1855.

DESPATCHES, of which the following are copies, have been received from Rear-Admiral Sir Edmund Lyons, Bart., G.C.B., Commander-in-Chief of Her Majesty's Ships and Vessels in the Mediterranean and Black Sea.

OPERATIONS IN THE SEA OF AZOF.

Royal Albert, Straits of Kertch,
June 12, 1855.

SIR,

I HAVE the honour to enclose, for the information of the Lords Commissioners of the Admiralty, copies of three letters from Captain Lyons, of the Miranda, reporting the destruction of Mariaupol, Ghiesk, and Kiten near Arabat, of immense quantities of grain, flour, and hay, destined for the supply of the enemy's army in the Crimea; so great was the quantity that in some cases the conflagration had not entirely subsided when last seen on the eighth day.

2. Thus, in the space of a fortnight, the Sea of Azof has been swept by the Allied squadrons under Captain Lyons's orders, and the enemy deprived not only of the supplies which already existed in the different depôts, but also of the means of transporting the coming crops.

3. I have also the honour to enclose a copy of a letter from Captain Lyons, speaking in terms of high praise of the officers and men employed in the launches of the fleet, and in the Danube and Sulina tenders.

4. Considerable skill, vigour, and promptitude have characterised these operations, and I trust that their Lordships may consider that credit is due to all employed in them. Opportunities offered for individual distinction, which were eagerly seized by the officers whom Captain Lyons particularly mentions, and whom I beg leave to recommend to their Lordships' favourable consideration.

I am, &c.,
(Signed) EDMUND LYONS,
Rear-Admiral and Commander-in-Chief.

> *To the Secretary of the Admiralty.*
> *Her Majesty's ship, Miranda,*
> *Mariaupol, 5th June, 1855.*

SIR,

I HAVE the honour to inform you that having anchored yesterday evening off this place with the ships under my orders, and six French steamers, I sent Lieutenant-Commander Horton of the Ardent, accompanied by a French officer with similar orders, at daylight this morning, to demand the surrender of the place, on exactly the same terms as those offered by us at Taganrog; and I desired him to express to the authorities, the earnest hope of myself and of the French senior officer, that they would not oblige us to resort to measures, which would endanger the whole town, as our object was to destroy all contraband of war, but to respect private property.

2. At the expiration of the delay granted, no authorised person appearing, I sent the line-of-battle ships' launches (lent to the squadron) and the boats of the ships under my orders, with all the marines under Lieutenant Macnamara, R.M.A., the whole commanded by Lieutenant J.F.C. Mackenzie, of this ship, to effect our object by force; the French boats accompanying ours.

3. On the marines and a body of French small-arm men landing, under cover of the launches' guns, 600 Cossacks, commanded by a Colonel, evacuated the town, and the marines and the French small-arm men advanced and took possession of it; the very extensive stores of grain were fired and destroyed by parties under the directions of Captain Lejeune, of the French Navy, and of Lieutenant Swinburne, of this ship, every care being taken to cause as little damage to the town as possible.

4. Thus was a considerable town on the military high road from the provinces of the Don to the Crimea (the only one left since our occupation of this sea), held

unmolested possession of by a small body of British marines and French small-arm men, for five hours, while immense stores of grain were destroyed.

5. The grain, plank, find other stores considered as contraband of war, being effectually destroyed, the whole party re-embarked without the slightest accident.

6. Lieutenant Mackenzie conducted this service with excellent judgment; and he speaks in high terms of the judicious manner in which First Lieutenant Macnamara, Royal Marine Artillery, posted the Royal Marines and Royal Marine Artillery under his orders, in presence of a superior force, who were thus deterred from venturing to molest them.

I have, &c.,
(Signed) E.M. LYONS,
Captain.
Rear-Admiral Sir Edmund Lyons,
Bart., G.C.B.

No. 2 Enclosure.

Her Majesty's ship, Miranda,
off the town of Gheisk, June 6, 1855.

SIR,

I HAVE the honour to inform you, that on my arrival here this morning with the vessels under my orders, and the launches of the line of battle ships, accompanied by four French steamers, I sent Lieutenant Commander Horton, of the Ardent, with whom was associated a French Officer, to demand the surrender of the place on the same terms as those offered by us at Taganrog and Mariaupol. These terms having been wisely acceded to by Colonel Borsikoff, the Military Governor, whose small force was quite inadequate to defend the town, the marines of this ship, under First Lieutenant Macnamara, R.M.A., and a French party, landed and destroyed a vast quantity of hay, stacked on the beach, ready for conveyance to the Crimea, and several thousand quarters of wheat, &c., &c. During this time Lieutenant Horton and the French officer went through the town, and had all the store-houses and magazines thrown open for their inspection, in order to see that no evasion of the terms was attempted, and that all contraband of war was destroyed.

6. On this as well as on the two former similar occasions, Lieutenant Horton conducted the interview with much judgment and firmness.

I have, &c.,
(Signed) E.M. LYONS,
Captain.
Rear-Admiral Sir Edmund Lyons,
Bart., G.C.B.

No. 3 Enclosure.

Her Majesty's ship Miranda,
off Kiten Bay, Sea of Azof,
June 10, 1855.

SIR,

I HAVE the honour to enclose a letter from Lieutenant Horton, commanding Her Majesty's ship Ardent, which I received on my arrival here this morning, informing me that he, yesterday, set fire to and destroyed 30,000 sacks of flour, stacked on the beach in Kiten Bay; this flour was the property of the Russian government, and evidently destined for the Russian army in the Crimea. Lieutenant Horton has performed this service judiciously and effectively.

I have, &c.
(Signed) E.M. LYONS, Captain.
Rear-Admiral Sir Edmund Lyons,
Bart., K.C.B.

Sub-Enclosure.

Her Majesty's ship Ardent, Kiten Bay,
June 10, 1855.

SIR,

I HAVE the honour to report that, on my arrival here yesterday, having failed of setting fire to the stores of flour by means of shells and carcases, I took advantage of a favourable state of weather in the evening, to drop the Ardent's bow close in shore, and to veer Mr. Roberts, the gunner, ashore in the dingy, with two men, under cover of musketry from aloft. I had previously ascertained that no ambuscade was there, and had cleared to a distance the 30 or 40 Cossacks who were watching, by firing round shot in their direction.

Mr. Roberts and his party very quickly and effectually fired all the stacks, and I anchored the Ardent off to watch the fires.

The whole stores are now consumed, estimated by the Lynx at 30,000 sacks.

I have, &c.,
(Signed) W. HORTON,
Lieutenant and Commander.
Captain Lyons,
Her Majesty's ship Miranda.

No 4 Enclosure.

Her Majesty's ship Miranda,
off Temrwick, June 9, 1855.

SIR,

I CANNOT allow the launches of the line-of-battle ships to return to their ships without requesting permission to bring to your notice the zeal and intelligence of the officers in command, and the excellent conduct and good discipline of all employed in them, which has enabled them to render such important service in the Sea of Azof, and which, if I may be permitted to say so without presumption, reflects so much credit on the ships they belong to.

I should also beg leave to bear similar testimony to the merit of the Commanding Officers of the Danube and Sulina, and those under their command, as well as to that of the Officers of Royal Marine Artillery who have been lent to this squadron during the same period.

I have, &c.,
(Signed) E.M. LYONS,
Captain.
Rear-Admiral Sir Edmund
Lyons, Bart., G.C.B.,
Commander-in-Chief.

Admiralty, June 25, 1855.

DESPATCHES, of which the following are copies or extracts, have been received from Rear-Admiral Sir Edmund Lyons, Bart., G.C.B., Commander-in-Chief of Her Majesty's Ships and Vessels in the Mediterranean and Black Sea.

Enclosure 1.

Royal Albert, Straits of Kertch,
June 6, 1855.

SIR,

CAPTAIN LYONS, of the Miranda, having informed me that the squadrons under his orders would be ready about the 2nd or 3rd instant, to commence operations in the shallow waters of the Gulf of Azoff, Vice-Admiral Bruat and I considered that the moment had arrived for reinforcing them with gun boats, which would only have embarrassed them in their previous rapid movements in deeper waters; we therefore despatched twenty launches of the line of battle ships armed with 24-pounder howitzers and rockets, and their Lordships will perceive by Captain Lyons's letter, of which I have the honour to enclose a copy, that their arrival on the spot was most opportune and attended with the happiest result; for, under the able management of the officers who commanded them, they mainly contributed towards the repulse of 3,500 of the enemy, and the destruction of the public buildings and government magazines of provisions at Taganrog.

Captain Lyons's account of the operations is so clear, and his appreciation of the merits of those acting under his orders on this important service so just, that I feel that it would only be weakened by any observations or recommendations of mine.

I am, &c.,

(Signed) E. LYONS,

Rear-Admiral and Commander-in-Chief.

The Secretary of the Admiralty.

REPORTS PROCEEDINGS AT TAGANROG.

Her Majesty's ship, Miranda,

Taganrog Roads, June 3, 1855.

SIR,

I HAVE the honour to inform you that I anchored in 18 feet water, with the squadron under my orders, in Taganrog inner roads, at about 8½ miles from the town, on the evening of the 1st instant, without any accident, although the enemy had removed the light vessels and beacons. During the night an easterly wind sprang up, and the water fell three feet, with every appearance of still falling; we were, therefore, obliged to remove a mile and a half further from the town.

2. The 2nd was employed in reconnoitring the town, which I was enabled to do satisfactorily in the Recruit; Lieutenant Day, commanding that vessel, having found a passage during the night.

I had arranged to proceed at 3 A.M. the following morning to summon the town, and in the event of a refusal to surrender, to endeavour to destroy the immense stores of grain and other Government property in that place.

3. Matters were in this state, when at sunset, to my great satisfaction, the Sulina, Danube, and Medina, with the twelve armed launches of the line of battle ships, hove in sight: this most welcome and opportune reinforcement of exactly the description of force required for the purpose in view, rendered success certain; and not long after the French steamers, with launches in tow, arrived.

4. Having concerted measures with Monsieur de Sedaiges, commanding the

French steamers, I preceded at 3 A.M. in the Recruit with the vessels and boats, and accompanied by the lightest French steamers (M. de Sedaiges being on board one of them), towing their launches. Having anchored the Recruit at 1400 yards from the Mole Head, and collected all the boats astern, I sent Lieutenant Commander Horton with a flag of truce, accompanied by a French officer with similar orders from M. de Sedaiges, to demand the surrender of all Government property of every description whatsoever, and of all grain, flour, and provisions (which I considered as contraband of war, knowing that even in the event of its not being government property, that it could only be intended for the supply of the Russian army in the Crimea), the whole to be delivered over to us to destroy; the troops to remove, during this necessary destruction, to a place five miles from the town, and within sight of the ships; the inhabitants to withdraw, except those appointed by the authorities to open the stores and assist us; any approach of troops, or any infraction of these terms, if accepted, to be considered as cancelling them, and to be punished with instant bombardment: one hour to be allowed for a decision, and no modification of the terms to be entertained. At the expiration of the hour, Lieutenant Horton and the French Officer were informed that the Governor refused the terms, and that, having troops at his disposal, he intended to defend the place. On this, these officers came off, and the flag of truce was hauled down from the Recruit.

5. Shortly afterwards the Recruit commenced firing, and the boats proceeded under the command of Commander Cowper P. Coles, of the Stromboli, in tow of one another, and accompanied by the French boats, until, having arrived in the required position, the tow was cast off, the boats' heads pulled round to the beach, and so heavy a fire opened, that, although the enemy made repeated attempts to get down to the houses lining the beach, so as to save the long range of storehouses from destruction, they never succeeded in doing so in sufficient numbers. Lieutenant Mackenzie (the senior lieutenanant of this ship) had charge of a separate division of light boats, with rockets and one gun, to cover the approach of Lieutenant Cecil Buckley, of the Miranda, who, in a four-oared gig, accompanied by Mr. Henry Cooper, Boatswain 3rd Class, and manned by volunteers, repeatedly landed and fired the different stores and government buildings; this dangerous, not to say desperate, service, when carried out in a town containing upwards of 3,000 troops constantly endeavouring to prevent it, and only checked by the fire of the boats' guns, was most effectually performed. The Recruit, from her light draught of water, was enabled to take an effective position at 1,400 yards, and so was the Mouette, French steamer, and the Danube, with 24-pounder howitzer and rockets, was very useful.

6. By 3 P.M., all the long ranges of stores of grain, plank, and tar, and the vessels on the stocks, were in a blaze, as well as the Custom House and other Government buildings, and unfortunately, but unavoidably, the town in many places; and our purpose being amply effected, the boats returned to the Recruit. The loss of the enemy in men must have been severe, as many were seen to fall; they deserve credit for the obstinacy with which they endeavoured to gain positions to prevent our effecting the object we had in view, but it was impossible to face the continuous and well directed fire kept up. Their loss in grain of different descriptions I cannot estimate, but as it comprises all, or very nearly all, in store at Taganrog, it must be enormous.

7. The only casualty in carrying out this service, was one private, Royal Marine-Artillery, severely wounded in the face by a musket ball.

8. I must now beg to be allowed to bring to your notice the very meritorious conduct of Commander Coles on this occasion, in command of so large a force of boats; and I cannot speak too highly of his energy, decision, and ability, which left me nothing to desire. He speaks in the highest terms of all under his orders, and particularly of Lieutenant J.T.C. Mackenzie, in charge of a separate division, who behaved with his accustomed spirit and judgment; and of Lieutenant Buckley, who so well carried out the hazardous service he had volunteered for. All the officers and men employed conducted themselves to my entire satisfaction, but as those above-mentioned were in such conspicious situations, I trust I may be pardoned for submitting their names to your favourable consideration.

9. I cannot refrain from bearing my testimony to the admirable conduct and cordial co-operation of our Allies, under the personal direction of Monsieur de Sedaiges; the boats being under the immediate command of Monsieur Lejeune, Capitaine de Frégate, and First Aide-de-camp to Admiral Bruat.

10. A Russian Serjeant, who deserted, and gave himself up to a French boat, states the number of troops in the town to have been 3,200, of which 800 arrived last night.

11. A Russian war-schooner, which had been run on shore near the town and abandoned, was set fire to and burnt, and so was a large raft of timber. The wreck of a large vessel (a sort of guard ship) which we observed to be fired by the enemy, and blown up on our first appearance in Taganrog Roads, was visited, but was found to be already effectually destroyed.

Many large buildings had the black flag hoisted, as a sign, I presume, of their being hospitals; these were most carefully respected by us, as were the churches, and, so far as possible, private houses.

I have, &c.,
(Signed) E.M. LYONS,
Captain.
Rear-Admiral Sir Edmund Lyons,
Bart., G.C.B.

EVACUATION OF ANAPA, &c.

Royal Albert, Straits of Kertch,
June 11, 1855.

SIR,

MY telegraphic message of yesterday, of which I have had the honour to enclose a copy, will have informed the Lords Commissioners of the Admiralty that Admiral

Bruat and I had received intelligence of Anapa having been evacuated by the enemy on the 5th instant.

2. I have now the honour to enclose a copy of a report which has just reached me from Rear-Admiral Stewart, whom I sent to Anapa to act in concert with Rear-Admiral Charner, to prevent the possibility of the place being occupied by a Russian force, leaving the political part of the question in the hands of Mr. Longworth, the Agent of Her Majesty's Government, whom I sent to the spot in the Highflyer, a few hours before Rear-Admiral Stewart left this anchorage.

I am, &c.,
(Signed) EDMUND LYONS,
Rear-Admiral and Commander-in-Chief.
To the Secretary of the Admiralty.

Enclosure.

Hannibal at Anapa,
June 11, 1855.

SIR,

IN pursuance of your orders of yesterday's date, I have the honour to inform you that I arrived at this anchorage at 10 A.M. to-day; Rear-Admiral Charner did not arrive till about 1 P.M. Admiral Bruat having last night informed me that he would be detained, and requested me not to wait for the Napoleon.

I enclose a return of the guns, by far the greater part of which have been rendered quite useless by the Russians themselves; the remainder are being made unserviceable or thrown over the cliffs, under the direction of Lieutenant Arthur, he gunnery officer of this ship.

The Russians have exploded nearly all the powder magazines in the place, and those which remain are empty.

The barracks were burnt by the Russians, as also a good number of buildings, and all the coal and grain, which appear to have been in considerable quantities.

The garrison is estimated by the Circassians at between seven and eight thousand, and they retired on the Kouban River, which they crossed by a bridge, destroying the latter behind them.

I have, &c.
(Signed) HOUSTON STEWART,
Rear-Admiral.
Rear-Admiral Sir Edmund Lyons,
G.C.B., K.C.H.
Commander-in-Chief.

Before Sevastopol,
June 2, 1855.

MY LORD,

THE reports which have been received from Kertch since I had the honour of writing to your Lordship on the 29th May, are of the most satisfactory character.

Five vessels, laden with corn, had come into Kertch in ignorance of the capture of the place, and had fallen into the hands of the Allies.

The French and English squadron had appeared before Berdiansk, and the enemy in consequence destroyed four of their war-steamers, and considerable depôts of corn.

They then exchanged a cannonade with the Russian forts at Arabat, and were so fortunate as to blow up a magazine with shells; and since, Captain Lyons, R.N., of the Miranda, has performed a most successful operation upon Genitschi. The Russian authorities of the town having refused to deliver up the Government depôt of corn, and ninety vessels, having on board supplies for their army in the Crimea, Captain Lyons bombarded the place with his squadron, and having driven the troops out of it, he landed the Sailors and Marines, and destroyed all the stores and the shipping.

This brilliant and decisive success marks the resolution and daring of Captain Lyons, and fortunately was accomplished with no other loss than that of one man wounded.

Admiral Sir Edmund Lyons states, that in no longer a period than four days the squadron has destroyed 241 vessels, employed exclusively in transporting provisions to the Crimea, besides four war steamers, and six millions of rations of flour and corn.

I beg leave to offer your Lordship my warmest congratulations on these important occurrences.

I have nothing of interest to report to your Lordship from hence, except that some more detachments of Sardinian troops have arrived.

A battery has arrived off the harbour.

I have, &c.,
RAGLAN.
The Lord Panmure, &c. &c.

Admiralty, August 13, 1855.

DESPATCHES, of which the following are copies, have been received from Rear-Admiral Sir Edmund Lyons, Bart., G.C.B., Commander-in-Chief of Her Majesty's Ships and Vessels in the Mediterranean and Black Sea.

No. 613. Royal Albert, off Sevastopol,
July 30, 1855.

SIR,

IN continuation of the proceedings of the steam squadron in the Sea of Azof, under the orders of Commander Sherard Osborne, of the Vesuvius, I beg leave to enclose, for the information of the Lords Commissioners of the Admiralty, copies of two letters from that officer, together with the several enclosures reporting the steps taken to deprive the enemy of the new harvest, and to cripple his resources of all kinds, since the proceedings which were communicated in my letter of the 7th instant (No. 538).

During the time the squadron was detained from stress of weather, under Berutch Spit, near Ghenitch, the vessels were, at every break of the weather, employed in destroying extensive fishing establishments which supplied the army in the Crimea with fish, as well as guard houses, barracks, stores of forage, and provisions on the Isthmus of Arabat, and the pontoon or only means of communication between Arabat Spit and the Crimea, at the entrance of the Kara-su River was burnt by Commander Rowley Lambert of the Curlew. The attack and destruction of Fort Petrovskoi, on the 16th instant, by the combined English and French squadrons named in Commander Osborn's letter, appears to have been accomplished with the usual skill and success which has attended the operations in the sea of Azof; and their Lordships will observe that particular mention is made of Lieutenant Hubert Campion, Senior Lieutenant of the Vesuvius, who commanded the landing party, and rendered great service. I would particularly beg leave to call their Lordships' attention to the high-minded conduct of Captain De Cintré, of His Imperial Majesty's steamer Milan, who, on seeing that the bulk of the squadron was under the orders of Commander Osborn, to whom he was senior, waived his right to plan the attack, and placed his ship, as well as the Mouette, in the positions pointed out by Commander Osborn.

In the meantime Lieutenant Hewett, in the Beagle, destroyed an extensive collection of fish stores and two large granaries full of corn in the neighbourhood of Berdiansk.

After destroying Fort Petrovskoi, the squadron proceeded to Glofira, where some extensive corn and fish stores were destroyed by vessels under the orders of Commander Rowley Lambert, of the Curlew, and a similar service was performed at the Crooked Spit, in the Gulf of Azof, by vessels under the orders of Commander F.A.B. Craufurd, of the Swallow. In the meantime Commander Osborn, reconnoitered various parts of the coast as far as Taganrog. The reports of Commander Osborn are so comprehensive that I will only remark that the admirable manner in which he has carried out my instructions "to clear the sea board of all fish stores, all fisheries and mills on a scale beyond the wants of the neighbouring population, and, indeed of all things destined to contribute to the maintenance of the enemy's army in the Crimea," fully corroborates the opinion I have before expressed, that he is an officer possessing a rare combination of high qualities, and I beg to recommend him to their Lordships' most favourable consideration.

I am, &c.

(Signed) EDMUND LYONS,

Rear-Admiral and Commander-in-Chief.

The Secretary of the Admiralty,

&c. &c. &c.

Her Majesty's ship Vesuvius,

Gulf of Azof, July 17, 1855.

SIR,

HEAVY gales and much sea obliged the squadron in this sea to take shelter under Berutch Spit for several days. Coaling, provisioning and completing stores was, however, proceeded with, and at every break in the weather the vessels were actively employed destroying some extensive fisheries upon Berutch Spit, as well as guard-houses, barracks, and stores of forage and provisions, to within an easy gun shot of Arabat Fort. The only pontoon or means of communication between Arabat Spit and the Crimea, at the entrance of the Kara-su River, has been burnt by Commander Rowley Lambert, H.M.S. Curlew, and we have now entire possession of the spit. A lull in the weather enabled me to put to sea upon the 13th July, for a sweep round the Sea of Azof; the Ardent, Weser, and Clinker being left under the orders of Lieutenant Horton to harass Genitch and Arabat, as well to cut off all communication along the spit.

Delayed by the weather, we did not reach Berdiansk until the 15th July; a heavy sea was running, but anxious to lose no time, the senior officer of the French Squadron (Captain De Cintré, of the Milan) and myself determined to go at once and endeavour to burn the forage and corn stacks upon the landward side of the hills overlooking the town.

No inhabitants were to be seen, but the occasional glimpse of soldiers showed that a landing was expected and that they were prepared for a street fight. I hoisted a flag of truce in order, if possible, to get the women and children removed from the town, but as that met with no reply and the surf rendered landing extremely hazardous, I hauled it down, and the squadron commenced to fire over the town at the forage and corn stacked behind it, and I soon had the satisfaction of seeing a fire break out exactly where it was wanted. The town was not touched except by an occasional shell. The wheat and forage being fired it became necessary to move into deeper water for the night, and from our distant anchorage the fires were seen burning throughout the night.

On the 16th July the Allied squadron proceeded to Fort Petrovski, between Berdiansk and Marianpol. As I approached the place there were evident symptoms of an increase to the fortifications since the Vesuvius silenced its fire three weeks ago. A redan, covering the curtain which faces the sea, shewed seven new embrasures, and much new earth led me to expect some masked works.

Captain De Cintré, commanding the French steamer Milan, although my senior, in the most handsome manner surrendered the right of planning the attack, and keeping alone in view the good of the allied cause, gallantly took up the position I wished him to do, followed by Captain De L'Allemand, in the Mouette.

At 9.30 A.M., all arrangements being made, the squadron, named in the margin*, took up their positions. The light draught gun-boats taking up stations east and west of the fort, and enfilading the works in front and rear; whilst the heavier vessels formed a semicircle round the front. The heavy nature of our ordnance crushed all attempts at resistance, and soon forced not only the garrison to retire from the trenches, but also kept at a respectable distance the reserve force, consisting of three strong battalions of infantry, and two squadrons of cavalry.

We then commenced to fire with carcases, and although partially successful, I was obliged to send the light boats of the squadron to complete the destruction of the fort and batteries; a duty I entrusted to Lieutenant Hubert Campion, of the Vesuvius, assisted by the officers in the annexed list.

In a short time I had the satisfaction of seeing all the cantonment, gun platforms, public buildings, corn and forage stores on fire, and the embrasures of the earthworks seriously injured; and although the enemy from an earthwork to the rear opened a sharp fire upon our men, Lieutenant Campion completed this service in the most able and perfect manner, without the loss of one man.

Lieutenant Campion reports that the fort was fully as formidable a one as it appeared from the ships; the platforms were laid ready, but the guns either had not yet arrived or had been withdrawn by the enemy. Leaving the Swallow, Commander Craufurd, to check any attempt of enemy to re-occupy the fort and extinguish the fire until the destruction was complete, the rest of the squadron proceeded to destroy great quantities of forage and some most extensive fisheries, situated upon the White House Spit, and about the mouth of the River Berda. By dark the work was done, and thirty fisheries, numbers of heavy launches, and great store of salted fish, nets, and gear, as well as much forage, had fallen into our hands in spite of considerable numbers of Cossack horse.

Nothing could exceed the zeal and energy displayed by every officer and man throughout the day; and the skilful manner in which the various officers in command of Her Majesty's vessels took up their positions in the morning, the beautiful accuracy of the fire, and the care with which the squadron was handled in shallow water, deserve to be called to your favourable notice. The able and cheerful co-operation of the French throughout the day was beyond all praise.

I have, &c.,
(Signed) SHERARD OSBORN,
Commander and Senior Officer.
Rear-Admiral Sir Edmund
Lyons, Bart., G.C.B.,
Commander-in-Chief.

Her Majesty's ship Vesuvius,
Gulf of Azof, July 21, 1855.

SIR,

THE day I closed, my last report to you, the Beagle, Lieutenant Hewett, was detached to Berdiansk.

Lieutenant Hewett rejoined me yesterday, and reports that one of the Russian sunken vessels was blown up. Lieutenant Hewett, the same evening, landed under cover of his vessel's guns, and destroyed an extensive collection of fish stores, and two large granaries full of corn.

On the 17th July, in consequence of information received of extensive depôts of corn and forage existing at a town called Glofira, upon the Asiatic coast, near Gheisk, I proceeded there with the squadron, accompanied by the French steamers Milan and Mouette. The Vesuvius and Swallow were obliged to anchor some distance off shore, I therefore sent Commander Rowley Lambert (Her Majesty's ship Curlew), with the gun-boats named in the margin† to reconnoitre in force, and if an opportunity occurred, to destroy any stores of provisions or of forage, he was to do so. Commander Lambert found Glofira and its neighbourhood swarming with cavalry; the town an open straggling agricultural village, and no appearance of corn or forage in it; he therefore very properly confined his operations to destroying, upon Glofira Spit, some very extensive corn and fish stores, but spared the town. The skill with which this service was executed in the face of large bodies of cavalry, reflects no small credit upon Commander Lambert; and he speaks most highly of the able assistance rendered him by the French officers and men under Captains De Cintré and L'Allemand. From Glofira I next proceeded to the Crooked Spit, in the Gulf of Azof, the French squadron parting company to harass the enemy in the neighbourhood of Kamiskeva and Obitotchna.

The squadron reached Crooked Spit the same day (July 18); and I immediately ordered Commander Frederick Craufurd, in the Swallow, supported by the gun-boats Grinder, Boxer, and Cracker, and the boats of Her Majesty's ships Vesuvius, Curlew, and Fancy, under Lieutenants Grylls, Rowley, and Sulivan, to proceed and clear the spit of the cavalry and Cossacks of the enemy, and then land and destroy the great fishing establishments situated upon it. Commander Craufurd executed this service with great vigour, and his report I have the honour to enclose. The extraordinary quantity of nets and stores of fish, and the scale of the works destroyed fully confirm the statements made by the work people that their occupation consisted in supplying food to the army in the Crimea, everything going to Simpheropol by the great northern road along the steppe. Whilst this service was being executed I reconnoitred the mouth of the river Mious, fifteen miles west of Taganrog, in Her Majesty's ship Jasper, Lieutenant J.S. Hudson. The shallow nature of the coast would not allow us to approach within a mile and three quarters of what in the chart is marked as Fort Temenos. The fortification was an earthwork of some extent and ditched but not pierced for guns. It was evidently of an old date, and as I could see no one within it, I again returned to the same place, accompanied by the boats of Her Majesty's ships Vesuvius and Curlew, and Her Majesty's gun-vessels, Cracker, Boxer, and Jasper.

Cavalry in large bodies, armed for the most part with carbines or rifles, were evidently much harassed by riding upon supposed points of attack; and when we got to Fort Temonos, and the usual Cossack picquet had been driven off, I and Commander Lambert, proceeded at once with the light boats into the river. When there, and immediately under Fort Temonos, which stands upon a steep escarpé of eighty feet, we found ourselves looked down upon by a large body of both horse and foot, lining the ditch and parapet of the work. Landing on the opposite bank, at good rifle-shot distance, one boat's crew, under Lieutenant Rowley, was sent to destroy a collection of launches and a fishery, whilst a careful and steady fire of Minie rifles, kept the Russians from advancing upon us. Assuring ourselves of the non-existence of any object worth hazarding so small a force any farther, we returned to the vessels, passing within pistol shot of the Russian ambuscade. The cool steadiness of the officers and men in the gigs, together with the wonderful precision of the fire from the covering vessels, distant as they were, doubtless kept the enemy in check, and prevented serious consequences. To Commander Lambert, Lieutenants Grylls and Rowley, and Mr. Tabuteau (Mate), who were in the gigs, as well as to Lieutenants Marryatt, Townshend, and Hudson, who commanded the gun-vessels, my best thanks are due.

The gig of the Grinder, under Lieutenant Hamilton, had a narrow escape upon the same day from a similar ambuscade, at a place called Kirpe, 10 miles east of Marianpol, the very proper humanity of Lieutenant Hamilton in not firing into an open defenceless town as it appeared to him, having nigh entailed the loss of a boat's crew when he attempted to land and destroy a corn store. A heavy fire of musketry at half pistol shot providentially injured no one, and Lieutenant Hamilton appears to have most skilfully escaped.

The 19th July, I reconnoitered Taganrog in the Jasper gun-boat. A new battery was being constructed upon the heights near the hospital, but although two shots were thown into it, it did not reply.

Every part the town showed signs of the injuries it had received when we visited it under the late Captain Edmund Lyons, of the Miranda. The long series of Government stores burnt by the Allied Flotilla had not been repaired, and the only sign of any communication being now held, by water, with the Don, was one large barge upon the beach.

To put a stop, however, to all traffic of this nature, and to harass the enemy in this neighbourhood, I have ordered Commander Craufurd to remain in the Gulf of Azof, with two gun-vessels under his orders.

That the squadron has not been idle, I trust this report will show; and without entering more into details than I have done, I can assure you, Sir, that from Ghenitch to Taganrog, and thence round to Kamiskeva, we have kept the coast in a state of constant alarm, and their troops incessantly moving. The good service done by the gun-boats in this way has been very great.

The total amount of provisions, corn, fisheries, forage, and boats, destroyed, has been something enormous.

Nothing can exceed the zeal and activity of the officers, or good conduct of the men, constituting this squadron; and constant work, does not, I am happy to say, appear as yet to impair their health.

I have, &c.,
(Signed) SHERARD OSBORN,
Commander and Senior Officer.
Rear-Admiral Sir Edmund
Lyons, Bart., G.C.B,
&c. &c. &c.

Her Majesty's ship Swallow,
off Crooked Spit, Sea of Azof,
July 15, 1855.

SIR,

IN compliance with your orders, I proceeded in Her Majesty's steam gun-boat Grinder, with Cracker and Boxer, and boats of the squadron to reconnoitre the Crooked Spit.

Having cleared the spit of some mounted troops who occupied it, I ordered a detachment of boats, with their respective officers, to land and destroy the immense fishing establishments and nets found upon the point of it. The country seemed swarming with cavalry, but, by the able management of the officers in command of the gun-boats, and by their good fire, they were effectually driven off the spit some distance inland.

Having reconnoitred as far into the land as we could see from the mast head of the Grinder, all the boats were ordered to land and set fire to very large and extensive government stores upon the upper part of the spit, including large fishing establishments, an enormous quantity of nets, haystacks, and several large houses used as government stores. I learnt from a Russian fisherman, that the fish caught on this spit and cured here was immediately forwarded to Simpheropol, for the use of the Crimean army; and I conclude that a very severe blow has been inflicted upon the enemy by the amount of property which was destroyed, including spars, timber, fish, nets, and boats; apparently the most extensive fishing establishment in the Sea of Azof; and I am happy to say without a casualty. My thanks are due to Lieutenants Hamilton, of Grinder, and Townsend, of Boxer, as also to Lieutenants Rowley, of Curlew; Grylls, of Fancy; Sullivan, of Vesuvius; Mr. Aldrich, Master of Swallow; Mr. Deare, Gunner of Curlew; and Mr. Windsor, Gunner of Swallow; who all and each by their zeal and activity rendered great service in destroying so large an accumulation of stores and houses in so short a space of time.

I have, &c.,
(Signed) FRED. A.B. CRAUFURD,
Commander.
Commander Osborne,
Senior Officer.

Vesuvius, Commander Sherard Osborn; Curlew, Commander Rowley Lambert; Swallow, Commander F.A.B. Craufurd; Fancy, Lieutenant C.G. Grylls; Grinder, Lieutenant F. Hamilton; Boxer, Lieutenant S.P. Townshend; Cracker, Lieutenant J.H. Marryatt; Wrangler, Lieutenant H. Burgoyne; Jasper, Lieutenant J.S. Hudson; Beagle, Lieutenant W.N. Hewett.
†Fancy, Grinder, Boxer, Cracker, Jasper, Wrangler. Boats of Vesuvius and Swallow.

Admiralty, August 18, 1855.

DESPATCHES, of which the following are copies have been received from Rear-Admiral Sir Edmund Lyons, Bart., G.C.B., Commander-in-Chief of Her Majesty's Ships and Vessels in the Mediterranean and Black Sea.

No. 633. Royal Albert, off Sevastopol,
August 4, 1855.

SIR,

IN continuation of the proceedings of the squadron in the Sea of Azof since those which were reported in my letter of the 30th ultimo, No. 613, I have the honour to enclose, for the information of the Lords Commissioners of the Admiralty, a copy of a letter from Commander Sherard Osborn, of the Vesuvius, the senior officer in that sea, reporting to me the steps he had taken to harass the enemy as much as possible, and to punish him at Berdiansk for having fired at some of our people, although the town had been previously spared on the plea of its being defenceless.

Commander Osborn does not fail to point out and to do justice to the merits of the officers by whom he has been so ably seconded, and he particularly mentions Commander Rowley Lambert, of the Curlew, the officer next in seniority to himself, who has on all occasions been conspicuous for his activity and gallantry.

Commander Osborn has also on several occasions borne the highest testimony to the merits of those gallant officers, Lieutenant William Horton, commanding the Ardent, and Lieutenant John E. Commerell, commanding the Weser.

I am, &c.
(Signed) EDMUND LYONS,
Rear-Admiral and Commander-in-Chief.
The Secretary of the Admiralty,
&c. &c. &c.

Her Majesty's ship Vesuvius,
Arabat Spit, July 25, 1855.

SIR,

SINCE my last letter I have fully succeeded in destroying, by means of submarine explosions, the four Russian steamers sunk in Berdiansk Bay, and as the enemy had, from the houses of the western suburb of Berdiansk, twice fired upon our people, whilst peaceably and unguardedly employed, I considered it right that such a dishonourable course, from a town which had been spared under plea of being defenceless, should be severely punished, and the more so as Berdiansk had been treated with unusual leniency upon the occasion of our former visits.

I therefore, on the 22nd of July, caused to be destroyed the western suburb, which had screened their riflemen, and succeeded in discovering and setting fire to no less than ten large granaries, filled with wheat, each averaging about two hundred tons in capacity, and several flour mills, which have been employed, night and day, grinding for the use of the Russians.

The church and major portion of the town I spared, although nearly every house we searched contained grain in large quantities, and the whole place might be considered little else than a general granary.

The dangerous service of landing in so large a town, with bodies of Cossacks threatening, was entrusted to Commander Rowley Lambert, Lieutenant Hubert Campion (senior of this ship), Lieutenant Hewett, Her Majesty's steam-vessel Beagle, and Lieutenant Marryat, Her Majesty's steam-vessel Cracker, and the skill with which it was executed reflects the highest credit upon their zeal and judgment.

The operations were admirably covered by the gun-boats under Lieutenants Grylls, Commerell, and Townsend, and Her Majesty's ships Vesuvius and Curlew; the latter under charge of her zealous First Lieutenant, C.J. Rowley.

On the 24th July I rejoined Lieutenant Horton, Her Majesty's steam-vessel Ardent. He, I found, had not been idle; and, with the assistance of the Clinker, Lieutenant Smithett, and Wrangler, Lieutenant Burgoyne, very much damage had been done to the enemy from Ghenitch to Obitotchna Spit, in the destruction of forage, fish, stores, and launches.

I have, &c.,

(Signed) SHERARD OSBORN,

Commander and Senior Officer.

Rear-Admiral Sir Edmund

Lyons, Bart., G.C.B.,

Commander-in-Chief.

CHAPTER 10

THE ASSAULTS UPON
THE REDAN

War-Department, June 6, 1855.

LORD PANMURE has this day received two Despatches and their Enclosures, of which the following are copies, addressed to His Lordship by Field-Marshal the Lord Raglan, G.C.B.

Before Sevastopol,
May 26, 1855.

MY LORD,

I HAVE the honour to report to your Lordship that a portion of the Allied Armies took up a position yesterday on this side of the Tchernaya, the left of the French resting under a redoubt established upon the edge of this ridge overhanging the valley, and opposite the Inkerman heights; the right extending beyond Tractir; and the ground more to the right, behind Chorgouna, being occupied by the Sardinian troops, aided in their advance by the 10th Hussars and 12th Lancers and the Horse Artillery, under Colonel Parlby.

Omer Pasha at the same time moved forward to the low heights in front of Balaklava, and thus afforded support to the French Divisions before him. These were commanded by General Canrobert, who pushed forward across the bridge of Tractir, and drove the enemy, who were not in great numbers, off, and having cleared his front, he withdrew to this side of the river, where he now remains.

Sir Colin Campbell advanced the Royal Marines from the high ridge on our extreme right to a point commanding the old Baidar-road; and Colonel Parlby, with the regiments I have mentioned, reconnoitred the country on the immediate right of General La Marmora's position, and patrolled along the Woronzow-road, in the direction of Baidar.

The appearance and bearing of the Sardinian troops are highly satisfactory, and I anticipate the greatest advantage from their addition to this army under their distinguished leader General La Marmora, whose zeal for the service and ardent desire to co-operate with us, I am happy to have so early an opportunity of acknowledging and recording. Nothing of importance has occurred in the British trenches since I wrote to your Lordship on the 19th instant.

The death of Colonel Egerton, of the 77th, on the night of the 19th ultimo, as already announced to your Lordship, prevented my receiving in due course the official report of the conduct of the officers serving immediately under him, and it is only a few days ago that I learnt that Captain Gilby was the next in seniority to him, of the 77th, on the occasion, and that he had highly distinguished himself.

I deem it an act of justice to a most deserving officer to bring his conduct under the notice of your Lordship.

I enclose the returns of casualties to the 24th instant. Your Lordship will regret to see that Lieutenant Williams, of the 17th, has been severely wounded.

I have the greatest pleasure in announcing to your Lordship the brilliant success which attended an attack by the French Army, of some ambuscades at the head of the Quarantine Bay, and in front of a cemetery near it. The attack was made on the night of the 22nd, and the operation was completed on the following evening. The enemy had collected a very large force on the first occasion to resist our Allies; but, notwithstanding, the French were enabled by their brilliant gallantry and determined resolution to maintain themselves in the pits at the head of the bay on the 22nd, and on the 23rd to occupy the whole with less resistance on the part of the Russians, who are stated to have sustained a very severe loss.

The French were necessarily exposed to a very heavy fire, and were assailed by vastly superior numbers. The achievement they accomplished redounds therefore highly to their renown, and is hailed with satisfaction by their Allies.

An expedition, composed of British, French, and Turkish troops, sailed for Kertch on Tuesday evening and Wednesday morning, and I hope soon to be able to announce the landing of the corps, and the result of its first operations. It is commanded by Lieutenant-General Sir George Brown, and has been conveyed in English and French ships, under the command of Admiral Sir E. Lyons and Admiral Bruat, whose exertions to carry out this important service have been most conspicuous.

The 31st Regiment has arrived from Corfu.

I am much concerned to have to report that Major-General Buller has been obliged by the failure of his health to leave the army. He has been constant in the discharge of his duty since he joined this army, distinguished himself both at Alma and Inkerman, and persevered in taking his turn in the trenches until driven by illness to withdraw.

I regret the loss of his services exceedingly.

I have, &c.

RAGLAN.

The Lord Panmure, &c. &c. &c.

War-Department, June 18, 1855.

LORD PANMURE has this day received two Despatches and their Enclosures, of which the following are copies, addressed to His Lordship by Field-Marshal the Lord Raglan, G.C.B.

Before Sevastopol,
June 9, 1855.

MY LORD,

I HAVE the great satisfaction of informing your Lordship that the assault which was made upon the Quarries in front of the Redan, from our advanced parallel in the right attack, on the evening of the 7th instant, was attended with perfect success, and that the brave men who achieved this advantage with a gallantry and determination that does them infinite honour, maintained themselves on the ground they had acquired, notwithstanding that during the night, and in the morning of yesterday, the enemy made repeated attempts to drive them out, each attempt ending in failure, although supported by large bodies of troops, and by heavy discharges of musketry, and every species of offensive missile.

The French on our right had shortly before moved out of their trenches and attacked the Ouvrages Blancs and the Mamelon. These they carried without the smallest check, and their leading column rushed forward and approached the Malakof Tower; but this it had not been in contemplation to assail, and the troops were brought back and finally established in the enemy's works, from which the latter did not succeed in expelling them, though the fire of musketry and cannon which was brought to bear upon them was tremendous.

I never saw anything more spirited and rapid than the advance of our Allies.

I am happy to say that the best feeling prevails between the two armies, and each is proud of and confident in the gallantry and high military qualities of the other.

I apprized your Lordship, by telegraph on the 6th, that our batteries reopened that afternoon.

The fire was kept up with the greatest energy until the day closed, when it was confined to vertical fire; but the next morning the guns resumed the work of destruction, and the effect was such that it was determined by General Pelissier and myself that the time had arrived for pushing our operations forward. Accordingly, soon after six o'clock on the evening of the 7th, the signal was given for the assault of the works I have enumerated, and the result was most triumphant.

The troops employed in storming the Quarries were composed of detachments from the Light and 2nd Divisions, and at night they were supported by the 62nd Regiment.

The command of these troops was entrusted to Colonel Shirley, of the 88th, who was acting as General Officer of the Trenches; and he was assisted in the arrangements and guided as to the points of attack and distribution of the troops by

Lieutenant-Colonel Tylden, of the Royal Engineers, the directing engineer officer of the right attack.

Although nothing could be more spirited than the attack of the Quarries, or more creditable to every officer and man engaged in the operation; yet I cannot refrain from drawing your Lordship's especial attention to the energy and determination which they all displayed in maintaining and establishing themselves after their first success in them. They were repeatedly attacked during the night, and again soon after daylight on the 8th, and it was in resisting these repeated efforts on the part of the enemy that a great portion of the heavy loss the Army has to deplore was sustained.

The mode in which Colonel Shirley conducted this very arduous service, and carried out his orders, entitles him to my highest commendation. I have great pleasure in mentioning the following officers, who are stated to have distinguished themselves on the occasion; viz: Lieutenant-Colonel Campbell, of the 90th, who commanded the storming party; Major Mills, Royal Fusiliers; Major Villiers, 47th; Major Armstrong, 49th; who are all severely wounded; Lieutenant-Colonel Maxwell, of the 88th; Major Bayley, of the same regiment, who was unfortunately killed; Lieutenant-Colonel Grant, 49th; Major Simpson, of the 34th; Lieutenant-Colonel Johnstone, of the 33rd; Major Herbert, of the 23rd; Captain Lowry, of the 47th; Captain Turner, of the 7th; Captain Lowndes, of the 47th; Captain Nason, of the 49th; Captain Le Marchant, of the 49th, who was wounded; Captain Wolseley,* 90th; and Lieutenants Chatfield and Eustace, of the 49th; and Palmer, Irby, and Waddilove, of the 47th; and Captain Hunter, 47th; and Lance-Corporal Quinn, 47th; who took a Russian officer prisoner in the most gallant manner.

I also feel it my duty to solicit your Lordship's notice to the eminent services of Lieutenant-Colonel Tylden, of the Royal Engineers; he has been indefatigable in the discharge of his peculiar duties from the commencement of the siege, and he has always been at hand to aid in the repulse of the enemy, when they have assaulted our trenches. He eulogizes the conduct of Captain Browne, of the Royal Engineers, Lieutenant Elphinstone, of the same corps, Lieutenant Anderson, 96th Foot (Acting Engineer), who is wounded; and he laments the death of Lieutenant Lowry, R.E., who conducted the storming party, and was afterwards killed by a cannon shot.

Notwithstanding the frequency of the endeavours of the Russians to regain possession of the Quarries, and the interruptions to the work to which these attacks gave rise, Lieutenant-Colonel Tylden was enabled to effect the lodgement and to establish the communication with the advanced parallel, and this redounds greatly to his credit and that of the officers and men employed as the working party; and I cannot omit this opportunity to express my approbation of the conduct of the Sappers throughout the operations. The exertions of the Royal Artillery, under Brigadier-General Dacres, and those of the Naval Brigade, under Captain Lushington, R.N., in serving the guns cannot be too warmly commended. The accuracy of their fire is the theme of universal admiration; and the constancy with which they applied themselves to their arduous duties under all circumstances, however dangerous, cannot be too strongly placed upon record.

It is deeply to be lamented that this success should have entailed so heavy a loss, as is shewn in the accompanying returns, which however, are still incomplete; but I have the assurance of the Principal Medical Officer that many of the wounds are slight, and that by far the greater portion of the sufferers are progressing most favourably.

I have just learnt that the enemy have abandoned a work in the rear of the "Ouvrages Blancs" which they constructed at the commencement of the month of May. The French took possession of it on the 7th, but did not retain it. In the other works they captured 62 pieces of artillery, and they have 14 officers, and about 400 men, prisoners.

We have a few prisoners, and amongst them a Captain of Infantry, who was wounded, and taken by Corporal Quinn, of the 47th Regiment.

I have, &c.,
RAGLAN.
The Lord Panmure, &c. &c. &c.

This officer is also recommended by Colonel Tylden.

War-Department, June 18, 1855.

LORD PANMURE has this day received three Despatches and their Enclosures, of which the following are copies, addressed to His Lordship by Field-Marshal the Lord Raglan, G.C.B.

Before Sevastopol,
June 5, 1855.

MY LORD,

I AM deeply concerned to have to inform your Lordship that Rear Admiral Boxer died on board the Jason last night, outside the harbour of Balaklava, after a very short illness.

He was removed to that ship in the hope that the pure sea air might prove beneficial to him; but this expectation was not fulfilled. His malady made rapid progress, and early in the afternoon of yesterday it was intimated to me that his life was despaired of.

His nephew died of cholera last week, and this melancholy event so deeply affected him that his health at once gave way, and he sunk under the same disease.

It is well known that this officer devoted his whole life to the public service. Since he under-took the appointment of Admiral Superintendent of the harbour of Balaklava he has applied himself incessantly to the discharge of his arduous duties, exposing himself in all weathers; and he has rendered a most essential service to the army by improving the landing-places and establishing wharves on the west side of the port, whereby the disembarkation of stores and troops has been greatly accelerated, and communications with the shore have been rendered much easier.

I have, &c.,
RAGLAN.
The Lord Panmure, &c. &c. &c.

Before Sevastopol,
June 5, 1855.

MY LORD,

I HAVE great satisfaction in informing your Lordship that I received intelligence the night before last, of the evacuation of Soujak Kali by the Russians on the 28th ultimo.

It appears that previously to their retirement from the place, the troops destroyed the principal buildings and the armament which consisted of about sixty heavy guns and six mortars, and it is concluded that they have joined the garrison of Anapa, from whence many of the inhabitants have removed.

Sir Edmund Lyons has been so good as to send me the detached report of the naval operations in the Sea of Azof, which will reach England either before or at the same time as this dispatch. They reflect the highest credit on Captain Lyons of the Miranda, and the officers and men serving under his orders, and are remarkable for the intelligence, gallantry, and judgment with which they have been conducted; and it is a matter of much gratulation, which will be peculiarly felt by Her Majesty, that whilst great injury has been inflicted on the enemy in the loss of resources of every description, the most brilliant and unwonted success has been achieved in an incredibly short time with only one casualty, and that not of a serious nature.

These gallant exploits of the navy, have spread joy in our camps and afforded vast satisfaction to every individual in the army.

A body of French troops under the command of General Morris and General Canrobert, and a column of the Sardinian corps under General La Marmora, made a reconnoissance on Baidar, on the morning of the 3rd.

The former proceeded along the Woronzow-road and pushed their cavalry several miles beyond Baidar; the latter operated on the left through a mountainous district, and advanced into Baidar, after a fatiguing march; only a small number of Cossacks shewed themselves.

Nothing has occurred in front of the town.

I have, &c.
RAGLAN.
The Lord Panmure, &c. &c. &c.

War-Department, June 28, 1855.

LORD PANMURE has this day received two Despatches and their Enclosures, of which the following are copies, addressed to His Lordship by Field-Marshal the Lord Raglan, G.C.B.

Before Sevastopol,
June 14, 1855.

MY LORD,

YOUR Lordship will be concerned to learn that the army still suffers from cholera, and that it has increased since the last report.

The men in general, however, look healthy, and I hope that the duration of this sad malady will not be long.

The reports of the state of the Sardinian army are to-day a little more satisfactory.

I have, &c.,
RAGLAN.
The Lord Panmure, &c. &c. &c.

Before Sevastopol,
June 16, 1855.

MY LORD,

I HAVE the honour to acquaint your Lordship that Lieutenant-General Sir George Brown and Admiral Sir E. Lyons, returned from Kertch yesterday, having fully and successfully accomplished the objects of the expedition to that part of the Crimea.

I have the highest satisfaction in drawing your Lordships' attention to the manner in which the Lieutenant-General conducted the duties I entrusted to his charge; and I entertain no doubt that if he had encountered the resistance which I was led to expect he would have met with, the result would have been equally advantageous, and would have reflected the same credit upon his arrangements, whilst the efficiency and gallantry of the troops would have been brought into stronger light. But it is a matter of great joy that so much should have been done without the loss of a life.

He feels greatly indebted to General Dautemarre and Reschid Pasha, who commanded the French and Turkish troops respectively, for their ready cooperation and assistance.

It has afforded me the most sincere pleasure to have the opportunity of personally congratulating Sir E. Lyons on the success of the expedition, for which he was from the first so warm an advocate, and to which he always attached the highest importance, and on the result of the attacks upon the enemy's possessions in the Sea of Azof. The excellence of the arrangements for the bombardment of Taganrog does infinite honour to Captain Lyons, of H.M.S. Miranda, and at once testifies his ability, determination and gallantry.

The progress of the works against Sevastopol since I reported to your Lordship on the 12th, has been perfectly satisfactory, and new batteries are completed, which will enable both the English and the French armies to resume the offensive with the utmost vigour.

I have, &c.

RAGLAN.

The Lord Panmure, &c. &c. &c.

P.S. I have just received a letter from Colonel Shirley, in which he expresses his regret at having omitted the name of Captain Peel, 34th Regiment, who was severely wounded in the successful attack of the Quarries on the 7th ultimo, where he highly distinguished himself.

RAGLAN.

War-Department, July 2, 1855.

LORD PANMURE has this day received a Despatch and its Enclosure, of which the following are copies, addressed to His Lordship by the late Field-Marshal Lord Raglan, G.C.B.

*Before Sevastopol,
June 19, 1855.*

MY LORD,

I INFORMED your Lordship, on the 16th, that new batteries had been completed, and that in consequence the Allies would be enabled to resume the offensive against Sevastopol with the utmost vigour.

Accordingly, on the 17th, at daylight a very heavy fire was opened from all the batteries in the English and French trenches, and maintained throughout the day, and the effect produced appeared so satisfactory, that it was determined that the French should attack the Malakoff works the next morning, and that the English should assail the Redan as soon after as I might consider it desirable.

It was at first proposed that the artillery fire should be resumed on the morning of the 18th, and should be kept up for about two hours, for the purpose of destroying any works the enemy might have thrown up in the night, and of opening passages through the abattis that covered the Redan; but on the evening of the 17th it was intimated to me by General Pelissier that he had determined, upon further consideration, that the attack by his troops should take place at three the following morning.

The French therefore commenced their operations as day broke, and, as their several columns came within range of the enemy's fire, they encountered the most serious opposition, both from musketry and the guns in the works, which had been silenced the previous evening; and, observing this, I was induced at once to order our columns to move out of the trenches upon the Redan.

It had been arranged that detachments from the Light, 2nd, and 4th Divisions, which I placed for the occasion under the command of Lieutenant-General Sir G. Brown, should be formed into three columns; that the right one should attack the left face of the Redan between the flanking batteries; that the centre should advance upon the salient angle; and that the left should move upon the re-entering angle formed by the right face and flank of the work; the first and last preceding the centre column.

The flank columns at once obeyed the signal to advance, preceded by covering parties of the Rifle Brigade, and by sailors carrying ladders and soldiers carrying woolbags; but they had no sooner shown themselves beyond the trenches than they were assailed by a most murderous fire of grape and musketry. Those in advance were either killed or wounded, and the remainder found it impossible to proceed. I never before witnessed such a continued and heavy fire of grape combined with musketry from the enemy's works, which appeared to be fully manned; and the long list of killed and wounded in the Light and 4th Divisions, and the seamen of the Naval Brigade, under Captain Peel, who was unfortunately wounded, though not severely, will shew that a very large proportion of those that went forward fell. Major-General Sir John Campbell, who led the left attack, and Colonel Shadforth, of the 57th, who commanded the storming party under his direction, were both killed, as was also Colonel Yea, of the Royal Fusiliers, who led the right column.

I cannot say too much in praise of these officers. Major-General Sir J. Campbell had commanded the 4th Division from the period of the battle of Inkerman, till the arrival very recently of Lieutenant-General Bentinck. He had devoted himself to his duty without any intermission, and had acquired the confidence and respect of all; I most deeply lament his loss.

Colonel Shadforth, had maintained the efficiency of his regiment by constant attention to all the details of his command, and Colonel Yea was not only distinguished for his gallantry, but had exercised his control of the Royal Fusiliers in such a manner as to win the affections of the soldiers under his orders, and to secure to them every comfort and accommodation which his personal exertions could procure for them.

I shall not be able to send your Lordship correct lists of the killed and wounded by this opportunity, but I will forward them by telegraph as soon as they are made out.

I have not any definite information upon the movements of the French columns, and the atmosphere became so obscured by the smoke from the guns and musketry, that it was not possible by personal observation to ascertain their progress, though I was particularly well situated for the purpose; but I understand that their left column, under General Dautemarre, passed the advanced works of the enemy, and threatened the gorge of the Malakof Tower; and that the two other columns, under Generals Mayran and Brunet, who both, I regret to say, were killed, met with obstacles equal to those we encountered, and were obliged in consequence to abandon the attack.

The superiority of our fire on the day we opened, led both General Pelissier and myself, and the officers of the Artillery and Engineers of the two Services, and the Armies in general, to conclude that the Russian Artillery fire was, in a great measure subdued, and that the operation we projected could be undertaken with every prospect of success. The result has shown that the resources of the enemy were not exhausted, and that they had still the power, either from their ships or from their batteries, to bring an overwhelming fire upon their assailants.

Whilst the direct attack upon the Redan was proceeding, Lieutenant-General Sir R. England was directed to send one of the brigades of the 3rd Division, under the command of Major-General Barnard, down the Woronzow Ravine, with a view to give support to the attacking columns on his right; and the other brigade, under Major-General Eyre, still further to the left, to threaten the works at the head of the Dockyard Creek.

I have not yet received their reports, and shall not be able to send them to your Lordship to-day; but General Eyre was very seriously engaged, and he himself wounded, though I am happy to say not severely, and he possessed himself of a churchyard, which the enemy had hitherto carefully watched, and some houses within the place; but as the town front was not attacked, it became necessary to withdraw his brigade at night.

I shall make a special report upon this by the next mail, and I shall avail myself of the same opportunity to name to you the officers who have been particularly mentioned to me.

I am concerned to have to inform you that Lieutenant-Colonel Tylden of the Royal Engineers, whose services I have had the greatest pleasure in bringing so frequently to your Lordship's notice, is very severely wounded. The account I received of him this morning is upon the whole satisfactory, and I entertain strong hopes that his valuable life will be preserved.

I feel greatly indebted to Sir G. Brown for the manner in which he conducted the duties I entrusted to him; and my warmest acknowledgements are due to Major-General Harry Jones, not only for his valuable assistance on the present occasion, but for the able, zealous, and energetic manner in which he has conducted the siege operations since he assumed the command of the Royal Engineers.

He received a wound from a grape shot in the forehead yesterday, which I trust will not prove serious.

I brought up the 1st Division from the vicinity of Balaklava as a reserve, and I shall retain them on these heights.

The Sardinian troops, under General La Marmora, and the Turkish troops, under Omer Pasha, crossed the Tchernaia on the 17th instant, and occupy positions in front of Chorgouna. They have not come in contact with any large body of the enemy.

I have, &c.,
RAGLAN.
The Lord Panmure, &c. &c. &c.

Admiralty, July 2, 1855.

DESPATCHES, of which the following are copies, have been received from Rear-Admiral Sir Edmund Lyons, Bart., G.C.B., Commander-in-Chief of Her Majesty's Ships and Vessels in the Mediterranean and Black Sea.

Royal Albert, off Sevastopol,
June 19, 1855.

SIR,

THE enclosed copy of a letter from Captain Lushington, who commands the Naval Brigade before Sevastopol, has just reached me in time to be transmitted for the information of the Lords Commissioners of the Admiralty, by this day's mail.

Their Lordships will readily perceive that the gallantry which has distinguished the Naval Brigade throughout the war, was never more distinguished then it was yesterday, during the attack on the Malakoff Tower and Redan; and on a future early occasion it will be my pleasing duty to bring under their Lordships' notice, the conduct of those engaged during the late bombardment and attack.

I regret to find the name of Lieutenant Thomas O. Kidd, of the Albion, amongst the killed yesterday; he was a zealous and gallant young officer, and had served a long time with the Naval Brigade.

Amongst the wounded is Captain Peel, of the Leander, whose chivalrous gallantry and cheerful readiness for every duty render his presence with the brigade invaluable, and I hope that Captain Lushington may not long be deprived of his services.

I regret also to find amongst the wounded Lieutenant William B. Urmston, of the Queen; Lieutenant John H. Cave, of the Diamond; Lieutenant Osborne W. Dalyell, of the Leander: Mr. George Parsons, Mate, of the Dauntless; and Mr. H.E. Wood, Midshipman, of the Queen, Aide-de-Camp to Captain Peel.

I am, &c.
(Signed) EDMUND LYONS,
Rear-Admiral and Commander-in-Chief.
To the Secretary of the Admiralty.
London.

Camp, Naval Brigade,
June 18, 1855.

SIR,

I HAVE the honour to report that on Sunday, at 3 A.M. we opened fire as before on the different forts of Sevastopol, which was very soon returned, but not with the spirit or skill that usually characterizes the enemy's fire. Towards 2 P.M. the fire became very slack and their batteries appeared much shaken.

The fire continued all day, and the Commander of the Forces having intimated to me his acceptance of my proposal to carry the ladders in case of an assault being made on the town and batteries, I told off four parties of 60 men each to accompany the four columns ordered for this service; and Captain Peel having volunteered his services on this occasion, I placed them under his command, and I beg to enclose a list of the officers under him. I regret to say that the assault which took place at 3

A.M., was not successful; but our severe loss shows too plainly that the seamen and officers of the Naval Brigade did their duty most gallantly, and their ladders were at their places in spite of the most murderous fire I have witnessed.

Captain Peel led one party in the most gallant style, and Lieutenant Cave led the other. The other two columns did not advance, and consequently the ladder parties, although exposed to a severe fire, as indeed was everyone, did not suffer much.

Captain Peel was shot through the arm, but was enabled to continue his duty until the affair was over. I have to regret as well that Lieutenant Urmston, Cave, and Dalyell, Messrs. Parsons, mate, and Wood, midshipman, were all wounded.

Lieutenant Kidd and 9 seamen were killed, and 41 seamen wounded, and 1 missing; these men, I trust, will be got in to-night after dark. The party under Lieutenant Cave, with the loss of Lieutenant Kidd and 5 seamen killed, Lieutenant Cave and 7 seaman wounded, equally performed the duty assigned. A heavy fire was kept up from our batteries with admirable precision, until the Commander-in-Chief ordered it to be slackened.

I have also to report the bursting of one of the 95 cwt. 68 pounders, which caused the death of four men, and wounded three.

The enemy's line of battle ships did not fire, but the steamers did. I have the honour to return a list of casualties for the last two days, and to inform you our sick list is 49, and all doing well.

Every officer and man engaged in this arduous service has done his duty most gallantly, and I only await your permission to recommend those whose conduct I have particularly noticed.

I have, &c.,
STEPHEN LUSHINGTON.

NIGHTLY ATTACK ON THE SEA DEFENCES OF SEVASTOPOL.

Royal Albert, off Sevastopol.
June 19, 1855.

SIR,

ON our return from Kertch, on the 15th instant, Vice-Admiral Bruat and I were informed by the Commanders of the Land Forces, that they intended to reopen the fire of the batteries on the following morning, and on the 18th instant to make further approaches towards Sevastopol, and endeavour to obtain possession of the enemy's positions of the Malakoff and Redan, and their Excellencies also informed us that they had ascertained that the nightly fire of our steamers had produced considerable effect.

2. On hearing this, my colleague and I at once determined to repeat the operation

on the two intervening nights, and accordingly on the 16th instant, the steam frigates and sloops named in the margin,* accompanied by several French steamers, discharged a heavy fire on the town and sea defences, whilst the Danube, Lieutenant R.P. Cator, and the launches of the Royal Albert, under the command of Lieutenants George W. Watson and Edmund Wilmot, poured in a shower of rockets, and happily without any casualty.

3. During the night of the 17th instant, the Princess Royal, and the steam-frigates and sloops named in the second marginal note†, and accompanied by a division of French steamers and the launches as before, renewed the firing, and on this occasion I am sorry to observe there was some loss, the Princess Royal having had one man killed, and two wounded; the Sidon, two men killed and eleven wounded; and Captain Lyons, of the Miranda, was so severely wounded in the leg by a shell, that I have been obliged to send him to Therapia Hospital.

4. Their Lordships will readily believe that a strong desire prevailed throughout the fleet to go under fire, but as only one ship of the line could do so with advantage, I thought it right that it should be the Princess Royal, commanded by Lord Clarence Paget, who having planned the course with infinite zeal and ability, was naturally best acquainted with it.

5. Returns of the casualties are herewith transmitted.

I am, &c.,
EDMUND LYONS,
Rear-Admiral and Commander-in-Chief.

*Tribune, Captain Hon. J.R. Drummond; Highflyer, Captain John Moore; Terrible, Captain J. McCleverty; Miranda, Captain E.M. Lyons; Niger, Commander H.W. Hire; Arrow, Lieutenant W.K. Jolliffe; Viper, Lieutenant H.W. Comber; Snake, Lieutenant H.F. McKillop; Weser, Lieutenant J.E. Commerell.

†Sidon, Captain G. Goldsmith; Highflyer, Captain John Moore; Miranda, Captain E.M. Lynne; Viper, Lieutenant [Final line illegible]

War-Department, July 4, 1855.

LORD PANMURE has this day received a Despatch and its Enclosures, of which the following are copies, addressed to His Lordship by the late Field-Marshal the Lord Raglan, G.C.B.

Before Sevastopol,
June 23, 1855.

MY LORD,

I INFORMED your Lordship in my despatch of the 19th instant, that I would make a more special report upon the movements of the 3rd Division, as soon as I should receive the reports of Lieutenant-General Sir R. England, and the Major-Generals commanding brigades under him.

The 1st Brigade, under Major-General Barnard, proceeded down the Woronzow-road, and was placed in position on the right of the ravine, ready to co-operate with the columns of attack on the right; whilst the 2nd Brigade, under Major-General Eyre, moved down the ravine which separates the left of the English from the right of the French advanced works, for the purpose of attacking the enemy's ambuscades, and making a demonstration on the head of the dockyard creek.

This service was performed with the utmost gallantry, and notwithstanding that they were exposed to a most galling fire, the troops maintained themselves in the position they had taken up during the day, and in the evening withdrew unmolested, leaving a post at the cemetery, which had been one of the objects of the attack in the morning. The action having from circumstances become a most serious one, I beg, as the most satisfactory way of making your Lordship acquainted with the particulars, to lay a copy of the Major-General's letter before your Lordship, and to solicit your attention to the officers whose services he particularly notices, and at the same time to his own distinguished conduct.

Your Lordship will see with concern that the loss sustained by this brigade is very considerable, and that Major-General Eyre is himself wounded but I have every reason to hope that the injury he has received is not very severe, and will not incapacitate him from the discharge of his duty with the same energy and devotion as he has already applied himself to its performance during the protracted operations before Sevastopol.

Lieutenant-General Sir G. Brown, to whose able assistance I referred in my former despatch, has specially brought to my notice the distinguished conduct of Colonel Yea, who was unfortunately killed, and pays a just tribute to the great merits of this deeply lamented officer; of Lieutenant-Colonel Lysons, of the 23rd; Lieutenant-Colonel Johnstone, of the 33rd; and Captain Gwilt of the 34th, all of whom are wounded; of Major-General Codrington, who commanded the Light Division; of Captain Blackett, of the Rifle Brigade, who has lost a leg; and of Captain Forman, of the Rifle Brigade, who fell upon the occasion; and Major-General Codrington mentions the admirable conduct of Captain Turner, of the 7th Foot; Major Macdonell, of the Rifle Brigade; Lieutenant Knox, of the Rifle Brigade, who is wounded; and Lieutenant Donovan, of the 33rd.

Lieutenant-General Sir R. England speaks highly of Colonel Cobbe, of the 4th Regiment, who commanded in the trenches of the left attack, and is severely wounded; and Lieutenant-General Bentinck eulogizes the conduct of Colonel Lord West, of the 21st Foot, who assumed the command of the left column after the death of Major-General Sir J. Campbell; of Lieutenant-Colonel Warre, who succeeded to the command of the 57th Regiment, on the death of Colonel Shadforth; of Lieutenant-Colonel Cole, commanding 17th Regiment ; and of Captains Croker (who was killed) Gordon, McKinstry, and O'Conor, and Lieutenant Thompson, of the 17th Regiment; and Lieutenant Shadwell Clerke, of the 21st Regiment; and Colour-Serjeant Colcliffe and Serjeant Pratt, of the 17th; and Captain the Honourable J. Stuart, and Lieutenants

Boileau (who is severely wounded) and Saunders, of the Rifle Brigade.

Major-General H. Jones reports most favourably of the services of the following officers of Engineers: Lieutenant-Colonel Gordon, Lieutenant-Colonel Chapman, Lieutenant-Colonel Tylden, Lieutenant Donnelly, Lieutenant Fisher, and he deeply laments the loss of Captain Jesse, Lieutenant Graves, and Lieutenant Murray, who fell upon the occasion.

I must express my obligations to Lieutenant General Sir R. England, Lieutenant-General Pennefather, Lieutenant-General Bentinck, and Major-General Codrington, for the able manner in which they conducted their duties; and I avail myself of the present opportunity to inform your Lordship, that Lieutenant-General Pennefather, who was then labouring under illness, is now in so bad a state of health as to be under the necessity of withdrawing from the army. I shall deeply regret his departure, entertaining the highest opinion of him, and knowing his devotion to Her Majesty's service.

I must not omit to mention the following officers of the Royal Navy, who particularly distinguished themselves on the 18th: Captain Peel, who commanded the whole of the sailors employed, and is severely wounded; Messrs. Wood (severely wounded) and Daniel, who have been through the whole siege; Lieutenants Urmston and Dalyell, who are both severely wounded; and Mr. Parsons, Mate, who is wounded; Lieutenants Cave and Kidd, both wounded, the latter mortally; and Mr. Kennedy, Mate.

I enclose the returns of casualties from the 18th to the 21st.

I have, &c.
RAGLAN.
The Lord Panmure, &c. &c. &c.

Enclosure 1.

Camp before Sevastopol,
June 19, 1855.

ЗIR,

I HAVE the honour to report, for the information of Lieutenant-General Sir Richard England, K.C.B., commanding the division, that, agreeably to his instructions, I moved off yesterday morning between one and two o'clock A.M. with my brigade, consisting of the 9th, 18th, 28th, 38th, and 44th Regiments – total strength about 2,000 bayonets, and proceeded down the ravine on our left, by the French Picquet-house, for the purpose of attacking the enemy's ambuscades, and of making a demonstration on that side.

In attacking the first of these ambuscades we were anticipated by the French, who cleverly took them on their left flank as we advanced in front, and made several prisoners. Beyond this the French had no instructions to co-operate with us; I, therefore, immediately pushed on an advanced guard under Major Fielden, 44th Regiment, composed of marksmen from each regiment, supporting it on the right by the 44th and 38th Regiments, and on the left by the 18th Regiment, keeping at first the 9th and 28th Regiments in reserve.

The enemy, whose strength I could not estimate, occupied a strong position; their right rested on a Mamelon, their left on a Cemetery. These points were occupied by marksmen.

The intervening ground was intersected and the road barricaded with stone walls, which our men were obliged to pull down, under fire, before they could advance.

In rear of this position, towards the fortress, the enemy occupied several houses, and there were bodies of the enemy seen in rear, as reserves, but of what strength I could not say. This position, under the fire of the guns of the fortress, was strong, and we could not expect to carry it and retain it without sustaining a considerable loss, and which, I regret to state, we have experienced both in officers and men; but it is gratifying to feel that they all most nobly performed their duty on this occasion. The 18th Regiment pushed on, and occupied some houses immediately under the Garden-wall Battery.

The 44th occupied some houses on the right, from whence they kept up a fire on the enemy's embrasures. Lieutenant-Colonel Lowth moved on with his regiment (the 33th), and after taking possession of some houses in front, endeavoured to turn the flank of a battery which annoyed us in front. These parties were afterwards from time to time reinforced or relieved by the 9th Regiment, the 28th Regiment being drawn up in line in rear to support the whole.

Having driven the enemy from these points, I continued to occupy them, with the view to ulterior movements, in the event of the attack on the right being successful, and until it was decided what portion of the ground should be retained for siege operations.

I cannot sufficiently express my sense of the conduct of the officers, non-commissioned officers, and men, on this occasion. They attacked the enemy in the first instance with the utmost gallantry, holding their ground until late in the evening, although exposed all day to a concentrated fire from the guns of the fortress, in addition to which I believe the enemy brought up some field-guns, and kept continually firing shells. The losses occasioned were considerable, the total being 31 officers, 44 Serjeants, and 487 rank and file, killed or wounded.

At about five o'clock in the evening, after giving orders for the removal of the wounded to the rear, the gradual withdrawal of the parties from the front – the ground being too far in advance to be permanently occupied for siege operations, I gave over the command of the brigade to Lieutenant-Colonel Adams, 28th Regiment, having received a wound in the head in the early part of the day, which prevented me latterly from attending properly to my duties. The enemy did not attempt to molest the troops on retiring. The conduct of all was so exemplary during this trying day, that I can scarcely with justice particularize individuals. I beg, however, to thank the officers commanding corps for the assistance they afforded me, viz., Lieutenant-Colonel

Borton, commanding 9th Regiment; Lieutenant-Colonel Edwards, commanding the 18th Royal Irish; Lieutenant-Colonel Adams, commanding the 28th Regiment; Colonel the Honourable A. Spencer, commanding the 44th Regiment, who was wounded; and to Lieutenant-Colonel Staveley, who succeeded to the command of the regiment on Colonel Spencer being obliged to quit the field; Lieutenant-Colonel Lowth, commanding 38th Regiment, who was also wounded, and to Lieutenant-Colonel Sparks, who succeeded him in the command of the regiment; and Major Fielden, 44th, commanding the advanced guard.

I received also the utmost assistance from my Brigade-Major Captain Faussett, 44th Regiment, and also on this, as on many other occasions from my Aide-de-Camp Captain Robertson, 4th Regiment. I was also indebted to Brevet-Major Stuart Wortley, Deputy Assistant Quartermaster-General, who kindly volunteered to act on my Staff.

I beg also to report the judicious arrangements of the Medical Department on this occasion, and especially to thank Assistant-Surgeon John Gibbons, 44th Regiment, and Assistant-Surgeon Jeeves, 38th Regiment, for their zealous and humane exertions in the field, while exposed to a most galling fire.

I have, &c.,
(Signed) WM. EYRE,
Major-General.

War-Department, July 11, 1855.

LORD PANMURE has received a Despatch, of which the following is a copy, addressed to his Lordship by Field-Marshal the late Lord Raglan, G.C.B.; and has also this day received two Despatches and their Enclosures, addressed to his Lordship by Lieutenant-General Simpson, Commanding Her Majesty's Forces in the East, of which copies are also subjoined.

Before Sevastopol,
June 25, 1855.

MY LORD,

I AM much concerned to have to announce to you the death of Major-General Estcourt, Adjutant-General of this army, which took place yesterday morning at nine o'clock, after an illness of little more than three days; he died of cholera, and I deeply lament the loss of so estimable a man, and of an officer so anxious to perform his duty.

I beg strongly to recommend that Lieutenant-Colonel the Honourable W. L. Pakenham may be placed at the head of the Adjutant-General's department. He has done the duty of Deputy-Adjutant-General since the army was formed; he is an excellent man of business, and well acquainted with the service in all its branches, and his appointment would not alone be agreeable to me, but would be equally so to General Simpson, who entertains a very high opinion of his qualifications, and reposes every confidence in him.

I have reported the death of General Estcourt to the General Commanding in Chief, and have mentioned to his Lordship my recommendation of Lieutenant-Colonel the Honourable W. L. Pakenham.

I have, &c.,
RAGLAN.
The Lord Panmure, &c. &c. &c.

Before Sevastopol,
June 30, 1855.

MY LORD,

IT is with the deepest regret that I announce to your Lordship the death of Field-Marshal Lord Raglan, G.C.B., which melancholy event took place a little before nine o'clock on the evening of Thursday last, the 28th instant, his Lordship expired without any suffering in the midst of the officers composing his personal staff.

I have further to report that being the next senior officer present, I have assumed the command of this army, until instructions shall arrive from England.

I have, &c.,
JAMES SIMPSON,
Lieutenant-General Commanding
. I have, &c.,
The Lord Panmure, &c. &c. &c.

CHAPTER 11

CONTINUING OPERATIONS AGAINST SEVASTOPOL AND THE BATTLE OF TCHERNAYA

War-Department, July 23, 1855.

LORD PANMURE has this day received a Despatch and its Enclosures, of which the following are copies, addressed to his Lordship by Lieutenant-General Simpson, Commanding Her Majesty's Forces in the East.

Before Sevastopol,
July 10, 1855.

MY LORD,

I HAVE the honour to enclose the returns of casualties to the 8th instant.

Your Lordship will regret to see that the lists of killed and wounded are heavy; but the nearer we approach the defences of the place the greater number of casualties must be expected.

Brevet-Major Harrison, 63rd Regiment, was killed on the evening of the 7th instant, whilst proceeding to the trenches; he was a most excellent officer, and is a serious loss to Her Majesty's service.

It will give your Lordship sincere pleasure to mark the improvement in the general health of the troops.

At five o'clock this morning a heavy fire was opened upon the Redan by the Allied batteries.

I have, &c.,
JAMES SIMPSON,
Lieutenant-General Commanding.
The Lord Panmure, &c. &c. &c.

Admiralty, July 23, 1855.

DESPATCHES, of which the following are copies, have been received at the Admiralty from Rear-Admiral Sir Edmund Lyons, Bart., G.C.B., Commander-in-Chief of Her Majesty's Ships and Vessels in the Black Sea.

Royal Albert, off Sevastopol,
July 10, 1855.

SIR,

THEIR Lordships will have great pleasure in learning that Commander Osborn, of the Vesuvius, mentions in favourable terms a letter he had received from Lieutenant W.N.W. Hewett, the Commander of the Beagle, reporting the destruction of the floating bridge in the Straits of Genitchi.

2. I have now the honour to enclose a copy of that letter, and to draw their Lordships' attention to the excellent arrangements made by Lieutenant Hewett, as well as to the gallant and able way in which his orders were executed by Mr. Martin Tracey, Midshipman, of the Vesuvius, Mr. John Hayles, Acting Gunner of the Beagle and the boats' crews, one of whom, Joseph Trewavas, Ordinary Seaman, lent from the Agamemnon, was wounded, and is particularly mentioned as having cut the hawsers.

I am, &c.
(Signed) EDMUND LYONS,
Rear-Admiral and Commander-in-Chief.
To the Secretary of the Admiralty.
London.

Beagle, off the town of Ghenitchesk,
4th July, 1855.

SIR,

I HAVE the honour to inform you that on my arrival off this place I immediately proceeded to minutely examine the communication between the town and Arabat Spit, and, on so doing, found it to be by means of a ferry of two large flats and hawsers, which I determined to destroy if possible.

Accordingly on the forenoon of yesterday I despatched my gig, under Mr. John Hayles, Acting Gunner of this ship, and paddle-box boat, under Mr. Martin Tracey, Midshipman, of the Vesuvius.

I have much pleasure in reporting that they succeeded entirely in destroying it by cutting the hawsers and casting the boats adrift, which was done under a very heavy fire of musketry at about 80 yards, the troops completely lining the beach, and the adjacent houses being filled with riflemen.

Great credit is due to Mr. Hayles for his activity and zeal in destroying the same, and to Mr. Martin Tracey for the effectual fire he kept up in covering his retreat, the firing from the ship and paddle-box boat at the same time causing great confusion and loss amongst the enemy as they retired from their exposed position.

Mr. Hayles speaks in the highest terms of the boat's crew, especially of Joseph Trewavas, Ordinary Seaman, lent from the Agamemnon, who cut the hawsers.

I enclose a list of casualties, which, I am happy to say, is very small, although the gig and paddle-box boat were riddled with musket balls.

I have &c.,
(Signed) W.N.W. HEWETT,
Lieutenant Commanding.
To Commander S. Osborne,
Senior Officer of Her
Majesty's ship Vesuvius.

War-Department, July 30, 1855.

LORD PANMURE has this day received two Despatches and their Enclosures, of which the following are copies, addressed to his Lordship by Lieutenant-General Simpson, Commanding Her Majesty's Forces in the East.

Before Sevastopol,
July 17, 1855.

MY LORD,

I HAVE the honour to submit for your Lordship's information the accompanying letters from Lieutenant-Colonel Campbell, 90th Regiment; the one referring to his personal services, and the other to those of a party of the 55th Regiment on the occasion of the capture of the Quarries in front of the Redan, on the night of the 7th ultimo.

With regard to Lieutenant-Colonel Campbell's own services I think it right to inform your Lordship that I find, upon enquiry, that the charge of holding the Quarries on the night in question, and of repelling the repeated attacks of the enemy was confided to that officer after he had led the assault, and was in fact a separate and detached command from that of Colonel Shirley, who acted as General of the day in the trenches of the right attack; the despatch of the late Field-Marshal Lord Raglan has already shewn how admirably that duty was performed by the brave men who were under the immediate direction of Lieutenant-Colonel Campbell.

The Lieutenant-Colonel's letter, recording the good conduct of the party of the 55th Regiment, speaks for itself.

I have, &c.,

JAMES SIMPSON,
Lieutenant-General Commanding.
The Lord Panmure, &c. &c. &c.

Enclosure 1.

Camp, Light Division,
July 13, 1855.

SIR,

THE despatch of the late lamented Field-Marshal Lord Raglan, of 9th June, mentions that I commanded the storming party on the Quarries on the evening of the 7th June. May I beg most respectfully that you will bring it to the notice of Lieutenant-General Simpson, Commanding the Forces, that I not only had the honour of commanding the storming party, but that having been twice wounded in the assault, I retained the sole and undivided command in the Quarries, not only of the original attacking force and supports, but of all reinforcements, during the whole night, until relieved at 7 A.M. on the 8th. The despatches must have explained already that the enemy made several desperate efforts, during the night, to regain the works, and that on three occasions overpowering numbers succeeded in re-entering, but were, on all occasions, driven back at the point of the bayonet. The entire night was, indeed, one continued struggle for this position, the fatigue and anxiety of which I have never recovered from. When Lord Raglan's despatch was completed, I have reason to suppose his Lordship had not received the details, as my own report to Colonel Shirley, General of the trenches, was unavoidably delayed in consequence of my wounds, and not being able to write. In justice to myself, conscious of having performed an important duty, to the best of my ability, and successfully, I now respectfully submit this statement to the Commander of the Forces, with the hope that he may be pleased to have my services on this occasion mentioned and particularized. At present, several officers have equal praise in the despatch who were not in the Quarries at all.

I have, &c.
ROB. CAMPBELL, Lieutenant-Colonel,
Commanding 90th Light Infantry.
Lieutenant-Colonel Brownrigg,
Military Secretary, &c. &c. &c.
Head Quarters.

Enclosure 2.

Camp, July 10.

SIR,

I HAVE the honour of forwarding the enclosed letter for the consideration of the Lieutenant- General Commanding the Forces; but I beg to remark, that in my report of the occurrences on the night of the 7th of June, I took care to mention the services of the 55th Regiment, which appear to have been overlooked in the late Field-Marshal's despatch.

I have, &c.,
H. SHIRLEY, Colonel, 88th Foot,
Commanding in the trenches on
the night of 7th June.
The Military Secretary,
Head Quarters.

Enclosure 3.

Before Sevastopol,
July 8, 1855.

SIR,

I BEG to draw your attention to the inadvertent omission, in Lord Raglan's despatch of the 9th June, of any mention of the 55th Regiment as sharing in the attack and defence of the Quarries, during the night of the 7th June. I did not mention the regiment in my report, as they were not given over to me as part of the attacking party; but the officer commanding the party informs me that they, being originally told off as a working party, were directed by the Engineer (Captain Browne) to throw down their tools, and that they were moved by you as a support to Egerton's Rifle-pit, whence they moved to support the attacking party, and did good service in clearing the Russian trenches, and in the defence throughout the night, as their severe list of killed and wounded attests (53 out of 160); many of the former not being found until the flag of truce, when their bodies were found in the trenches they had gained.

The officer in command of the party, Captain, now Major, Cure, reports that the gallant conduct of Lieutenant Stone, who was killed at the head of his men, charging the Russians in their trench with the bayonet, and of Captain Elton, who, with a small body of men, formed a covering party on the right to those who were reversing the trench, is particularly deserving of mention, as is that also of Lieutenants Scott and Williams, who were most active in performing their duties.

Hoping that the Commander of the Forces may deem this statement sufficiently satisfactory to enable him to move in the subject,

I have, &c.,
ROB. CAMPBELL, Lieutenant-Colonel,
90th Regiment, Commanding Assault.
To Colonel Shirley, Commanding
2nd Brigade, Light Division.

Before Sevastopol,
July 17, 1855.

MY LORD,

I HAVE the honour to transmit herewith the Nominal and Numerical Return of Casualties in this army, from the 13th to the 15th instant; also, the Weekly Report of the Inspector-General of Hospitals, which will be most gratifying to your Lordship, as shewing a steady decrease in the number of cases of spasmodic cholera.

I have but little to report to your Lordship: our siege operations are steadily progressing.

Last night, about eleven o'clock, a sortie was made by the enemy on the right of the French works, in front of the Mamelon; the cannonade and fire of musquetry was exceedingly heavy, but I have not as yet been made acquainted with any particulars of the attack.

I regret to have to announce to your Lordship the death of Captain Rowland A. Fraser, of the 42nd Highlanders, a very talented young officer, who was killed in the trenches of the right attack, last night, by the splinter of a shell.

I have, &c.,
JAMES SIMPSON,
Lieutenant-General Commanding.
The Lord Panmure, &c. &c. &c

War-Department, August 1, 1855.

LORD PANMURE has this day received a Despatch and its Enclosures, of which the following are copies, addressed to his Lordship by Lieutenant-General Simpson, Commanding Her Majesty's Forces in the East.

Before Sevastopol,
July 21, 1855.

MY LORD,

I HAVE great pleasure to inform your Lordship that the health of the Army has greatly improved; cholera has nearly disappeared, and although more sickness has appeared amongst the officers, it is not of that character to cause uneasiness.

With reference to the exterior army, the Russians hold their strong position on the Mackenzie Heights, extending by Aitodor to Albat, with advanced posts by Chouli, Ogenbash, and the strong range of heights overhanging Urkusta and the valley of Baidar. It is reported they have also a force of artillery and infantry at Alupka. The French have pushed forward the whole of their cavalry into the Valley of Baidar, resting upon the Sardinians, upon the left bank of the Souhai river, and communicating with the French upon the Tchernaya, whilst the high ridge protecting Balaklava is guarded by the Turkish Army.

I propose sending four squadrons of light cavalry into the Valley of Baidar to-morrow, to protect and afford convoys to the commissariat for the purpose of bringing in forage and supplies for the use of the army.

Major-General Markham, arrived on the 19th instant, and, agreeable to the instructions conveyed in your Lordship's telegraphic message, I have appointed him to the command of the 2nd Division.

Sir Stephen Lushington, K.C.B., having been promoted to the rank of Admiral, has been relieved in the command of the Naval Brigade, by Captain Honourable Henry Keppel. I take this opportunity of recording my sense of the ability and zeal with which he has throughout conducted his arduous and responsible situation of commanding the Naval Brigade, which has rendered such excellent service in our batteries.

I beg also to report to your Lordship that Mr. Commissary-General Filder has been obliged to relinquish the command of his important department, and will have to return to England upon the recommendation of a Medical Board.

I inclose the list of casualties to the 19th instant.

I have, &c.,
JAMES SIMPSON,
Lieutenant-General Commanding.
The Lord Panmure, &c. &c. &c.

War-Department, August 6, 1855.

LORD PANMURE has this day received a Despatch and its Enclosures, of which the following are copies, addressed to his Lordship by General Simpson, Commanding Her Majesty's Forces in the East.

Before Sevastopol,
July 24, 1855.

MY LORD,

I HAVE the honour to enclose the weekly return from Dr. Hall of the state of the sick. Your Lordship will read with satisfaction the improved condition of the health of the Army. I had entertained fears, from the very great heat of the last few days, that cholera would have assumed a more virulent form, but such has fortunately not been the case.

I have nothing to relate of importance respecting the siege. On the night of the 22nd the enemy opened a very heavy fire of musketry from the parapets of the Malakoff and adjacent works, but they did not attempt an attack. They opened a similar fire in the course of the night on the left of the French. I have every reason to believe that they were apprehensive of an attack on the part of our Allies, and for this reason opened the fire above described, which did no damage to either the works or soldiers.

The troops in the Baidar Valley have not altered their positions from the date of the last time I had the honour to address you.

I have, &c.,
JAMES SIMPSON,
Lieutenant-General Commanding.
The Lord Panmure, &c. &c. &c.

War-Department, August 13, 1855.

LORD PANMURE has this day received a Despatch and its Enclosures, of which the following are copies, addressed to his Lordship by General Simpson, Commanding Her Majesty's Forces in the East.

Before Sevastopol,
July 31, 1855.

MY LORD,

I BEG to enclose the list of casualties to the 29th instant, which I regret to say are very heavy.

The proximity of our works to those of the enemy, together with the lightness of the night, and rocky nature of the ground, making it impossible to obtain rapid cover, materially contributes to such a result; notwithstanding which disadvantages our engineers continue steadily, though slowly, to advance in the direction of the Great Redan.

An agreeable change has taken place the last few days in the temperature of the weather; heavy showers of rain have occasionally fallen.

Several reconnaissances have been made from the valley of Baidar towards Ozenbash, Aitodor, and through the Phoros Pass towards Alupka, the enemy nowhere appearing in any force; but the narrowness of the mountain roads, with the exception of the Woronzow, makes it unnecessary for them to alter their concentrated position on the heights of Mackenzie and plateau of the Belbek.

The health of the troops continues very satisfactory.

I have, &c.,
JAMES SIMPSON,
Lieutenant-General Commanding
The Lord Panmure, &c. &c. &c.

War-Department, August 16, 1855.

LORD PANMURE has this day received a Despatch and its Enclosures, of which the following are copies, addressed to his Lordship by General Simpson, Commanding Her Majesty's Forces in the East.

Before Sevastopol,
August 4, 1855.

MY LORD,

I HAVE the honour to acquaint your Lordship that on the night of the 2nd instant, between ten and eleven o'clock, the enemy made a sortie in considerable force by the Woronzoff-road. The strength of the enemy is computed to be about 2000. Their object was to destroy a heavy iron chevaux de frize, made across the Woronzoff-road, between our right and left attacks, and being further supported by heavy columns in rear, to take advantage of such circumstances as might present themselves.

They came on with loud cheers and bugling, and were received with great gallantry by our advanced picquet, under the command of Lieutenant R.E. Carr, of the 39th Regiment, who withdrew his men, firing at the same time upon the enemy, to the main body, under the command of Captain Leckie, 39th Regiment.

A heavy and well directed fire was opened upon the enemy by the party under Captain Leckie on the Woronzoff-road, as also by the guards of the trenches on the right of the fourth parallel, under the command of Captain Boyle, of the 89th Regiment, and Captain Turner, of the 1st Royals, which, in about ten minutes, caused the enemy to retire from an attack which, if it had not been so well met, might have been a serious affair.

The enemy left four men killed, and some wounded were carried away. We had only one man slightly wounded in this affair.

I have the satisfaction of informing your Lordship of the return to this Army of Captain Montagu, of the Royal Engineers, from being a prisoner of war. He expresses himself highly grateful for the kindness with which he was treated by the Russians during his captivity.

It is with great regret that I have to communicate to your Lordship that Lieutenant-General Sir R. England, G.C.B., has been compelled, upon the recommendation of a Medical Board, to return to England. Sir R. England is the last of the General Officers who left the United Kingdom in command of a Division; he has remained at his post throughout the trying heats of Bulgaria, and the severities and hardships of the winter's campaign in the Crimea; and great credit is due to this officer for the constancy and untiring zeal he has exhibited in carrying out arduous and difficult duties on all occasions.

I have, &c.,
JAMES SIMPSON,
General Commanding.
The Lord Panmure, &c. &c. &c.

War-Department, August 23, 1855.

LORD PANMURE has this day received a Despatch and its Enclosures, of which the following are copies, addressed to his Lordship by General Simpson.

Before Sevastopol,
August 11, 1855.

MY LORD,

I HAD the honour to acquaint you that during the past week the Army has been unceasingly employed in strengthening and improving the advanced works, which are now so close to the enemy, that it is with the greatest difficulty any approach can be made. By the casualty return which I enclose, your Lordship will regret to see a large number, though the proportion of wounded over the killed is considerable.

Brevet-Major Macgowan, of the 93rd, is supposed to have fallen a prisoner into the hands of the enemy. I have caused a letter to be addressed to the Governor of the place, to ascertain his fate, but up to this time I have received no answer.

The health of the Army is, on the whole, good, although the cholera still continues to take daily several victims.

I have, &c.,
JAMES SIMPSON,
General Commanding.
The Lord Panmure, &c. &c. &c.

War-Department, August 27, 1855.

LORD PANMURE has this day received a Despatch and its Enclosures, of which the following are copies, addressed to his Lordship by General Simpson.

Before Sevastopol,
August 14, 1855.

MY LORD,

DURING the last few days considerable activity has been exhibited in the movements of the enemy, both in the town and on the north side; and, from the information we have received from the country, as well as the examination of deserters, I have reason to believe that the Russians may attempt to force us to raise the siege by a vigorous attack from without.

Every precaution is taken on the part of the Allies, and the ground occupied by the Sardinians above the village of Tchorgouna, and in its front, has been made very strong through the energy and skill of General La Marmora, who is unceasing in his precaution, and shews the utmost disposition to co-operate in the most agreeable manner with the Allies.

The fire has, if anything, been rather less during the day, since my last despatch. At times, however, the enemy open heavily for a short period, causing many casualties; and amongst them I regret to have to announce that of Brevet-Major Hugh Drummond, Scots Fusilier Guards, who was killed yesterday afternoon by a fragment of a shell. His loss is deeply felt by all who knew him, and Her Majesty has lost the services of a most promising officer.

The firing on our side has been directed in a great measure against the large barracks, dockyard buildings, and the town, all of which shew visible signs of the admirable practice of the Royal Artillery.

I further beg to enclose the returns of casualties to the 12th instant.

I have to apologize to your Lordship for having omitted to inform you before that I had despatched the steamer Indiana, on the 8th instant, to Corfu, for the purpose of conveying the 82nd Regiment from that island to the Crimea.

Drafts for the Light Division and 71st Regiment, to the number of 800 men, the remainder of the Carabineers, and one squadron of the 1st Dragoon Guards, have arrived.

I have, &c.,
JAMES SIMPSON,
General Commanding.
The Lord Panmure, &c. &c. &c.

War-Department, August 29, 1855.

LORD PANMURE has this day received two Despatches and their Enclosures, of which the following are copies, addressed to his Lordship by General Simpson.

Before Sevastopol,
August 18, 1855.

MY LORD,

In my despatch of the 14th instant, I informed your Lordship that I had reason to believe that the Russians would attempt, by a vigorous attack, to force us to raise the siege.

This they endeavoured to do on the morning of the 16th, but the result was most glorious to those of the Allied troops who had the good fortune to be engaged.

The action commenced before daylight, by a heavy column of Russians, under the command of General Liprandi, and composed of the 6th and 17th Divisions, with the 4th and 7th Divisions in reserve, attacking the advanced posts of the Sardinians.

The ground occupied by them is on commanding hills on the right of the position, on the left bank of the Souhaia river, where it forms its junction with the Tchernaya, with two advanced posts on the opposite side. These were held with very determined gallantry for a considerable time, but being separated from their supports by the river, and not having the protection of artillery, they were compelled to leave the most advanced one.

About the same time, the 5th and 12th Divisions, to which was added a portion of the 17th; advanced against the bridge of Tractir, held by one battalion of French infantry of the line, who were for a short time obliged to yield and fall back upon the main supports; with these, however, they quickly retook the bridge at the point of the bayonet.

Again the Russians attacked with persevering courage, and were enabled to follow up their advantage by gaining the heights which rise precipitously on each side of the road; their success was but momentary – they were driven back across the river, leaving the ground covered with dead and wounded.

The Russian General, in no way daunted by the failure of his two attempts, ordered a second column, of equal force to the first, to attack; they advanced with such impetuosity, covered by the fire of their numerous artillery, that a third time the bridge was carried, and the heights above it crowned, but they were again repulsed, and retired in great confusion into the plain, followed by the bayonets of our gallant Allies.

The General Officer who commanded the Russian column, and who is supposed to be General Read, was killed, and in his possession was found the orders for the battle, signed by Prince Gortchakoff, who commanded in person.

From these it would appear that it was a most determined attempt to force us to raise the siege. Had they succeeded, Balaklava was to have been attacked by one portion of their army, whilst the heights on which we now are, were to have been stormed with the other; at the same time a vigorous sortie was to have been made from the town on the French works, on our extreme left, from the Quarantine, and another on the works on our extreme right on Mount Sapoune.

The action which I have endeavoured to describe is most glorious to the arms of the French and Sardinian troops. To meet the force of the Russians, the former had but 12,000 infantry, and 4 batteries of artillery engaged; the latter had 10,000 men in position, 4,500 actually engaged, and 24 pieces of cannon.

The Russian force consisted of from 50,000 to 60,000 men, with 160 pieces of artillery, and cavalry to the amount of 6,000.

This disparity of numbers will readily explain to your Lordship the difficulty that would have been experienced, had an attempt been made to follow up the advantage by a pursuit. The Russian retreat, moreover, was protected by the fire from the heavy guns in position on the Mackenzie heights.

The loss sustained by the Russians is estimated at between 5,000 and 6,000 men, including 600 prisoners, whilst on the part of the Allies it does not amount to more than 1,000 men.

This brilliant affair has caused the greatest delight amongst the ranks of the allied army; and while it adds fresh lustre to the gallant achievements of the French arms, it is with the utmost pleasure that I have to record the intrepid conduct and gallant bearing of the Sardinian troops, under General de la Marmora, who have for the first time met, conquered, and shed their blood against our common enemy, who is now disturbing the peace of Europe.

Captain Mowbray's battery of 32-pounder howitzers was placed in advance with the Sardinian troops, and did most excellent service in preventing the advance of the enemy's artillery.

Our cavalry, under Lieutenant-General Sir J. Scarlett, K.C.B., was placed in the plain of Balaklava, prepared to take advantage of any circumstance that might present itself, but the opportunity did not arise for calling upon their services.

I regret that I am unable to give a more detailed account of the part performed by the Sardinians, as up to this time I have not received General Delia Marmora's report.

I have, &c.,
JAMES SIMPSON,
General Commanding.
The Lord Panmure, &c. &c. &c.

War-Department, September 3, 1855.

LORD PANMURE has this day received a Despatch and its Enclosures, of which the following are copies, addressed to his Lordship by General Simpson.

Before Sevastopol,
August 21, 1855.

MY LORD,

IN my despatch of the 18th, instant I was unable to give as detailed an account of the part taken by the Sardinian troops, in the battle of the Tchernaia, as I could have wished. I have since received General La Marmora's report, of which I have now the honour to send you a copy.

The killed and wounded of the Russian army exceed, if anything, the number I originally stated. An armistice was granted, to enable the enemy to bury the dead, and vast quantities were carried away.

The fire from the batteries of the Allies has been very effective, and the result attained has been sufficient to enable the works against the place to progress satisfactorily.

Major McGowan, 93rd Highlanders, who was reported by me as missing, in my despatch of the 11th August, I have since ascertained was attacked whilst posting his sentries in advance of the trenches, wounded severely, and made prisoner.

I have, &c.,
JAMES SIMPSON,
General Commanding.
The Lord Panmure, &c. &c. &c.

War-Department, September 5, 1855.

LORD PANMURE has this day received a Despatch and its Enclosures, of which the following are copies, addressed to his Lordship by General Simpson.

Before Sevastopol,
August 25, 1855.

MY LORD,

HAVING been engaged since daylight in a careful observation of the position in front of Balaklava, I am unable to address your Lordship at any length this day.

The enemy have been concentrating troops at the Mackenzie, Tasova, and Karales, their left extending as far as the village of Makoul, and are supposed to have received considerable reinforcements, which probably consist of two divisions of Grenadiers, which have been conveyed in carts from Bakshiserai and Simpheropol.

The bridge across the Great Harbour is nearly completed, and large bodies of men are employed in erecting earthworks on the north side of the harbour. Intrenchments have been thrown up on the Sievernaya Hill, extending from the sea coast to the site of the first lighthouse, facing the north.

From various sources, we learn that the Russians on the right bank of the Tchernaya, are held in perfect readiness for an offensive movement.

Our siege operations progress steadily, with I regret to say heavy casualties on our side, as your Lordship will see by the accompanying lists.

I have, &c.,
JAMES SIMPSON,
General Commanding.
The Lord Panmure, &c. &c. &c.

PROCEEDINGS OF NAVAL BRIGADE.

No. 754. Royal Albert, off Sevastopol,
September 10, 1855.

SIR,

I BEG leave to enclose, for the information of the Lords Commissioners of the Admiralty, copy of a Letter from Captain the Honourable Henry Keppel, reporting the proceedings of the Naval Brigade under his command, on the 7th and 8th instant, and enclosing a list of casualties.

I am, &c.
(Signed) EDMUND LYONS,
Rear-Admiral and Commander-in-Chief,
The Secretary of the Admiralty.

REPORTING PROCEEDINGS.

Royal Naval Brigade,
No. 16. before Sevastopol,
September 9, 1855.

SIR,

I HAVE the honour to inform you that, in pursuance of instructions, a vigorous fire was opened from the batteries at six o'clock on the morning of the 7th, and was maintained throughout the day; the fire was recommenced yesterday morning with increased vigour, preparatory to an assault to be made by our Allies on the Malakoff, and subsequently by ourselves on the Redan.

2. At noon the French were observed to start *en masse* from their trenches and

possess themselves in gallant style of the Malakoff Battery, on which the tricolor flag was hoisted and the imperial eagles planted within ten minutes of their quitting their trenches.

3. The French flag was no sooner displayed on the Malakoff than our storming party issued from their trenches and assailed the salient angle of the Redan, but the enemy were by that time prepared to meet them, and as the supporting party advanced, a heavy fire of grape and canister was opened on them, in spite of a brisk fire kept up from our batteries on all parts of the Redan not assailed, as well as on the flanking batteries.

4. After maintaining the footing they had gained for some time, our troops were obliged to retire, the killed and wounded left on the ground sufficiently testifying how gallantly they had fought.

5. The fire from our batteries was kept up until dark, and at about eleven o'clock the enemy evacuated the Redan after having fired a train that exploded the magazines.

6. This morning's light showed how successful and complete had been the victory gained by the Allied Forces.

7. The enemy had evacuated all their positions on the south side of the harbour; the town, Fort Nicolai, Fort Paul, and dockyard, were in flames, and their line of battle ships had been sunk in the positions they were last seen in when at anchor.

8. The conduct of the officers and men of the brigade under my command has been such as to continue to merit the high opinion you have been pleased to express of them.

9. I have the honour to enclose a list of casualties for the 7th and 8th.

I am, &c.,
(Signed) HENRY KEPPEL,
Captain Commanding Royal Naval Brigade.
Rear-Admiral Sir Edmund
Lyons, Bart., &c. &c. &c.,
Commander-in-Chief.

War-Department, September 10, 1855.

LORD PANMURE has this day received a Despatch and its Enclosures, of which the following are copies, addressed to his Lordship by General Simpson.

Before Sevastopol,
August 28, 1855.

MY LORD,

SINCE the attempt of the enemy to force the passage of the Tchernaya, on the 16th instant, no movement of aggression has taken place; but all the accounts I have received tend to shew a disposition on their part to renew the attack. I have considered it necessary to send the Highland Division, composed of the 42nd, 71st, 79th, and 93rd Regiments, under the command of Lieutenant-General Sir C. Campbell, to reinforce our extreme right, and they are now encamped on the slopes of the heights overhanging the village of Kamara.

I have likewise placed 50 guns and the cavalry in reserve, to act on the first appearance of the enemy.

The 56th Regiment has arrived, and I have attached it to the 1st Division.

The siege operations are progressing favourably; but, owing to the brightness of the nights, a large amount of work cannot be executed.

The raft bridge from the north side to the south shore has been completed, and is actually in use by the enemy; and a considerable increase of troops, with a good deal of movement, is observable in the town.

The installation of the Knights of the Bath took place yesterday at my headquarters, and was conducted with great dignity and solemnity by Viscount Stratford de Redcliffe.

The effect was most imposing, attended as the ceremony was by the Naval and Military Commanders-in-Chief of the Allied Forces; and after the delivery by Her Majesty's Ambassador of a peculiarly eloquent discourse upon the character and history of the Most Honourable Order, the several Knights were respectively invested with the insignia of their Class.

I have, &c.,

JAMES SIMPSON,

General Commanding.

The Lord Panmure, &c. &c. &c.

CHAPTER 12

THE FALL OF SEVASTOPOL

War-Department, September 12, 1855.

LORD PANMURE has this day received a Despatch and its Enclosures, of which the following are copies, addressed to his Lordship by General Simpson.

Before Sevastopol,
September 1, 1855.

MY LORD,

THE siege operations during the past week have progressed slowly, the brightness of the nights rendering the work to be performed a task of great difficulty. The head of the sap is now about 150 yards from the salient of the Redan, and the enemy interrupt the work by every means in their power.

On the night of the 28th, a 13-inch shell fell into a magazine on the left face of the Mamelon, which exploded, causing some few casualties, but in no way interrupting the continuance of the fire.

On the night of the 30th ultimo, the Russian pickets made a rush at our advanced trench, upset a few gabions, and unfortunately killed Lieutenant Preston, of the 97th Regiment. In this affair, Captain Pechell, of the 77th Regiment, who commanded the advanced party, and Lieutenant Colonel Bunbury, of the 23rd Regiment, who commanded the supports, behaved with great gallantry.

Great activity prevails on the part of the garrison in making use of the new raft bridge across the harbour, and stores of all kinds are daily transported to the north side.

Large working parties are employed in throwing up works on the north side, but as yet they are in too unfinished a state to judge of their exact nature.

From the information we continue to receive, it appears that the enemy is concentrating his force between the Mackenzie Heights and Fort Constantine; and although several minor changes of position have been made, no movement of importance has occurred to indicate a positive intention to attack.

All our accounts confirm the reports of the great losses of the enemy daily in Sevastopol, and that some discontent prevails in their ranks.

I have the honour to enclose the lists of casualties.

I have, &c.,
JAMES SIMPSON,
General Commanding.
The Lord Panmure, &c. &c. &c.

War-Department, September 19, 1855.

LORD PANMURE has this day received Despatch (of which the following are extracts), and the subjoined returns of casualties from the 31st ultimo to the 2nd instant, addressee to his Lordship by General Simpson:

Extract of a Despatch from General Simpson to Lord Panmure, dated, before Sevastopol, September 4, 1855.

"FROM the heavy fire maintained by the enemy on the head of our sap, the progress made has been slow, and accompanied, as must be expected, by several casualties amongst the sappers and working parties; and it is with great regret that I have to report the death, last night, of Captain Pechell, 77th Regiment, whose conduct I had occasion to bring before your Lordship's notice in my despatch of the 1st instant.

"Within the last few days a second bridge has been commenced from the north shore to Karabelnaia, the object being evidently to expedite the removal of stores from the dockyard.

"The continued reports we receive, induce General Pelissier and myself to believe that the enemy still meditate an attack in force on our positions on the Tchernaya, to meet which the troops are kept in a continued state of readiness.

"The 82nd Regiment have arrived from Corfu, and have disembarked this day. I intend them to relieve the 13th Regiment at Balaklava, which has joined the 1st Division under Lord Rokeby.

"The health of the troops is excellent."

War-Department, September 21, 1855.

LORD PANMURE has this day received a Despatch and its Enclosures, of which the following are copies, addressed to his Lordship by General Simpson.

Before Sevastopol,
September 8, 1855,

MY LORD,

AT daylight on the 5th instant, the batteries of the Allied Armies opened a steady and continuous fire against the enemy's works.

During the night one of the vessels, supposed to be a frigate, stationed on the north side of the harbour, was set on fire by, it is believed, a shell from a French battery in their right attack. The firing, during the 6th, 7th, and up to the present moment, has continued uninterrupted, and but feebly responded to by the Russians.

Another frigate was discovered yesterday afternoon to be on fire, and has been entirely destroyed.

From the length of time it continued burning, it is supposed to have contained stores.

About eleven o'clock last night a heavy explosion took place, but I have not as yet been able to ascertain in which part of the enemy's works.

I have, &c:,
JAMES SIMPSON,
General Commanding.
The Lord Panmure, &c. &c. &c.

War-Department, September 22, 1855.

MAJOR the Honourable Leicester Curzon arrived this morning with a Despatch from General Simpson to Lord Panmure, of which the following is a copy.

Before Sevastopol,
September 9, 1855.

MY LORD,

I HAD the honour to apprize your Lordship in my Despatch of the 4th instant, that the Engineer and Artillery Officers of the Allied Armies had laid before General Pelissier and myself a report recommending that the assault should be given on the 8th instant, after a heavy fire had been kept up for three days.

This arrangement I agreed to, and I have to congratulate your Lordship on the glorious results of the attack of yesterday, which has ended in the possession of the town, dockyards, and public buildings, and destruction of the last ships of the Russian Fleet in the Black Sea. Three steamers alone remain, and the speedy capture or sinking of these must speedily follow.

It was arranged that at twelve o'clock in the day the French columns of assault were to leave their trenches, and take possession of the Malakoff and adjacent works. After their success had been assured, and they were fairly established, the Redan was to be assaulted by the English; the Bastion, Central, and Quarantine Forts, on the left, were simultaneously to be attacked by the French.

At the hour appointed our Allies quitted their trenches, entered and carried the apparently impregnable defences of the Malakoff with that impetuous valour which characterizes the French attack; and, having once obtained possession, they were never dislodged.

The Tricolour planted on the parapet was the signal for our troops to advance.

The arrangements for the attack I entrusted to Lieutenant-General Sir William Codrington, who carried out the details in concert with Lieutenant-General Markham.

I determined that the second and light divisions should have the honour of the assault, from the circumstance of their having defended the batteries, and approaches against the Redan for so many months, and from the intimate knowledge they possessed of the ground.

The fire of our artillery having made as much of a breach as possible in the salient of the Redan, I decided that the columns of assault should be directed against that part, as being less exposed to the heavy flanking fire by which this work is protected.

It was arranged between Sir W. Codrington and Lieutenant-General Markham that the assaulting column of 1000 men should be formed by equal numbers of these two divisions, the column of the light division to lead, that of the 2nd to follow. They left the trenches at the pre-concerted signal, and moved across the ground preceded by a covering party of 200 men, and a ladder party of 320. On arriving at the crest of the ditch, and the ladders placed, the men immediately stormed the parapet of the Redan, and penetrated into the salient angle. A most determined and bloody contest was here maintained for nearly an hour, and, although supported to the utmost, and the greatest bravery displayed, it was found impossible to maintain the position.

Your lordship will perceive, by the long and sad list of casualties, with what gallantry and self devotion the officers so nobly placed themselves at the head of their men during this sanguinary conflict.

I feel myself unable to express in adequate terms the sense I entertain of the conduct and gallantry exhibited by the troops, though their devotion was not rewarded by the success which they so well merited, but to no one are my thanks more justly due than to Colonel Windham, who gallantly headed his column of attack, and was fortunate in entering, and remaining with the troops, during the contest.

The trenches were, subsequently to this attack, so crowded with troops that I was unable to organize a second assault, which I intended to make with the Highlanders under Lieutenant-General Sir Colin Campbell, who had hitherto formed the reserve, to be supported by the third division under Major-General Sir William Eyre. I, therefore, sent for these officers, and arranged with them to renew the attack the following morning.

The Highland Brigade occupied the advanced trenches during the night. About eleven o'clock the enemy commenced exploding their magazines, and Sir Colin Campbell having ordered a small party to advance cautiously to examine the Redan, found the work abandoned; he did not however, deem it necessary to occupy it until daylight.

The evacuation of the town by the enemy was made manifest during the night. Great fires appeared in every part, accompanied by large explosions, under the cover of which the enemy succeeded in withdrawing their troops to the north side by means of the raft-bridge recently constructed, and which they afterwards disconnected and conveyed to the other side.

Their men-of-war were all sunk during the night.

The boisterous weather rendered it altogether impossible for the Admirals to fulfil their intention of bringing the broadsides of the Allied Fleets to bear upon the Quarantine Batteries; but an excellent effect was produced by the animated and well-directed fire of their mortar vessels, those of Her Majesty being under the direction of Captain Wilcox, of the Odin, and Captain Digby, of the Royal Marine Artillery.

It now becomes my pleasing duty, my Lord, to place on record the high sense I entertain of the conduct of this Army since I have had the honour to command it. The hardships and privations endured by many of the Regiments during a long winter campaign are too well known for me to comment upon. They were borne both by officers and men with a patience and unmurmuring endurance worthy of the highest praise, and which gained them the deserved applause and sympathy of their country.

The Naval Brigade, under the command of Captain the Honourable Henry Keppel, aided by Captain Moorsom, and many gallant officers and seamen who have served the guns from the commencement of the siege, merit my warmest thanks.

The prompt, hearty, and efficacious co-operation of Her Majesty's Navy, commanded by Rear-Admiral Sir Edmund Lyons, and ably seconded by Sir Houston Stewart, has contributed most materially to the success of our undertaking; and here, perhaps, I may be permitted to say that, it had pleased God that the successful result of this memorable siege should have been reported by my ever to be lamented predecessor in this command, I am sure that it would have been one of his most pleasing duties to express the deep sense which I know he entertained of the invaluable assistance and counsel he received on all occasions from Sir Edmund Lyons. When at times affairs looked gloomy and success doubtful, he was at hand to cheer and encourage; and every assistance that could tend to advance the operations was given with the hearty good will which characterizes the British sailor.

Nothing has contributed more to the present undertaking than the cordial co-operation which has so happily existed from the first between the two services.

I cannot sufficiently express my approbation of the conduct of the Royal Engineers under Lieutenant-General Sir Harry Jones, who has conducted the siege operations from the beginning of this year. For some time past he has been suffering on a bed of sickness, but the eventful hour of the assault would not permit him to remain absent; he was conveyed on a litter into the trenches to witness the completion of his arduous undertakings.

My warmest thanks are due to the officers and soldiers of the Royal Artillery under the command of Major-General Sir R. Dacres, who, during the arduous operations of this protracted siege, have so mainly contributed to its ultimate success.

I must beg further to record my thanks for the cordial co-operation and assistance I have received in carrying out the details of the service from the Chief of the Staff, the Adjutant and Quartermaster-Generals, and General Staff, as well as Generals commanding Divisions and Brigades of this Army.

I must reserve to myself, for the subject of a future despatch, bringing before your Lordship the particular mention of officers of the various branches of this Army, whom I shall beg to recommend to your favourable notice.

I entrust this despatch to the care of Brevet-Major the Honourable Leicester Curzon, who has been Assistant Military Secretary to my noble predecessor and myself since the commencement of this war, and who will be able to give your Lordship more minute details than the limits of a despatch will allow.

I have, &c.,
JAMES SIMPSON,
General Commanding.
The Lord Panmure, &c. &c. &c.

Admiralty, September 22, 1855.

DESPATCHES, of which the following are copies, have been received from Rear-Admiral Sir Edmund Lyons, Bart., G.C.B., Commander-in-Chief of Her Majesty's Ships and Vessels in the Mediterranean and Black Sea.

No. 753. Royal Albert, off Sevastopol,
September 10, 1855.

SIR,

OF the operations on shore, which have produced the successful result of the singular and memorable siege of Sevastopol, Her Majesty's Government will be informed by General Simpson; but it is my duty to report to the Lords Commissioners of the Admiralty what has taken place afloat and on the seaboard under my own observation.

It had been arranged by Generals Simpson and Pelissier, Admiral Bruat and myself, that precisely at noon on the 8th instant the Allied Fleets should open fire upon the Quarantine Batteries that enfiladed the approach of the assaulting columns; but unfortunately the weather, which had been fine for some days, changed on the morning of the attack, and a north-west gale and heavy sea rendered it impossible for any vessels to act upon batteries situated on the lee shore of this exposed roadstead. It will, however, appear by the enclosed reports from Captain Wilcox, of the Odin, and Captain Digby, of the Royal Marine Artillery (whom, as well as the junior officers mentioned by them, I beg leave particularly to recommend to the favourable consideration of their Lordships), that the mortar vessels attached to the fleets kept up a very effective fire from their position in the Bay of Strelitzka.

As the day closed, things in the harbour seemed to be in the same state as they were in the morning, but, during the night, several heavy explosions were heard, and at dawn we observed that the fortifications on the south side were in flames, and that the 6 remaining ships-of-the-line had been sunk at their moorings, leaving afloat no more of the late Russian Black Sea Fleet than two dismasted corvettes and 9 steamers, most of which are very small.

Soon afterwards the enemy were seen retreating across the newly constructed bridge, until the south side of the harbour, on which the naval and military arsenals, the public buildings, and the town of Sevastopol are situated, appeared to be completely evacuated, and then the southern portion of the bridge was hauled over to the north shore.

It is now my pleasing duty to render justice to the admirable conduct of all whom I have had the honour and happiness to command during the last nine months of this arduous struggle, and whose duties I shared in before; for although, with the exception of the Naval Brigade in the camp, whose gallant bearing from the beginning under the command of Sir Stephen Lushington, has been beyond all praise, and never more so than during the last two bombardments under the command of the Honourable Captain Keppel, it has not fallen to the lot of the Navy, on this occasion to perform distinguished deeds of arms such as those of their gallant brethren in the Army; still, whilst straining every nerve, night and day, under very trying circumstances, to supply the means for carrying on the siege, in the glory of which they could not share, the generous cheer of encouragement, unalloyed by envy, has always been heartily given in the day of triumph; nor have sympathy and assistance ever been wanting in the hour of distress and suffering; the same sentiments have pervaded all ranks – captains, officers, seamen and marines, all agreeing with each other in following, as I believe I have said once before, the excellent example set them by my able second in command and coadjutor Rear-Admiral Houston Stewart.

Perhaps in closing this letter I may be permitted to indulge in the expression of the gratification I feel in reflecting that under all the circumstances to which it relates, my gallant colleague Vice-Admiral Bruat and I have gone heart and hand together, and that the most perfect understanding and hearty co-operation in the great cause of humanity in which we are all engaged, have invariably prevailed throughout both fleets.

I am, &c.,

(Signed) EDMUND LYONS,

Rear-Admiral and Commander-in-Chief.

To the Secretary of the Admiralty.

Admiralty, September 26, 1855.

A DESPATCH, of which the following is a copy, has been received from Rear-Admiral Sir Edmund Lyons, Bart., G.C.B., Commander-in-Chief of Her Majesty's Ships and Vessels in the Mediterranean and Black Sea.

No. 771. Royal Albert, off Sevastopol,
September 15, 1855.

SIR,

THE Lords Commissioners of the Admiralty will have been already informed by my letters from Kertch of last June, and by my recent telegraphic messages from hence, that the Russians had annihilated their fleet in this part of the world, leaving the Allies undisputed masters of the Sea of Azof, as well as of the Black Sea; that they had blown up and abandoned their last holds on the coast of Circassia, and that after a gallant defence against an unparalleled siege they had been defeated and obliged to evacuate the south side of the Harbour of Sevastopol, on which are situated the naval and military arsenals, the public buildings, and the town.

2. I have now to request you to acquaint their Lordships that the enemy has not succeeded in his endeavours to destroy all the forts on the south side. Fort Paul, it is true, is literally blown to atoms, and Fort Alexander is very much damaged, but the Quarantine Fort has not suffered considerably by the explosion of the magazine, the sea face remaining perfect, and most of the guns being fit for use, few of these being even spiked. At Fort Nicholas the preparations for blowing it up had not been completed, and though the flames have made some havoc in the interior, the stone work appears to be uninjured, and the earth works on the sea-defences remain in a perfect state.

3. The five docks and the adjoining basins are magnificent, and together with the steam machinery for filling them from the Tchernaya and for pumping them out, are in excellent order; and the resources of all kinds still remaining after the enormous expenditure during the siege, showed very plainly the importance the enemy attached to having a large depôt at the threshold of the Bosphorus.

4. The bottom of the splendid harbour is now encumbered with more than 50 sunken vessels, including 18 sail of the line and several frigates and steamers, whose menacing attitude but a short time ago materially contributed to bring on the war in which we are now engaged.

(Signed) EDMUND LYONS.

Admiralty October 1, 1855.

A DESPATCH, of which the following is a copy, has been received from Rear-Admiral Sir Edmund Lyons, Bart., G.C.B., Commander-in- Chief of Her Majesty's Ships and Vessels in the Mediterranean and Black Sea.

EMBARKATION OF NAVAL BRIGADE.

Royal Albert, off Sevastopol,
September 18, 1855.

SIR,

I HAVE the honour to enclose, for the information of the Lords Commissioners of the Admiralty, a printed copy of a General Order which has been issued to the Army on the re-embarkation of the Royal Naval Brigade.

I am, &c.,
(Signed) EDMUND LYONS,
Rear-Admiral and Commander-in-Chief.
To the Secretary of the Admiralty.

GENERAL ORDER.

Head Quarters, Sevastopol,
September 17, 1855.

No.1. The service for which the Naval Brigade was attached to this Army having been completed by the fall of Sevastopol, the Force has been ordered to rejoin the Fleet.

The Commander of the Forces heartily thanks the Officers, Petty Officers, and Seamen, for the very efficient services they have rendered in the batteries, and on all occasions when their aid against the enemy was required; and he has to notice the patience and courage with which, side by side with the Soldiers of this Army, they have endured the dangers and hardships of nearly a year's duty in the trenches.

General Simpson cordially acknowledges the obligations he is under to Rear-Admiral Sir Stephen Lushington, K.C.B., who so ably commanded the Brigade, from its formation until his removal by promotion to a higher rank, and to Captain Honourable H. Keppel, R.N., who succeeded him, and retained the command until the conclusion of this ever-memorable siege.

By order,
(Signed) H. W. BARNARD,
Chief of the Staff.

War-Department, October 11, 1855.

LORD PANMURE has this day received a Despatch and its Enclosures, of which the following are copies, addressed to his Lordship by General Simpson.

Sevastopol,
September 29, 1855.

MY LORD,

SINCE my last despatch the troops have been employed, to the number of 9,500 men, daily, in making the road from Balaklava to the camp; and as, after a few hours of rain the whole distance is converted into a mass of deep mud, the work that has to be performed, from this reason as well as the great distance that the stones have to be transported, render it one of great labour and difficulty.

Large fatigue parties are daily employed in the town, dismantling and conveying timber and other materials from the ruins of the buildings, and I hope, by this means, to get a considerable portion of the troops under cover previous to the commencement of the bad weather.

The enemy have been firing from the batteries on the north side at the working parties in the town, and, although causing some little annoyance, they have not prevented the work being carried on, and, I am happy to add, that one man killed and one wounded are the only casualties occasioned by their fire.

I regret to have to report to your Lordship that owing to the explosion of a Russian magazine on the 27th instant one officer and 19 men were wounded. I ordered an investigation to be made, and, from the report I have received, the origin was from the explosion of a hidden fougass, a number of which have been dug up in various parts of the town and batteries.

The invention of this machine is peculiarly Russian.

I have received a letter from Lieutenant-Colonel Ready, 71st Regiment, commanding Her Majesty's troops at Yenikale, reporting the proceedings of a trifling affair, in which a detachment of the 10th Hussars, in company with the Chasseurs d'Afrique, were engaged on the 21st instant with the Cossacks.

Colonel D'Osmont, commanding the French troops, at Kertch, received information that the Cossacks were collecting and driving away all the arabas from the neighbourhood, and, as he determined to endeavour to prevent this, he invited the assistance of the English cavalry to cooperate with the Chasseurs d'Afrique. For this service, Lieutenant-Colonel Ready ordered two troops, commanded by Captains the Hon. F. FitzClarence and Clarke, of the 10th Hussars.

The Cossacks were supposed to have assembled their arabas at two villages, named Koss-Serai Min and Seit Ali, equidistant from Kertch about 15 miles, and from one another, 6½. Captain FitzClarence's troop was ordered to the first village, and Captain Clarke's to the latter. At each of these villages they were to join a troop of the Chasseurs d'Afrique who had preceded them. On arriving at Koss-Serai Min, Captain

FitzClarence found both troops of the French Dragoons, and immediately sent off an order to Captain Clarke to join him that night; the letter was unfortunately not delivered until the following morning. In complying with this order, Captain Clarke, whose troop consisted only of 34 men, fell in with a body of about 50 Cossacks, which he immediately charged and pursued, but as they were soon reinforced by upwards of 300, he was forced to retire upon the village, with a loss of his serjeant-major, farrier, and 13 men taken prisoners.

Captain FitzClarence's troop, with the Chasseurs, the whole under the command of the Officer commanding the French troops, having seen a large body of the enemy, skirmished with them at some distance, and moved in the direction of the village of Serai Min; where, after having joined Captain Clarke's troop, the whole force commenced their march upon Kertch.

At about the distance of half a mile front the village they were attacked by a large body of Cossacks, who were, however, beaten back by repeated charges. The loss of the 10th Hussars

consisted of-

2 Privates, supposed to have been killed.

1 Wounded.

1 Troop Serjeant-Major, 1 Farrier, 13 Men, 15 Horses, Missing.

From information that has since been received, the Cossacks were supported, within a quarter of an hour's march, by eight squadrons of Hussars and eight guns.

Colonel Ready informs me that nothing could exceed the coolness and courage of the troops in the presence of such overwhelming numbers of the enemy, who were only kept at bay by their steady movements.

I have the honour to enclose the lists of casualties.

The health of the Army, I am rejoiced to say, is excellent.

I have, &c.,
JAMES SIMPSON,
General Commanding.
The Lord Panmure, &c. &c. &c.

War-Department, October 18, 1855

LORD PANMURE has this day received a Despatch and its Enclosures, of which the following are copies, addressed to his Lordship by General Simpson.

Sevastopol,
October 6, 1855.

MY LORD,

MARSHAL PELISSIER having signified to me his wish that the cavalry force under

General d'Allonville, at Eupatoria, should be reinforced by some English Cavalry, I at once acceded to his request, and have ordered the brigade of light cavalry, under Brigadier-General Lord George Paget, composed of the Carbineers, 4th and 13th Light Dragoons, and 12th Lancers, and one troop of the Royal Horse Artillery, under Captain Thomas, to be sent for this service.

I am in hopes that transport will be found to convey them early next week.

I have the honour to transmit to your Lordship the copy of a report I have received from Lieutenant-Colonel Ready, with the details of an expedition undertaken against a fort and buildings on the island of Taman. The object was entirely carried out, and the troops have been enabled to supply themselves with a large amount of firewood and building materials.

Since I last had the honour of addressing you, I have seen Lieutenant-General Vivian, and I am happy to inform your Lordship that he quite approves of the decision I had formed of uniting the Contingent at Kertch. Some few thousand men have already arrived there, and every exertion is being made to ensure them their supplies of food and fuel for the winter.

The corps of General de Salles have, during the past week, pushed forward their advanced posts to the high ground on the left bank of the Belbek, overlooking Foti Sala.

Their supports occupy a ridge from this place, stretching towards the south to Markul.

The main position of the army is on high, bold ground, extending from Aitoda to Markul, with the reserves posted between the village of Urkusta and the Bridge of Tinli.

The corps is further to be reinforced with the view next week of making a strong reconnaissance of the ground from Foti Sala towards Wyenbash, on the left bank of the Katcha.

I have omitted to report that Lieutenant-General Markham has been compelled, by illness, to return to England for a few months. He sailed on the 29th ultimo.

I have, &c.,
JAMES SIMPSON,
General Commanding.
The Lord Panmure, &c. &c. &c.

CHAPTER 13

FINAL OPERATIONS IN THE CRIMEA AND THE BLACK SEA

War-Department, November 1, 1855.

LORD PANMURE has this day received a Despatch and its Enclosures, of which the following are copies, addressed to his Lordship by General Sir James Simpson, G.C.B.

Sevastopol,
October 20, 1855.

MY LORD,

I AM happy to be able to congratulate your Lordship on the successful termination of the expedition to Kinbourn. I transmit a copy of the report of Brigadier-General the Honourable A. Spencer. This contains all the information I have received on the operations, with the exception that in a private note, Sir E. Lyons mentions that the enemy have exploded the three forts at Ochakoff, commanding the northern entrance into the Dnieper.

In consequence of the continued fineness of the weather, great progress has been made in the construction of the road and railway. The divisions have all got some weeks' supply of rations in their camp; and I entertain no anxiety of there being a scarcity of anything during the approaching winter.

I informed your Lordship, in my despatch of the 13th instant, that the Highland Division, under Lieutenant-General Sir Colin Campbell, were to proceed to Eupatoria, and co-operate with the French; but upon the receipt of your telegraphic despatch of the 13th instant, apprizing me that the Russians had resolved to hazard a battle, and attack the Allies, I did not consider myself justified in weakening the force under my command by so many men, and I therefore counter-manded the movement.

I have the honour to enclose the weekly reports of Colonel McMurdo and Dr. Hall.

I have, &c.,
(Signed) JAMES SIMPSON,
General Commanding.
The Lord Panmure, &c. &c. &c.

Enclosure 1.

Camp before Kinbourn,
October 17, 1855.

SIR,

IN reporting, for the information of the General Commanding the Forces, the fall of the garrison of the Fortress of Kinbourn, this day, I have the honour to state, that the force under my command, as per state enclosed,* effected their landing on Monday, the 15th, unopposed.

Owing to a heavy surf, and which continued all day yesterday, the landing has been accomplished with some little difficulty. The troops, however, were all got on shore on the first day, and have since been employed in entrenching our position. There are rumours of a force of the enemy collecting at Kherson, about 40 miles from here, but our immediate neighbourhood appears to be clear.

The advanced line of the position, flanked on both sides by the sea, is held by the force under my command, and is about a mile in extent.

I have, &c.,
(Signed) AUGUSTUS SPENCER,
Brigadier-General Commanding English
Land Force.
The Military Secretary, &c.,
Head Quarters.

Enclosure 2.

Head-Quarters, Land Transport Camp,
Crimea, October 15, 1855.

WEEKLY REPORT. – No. 16.

THE arrivals during the week have been limited to railway horses. 19 landed from Her Majesty's ship Assistance, and 79 from the steam transport Arabia.

Each vessel lost a horse on the passage; but on the whole they have arrived in fair condition.

I have had them put under cover; and hope, with care, to have them in working order in the course of a week.

The work of ballasting is progressing favourably, and as many waggons and teams are supplied for this service as are required without much prejudice to the ordinary demands.

The precautions taken by Mr. Beatty are likely to be effectual in securing the line for the winter; and I only regret that the state of this able engineer's health will compel him to relinquish his work for a while. He will leave it in able hands, however. Mr. Campbell has served with Mr. Beatty from the beginning, and is now actively engaged in carrying out his plans upon the line.

Nothing but the application of science could enable the British Army to exist in its present position.

The little harbour of Balaklava which I can liken to nothing than the eye of the needle, through which the camel *must* pass, is now embraced on either side by the railway – its branches leading from the various wharves and storehouses, to depôts outside the town, where room (though not sufficient) is afforded to the transport to load up. Waggons and their teams are thus allotted for the special service of drawing supplies of fuel, hay and corn, to these depôts, independent of the trains which proceed to the front. The narrow ways of the little town are thus relieved in a great measure from the interminable crush of animals and carriages throughout the day, which effectually impeded one another, and caused the death of many.

The road is another important work, the progress of which I watch with the greatest interest. I am an old road maker myself, and believe the line to be good.

But the most important work of all will, in my opinion, be the floating factory.

This is a measure worthy of England; for her base is on the waters, and she has now floated Woolwich to her army in the Crimea.

I have minutely inspected this vessel and her fittings (and moreover drawn largely from her stores), and have been struck with admiration at her capacities.

I have had the fashion of the boxes of wheels taken, and I hope to have them cast in large numbers.

Iron axles can be welded and turned, engines fitted, and timbers sawn; in short, I have no longer to look 3,000 miles for the source of vitality. I hope now to be enabled to make provision for the Spring; for the transport is so situated that the material parts of all the carriages must become worn out by the incessant traffic to which it will necessarily be exposed throughout the entire winter.

I reckon that every waggon, with its horse, harness, and driver, must travel on an average of 14 miles daily, over indifferent roads, and that this wear and tear must extend over a period of six months; at the end of which time, when the army, refreshed, will call upon this corps to take it into the field, neither waggons nor harness will be in a serviceable state. It is absolutely necessary, therefore, that strong reserves of wheels, axles, shafts, poles, and harness of every kind should be ready; and although I see that the floating factory can do much, it will be necessary for the arsenals at home to help, especially with harness, which should be very strong, and serviceable.

I think it would be worth while to ascertain, by comparison, the relative quality and prices of the English and Sardinian mule waggon harness. It may be found that the advantage, as to cost, is on the Sardinian side, and that the stout white leather of which it is composed is more durable than that furnished to this corps.

The general organization of this corps proceeds satisfactorily. I was glad of an opportunity lately, when a division of the army was under orders for Eupatoria to try the efficiency of the corps. Two divisions of transport, composed of 3,000 animals, with their proportion of waggons, carts, ambulances and artificers, were ready for embarkation in a very short time, and appeared very efficient and complete.

The scope of the intended operations of the force being afterwards limited to three or four days, the amount of transport was proportionally reduced to nearly one half.

The bulk of the transport of an army is entirely regulated by the radius of intended operations – it is solely a question of supply. Thus, for these three days, which were intended to be the scope of the operations at Eupatoria, the Commissary-General made a requisition on this department for 1,500 pack animals and 20 carts. The requirements of the other branches of the force were trifling compared to this demand, and it will enable his Lordship to form some idea of what the requirements of the whole army will be, when it takes the field in a country devoid of resources.

I will here venture to express an opinion, as it bears materially upon the subject of transport; it is that our soldiers should habitually move with three days' provisions on their person, whether it be in war or peace, the weight should never be diminished.

The Roman soldiers used to be clad in heavier armour during peace, than they wore on a campaign, so that war with its burdens and toils should sit lightly upon them. The French soldiers in the present campaign carry four days' provisions, besides their tents; and if the British soldier should do the same, 1,500 animals to every 6,000 men that take the field, would be saved to the transport of the army.

I make these observations with profound respect to the opinions of my superiors, and in the spirit and intention of these reports, viz., to do all that lays in my power to make the British army moveable and efficient.

To return to the corps. The arrival of the young English drivers is a timely resource, as the natives had begun to desert in great numbers, notwithstanding the precautions I have taken to prevent them, in communication with the police and Admiral Freemantle.

I have obtained labourers from Constantinople to aid in building stables, and I hope that the most valuable of the animals will soon be under cover.

I have adapted the constructions entirely to the nature of the ground on which the several camps are pitched, which, being principally rocky, I find the simplest mode to be that of excavating a couple of feet, and running a centre wall with a roof on either side. The earth thrown out by the excavation being mixed with manure, forms everyday a higher bank outside, so as to increase the protection and warmth of the stables.

Stone is abundant, and I am making use of the materials of the packing cases, in which the bat saddles are sent out, for planking.

M. McMURDO,
D. G.

* 1st Brigade, 4th Division; Royal Marines, 1,200 men, rank and file; Royal Engineers, Artillery, and detachment of Cavalry.

Admiralty, November 1, 1855.

DESPATCHES, of which the following are copies, have been received from Rear-Admiral Sir Edmund Lyons, Bart., G.C.B., Commander-in -Chief of Her Majesty's Ships and Vessels in the Mediterranean and Black Sea.

No. 859. Royal Albert, off Kimburn,
October 18, 1855.

SIR,

MY letter of the 6th instant, No. 834, will have informed the Lords Commissioners of the Admiralty, that an allied naval and military expedition was to leave the anchorage off Sevastopol, on the following day, for the purpose of taking and occupying the three Russian forts on Kimburn Spit, at the entrance of Dnieper Bay; and the telegraphic message, which I forwarded to Varna last night, will soon communicate to their Lordships the success which has attended this enterprize.

It is now my duty to give a more detailed account of the proceedings of the expedition.

I have therefore the honour to state, that we arrived at a rendezvous off Odessa, on the 8th instant, but owing to strong south-west winds, which would have prevented the troops from landing, it was not until the morning of the 14th instant, that the expedition was enabled to reach the anchorage off Kimburn.

During the night the English steam gun-vessels, Fancy, Boxer, Cracker, and Clinker, and four French gun-vessels, forced the entrance into Dnieper Bay, under a heavy but ineffectual fire from the Spit Fort, and on the following morning the British troops, under the orders of Brigadier-General Honourable A.A. Spencer, together with the French troops, under the command of General Bazaine, were landed about three miles to the southward of the principal fort, and thus, by these nearly simultaneous operations, the retreat of the garrisons and the arrival of reinforcements were effectually cut off.

In the evening the English and French mortar vessels tried their ranges against the main fort with excellent effect.

The wind having again veered round to the southward, with a great deal of swell, nothing could be done on the 16th; but in the forenoon of the 17th, a fine northerly breeze, with smooth water, enabled the French floating batteries, mortar vessels, and gunboats, and the Odin and the mortar vessels, and gunboats named in the margin,* to take up positions off Fort Kimburn; and their fire was so effective, that before noon the buildings in the interior of the fort were in flames, and the eastern face had suffered very considerably.

At noon, the Royal Albert, Algiers, Agamemnon and Princess Royal, accompanied by Admiral Bruat's four ships of the line, approached Fort Kimburn in a line abreast, which the shape of the coast rendered necessary, and the precision with which they took up their positions in the closest order, with jib-booms run in and only two feet of water under their keels, was really admirable. At the same moment the squadrons under the orders of Rear-Admirals Sir Houston Stewart and Pellion pushed through the passage between Ochakoff and the spit of Kimburn, and took the forts in reverse, whilst the St. Jean d'Acre, Curaçoa, Tribune and Sphinx, undertook the centre battery, and the Hannibal, Dauntless and Terrible, that on the point of the spit.

The enemy soon ceased to reply to our overwhelming fire, and, though he made no sign of surrender, Admiral Bruat and I felt that a garrison which had bravely defended itself against so superior a force deserved every consideration, and we therefore made the signal to cease firing, hoisted a flag of truce, and sent on shore a summons, which was accepted by the Governor, Major-General Kokonovitch, and the garrisons, consisting of 1,400 men, marched out with the honours of war, laid down their arms on the glacis, and, having surrendered themselves as prisoners of war, they will be embarked in Her Majesty's ship Vulcan to-morrow.

The casualties in the allied fleets are very few, amounting in Her Majesty's ships to only two wounded. The loss of the enemy in killed and wounded is, I fear, very severe.

In the three forts, which have suffered considerably by our fire, we found eighty-one guns and mortars mounted, and an ample supply of ammunition.

This morning the enemy has blown up the forts on Ochakof Point, which mounted twenty-two guns, and we learnt from a Polish deserter, who escaped in a boat from them during the night, that the Commandant apprehended an attack from our mortar vessels, which would not only have destroyed the forts, but also the neighbouring dwellings.

I have abstained from entering into the particulars of the proceedings of the squadron under the orders of Rear-Admiral Sir H. Stewart, as he has so ably described them in the letter which I have the honour to enclose, from which their Lordships will perceive that I have received from him on this occasion, as, indeed, I have on all others since I have had the good fortune to have him as second in command, that valuable assistance which might be expected from an officer of his distinguished and acknowledged merits; and I beg leave to add my testimony to his in praise of all the officers, and especially Lieutenant Marryat and Mr. Brooker, whom he recommends to their Lordships favourable consideration.

To particularize the merit of the officers under my command, where all have behaved admirably, would be a difficult task indeed; but I beg leave to mention that the same officers of the Navy and the Royal Marine Artillery, who were in the mortar vessels at the fall of Sevastopol, are in them now, and that on this occasion, as before, they have been under the direction of Captain Willcox of the Odin, and Captain Digby of the Royal Marine Artillery. Nor can I refrain from stating what I believe to be the feeling of the whole fleet, that on this expedition, as on that to Kertch, the talents and indefatigable exertions of that very valuable officer, Captain Spratt, of the Spitfire, and of those under his command, entitle them to our warmest thanks, and deserve to be particularly mentioned.

I need hardly say that my distinguished colleague, Admiral Bruat, and I have seen with infinite satisfaction, our respective squadrons acting together as one fleet.

> I am, &c.
> (Signed) EDMUND LYONS,
> Rear-Admiral and Commander-in- Chief.
> *The Secretary of the Admiralty.*

> *Valorous, in Dnieper Bay,*
> *October 18, 1855.*

SIR,

I HAVE the honour to inform you, that, in pursuance of your orders, I hoisted my flag in Her Majesty's steam frigate Valorous, on the afternoon of the 14th instant, immediately after the arrival of the allied fleets off Kimburn Spit, and proceeded, under the able guidance of Captain Spratt, of the Spitfire, to take up positions at the entrance of Dnieper Bay, where, with the division of steam vessels, placed under my orders (as per margin),† and in company with those under the orders of my colleague, Rear-Admiral Odet Pellion, we remained in readiness to force an entrance into the Dnieper, for the purpose directed by you, of preventing, as far as possible, any reinforcements being thrown into the forts on Kimburn Spit, as well as to cut off the retreat of the garrison, should either be attempted.

At 9 P.M. I instructed Lieutenant Joseph H. Marryat, of the Cracker, to take on board Mr. Edward W. Brooker, additional Master of the Spitfire, and endeavour with him to determine the course of the intricate channel through which we were to pass, and to lay down buoys along the south side of it; the French having undertaken to perform the same service on the north side.

I likewise directed Mr. Thomas Potter, Master of the Furious (lent to do duty in the Valorous), to proceed with two boats of the Tribune, and, protected by the Cracker, to search for the spit on the north bank, and on his return endeavour to place a buoy on the edge of the shoal off Kimburn Spit, that the entrance of the channel might be assured.

As soon as the preconcerted signal was given, indicating that this operation was effected, I despatched the Fancy, Boxer, and Clinker, into Dnieper Bay, with orders to anchor in such positions as would best protect the right flank of our troops, upon the disembarkation taking place, and to make that their chief care, as long as there was any possibility of the enemy threatening them.

During the night, Rear-Admiral Odet Pellion also sent in the French gunboats for the same purpose.

At daylight on the following morning I had the satisfaction of observing all the gunboats, French and English anchored safely to the north-east of Kimburn Fort, and without any of them having sustained damage, although the enemy had fired both shot and shell and musketry at them during their passage in. Thus the chief part of the object you had most anxiously in view was accomplished.

While still in considerable doubt as to the extent to which the channel for the larger ships was buoyed, at ten A.M. Lieutenant Marryat and Mr. Brooker came to inform me that the work entrusted to them had been completed, and that the latter officer was ready to pilot the ships in. The zealous desire evinced by these officers to furnish me personally with their report on the difficult navigation of the Dnieper deserves my warmest thanks, and the gallant manner in which Lieutenant Marryat brought the Cracker out for that purpose, under a very heavy fire from the whole of the forts and batteries, elicited the admiration of all who witnessed the proceeding.

We were now fully prepared to advance, and, in obedience to your directions, awaited the signal for general attack.

The whole of the proceedings of yesterday must be already fully known to you; but it is right that I should state briefly the share taken in them by the division you did me the honour to place under my orders, which consisted of the ships and vessels as already stated, reinforced by those named below.

It being necessary to advance in single line, it was arranged that the ships should do so in the following order.

Valorous – Captain C.H.M. Buckle, C.B., bearing my flag.
Furious – Captain William Loring, C.B.
Asmodée (French), bearing the flag of Rear-Admiral Odet Pellion.
Cacique (French).
Sidon – Captain George Goldsmith.
Leopard – Captain George Giffard, C.B.
Sané (French).
Gladiator – Captain C.F. Hillyar.
Firebrand – Captain E.A. Inglefield.
Stromboli – Commander Cowper Coles.
Spiteful – Commander F.A. Shortt.

At noon, the signal being made from your flagship to weigh, we proceeded through the channel, each ship engaging the Spit batteries and Kimburn Fort as they came within range.

To Lieutenant Marryat, of the Cracker, is due the merit of preceding and piloting us through, which he did with great judgment.

Had the enemy continued his defence of the Spit batteries, the Sidon, Leopard, Sané, and Gladiator were directed, in that case, to remain in front of them until their fire was completely silenced; but as they were subdued by the accurate and well sustained fire which was poured upon them by the ships which you had placed to the westward of the Spit, and by those of our own squadron on passing to the eastward, this became unnecessary; the whole division, therefore, continued its course through the channel, and anchored well inside Fort Nicolaev and Ochakof Point.

During this time the four gunboats, Fancy, Grinder, Boxer, and Clinker, did good service, by placing themselves in such position as to throw a flanking fire on the middle battery and Kimburn Fort at the time our division passed within short range.

Immediately on anchoring, I transferred my flag to the Cracker, and followed by the other gunboats, proceeded close off the east front of Kimburn Fort, to be ready to act as circumstances required, should the enemy's fire, which at that moment had entirely ceased, be renewed; however, the necessity for further action did not arise.

As the service entrusted to me was carried out under your own observation, I feel it to be unnecessary to do more than to record my grateful sense of the very satisfactory manner in which the whole of the ships under my orders took up their appointed stations, and of the manner in which all employed performed their duty.

I think myself fortunate in having for my temporary flagship so efficient and well ordered a man-of-war as the Valorous, and I feel much indebted to Captain Buckle and his zealous First Lieutenant Joseph Edye, for their unremitting attention and assistance.

1 am delighted to add, that in concerting with our gallant Allies the arrangements necessary for carrying into effect the present successful operations, I have received the cordial support and concurrence of my excellent colleague, Rear-Admiral Odet Pellion.

The anxiety which you yourself ever feel to do full justice to merit and exertion must be my excuse for presuming to request your most favourable notice of Lieutenant Marryat and Mr. Brooker. They have had anxious, difficult and dangerous work to perform, and they have each of them executed it admirably.

I have, &c.,

(Signed) HOUSTON STEWART,

Rear-Admiral.

Rear-Admiral Sir Edmund

Lyons, Bart., &c., &c., &c.,

G.C.B.

No. 843. Royal Albert, off Odessa,
October 9, 1855.

SIR,

I TRANSMIT, to be laid before the Lords Commissioners of the Admiralty, copy of a letter from Captain Robert Hall, of the Miranda, Senior Officer in the Straits of Kertch, detailing the proceedings of an Anglo-French naval and military expedition to Taman and Fanagoria, on the 24th ultimo, for the purpose of depriving the enemy of his means of sheltering troops in the ensuing winter, and in order to procure materials for housing our troops at Cape St. Paul's and Yenikalé.

I also enclose, for their Lordships' information, copy of a letter from Captain Osborn, of the Vesuvius, detailing the proceedings of an Anglo-French attack on Temriouk, which, by previous arrangement, was made simultaneously with that on Taman and Fanagoria.

Both expeditions were conducted in a most satisfactory manner, and were accomplished with the loss of only one man wounded. Three of the 71st Regiment and three of the (French) Infantry of the Marine were taken prisoners, in consequence of their own imprudence.

I am, &c.,
(Signed) EDMUND LYONS,
Rear-Admiral and Commander-in-Chief.
To the Secretary of the Admiralty.

No. 9. Her Majesty's ship Miranda, off
St. Paul's, October 3, 1855.

SIR,

I HAVE the honour to report, that according to your directions of the 25th August I put myself in communication with Captain Bonet, of His Imperial Majesty's ship Pomone, commanding the French naval station here, relative to an expedition to destroy the Russian establishments at Fanagoria and Taman; and also arranged with Captain Osborn, that a simultaneous attack should be made on Temriouk by the Azof Squadron.

On the 24th ultimo, at daylight, the military part of the expedition, under command of Major Hunter (71st), embarked, consisting of 300 of the 71st Highland Light Infantry, carried by the Sulina, and 600 French, of the Infantry of the Marine, placed on board six gunboats of that nation; and at 8.30, the flotilla, as per margin‡, proceeded.

Arriving at Taman at noon, swarms of cavalry were seen near it and Fanagoria, and a strong body marched into the powerful earthwork at the latter place.

The gunboats appointed to cover the landing, as per margin,* immediately opened fire, and in a short time forced the enemy to retire, leaving the troops to land without opposition at the spot previously agreed upon, about a mile east of Fanagoria.

By 4, P.M., we were completely established in the fort, in which the field-piece of this ship, and four light mountain howitzers from the Pomone were placed in position. A large body of cavalry, numbering at least 600, continuing drawn up in front of Fanagoria, were dispersed by some Lancaster shells beautifully thrown from the Lynx and Arrow.

During the night a small body of the enemy fired upon our sentries and wounded a seaman of the Miranda.

The buildings within the earthwork were found to be much more extensive than was anticipated, consisting of a large hospital, some storehouses, and two very large powder magazines, in perfect order but quite empty, composing, with the houses of the employés, a very considerable establishment: sixty-six guns, chiefly of 6, 9, and 12-pounders, and four cohorn mortars were lying disabled with the work.

The storehouses were all empty except one, which contained some hospital necessaries, and the dispensary, which contained some medicines which have been preserved for the use of the squadron.

Taman was found to be completely deserted, and the houses quite empty. A large magazine of flour and another of corn were fired by the Russians before they retired, and 11 iron guns, 30 and 36-pounders, which were found buried at Taman, and were said to have been a present from the Empress Catherine, have been destroyed by us. Considerable bodies of the enemy's cavalry hovered about during the time of our being occupied in taking down and removing the material of the building, but did not approach within gunshot.

I regret to have to report that they succeeded in cutting off three stragglers of the 71st, and three of infantry of marine.

I have much pleasure in bearing testimony to the zeal and activity of the officers and men of the squadron, especially of Lieutenant Aynsley, commanding the Lynx, who, during my absence, superintended the duties of the squadron afloat, and of Lieutenant Fitzroy, of the Miranda, who had the direction of the disembarkation, &c., of the troops, as well as the shipment of the wood, &c., for removal to Yenikalé. Nothing could exceed the good feeling and cordiality existing between the officers and men of our Allies, and our own.

On the morning of the 3rd every building at Fanagoria and Taman which could shelter an enemy having been destroyed, and large quantities of the material removed to Yenikalé and St. Paul's, the troops re-embarked; and returned to their quarters at Kertch and St. Paul's.

I have, &c.,
(Signed) R. HALL.
Captain.

Her Majesty's ship Vesuvius, Sea of Azof,
No. 35. September 26, 1855.

SIR,

I HAVE the honour to report that, in pursuance of arrangements made with Captain Hall, Her Majesty's ship Miranda, I proceeded, on the 23rd September, with the vessels named in the margin**, to harass and keep in check the enemy's troops at Temriouk, whilst the allied squadron at Kertch attacked Fanagoria and Taman.

On the 24th September, at daybreak, we arrived off Temriouk Lake, and were there joined by the French steamers Milan, Caton, and Fulton.

We failed in reaching the town with our boats, the lake proving too shoal for even those of the lightest description; up to noon however we kept a large body of horse, foot and artillery in the town, the latter opening a sharp but harmless fire at us to prevent the destruction of a fine brig which was secreted just inside the lake's entrance. Weighing from thence, the squadron, accompanied by that of our gallant Allies, under Capitaine de Frégate De Cintré, proceeded to cut off the communication between Temriouk and Taman by the narrow belt of land lying north of the lakes. In this we perfectly succeeded; for at 1 P.M. a heavy column of troops, with nine field-guns, were discovered on the march, proceeding towards Taman. Opening fire on them at 2,500 yards, we stopped their march; and after suffering severely, as it appeared to us, they retreated upon Temriouk, the Wrangler with her Lancaster guns keeping up an effective fire upon them to an extraordinary distance. Some of the enemy's riflemen, who with much gallantry fruitlessly endeavoured to keep the beach, and save a quantity of forage, must have lost a number of men by the admirable shell practice of the French squadron. Whilst this was doing, I detached the Ardent, Beagle, and Cracker, to watch another favourable part of the neck of land. Lieutenant Campion was fortunate enough to discover that the road lay over a fine wooden bridge, which spanned a channel connecting the Sea of Azof with Lower Temriouk Lake.

The bridge was 180 feet long and 30 feet wide, composed of strong wooden piles, and sleepers at each end, and four pontoons in the centre, the whole well planked over and apparently much used. It was evidently the route of communication between Temriouk and Taman, except by the very circuitous round of the extensive lakes. The burning of this bridge effectually stopped the garrison of Temriouk, who could not be under 2,000 men and some 10 or 12 guns, arriving in time to resist the landing at Taman.

I therefore weighed, as the weather was threatening, and have since driven in and destroyed the Cossack posts which had been established in this neighbourhood, and to watch our garrison at Enikale.

Two French flags (tricolors) were found by Lieutenant Strode at one of these posts, the Russians having left them, as well as some of their arms, in making a hasty retreat. I am unable to say under what circumstances they could have got into the enemy's possession.

Throughout these operations I have received the greatest assistance from

Commander Rowley Lambert, of Her Majesty's ship Curlew, and the zealous exertions of the officers and men in the squadron generally.

The Recruit has been left to watch the Straits of Ghenitch, and Lieutenant Day, her commander, alone, on the nights of the 18th and 21st September, passed the enemy's picquets there, and waded up to their gun-vessels and guards in the channel. His reconnaissance confirms my opinion of their perfect readiness to resist an attack in that direction. I am sorry to say the exposure and excessive labour has caused Lieutenant Day to be laid up with a severe attack of illness.

The two Russian fishermen taken at the mouth of the Don, having quite recovered from the effects of their wounds, I caused Commander Rowley Lambert to proceed with them on the 23rd instant to Arabat Fort, under a flag of truce, for the purpose of offering to land them there if General Wrangel wished. The offer was accepted and the prisoners landed.

The squadron is now proceeding to Ghenitch to complete ammunition from the Durham, and I am in hopes that fine weather, which may be shortly expected by general account, will enable us to do more service in the coming month than that of the present one.

I have, &c.,

(Signed) SHERARD OSBORN.

Captain and Senior Officer.

Rear-Admiral Sir Edward

Lyons, Bart., &c., &c., &c.

G.C.B.

Mortar vessels – Raven, Magnet, Camel, Hardy, Flamer, Firm. Gun vessels – Lynx, Arrow, Viper, Snake, Wrangler, Beagle.

†*Valorous, Gladiator, Fancy, Cracker, Grinder, Boxer, Clinker.*

‡*Lynx, Arrow, Snake, Harpy, Sulina, and 10 French gun-boats.*

□ *Lynx, Arrow, Snake, and two French gunboats.*

**Vesuvius, Curlew, Ardent, Wrangler, Beagle, Fancy, Grinder, Cracker.*

Admiralty, November 20, 1855.

DESPATCHES, of which the following are copies, have been received from Rear-Admiral Sir Edmund Lyons, Bart., G.C.B., Commander-in-Chief of Her Majesty's Ships and Vessels in the Mediterranean and Black Sea.

Royal Albert, off Sevastopol,

November 6, 1855.

SIR,

THE accompanying copy of a letter from Captain Sherard Osborn, of the Vesuvius, with its several enclosures, will place the Lords Commissioners of the Admiralty in possession of a detailed account of the active and energetic proceedings of the squadron in the Sea of Azoff, under the command of that valuable officer.

The enterprize, which was undertaken and so successfully carried out by Commander J.E. Commerell, of the Weser, in crossing the Isthmus of Arabat, and in destroying a large quantity of forage on the Crimean shore of the Sivash, reflects great credit on that officer, and adds still further proof of his having deserved that promotion which their Lordships have lately been pleased to confer upon him. The gallantry of William Rickard, Quartermaster, of the Weser, deserves to be particularly mentioned; and I beg leave to recommend him to their Lordships' favourable consideration for the medal and gratuity for distinguished service.

Lieutenant Geo. F. Day, commanding the Recruit, has also displayed his usual activity and zeal in harassing the enemy on the north-east coast of the Sea of Azoff; and I regret to find that his foot has been severely injured by the recoil of a gun.

I am, &c.
(Signed) EDMUND LYONS,
Rear-Admiral and Commander-in-Chief.
The Secretary of the Admiralty.

Her Majesty's ship Vesuvius,
At Sea, October 25, 1855.

SIR,

I AM now returning westward towards Ghenitch, having been employed with Her Majesty's ships named in the margin,* since the 9th October, 1855, along the north coast of this sea as far as Taganrog.

On Crooked Spit, as well as Bielosarai or White House Spit, the enemy had established a large force in the remains of the old fishing establishments, and constructed a series of rifle pits and breastworks, from which they opened fire upon any of our vessels taking shelter under those points; and as the enemy had a number of boats with them, with which they could easily board a vessel in distress, I thought it right to destroy the latter and dislodge the men.

The Recruit, Lieutenant Geo. F. Day, came in collision with them on the 15th instant, and although he could not dislodge the riflemen, he succeeded in destroying seven launches and five large fisheries, in spite of the enemy's cavalry and infantry.

Lieutenant Day, I am sorry to say, received a severe injury of the foot, by the accidental explosion of an 8-inch gun, but he speaks in high terms of the satisfactory manner in which Mr. Wm. Parker, Second Master of the Recruit, executed the service entrusted to him.

On the 20th October, the Ardent, Lieutenant Hubert Campion, drove in a large force of cavalry which attempted to prevent him approaching Crooked or Krivaia Spit, and he likewise destroyed three boats.

On the 24th October, the weather was sufficiently favourable to enable me to get the Vesuvius close enough to force the enemy from their rifle-pits upon the Bielosarai

Spit; at 1 P.M., the small-arm men and marines of this ship landed, under Lieutenant Chetham H. Strode, Mr. R.R. Armstrong, Mate, and Mr. H.D.R. Farquharson, Midshipman, supported by the ship and boats.

Directly the enemy saw their escape threatened, they beat a rapid retreat, though fully 150 in number, and effected their escape by a superior knowledge of the paths through the swamps. Lieutenant Strode then destroyed their posts, which had been recently re-constructed; they were eight in number, and calculated to house 200 men; besides these, eleven fine boats and an extensive fishery were set fire to, near the town of Alti.

The Recruit, Lieutenant Day, at the same time destroyed, in the neighbourhood of Marianpol, two large fisheries and some fine launches, mounted on regular travelling land-carriages, and in the evening we were complete masters of the only portion of the coast the enemy have attempted to re-establish themselves upon; and, as the frosts have already set in, I am in hopes that they will not be able to recover their ground before next spring.

The extraordinary efforts made by the enemy to prosecute their fisheries upon this coast, are the best proof of their importance.

They sometimes move down two or three hundred soldiers, who escort large launches placed upon carriages and arabas drawn by oxen laden with nets and gear, as well as fishermen to work them.

The fish directly they are caught are carted off into the interior; and when it is remembered that we have destroyed some hundred and odd launches upon one spit alone, some idea can be formed of the immense quantity of fish consumed on this coast; and in proof of its being a large item in the sustenance of Russian soldiers, I would remind you that hundreds of tons of salted and dried fish were found and destroyed by us in the first destruction of the military depôts at Ghenitch in May last.

This report is closed at Ghenitch, where I had the satisfaction of learning, as the enclosed letter from Lieutenant Commerell will shew, that he had succeeded in destroying a large collection of forage and corn at the entrance of the Solgar or Kara-Su River.

The zeal and enterprize displayed by Lieutenant Commerell on this occasion, as well as whenever any service has to be performed, is most conspicuous; and his judgment in seizing the only good opportunity that has occurred for some time to cross Arabat Spit, and traverse the Putrid Sea, deserves to be particularly called to your notice. The Quartermaster, William Rickard, praised so highly by Lieutenant Commerell, was one of my boat's crew. I fully concur in the high character given of him.

I have, &c.,
(Signed) SHERARD OSBORN,
Captain and Senior Officer in the Sea of Azoff.
Rear-Admiral Sir Edmund
Lyons, Bart., &c., &c., &c.
G.C.B.

Her Majesty's steam gun-vessel Weser,
Genitchi, 12th October, 1855.

SIR,

I HAVE the honour to inform you that on the evening of the 10th instant, I determined, in obedience to your discretionary orders, to launch a boat across the Spit of Arabat, and destroy large quantities of corn and forage, stored on the banks of Kara-Su and Salghir Rivers, on the Crimean shore of the Sivash; the proximity of a guard signal house and signal station, also the distance the corn lay from the beach, rendered anything but a night surprise impracticable.

Having left the Weser in charge of Mr. Haswell, Second Master, and, accompanied by Mr. Lillingston, Mate, a Quartermaster, and two seamen, assisted by a party we hauled a small prize boat across the spit, embarked in her, and at half past four A.M., reached the opposite side.

Landing with the petty officer and one man, I forded the above-mentioned rivers, and at a distance of about two miles and a half from the boat, arrived at the corn and forage we were in search of, stacked on the banks of the Salghir River, evidently for transmission by water, as the river was perfectly navigable for barges, the sides being cut, and towing paths on either bank.

In a short time the forage and corn, amounting to about 400 tons, was totally destroyed, not however without alarming the guard, and from 20 to 30 mounted cossacks, who were encamped in a village close at hand. On our retreating, we were so hard pressed by them, that, but for the circumstance of the last 200 yards being mud, and the cover of rifles from Mr. Lillingston, and a man who remained in the boat, we could hardly have escaped capture. Having re-crossed the Spit, we returned to the Weser by 8 A.M.

I must bring to your notice the excellent behaviour of the small party who accompanied me, more especially that of William Rickard, Quartermaster, who, though much fatigued himself, remained to assist the other seaman who, from exhaustion, had fallen in the mud, and was unable to extricate himself, notwithstanding the enemy were keeping up a heavy fire on us, at the distance of 30 or 40 yards, as we crossed the mud.

Trusting my proceedings will meet with your approval, I have, &c.

(Signed J.E. COMMERELL,
Lieutenant Commanding.
To Captain Sherard Osborn,
Senior Officer.

Her Majesty's ship Recruit, off
Berdiansk, October 18, 1855.

SIR,

I HAVE the honour to forward you a report of my proceedings since leaving Her Majesty's ship Curlew at this place on the 15th. According to my orders, I steered for my cruizing ground between the Dolga Bank and Whitehouse Spit. When off the latter place, observing a number of men and boats engaged in fishing, and also that many large fishing store-houses had been built since my last visit here on the 14th of last month, I hauled close in to the shore, anchoring the Recruit about 700 yards off, with the intention of landing with my boats and destroying all I could, as soon as I had driven back the troops, who were coming down in great numbers, both cavalry and infantry, to prevent us; the former we soon disposed of, but the latter, scattering themselves about in twos and threes, threw themselves on the ground, creeping along so that we could not see them to stop their advance with our shells from the ship; I therefore resolved to land at once, in hopes, by the quickness of our movements, to get our work over before they could possibly close on us. Unfortunately for me, I regret to say, that whilst directing the pointing of an 8-inch gun to where I believed some of these riflemen to be, (just as I was on the point of going into the boat to land) the gun, from some unaccountable cause, went off, and, in recoiling, the whole weight of both gun and carriage came down on my left foot, injuring it very severely and breaking several bones, which I fear will lay me up for some time.

I was thus rendered incapable of landing, so sent Mr. Parker, Second Master of this ship, on shore in charge of the boats and landing party, who succeeded in carrying out my instructions as to the destruction of all the boats there (seven in number), many new fishing nets of great length, five large new fishing establishments, full of quantities of fishing tackle and other gear: this service he performed in a most gallant manner, and much to my satisfaction, as they were the whole time exposed to a very smart and annoying fire from the enemy's concealed infantry (at a very short distance), who, in spite of our fire from the ship, had managed to creep down close to them, favoured by the inequality of the ground and the long grass, so that our party had to make a long detour (covered by a hot fire of rifles from the Recruit) to prevent them being cut off, and to get to their boats. The Russians kept up a constant fire of rifles from the lighthouse, in which they had succeeded in lodging themselves, upon the boats, and then upon the ship, which we returned with rifles only, and I think to some purpose, until we weighed and shifted further out. Not a man was hit, though ship and boat were many times. As I did not wish to injure the lighthouse, I did not attempt to fire, so as to dislodge them, with shot or shell from the guns.

The 17th I stood along the spit to see if anymore boats or nets could be found along the shore where I could destroy them, as also to drive away a number of troops I saw hidden behind some banks, and at the same time to try and set fire with carcases to a number of new stores, built on the broad part of the spit high up but too far off for me with my small force to attempt to land and destroy.

I could see no more boats, but their perseverance in thus rebuilding these houses, boats, and nets, with the fact of so many troops being there to protect them, tells its own tale, that they must be much in want of provisions.

I have, &c.,
(Signed) GEO. F. DAY,
Lieutenant-Commander.
Captain Osborn, Senior Officer.

*Curlew, Recruit, Ardent

War-Department, November 27, 1855.

LORD PANMURE has this day received a Despatch, and its Enclosures, of which the following are copies, addressed to his Lordship by Sir Wm. Codrington.

Sevastopol, November 13, 1855.

MY LORD,

HAVING so lately assumed the command of the Army, I have not sufficient materials, nor do I consider it necessary to write a separate despatch.

The return of the troops from the expedition against Kinburn was announced to your Lordship by electric telegraph, on the 3rd instant.

I do myself the honour to transmit the copies of reports received from Brigadier-General Honourable A. Spencer, giving a more detailed account of the proceedings of the force under his command than he had hitherto been able to make, and two reports from Brigadier-General Lord George Paget, with an account of two reconnaissances that were made by the allied cavalry from Eupatoria.

I have, &c.
W. CODRINGTON,
General Commanding.
The Lord Panmure, &c. &c. &c.

Enclosure 1.

Her Majesty's ship Royal Albert,
off Sevastopol, November 4, 1855.

SIR,

IN reporting the return of the Expeditionary Land Force under my command from Kinburn, I am now enabled to make, for the information of the Commander-in-Chief, a more ample report of their proceedings, than in my previously hurried despatch I was able to do.

The landing of the troops, three miles from Kinburn Fort, was effected without opposition on the 15th October. Owing to a heavy surf there was considerable difficulty in it, but the infantry were all on shore by 11 o'clock (it commenced at 8 A.M.), and from the activity of the Royal Navy employed, the cavalry and most of the artillery were landed in the course of the day, though the first portion of the commissariat was only landed, and with great difficulty, on the evening of the second day.

The whole force was very shortly in position. The orders I had received from the French General Bazaine were, to protect with the English troops the right flank from any attack the enemy might make, for the relief of the garrison, from Nicolaieff or Cherson; whilst the French line was to be in our rear but facing the fort.

The ground I occupied was about a mile in extent; the regiments were deployed into line, every advantage being taken of the nature of the ground, which was undulating.

The tents were pitched in rear of the battalions as they arrived from the landing-place. The regiments were employed immediately after landing in entrenching their own fronts, thus making our general line of field works from the sea on either side. A work was also thrown up in the course of the following day, on the left flank of the line, to be occupied by field pieces or by ship guns, should the fort not fall immediately. The nature of the ground rendered any assistance from the allied gun-boats impossible.

The French had hastily thrown up a place d'armes in rear of our right, from which a re-embarkation, if necessary, might have been satisfactorily accomplished.

The bombardment from the ships commenced on the afternoon of the 15th, but from the state of the weather it was discontinued; and on the 16th they were unable to resume it from the same cause.

By the morning of the 17th, the field works thrown up by the troops were, as far as circumstances would admit of, very defensible, although too extensive. The outlying pickets had also thrown up small entrenchments at their respective posts: that morning at daybreak I made a reconnaissance with the detachments of French and English cavalry and the 57th Regiment. The weather becoming thick the infantry returned after a march of four miles out. The cavalry proceeded to the village of Paksoffka, a few miles further, which they found deserted: at 10 A.M. the ships opened fire, and at three o'clock the forts surrendered, with about 1,400 prisoners; 17 officers, and 739 men were given over to me by General Bazaine, and were subsequently sent on board Her Majesty's ship Vulcan, to proceed to Constantinople. On the following morning the forts at Ochakoff were blown up by the enemy. French and English Commissioners were appointed for the taking over of the materiel found in the forts of Kinburn, and for the temporary division of the place. On the 19th, I moved the English camp to the immediate neighbourhood of the fort, and occupied the southern shore; the ground is here nearly level with the sea, and so perfectly smooth that it is easily protected by ships on both flanks. On the 20th the English force, with the exception of the 21st Regiment, who were left to do the duties at Kinburn, joined the French in a reconnaissance under General Bazaine. The troops carried three days' provisions, and the Commissariat were able to carry three more. We halted and bivouacked that night at the village of Paksoffka, about eight miles' march of sandy soil. The French occupied a village at a short distance. We had no tents, but the weather was fine, and there was plenty of wood and hay, and a large supply of cabbages, and other vegetables. The inhabitants had all left. On the 21st, halted. The following day, with the cavalry, artillery, and three battalions, I accompanied General Bazaine, with a part of the French force, to the village, of Skadoffka, about five or six miles; country very open, with occasionally deep sand; always plenty of water in the villages. Having burnt the village, we returned that day to Paksoffka. The detachment of Carabineers, under Captain Wardlaw, had pushed on by my direction to a village about three miles further, where they found inhabitants, who told them that some Russian cavalry had left them that morning.

On the 23rd the whole force returned to Kinburn. On the march our rear was threatened by about 250 of the enemy's cavalry, who, however, soon retired. On the 27th the cavalry and artillery were embarked, and on the 30th the whole of the infantry, to return to the Crimea, leaving French troops to garrison the fort.

I cannot speak too highly of the assistance I have received from the co-operation and counsel of Admiral Sir Edmund Lyons, and of the support afforded me by him and the Officers of the Royal Navy under his command, – to whose excellent arrangements, for the landing and re-embarkation of the troops, I have been much indebted.

I beg to assure the Commander-in-Chief of the great satisfaction I have felt in serving under the orders of General Bazaine in this expedition.

I have received every assistance from Colonel Hurdle, Royal Marines, who commanded a brigade (2 battalions Royal Marines and 63rd Regiment); 500 marines were added, through the consideration of Sir Edmund Lyons, to this force.

Also from Colonel Lord West, 21st Fusiliers, commanding a brigade (17th, 20th, 21st, and 57th Regiments); who mentions his Brigade-Major, Captain Earle, 57th Regiment, and his Aide-de-Camp, Captain Carleton, 21st Fusiliers. Colonel Hurdle mentions Captain Rodney, Royal Marines, and Captain Ellis, Royal Marines, his Brigade-Major and Aide-de-Camp.

I was also ably supported by Brevet-Major Best, commanding Royal Engineers; Captain Johnson, commanding Royal Artillery; Captain Wardlaw, commanding detachment 6th Dragoon Guards; Brevet-Major Gordon, commanding 17th Regiment; Captain Gray, commanding 21st Fusiliers; Lieutenant-Colonel Evelegh, commanding 20th Regiment; Lieutenant-Colonel Warre, commanding 57th Regiment; Lieutenant-Colonel Lindesay, commanding 63rd Regiment; Lieutenant-Colonel Campbell, commanding battalion Royal Marines; Lieutenant-Colonel Holloway, commanding battalion Royal Marines; Brevet- Major Smith and Brevet-Major Hallewell, Assistant Adjutant and Quartermaster-Generals, were of great use to me; as also my personal Staff, Captain Robinson and Captain Baillie, 44th Regiment; and Lieutenant St. Clair, 4th Regiment, acting as interpreter.

Dr. Gordon, Principal Medical Officer, Deputy Assistant-Commissary-General Power, Captain Clavell, Royal Marines, acting as Provost Marshall, and Lieutenant Young, Land Transport Corps, were all most zealous in their several departments.

I have, &c.,
(Signed) AUGS. SPENCER,
Brigadier-General.
To the Quartermaster-General,
&c., &c., &c.

Enclosure 2.

Eupatoria, October 30, 1855.

SIR,

I HAVE the honour to report that the allied forces stationed here, disposed as per margin,* marched on the small town of Sak, on the morning of the 27th instant, under the command of General of Division D'Allonville.

At the further extremity of the strand that divides the sea from the lake of Sazik Gualoie (by which route the column marched), the ground rises to the level of the steppe land that universally prevails. On reaching this point the allied cavalry and horse artillery made a rapid advance to the front, for about five miles, in an easterly direction, passing to the left of Sak.

We there found the enemy in much the same position in which we had left them on the 23rd instant, though they had, to a certain extent, entrenched themselves.

General D'Allonville from this point opened a fire with much effect, which continued for nearly an hour, and which was warmly responded to by the enemy.

Captain Thomas's troop of Horse Artillery being supported by the 12th Lancers; the Carabineers, 4th and 13th Light Dragoons being in second line, in reserve.

The loss to the Allies on this occasion was 30 killed and wounded; one English Artillery-man having been slightly wounded, two horses killed, and three wounded.

We then withdrew to the town of Sak, where we bivouacked for the night.

At daybreak, on the 28th instant, the cavalry and horse artillery made another advance in rather a more northerly direction (to the south of the village of Temesh), in the endeavour to turn the right of the enemy, or to draw him into action, which, however, he appeared to shew no disposition to respond to, and we consequently returned to our bivouack at Sak, in front of which the infantry had remained to secure our rear.

On this second night there was a total want of water, in consequence of the drain upon the wells the night before, and there was an absence of water for a circumference of many miles to our front. The column therefore returned to Eupatoria yesterday, the 29th instant.

I beg to report that I have attached Captain the Honourable Charles Keith, 4th Light Dragoons, to General D'Allonville, during the time the troops are in the field, and that I sent Captain Clifton, 12th Lancers, on board Her Majesty's ship Diamond, to assist Captain Hamilton, R.N., in his operations.

I have, &c.
(Signed) GEO. PAGET,
Brigadier-General, Commanding British
Troops at Eupatoria.
To his Excellency,
The General Commanding-in-Chief.

Enclosure 3.

Eupatoria,
November 3, 1855.

SIR,

I HAVE the honour to report that a portion of the allied troops stationed here, under the command of General of Brigade Ali Pasha, strength as per margin,† were sent yesterday to the village of Tchotai, fifteen miles to the north of Eupatoria, in consequence of information of some stores of hay, live stock, &c., having been collected there by the enemy.

The two squadrons of the 12th Lancers with this force, were commanded by Lieutenant-Colonel Tottenham of that regiment, whose report I have the honour to enclose, and by which it will be gratifying to observe, that this operation met with the most complete success.

The remainder of the allied forces here made at the same time a demonstration to the right of this village, for the purpose of drawing off the attention of the enemy; the English Brigade of Cavalry advancing as far as Yultschuk, the French on their right.

Colonel Pole, 12th Lancers, was in command, an attack of fever having for some days confined me to my bed, and he reports that no enemy made its appearance in any force.

I have, &c.,
(Signed) GEO. PAGET,
Brigadier-General, Commanding British
Troops at Eupatoria.
To his Excellency,
The General Commanding-in-Chief.

Enclosure 4.

Eupatoria, November 3, 1855.

MY LORD,

I HAVE the honour to report that, agreeably to Brigade Orders of the 1st instant, I proceeded at 4 A.M. yesterday, in command of two squadrons of the 12th Royal Lancers, to join the force under Ali Pasha, ordered to assemble in front of the Turkish cavalry camp.

At daylight we marched through Alchir to Tchotai, a village about 15 miles from this. The Turkish cavalry were in advance, supported by the English and French squadrons. We arrived at Tchotai about half-past eleven, and captured 1 Russian Commissariat Officer (as it is supposed), 1 Cossack, about 40 arabas, and about 3000 head of horses, camels, oxen, and sheep; 3 Russian carriages were also brought in, and a considerable number of the inhabitants of the village.

We started on our return at half-past one, having set fire to the villages and destroyed 30 large ricks of hay. We arrived in camp about 8½ P.M.; no resistance was offered by the enemy.

I have, &c.,

(Signed) W.H. TOTTENHAM.

Lt.-Colonel, 12th Royal Lancers.

Brigadier-General Lord George Paget,

Commanding the Light Brigade,

Eupatoria.

*1st Column, under the command of Mushir Achmed Pasha:-
    Division of Turkish and Egyptian Infantry, each with a battery of Artillery.
    1 brigade of Turkish Cavalry, with a troop of Horse artillery.
2nd Column, under the command of General of Division de Failly:-
    A section of French Engineers.
    9 battalions of French Infantry.
    2 battalions of Artillery.
3rd Column, under the command of General of Division d'Allonville, Commander-in-Chief:-
    A brigade of Turkish Cavalry (Ali Pasha).
    Division of French Cavalry, with its troop of Horse Artillery (General Esterhazy).
    Brigade of British Cavalry, with its troop of Horse Artillery (Brigadier-General Lord George Paget).
†Under the orders of General of Brigade Ali Pasha:-
Bashi Bazouks.
2 Regiments of Turkish Cavalry.
2 French squadrons (Hussars).
2 English squadrons (Lancers).

War-Department, November 29, 1855.

LORD PANMURE has this day received a Despatch and its Enclosures, of which the following are copies, addressed to his Lordship by General Sir William Codrington, K.C.B.

Sevastopol, November 17, 1855.

MY LORD,

ON the 15th instant, about 3 P.M., a terrific explosion shook the camp of the army and spread heavy destruction in the immediate neighbourhood of its force; even here, at Head-Quarters, two and a half miles perhaps distant, it burst open and broke windows, all felt the power of it, and the high column of smoke, with shells bursting in the midst and around it, told too well the cause, and showed the danger of all within its reach.

It was not long before we were on the spot: to the sudden burst had succeeded a continued and dark drift of smoke, which told its tale of continued fire and of danger; constant bursting of shells was going on, and the ground was covered with bits of wood, musquet balls, and splinters of shells from the first heavy explosion, which had strewed the ground with destruction, and killed and hurt very many people.

100,000 pounds of powder had exploded in the French siege train, set fire to all the stores there, and to our neighbouring English park where all was fiercely burning, whilst the tendency of the light air at first threatened a second and as serious an accident from powder, not eighty yards off, for the roof of the building had been damaged and the door blown in by the shock.

Some General Officers had fallen in and marched part of their divisions down, others sent some in fatigue, some with stretchers for the wounded, all exerted themselves with the French with an energy and disregard of danger that was admirable; blankets were taken to the exposed store, placed and wetted on the roof by water being passed up in buckets; the doors were covered with wet blankets and sandbags, and in a short time it was reported and looked safe, though the closeness of the fire and frequent explosions could not allow the feeling of security. Many detached though small fires were burning, and the ground of both the French and English parks, a space of 150 yards across, was a mass of large fires, some of fuel, some of huts, some of gun carriages, boxes, handspikes, and rope.

The fortunately light air had rather changed its direction, and by breaking up and dragging away things, a sort of lane was at last formed, the fires cut off, and gradually got under control, because confined to smaller though fierce fires, but manageable.

I saw every one working well, and I know that French and English took live shells from the neighbourhood of danger to a more distant spot, and at a later period parties threw what earth the rocky soil could give, upon the fires, and helped much to subdue them; all was safe about 7 P.M., and a strong guard and working party posted for the night.

The army was under arms, the following morning before daylight, and everything being quiet, I ordered the divisions to turn in, and continue the working parties in the roads, which I had counter ordered for that morning.

The exploded powder store was situated in the ruins of some walls which had advantageously been made use of for the purpose of shelter; it had been the store of supply to the French attack on the Malakoff front, and it contained the powder which had been brought back from their batteries.

It is at the head of the ravine, which, as it gets towards Sebastopol, forms the steep and rocky valley of Ravin du Carénage.

The Light Division was on the ground which it first took up in October, 1854; the Rifles on the right, then the 7th, the 33rd, and 23rd; on their left the 34th Regiment, which subsequently joined, was on the right front in advance; and the vacating of a spot of ground by the Sappers' camp, enabled me when commanding the division to place the Artillery and Small-arm Brigade on the immediate right of the Rifles.

The French subsequently brought their main siege train and store to the position it has now for some time occupied.

Daylight showed the damage, of which I have given your Lordship an outline in another letter.

But the more important and sad part is the loss of life, and the wounded who have suffered. One officer and 20 non-commissioned officers and men, killed; 4 officers and 112 non-commissioned officers and men, wounded; with 7* missing, show the sudden and fatal power of the shock, which not only destroyed in its immediate neighbourhood, but wounded, by shell and splinters, some at a distance of three-quarters of a mile.

The loss of our Allies is distressingly heavy.

I have, &c.,

W.J. CODRINGTON,

General Commanding.

The Lord Panmure, &c. &c. &c.

*Six artillery men since accounted for and alive. – W.C., 1 P.M. November 17.

Admiralty, December 7, 1855.

DESPATCHES, with Enclosures, of which the following are copies, have been received from Admiral Sir Edmund Lyons, Bart., G.C.B., Commander-in-Chief of Her Majesty's Ships and Vessels in the Mediterranean and Black Sea.

REPORTING DESTRUCTION OF CORN, &c.,
IN GHEISK-LIMAN.

No. 951. Royal Albert, Kazatch Bay,
November 24, 1855.

SIR,

THEIR Lordships are aware that when the small gun-boats were no longer required at Kinburn I sent them back to Captain Osborn, to afford him the means of destroying, at the latest period of the season, the harvest of this year, which I understood to be collecting in the neighbourhood of Gheisk-Liman, for the purpose of being transported in the winter months, partly to the enemy's army in the Crimea over the frozen Gulf of Azof, and partly to his army in the Caucasus by the military road.

2. The enclosed copy of a letter from Captain Osborn will show their lordships that in this, as on many former occasions, he has fully justified the confidence I have placed in him. The skilfulness of the arrangements made by him, and the admirable manner in which they were executed by himself, by Commander Kennedy, of the Curlew, and by the officers and men under their orders, completely frustrated the efforts of the large force that was brought against them in defence of the stores, which the enemy appears to have considered safe from any naval attack, in consequence of the shallowness of the water.

3. The effects of this brilliant enterprize, in the destruction of so much corn and forage at the commencement of winter, cannot fail to be severely felt by the Russian armies both in the Crimea and the Caucasus.

4. Commander Kennedy, in reporting his large share in the proceedings of the day in the command of the Curlew, states to Captain Osborn that at one place alone the rows of stacks were six deep and extended two miles, and it appears that for economy in transport and storage the straw was cut near to the ears of the corn,

5 As the ice is now forming on the shores of the Sea of Azof and the squadron is withdrawn, I feel it to be due to Captain Osborn to record that under circumstances of great difficulty, occasioned by unusually tempestuous weather, he has most ably continued through the summer, and brought to a successful close in the autumn, operations novel in their nature and extremely detrimental to the enemy, which commenced auspiciously in the spring under the direction of the late Captain Lyons of the Miranda; nor is it too much to say, that both commanding officers were supported throughout, by as dashing and as intelligent a band of young officers, seamen, and marines, as ever shone in the British Navy.

I am, &c.
(Signed) EDMUND LYONS,
Rear-Admiral and Commander-in-Chief.
The Secretary of the Admiralty, London.

No. 41. Her Majesty's steam-sloop Vesuvius,
off Gheisk, November 7, 1855.

SIR,

AFTER dark on the evening of the 3rd instant, the squadron under my command was assembled and anchored in 16 feet water, off Gheisk-Liman, and I made arrangements for the morrow to operate against the extensive collection of corn, forage, and fuel, belonging to the enemy, stacked along its shores, so as to distract the attention of the large force which, from previous observation, I knew to be in the neighbourhood.

Under Lieutenant Ross, of the Weser, I placed the Curlew in the temporary charge of Lieutenant Miall and the Ardent in charge of Mr. Tilly, Second Master, each vessel having sufficient men left in her to weigh an anchor, or fight a gun, and man a few boats, giving orders to Lieutenant Ross to close in on the northern face of Gheisk, and to be prepared to co-operate with me inside the Liman.

The Vesuvius I left in the offing, denuded of every available person; embarking officers and men as in the annexed list, from the Vesuvius, Curlew, Weser, and Ardent, with their boats, we left at daylight, towed by Her Majesty's gun-boats,

Recruit, Lieutenant G. Day.

Boxer, Lieutenant S.P. Townsend.

Cracker, Lieutenant J.H. Marryat.

Clinker, Lieutenant J.S. Hudson.

By 6.30 A.M. the flotilla was off Vodina, three miles north of Glofira; here long tiers of corn-stacks and much fuel was stored along the coast, with a Cossack guard for its protection; I immediately detached Commander Kennedy with the boats, covering him with the gun-vessels, and in a short time all was in flames, and the party cleverly re-embarked at the moment that a large body of Cossacks rode up from Lazalnite.

The town of Glofira became the next point of attack; it was greatly changed in appearance since visited by Captain Rowley Lambert in July last. Corn stacks, for some miles in extent, might now be seen along its southern and eastern face, placed close to the water's edge ready for transport; and between the rows of houses tier on tier were to be seen.

An entrenchment had been cut along the edge of the cliff commanding the spit; large bodies of dismounted cavalry were seen lining it, and armed men shewed in the rear of every house.

To endeavour to flank the defences, as well as destroy the corn stacks stored on a high hill east of Glofira, I despatched Commander Kennedy, with the boats of Her Majesty's ship Curlew, a paddle-box boat and cutter of the Vesuvius, the whole towed by the Clinker, Lieutenant Hudson, with orders to turn the spit end, and then attack in that direction, after giving a certain time to allow the enemy's attention to be divided by the other attack. The gun-boats Recruit, Grinder, Boxer, and Cracker, opening fire on the entrenchments with Shrapnell shell, and on the corn ricks with carcases.

As the enemy could only be dislodged from the extreme west, and the carcases did not well answer, and moreover endangered the whole town, I despatched Lieutenants Day and Campion with the small force of marines available, a howitzer boat and two rocket boats, to aid more effectually in carrying out my object.

Lieutenant Campion, with Mr. Verey, gunner, charging at the head of the marines, supported by Lieutenant Day and the seamen, all being under a sharp fire of musketry, succeeded in driving the enemy, with considerable loss, out of their trench work, and captured a small brass piece, and then steadily forced them back, with loss, from store to store, until the whole of the vast quantity of corn, stacked ready for thrashing and transport, was in flames.

The gallant manner in which Lieutenant Campion led the marines deserves to be brought under your notice.

Seeing the enemy collecting a number of men, ready to charge our men if they advanced beyond a ravine on the east face of the town, I recalled my force, and had the satisfaction of seeing all embarked, with only one man wounded.

The vessels off Gheisk were now seen to be engaged, Lieutenant Ross, of the Weser, having placed them in capital positions; and, as the enemy moved down large bodies of troops, especially cavalry, to resist his landing, and opened fire on him, he very unwillingly had to fire on the town, to dislodge them.

The proceedings of Lieutenant Ross were ably executed, and he fully succeeded in keeping in check a heavy body of cavalry which might have much incommoded the small force under Commander Kennedy, who, by the most strenuous exertions, had reached his position, and finding the cliff too steep to scale in the face of a large number of troops, who were firing on him from its crest, he very judiciously executed the duty I had entrusted to him, with the gun and the carcase rockets of the ship's boats, setting every store in flames, except one large government building considerably in the rear.

Commander Kennedy speaks in the highest terms of his party, for the shallowness of the water obliged the crews of the boats to be rowing and wading through the water from noon until midnight, the season too being now very cold.

Throughout the night the stores were burning fiercely, a sheet of flames extending fully two miles, but the town of Glofira, *except where the troops had used the houses against us,* remained untouched.

At an early hour on the 6th November, we weighed and proceeded into the Liman, steering towards Gheisk; the valuable services of Mr. George Perry, Acting Master of the Vesuvius, and Mr. Parker, Second Master of the Recruit, came here into play; and, at an early period, I had the satisfaction of seeing all the gun-boats anchored just in their own draught of water, within long gun-shot of the east extreme of Gheisk and the neighbouring steppe, along the edge of which, for four miles, corn and hay was stacked in quantities far beyond what I had conceived to be possible, and at the base of the steppe, as well as that part of the spit commanded by the town, timber yards, fish stores, boats, &c., in numbers were accumulated.

To attack upon as many points as possible was, I thought, the only way to foil the troops that had now had 36 hours to prepare for us; the gun-boats Grinder, Boxer, Cracker, and Clinker, were left to cover the landing party. To Lieutenant Ross of the

Weser, I signalized to prepare to land, and divided the force in the Liman into three bodies; the left under Lieutenants Day and Townsend, consisted of boats and men of Recruit and Boxer; the centre I entrusted to Commander Kennedy, having under him Lieutenants Hamilton, Campion, Marryat, and Mayne, with all the boats of the Curlew, Ardent, Grinder, and Cracker, and port rocket and gun-boats of the Vesuvius, in charge of the officers named in the margin;* the right division under Lieutenant Chetham Strode, and Lieutenant Hudson, consisted of the starboard gun-boats of Vesuvius, and those of Clinker, together with some marines, Mr. R. Farquharson, Midshipman, in charge of the latter. Lieutenant Ross, on the west side of Gheisk Spit, had the boats and small-arm men of the Weser, with a small force from Curlew and Ardent, under Lieutenant Miall, and Mr. Tilly, Second Master, in readiness to co-operate.

The different parties pulled in and effected a landing at appointed places, fully a mile apart; the Russian troops, within light breastworks, attempted to prevent them, but failed, and in a few moments a screen of flames and smoke rolling from our men towards the enemy, prevented the latter seeing where or how to manoeuvre, in order to cut off any of our small detachments.

On the right and centre the enemy mustered strongest, and at one time observing a column of some 1500 Cossacks moving rapidly off the left, I directed Commander Kennedy (who by that time had connected his fires with those of Lieutenant Day) to re-embark all but the marines, and with them to proceed to his right, and I reinforced him with the marines of the Recruit and Weser, under Lieutenant Campion. This answered perfectly; the enemy arrived too late to save anything on the left, whilst our men steadily worked towards the right division, under Lieutenants Strode and Ross, who, in spite of a heavy but badly directed fire from the houses on the heights, steadily held their ground, and effectually destroyed a great accumulation of materials for boats and ship building, fish stores, cavalry camp gear and granaries.

When everything but the town of Gheisk was destroyed, I ordered the embarkation to take place, and detached some boats to cover Lieutenant Ross, between whom and his boat the enemy were throwing a body of men, who, by their uniform, I believed to be regular infantry. By 2 P.M., everything was finished, and all the parties safely re-embarked on board their respective gun-boats, the casualties amounting to only six men wounded in all, one of them dangerously and another severely.

Nothing further being left within our reach in Gheisk-Liman, except the store of corn which escaped on the previous day at Glofira, I, therefore ordered Commander Kennedy with the moiety of the boats to return to their respective ships, and remained with the Recruit, Ardent, Boxer, and Cracker's boats to finish what had escaped east of Glofira.

On the 6th the weather, which had favoured us most providentially, changed; fogs and strong breezes came on, but directly I was able, the rocket boats and carcases were again employed upon Glofira until the fires extinguished yesterday were re-lighted, and another extensive accumulation of corn in flames; I then weighed and returned to the Vesuvius, reaching her the same afternoon.

I despair of being able to convey to you any idea of the extraordinary quantity of corn, rye, hay, wood and other supplies, so necessary for the existence of Russian armies both in the Caucasus and the Crimea, which it has been our good fortune to destroy.

That these vast stores should have been collected here, so close to the sea, whilst we were still in the neighbourhood, is only to be accounted for, by their supposing that they could not be reached by us, and judging by the position the squadron under the late Captain Edmund Lyons, took up in May last, the Russians had established a camp and fortified their town only to meet a similar attack.

During these proceedings we never had more than 200 men engaged; the enemy had, from the concurrent testimony of Lieutenants Ross and Strode, and my own observation, from 3,000 to 4,000 men in Gheisk alone.

Where every officer exerted himself to the utmost, and did all and more than I expected of them, it would be invidious for me to mention, one more than another; it was their coolness, zeal, and example, that rendered steady many of the younger men; who for the first time were under fire, and but for their general intelligence and zeal, the enemy would have easily frustrated our operations.

The zeal, good conduct, and gallantry of the men, was deserving of every praise.

Commander Kennedy, my second in command, gave me the most valuable co-operation, and from him as well as the reports of the other officers, I feel justified in placing before you the names of the following warrant officers and men, who, under fire, behaved remarkably well, viz.: Mr. Richard Verey, Acting Gunner of Her Majesty's ship Ardent; Thomas Kerr, Gunner, Royal Marine Artillery, Her Majesty's ship Vesuvius; Peter Hanlan, A.B., Her Majesty's ship Curlew; David Barry, A.B., Her Majesty's ship Cracker.

The enclosed pian, illustrative of our operations, by Mr. George Perry, Acting Master of the Vesuvius, will, I trust, be of use, and I beg you will allow me to call your attention to the unvarying zeal of that officer.

I have, &c.,
(Signed) SHERARD OSBORN.
Captain and Senior Officer in the
Sea of Azof.
Rear-Admiral Sir Edmund
Lyons, Bart., &c., &c., &c.
G.C.B.

Mr. Armstrong, Mate; Mr. Scott, Gunner; Mr. Verey, Gunner.

Admiralty December 14, 1855.

DESPATCHES, of which the following are copies, have been received from Admiral Sir Edmund Lyons, Bart., G.C.B, Commander-in-Chief of Her Majesty's Ships and Vessels in the Mediterranean and Black Sea.

No. 962. Royal Albert, Kazatch Bay, December 1, 1855.

SIR,

I REQUEST that you will lay before the Lords Commissioners of the Admiralty the enclosed copy of a letter from Captain Sherard Osborn, of the Vesuvius, dated the 24th ultimo, informing me that as the formation of ice had commenced in the Sea of Azof, and as he had been informed by both M. Gopcevitch, the Austrian merchant, charged with the shipment of corn in Austrian vessels, and by the Russian authorities at Mariaupol, that all chance of neutral vessels obtaining cargoes this year was at an end, he had withdrawn to Kertch with the squadron under his orders, after assuring himself that no merchant vessels remained in that sea.

I have so frequently had occasion to bring the merits of Captain Osborn under their Lordships'notice, that it is perhaps unnecessary, on the present occasion, that I should say more than that he has maintained his high character up to the close of the service upon which he was employed for six months, and he brings under my favourable notice the gallant and zealous support he has received, from first to last, from the officers and men under his orders.

I am, &c.
(Signed) EDMUND LYONS,
Rear-Admiral and Commander-in-Chief.
The Secretary of the. Admiralty, London

No. 42. Vesuvius, off Kertch November 24, 1855.

SIR,

BEING now, in accordance with your instructions, on my road to rejoin your flag, I have the honour to report the close of operations in the Sea of Azof, and the proceedings of the squadron in that sea subsequent to my Last letter dated off Gheisk, 7th November, 1855.

On the 7th, I received your instructions, with notices relative to neutrals quitting the Sea of Azof on the 20th November, 1855.The weather became most severe, and I could only succeed in serving the notices upon the authorities on shore at Mariaupol. But on the 8th November, 1855, the shipping anchored off Mariaupol were duly warned, and on the 9th those off Taganrog likewise.

A gale of extreme violence from the eastward blew continually from that date until the 18th November, I then immediately served a notice upon the neutral shipping in Berdiansk.

There, from Mr. Gopcevioh, as well as previously at Taganrog and Mariaupol, we learnt that the Russian authorities had kept the neutrals in quarantine ever since their arrival, and that the likelihood of cargoes being procured was almost at an end.

A Russian officer at Mariaupol laughed at the idea of the neutrals believing they would get wheat this year, and told Commander Kennedy, whom I sent in there with a flag of truce, that the neutrals must stay the winter.

Under these circumstances, looking to your wishes and instructions upon the subject, it became a cause of great anxiety for me lest, by the sudden commencement of winter, or intentionally, the neutral vessels should fail to quit the sea on the 20th November, 1855.

I, therefore, as the ice had begun to make and the temperature to fall rapidly after the 13th, despatched all the squadron to Kertch except the Ardent, Snake, and Clinker, and with them proceeded up the Gulf of Azof.

We arrived off Mariaupol on the 19th and found all the neutrals had sailed for Kertch, and on the 20th I sighted Taganrog and found the roads empty, all the vessels that were there having likewise left.

The ice already extended on either hand some miles from the shore, the Don appeared to be frozen, and every indication of winter having set in, in that neighbourhood, was apparent.

At Mariaupol the river or harbour was frozen, and much ice lined the coast as far down as Bielosarai Lighthouse; the temperature at mid-day as low as 29° Fahrenheit. From thence I separated the squadron so as to examine the whole coast from Gheniteh to Enikale Lighthouse, most minutely, and not a single boat of the smallest description was to be seen.

In surrendering into your hands the prominent position in which you have been pleased to employ me for the last five months, that of Senior Officer of a detached squadron, allow me, Sir, to express, most respectfully, my deep sense of the honour you conferred upon me, and the grateful recollection of the unvarying kindness, confidence, and consideration I have experienced at your hands; without it I feel I never should, as I trust I have, succeeded in carrying out your views and instructions.

Next to that let me again remind you that my anxiety to execute your plans has ever been an easy task, supported as I have ever been by the gallant and zealous exertions of every officer and man serving in this squadron; I know not how sufficiently to express my approbation of their conduct.

And it is not the less pleasing part of my duty to assure you of the kindly co-operation I have ever received from the officers of the French Navy serving in the Sea of Azof. Among those more especially known to me, I feel justified in mentioning Lieutenant Cloue, commanding the Brandon; Lieutenant La Juchette, Fulton; and Lieutenant Vidal, of the Caton.

&c.,

(Signed) S. OSBORN

War-Department, December 18, 1855.

LORD PANMURE has this day received a Despatch and its Enclosures, of which the following are copies, addressed to his Lordship *by* General Sir William Codrington, K.C.B.

Sevastopol, December 4, 1855.

MY LORD,

THE enemy continue to fire occasionally, and sometimes heavily, on parts of the town. They must have expended a considerable quantity of valuable ammunition without causing us any loss or inconvenience. The enclosed Casualty Return is the first of the sort I have had occasion to report to your Lordship.

It may seem unimportant to refer to the state of roads and weather here, but their condition affects the essential communications and well-being of the army. The winter broke upon us suddenly on the 26th and 27th with snow, and has varied with gales and rain; and a very deep state of the ground has damaged all communications.

Constant presence of labourers and constant attention are requisite, and are being given to the road, which, from a peculiarity of soil and condition, was worked into holes, but which is and will continue to be of the greatest service to the army and its supplies.

I have, &c.,
W.J. CODRINGTON,
General Commanding.

P.S. – I beg leave also to forward the weekly report of Dr. Hall, the principal Medical Officer, by which your Lordship will perceive that the general state of health of the army continues favourable.

W.J. CODRINGTON,
General Commanding.
The Lord Panmure, &c. &c. &c.

War-Department, January 8, 1856.

LORD PANMURE has this day received a Despatch, of which the following is a copy, addressed to his Lordship by General Sir William Codrington, K.C.B.

Sevastopol, December 25, 1855.

MY LORD,

NOTWITHSTANDING the recent severe weather, the thermometer a few nights ago having fallen nearly to zero, the general state of health of the Army has continued good. The roads are in fair working order; and though the efficiency of the locomotive engines was impaired by the frost, the damage has been made good.

The final operations on the Docks have been somewhat delayed on our side, by the influx of water, and by the freezing of pumps.

The fire from the forts on the northern side of the harbour continues, and it is at times heavy; but the casualties, I am happy to say, are few.

There has been no movement of importance on the part of the enemy in our neighbourhood of late. A detachment of French troops surprised a Cossack post near Teilion, a few days ago, killing several men, and taking the rest prisoners.

The general drill of the Army makes good progress.

I have, &c.,
W.J. CODRINGTON,
General Commanding.
The Lord Panmure, &c. &c. &c.

Head Quarters, Kertch, December 21, 1855.

MY LORD,

I HAVE with much regret to report to you the death of Captain R. S. Sherwood, of the cavalry of this force.

This officer was engaged in a skirmish, that took place on the 16th instant, between a detachment of our cavalry and a party of Russian cavalry; his gallantry in this affair was most conspicuous, as is reported to me by the officer who commanded the detachment. Captain Sherwood was severely wounded, and was carried off by the Russians; and, as I have since learnt, died on the 19th from his wounds.

I deplore his loss, for he was an intelligent and very promising young officer.

I have reason to believe that the treatment he received from the Russians was most humane and considerate.

I have, &c.,
R. J. H. VIVIAN,
Lieutenant-General, Commanding
Turkish Contingent.

CHAPTER 14

THE END OF THE WAR

War-Department, February 15, 1856.

LORD PANMURE has this day received a Despatch and its Enclosure, of which the following are copies, addressed to his Lordship by General Sir William Codrington, K.C.B.

Head Quarters, Sevastopol,
2nd February, 1856.

MY LORD,

THE destruction of the Docks of Sevastopol is now completed; the sides of the last dock were blown in yesterday morning, small parts of the wall here and there only remaining. Thus the whole of the canal of entrance and north docks in charge of the French, the basin in our mutual charge, and the south docks in English charge, are separate, but shapeless masses of dirt, heavy broken stones, split beams of timber, and shattered gates protruding from the heap of confusion.

The labour of destruction has been difficult; these fine works were formed in the middle ravine at its outlet in an inner and sheltered part of the harbour, one of the natural watercourses from the plateau on which we are encamped. This end of the ravine, about 700 yards from its mouth, seems to have been filled in so as to create a great artificial dam of earth, which, with the steep banks on each side, form three sides of a raised enclosure looking down upon the docks. A solid stone wall, much struck by shot, crowns this sort of natural square; the fine but shattered barracks, standing still higher on the left, with the sheds and dockyard buildings, the masting shears, and a long quay to Fort Paul in front jutting into the harbour, show how well adapted all was for its purpose. It is now a picture of destruction, desolation, and silence; there lies against the quay the half sunken hull of a vessel; and, in the harbour beyond, the only things breaking the surface of the water are the lower masts of sunken ships of war.

The drainage of the water of the middle ravine must, however, pass through to the harbour somewhere, and it was this that has so much impeded the shafts; for the water from rains often stood two feet high over the floor of the docks, and thus of course filled the shafts themselves. Some details of the execution of these are given in the enclosed summary from Colonel Lloyd, Commanding the Royal Engineers, the immediate executive officers being Colonel Gordon and Major Nicholson.

Amidst great difficulties of cold and wet, very severe frost at one time, and perpetually recurring pressure at another, the work went steadily on; and great praise is due to all those concerned, the Engineers and Sappers, parties of the Royal Artillery, the 18th Regiment, and latterly of the 48th Regiment. These parties return to their duty to-morrow after constant and laborious work.

The casualties have been but six, of which two only have been fatal, and one man of the 48th Regiment lost by foul air in a shaft; after several vain attempts by Major Nicholson, other officers and men, themselves descending at great risk, the poor fellow's body was brought up, but life was gone.

Your lordship will see that Colonel Lloyd expresses his obligation to Mr. Deane, and the Chief Engineer of Her Majesty's ship Royal Albert, for their assistance.

The Voltaic Battery, we must confess, did not always succeed, it seems to require great nicety in preparation, but in those cases in which I saw it succeed the effect was perfect – ignition and its result, the shake of the ground, the heaving up of the mass seemed to be instantaneous.

The destruction of other things will continue.

I have, &c.,
W.J. CODRINGTON,
General Commanding.
The Lord Panmure, &c. &c. &c.

Enclosure.

Head Quarters, Camp, Sevastopol,
February 1, 1856.

SIR,

AFTER a period of three months' unceasing labour in the dockyard, for the destruction of the docks, in compliance with Lord Panmure's orders, it affords me very great satisfaction to report, for your Excellency's information, the termination of our exertions in the demolition of that portion allotted to the English, which consisted of the three docks on the south side, and one half of the east and west sides of the basin.

The result of our operations has been the perfect destruction of the whole, the foundations being completely torn up. The length of time occupied in effecting the above object has, I regret, far exceeded what had been anticipated, owing to many circumstances over which no human being could have any control. Your Excellency, I believe, is aware that on the morning of the 16th December, 1855, after a very heavy and continuous fall of rain, all the shafts which had been sunk behind the revetment walls of the docks, were found to have twenty feet of water in them, the shafts being thirty feet deep; and the shafts along the bottoms of the docks, which had been sunk to a depth of twelve feet, were not only quite full of water, but had 2 feet 6 inches of water above the floors of the docks themselves.

A very large party was employed day and night endeavouring to reduce the water, and effected this object but slowly, as the water continued to find its way in by percolation. At this stage of the work, the wet weather was suddenly succeeded by intense frost, which for some days rendered our pumps useless, thus causing a further delay and obliged us to bale the water out of the shafts, resuming the pumping as soon as the pumps would work again, which has been continued to the very last.

It was the intention to have destroyed one entire dock at a time, but owing to the influx of water such an arrangement was obliged to be abandoned, and such charges only as could from time to time be prepared were fired, the pumping in very many cases being kept up day and night until the last moment. The bottoms and sites were blown up before the sides were destroyed, which enabled us to be satisfied that the former were thoroughly demolished.

I must observe that, as the demolition of the northern portion was carried out by the French, it is incumbent on me to explain why their operations were not subjected to as many difficulties as fell to our lot. Their docks were four feet higher in level than ours, and in no instance had they, I understand, any water to contend against, or at least so small a quantity as to be scarcely appreciable. Their charges in the bottoms were not more than 6 ft. deep, whereas our's averaged 10 ft. 6in. in depth.

Though the external effect of some of our explosions may not appear great, I am happy to say that every portion of the masonry is either absolutely torn down or left in so dangerous a condition that it will add very much to the difficulties of re-building.

I was extremely anxious that the facilities afforded by Her Majesty's Government for the employment of voltaic batteries on a large scale, as sent out by the Admiralty under Mr. Deane, should be fairly tested under the most favourable circumstances. I applied to Vice-Admiral Sir E. Lyons, who kindly offered the services of Mr. Deane, Submarine Engineer, to carry out the voltaic operations, and this gentleman had every assistance in skilled labour afforded him from the Royal Sappers and Miners.

Many failures having taken place in firing the charges by electricity, owing to different causes, I am inclined to doubt its advantages as applicable generally to military purposes.

The pair of dockgates ordered to be taken down and sent as trophies to England were removed with considerable difficulty, being so very massive and strongly put together with bolts, nuts, &c., which had become rusty.

I cannot say too much in praise of the exertions both of officers and men, including a party of 350 of the 18th and 48th Regiments, in addition to the Royal Sappers and Miners, amounting to 85, in the destruction of the docks, though they had to work, for the greater part of the time, day and night during the severest weather, and for having brought this service to a successful issue, after so many drawbacks, which, instead of causing despair and dispiriting those employed, only stimulated them to renewed exertions.

I should be remiss in my duty were I to omit acknowledging the very valuable assistance I have received throughout, from Colonel Gordon, C.B., the Executive Officer, Major Nicholson, who was the resident Engineer, and Lieutenants Cumberland, Graham, and C. Gordon, Royal Engineers; their unremitting zeal, attention, and devotion to the work, in accomplishing this troublesome task, under difficulties of no ordinary nature, claim my warmest thanks. I am also much indebted to Mr. Deane, Submarine Engineer, whose valuable services in preparing and firing most of the mines by voltaic action, were kindly placed at my disposal by his Excellency Vice-Admiral Sir E. Lyons.

I must not omit to acknowledge the professional aid received from the Chief and Assistant Engineer of Her Majesty's ship Royal Albert (until that ship sailed for Malta), in the taking to pieces of the dock gates. In connexion with this service, the assistance afforded by a large party of the Royal Artillery, placed at my disposal by Lieutenant-General Sir Richard Dacres, and under the superintendence and direction of Lieutenant-Colonel Bent, Royal Engineers, I cannot but greatly appreciate.

I have, &c.,
EDWD. T. LLOYD,
Lieutenant-Colonel Commanding Royal
Engineers.
His Excellency General Sir Wm.
Codrington, K.C.B., Commander
Of the Forces.

War-Department, February 19, 1856.

LORD PANMURE has received a Despatch, of which the following is a copy, addressed to his Lordship by General Sir William Codrington, K.C.B.

Sevastopol, February 4, 1856.

MY LORD,

MARSHAL PELISSIER informed me a few days ago that this day Fort Nicholas would be destroyed; and he sent again to say that at one o'clock P.M. the mines for this purpose would be fired.

The view over the whole harbour is well obtained from the interior slope of the Redan Hill, and from other points within the Russian lines.

The day was magnificently clear; every sentry on the opposite side could be seen, every working party watched, every soldier that was lounging in the sun; occasional shot and shell were sent from the enemy to the Karabelnaia and the town, but otherwise nothing disturbed the usual appearance of quiet, almost of desolation.

On our (the south) side, we looked down on the large ruined barracks in front, on the inner creek of the Dockyard, the Quay, and the remains of Fort Paul, the spacious inlet from the harbour on our left, beyond which stand the roofless buildings of Sevastopol itself. There also is the well-remembered long line of pointed arches, the casemates of the interior of Fort Nicholas, of which the embrasures in double tier pointed to seaward and away from us.

It juts out into the harbour built on an inner tongue of land; Fort Constantine forming a similar but more outward defence for the sea approach on the north.

The scene and feeling of expectation were of great interest, for another tangible proof of power and success was to take place, and 106,000 lbs. of powder were in the several mines. At the hour named a burst of smoke, dark and thick, rolled from our left of the building; it was followed by another; the heavy sound arrived, the stones were shot into the air and to the sea; the explosions of the extreme right and the centre mingled at little interval into one drifting cloud, which veiled the destruction below.

The light of the sun played beautifully on the mass of smoke, of which the lower part lay long and heavily on its victim. The breeze passing it away over the remains of the town, showed that a low line of ruin was all that remained of the pride of Fort Nicholas, and one standing menace of the harbour lay buried under its waters.

The state of the docks has been given in detail in my letters. They are all destroyed, whilst the earth surrounding them is shaken into cracks; basin, docks, masses of broken granite, capstans, gates, beams of iron, and of timber are tumbled into one mass of destruction.

> I have, &c.,
> W.J. CODRINGTON,
> General Commanding.
> *The Lord Panmure, &c. &c. &c.*

War-Department, March 3, 1856.

LORD PANMURE has this day received three Despatches, and an Enclosure, of which the following are copies, addressed to his Lordship by General Sir William Codrington, K.C.B.

Sevastopol, February 16, 1856.

MY LORD,

I HAVE the honour to acquaint your Lordship that a Russian force, estimated at about 3,000 infantry and cossacks, appeared on the morning of the 12th instant, on the ridge of Kardoubel, above the valley of Baidar, but retired after a short reconnaissance.

The French Engineers blew up, on the 12th instant, two portions of the aqueduct which formerly supplied the docks of Sevastopol.

Some blasting experiments have been made on the walls of the large barracks, near the dockyard, and the mining is in progress.

The weather, for some days past, has been showing the gradual approach of spring, and the health of the Army continues excellent.

General Sir Colin Campbell rejoined this Army on the 14th instant.

I have, &c.,

W.J. CODRINGTON,

General Commanding.

The Lord Panmure, &c. &c. &c.

Sevastopol, February 19, 1856.

MY LORD,

THE health or the Army remains good, and we have been enabled lately to continue ball practice and the assembling of regiments for exercise during the very favourable weather of the last ten days. On the evening of the 17th orders were given for the assembly of the whole infantry of the English Army in contiguous columns, on the brow of the plateau; but fog and drizzling rain in the night turned to sleet in the morning, changed the state of the ground, and sent the thermometer down to 18°, and to 9° last night.

The parade had been of course put off; but it would have shown to us all troops rendered efficient in health and strength by the care of the Government at home, and by the exertions and superintendence of the Officers commanding divisions, brigades, and regiments.

I am quite sure that any of our Allies, inclined to be present, would have been glad to see the efficiency of part of the Army which acts with them.

To day is a fine clear day of a Canadian winter, thermometer at 14°, bitterly cold from the strong breeze; and this change having come so suddenly, want of caution may very probably have produced some frost bites.

We shall be enabled soon to add to the interest taken in the ball practice with that beautiful arm the Enfield Rifle, by giving a few prizes, subscribed for among ourselves, to the best shots.

I have, &c.,

W.J. CODRINGTON,

General Commanding.

The Lord Panmure, &c. &c. &c.

War-Department, March 10, 1856.

LORD PANMURE has this day received a Despatch and its Enclosure, of which the following are copies, addressed to his Lordship by General Sir William Codrington, K.C.B.

Sevastopol, February 26, 1856.

MY LORD,

I HAVE the honour to inform your Lordship that a large portion of the infantry of the English Army paraded, on the 24th instant, on the ridge of the plateau overlooking the plain of Balaklava, where the ground had become sufficiently dry for the purpose.

The troops were formed, by divisions, in a line of contiguous columns of battalions at quarter distance, extending for nearly a mile, and marched past at half distance.

They were subsequently formed on a slope to the rear of the original line, in masses of columns by divisions, and again marched past in quarter distance.

The day was fine, but cold, and the general appearance, cleanliness, and steadiness of the troops afforded all the utmost satisfaction, for the men looked in the finest health and vigour. Marshal Pélissier, General Durando, and a large number of officers of the French and Sardinian Armies were observers of the fine bearing and efficiency of the troops.

I enclose the Weekly Report of Sir John Hall, Inspector-General of Hospitals, in which your Lordship will see recorded the excellent state of health of the Army generally.

I have, &c.,
W.J. CODRINGTON,
General Commanding.
The Lord Panmure, &c. &c. &c.

War-Department, July 30, 1856.

LORD PANMURE has this day received a Despatch, of which the following is a copy, addressed to his Lordship by General Sir William Codrington, K.C.B.

Sevastopol, July 16, 1856.

MY LORD,

FINDING that all arrangements would be completed for evacuating the Crimea on the 12th instant, I wrote, the previous day, to the officer in command of the Russian troops, a Colonel of the Gendarmerie, at Kamiesh, that I should be ready to hand over the Dockyard of Sevastopol and the port of Balaklava on that day.

Her Majesty's ship Algiers had entered the port of Balaklava on the 7th instant; the 56th Regiment embarked in that ship on the evening of the 11th; the only troops remaining were one wing of the 50th Regiment, which formed the guard of the town that night.

The following day, the 12th, at One P.M., all the remaining stores and establishments having been embarked, a company of the 50th was posted outside of the town to receive the Russian troops, and on their approach, marched in with the Russian Guard, composed of about 50 mounted Cossacks and a similar number of Infantry Cossacks.

The usual form of salutes took place, the Russians placed sentries where they wished, and the four companies of the 50th marched on board the Algiers. I embarked with my personal staff at the same time.

Although the weather was unfavourable we were enabled to quit the harbour of Balaklava that evening.

Admiral Sir H. Stewart and Admiral Freemantle were at anchor outside the harbour; they weighed, and we all sailed for this place, where I arrived to-day.

I have, &c.,
W.J. CODRINGTON,
General Commanding.
The Lord Panmure, &c. &c. &c.

INDEX OF PERSONS

INDEX OF MILITARY AND NAVAL UNITS